THE BIPOLAR EXPEDITIONIST

THE BIPOLAR EXPEDITIONIST

Keith Alan Steadman

Revised Edition

iUniverse, Inc.
New York Bloomington

THE BIPOLAR EXPEDITIONIST

iUniverse books may be ordered through booksellers or by contacting:

iUniverse
1663 Liberty Drive
Bloomington, IN 47403
www.iuniverse.com
1-800-Authors (1-800-288-4677)

Because of the dynamic nature of the Internet, any Web addresses or links contained in this book may have changed since publication and may no longer be valid.

The views expressed in this work are solely those of the author and do not necessarily reflect the views of the publisher, and the publisher hereby disclaims any responsibility for them. In order to preserve the anonymity of persons mentioned in this book I have made subtle alterations to their names.

Cover photography by Steadman
Cover design by Keith Alan Steadman

ISBN: 978-0-595-48147-7 (pbk)
ISBN: 978-0-595-60912-3 (cloth)
ISBN: 978-0-595-60241-4 (ebk)

Printed in the United States of America

To Susan Carol Rose

Contents

Acknowledgements

Without the encouragement of so many, this book may never have come to fruition. I would especially like to thank my wonderful team of general practitioners, psychiatrists, psychologists and support workers who have put me back on track more times than I probably deserve.

I am so grateful and blessed to have family and friends in the United Kingdom and in the United States who have been so supportive and understanding, especially when I underwent lengthy episodes of mania and depression during the course of writing.

Most of all, I want to express my gratitude and love to Susie, one of life's true angels. She never stopped believing in my abilities, and also in my quest to create something positive out of what can often appear to be a negative situation.

Introduction

Can you imagine what it must be like to stay wide awake for endless nights, lapping up mankind's richest cream, and still be able to prance and dance around town with the energy of a five year old? Teetering on the brink of an excessive lifestyle and a depressing death is an occupational hazard for a bipolar affected traveller. This project is dedicated to all of those human beings who took their moods a step too far and never returned.

My name is Keith, and I shall be taking you on a fascinating journey through my yo-yoing mind, while at the same time attempting to highlight the effects that this two-faced pig of an illness can have upon the support network of caregivers and loved ones. This true story of my first encounter with bipolar affective disorder contains every emotion known to man, and I guarantee that your senses will be stretched to unimaginable limits just as mine were. You are about to experience my naked pleasure and my raw pain, as I am not about to pull any punches or dodge any issues. To begin with, you may understandably struggle to comprehend the sheer intensity and amount of stamina required by myself and millions of others to become fully paid up members of the bipolar survivors club, but I promise that will change as you become more and more enlightened. What you are about to receive will fire up your mind and take your breath away. I am going to tell it to you straight, with no frills attached, in the hope that you will come away with a little more understanding of this illness than you had to begin with. Another important matter to deal with is the ridding of the stigma and taboo elements that often accompany anything mentally related. Bipolar affective disorder is an *illness* that scares some people because of its unpredictability, but there is nothing to be frightened of. Mankind has always been afraid of what they cannot actually see or easily explain, so a wall is built or an attack is mounted that the attacker hopes will erase the imagined problem. There are always the ignorant few who attempt to make life even tougher for a mentally ill person, and I intend to play my part in firmly stamping it out.

If only one soul can glean some inspiration from my efforts, then I will consider this project a success. There are millions of human beings across the globe who are manic-depressive, most of whom manage to cope very well so long as they take their daily medication and don't pull their personal trigger. My trigger of choice was alcohol; blurred, slurred gallons of the confrontational stuff. Don't be alarmed, but a mentally related illness, including minor stress related problems, will strike most of us at some point during our privileged stay here on Planet Earth. I could reel off statistic after statistic, but suffice to say that in the United States alone there are over two-million diagnosed bipolar affected people who are either roaming around free, or are in a secure psychiatric unit. The vast majority are conducting perfectly normal lives, and you would never know that they are bipolar. This is because they stick to their medication and try their best to avoid the triggers. Although mania and depression can be rather alarming when they are in full flow, they can be controlled with the help of prescribed medication and the appropriate therapy.

This project has been put together so that every type of reader can connect easily with it, hopefully picking up a few useful tips along the precarious way. There is an uplifting message to be found among the pages of what can sometimes become a rather heavy subject. My earthy views and opinions may not be to everybody's taste, but they will certainly make you think. Depression is such a horrible place to be sucked into. It creeps up and smacks you in the face like nothing else I know, yet it will always subside, I promise. The most extreme outcome is of course death, whether it be on the end of a sad makeshift rope or because a misjudged manic prank too many went tragically wrong—I came close on numerous occasions. There isn't always that special somebody around to bail you out from your latest ship, whether it be sinking in the choppy seas or floating around in space.

In retrospect I made it around the block too many times for my own good, although in a perverse sort of way I wouldn't alter a single thing. The rounded knowledge and deep insights that I have gained through the experiences of not only myself, but from so many others, are absolutely priceless. All of this valuable information has contributed toward making me a better rounded and much more open minded soul. Learning the hard way has helped to mould me into an understanding and tolerant 43 year old man who appreciates the simple things in life, as well as the occasional not quite so simple. The baggage accumulated with a quest for knowledge also contains many faults. We all have so much untapped intelligence just waiting to be freed at the right time. Some of us have been on an expedition to explore the unknown recesses of our minds, and have come back down to earth with an almighty bump, but otherworldly the wiser. It doesn't always pay to share these experiences, unless you want to eat corned beef sandwiches and obey the routine cry of "Medication time" from within the hollow confines of a key jangling psychiatric institution.

Alas, not all of us survived the rigors of manic depression. So many have fallen along the way. For all we limited human beings know, they may have been elevated to a much higher, incomprehensible level of existence where one can experience and use productively, not destructively, the benefits of a fully operational brain.

This book also goes out to those who crashed one time too many while going up and down an ever changing street, only to find themselves getting nowhere fast and somewhere prematurely. What would millions of us manic-depressives do without the superb scientists, psychiatrists, psychologists, nurses, general practitioners and pharmacists? Without their dedication and progress we wouldn't have the medicines and the specialist care that we have now. More than anything, they provide people like myself with stability and hope for a better future. At the end of the day the buck stops with the beholder. Only so much assistance, medication and strong advice can be issued, and then it's down to the likes of me to put into action a responsible plan to make my life as fulfilling as it was originally designed to be.

I hope that you are more aware, enlightened, inspired and ultimately uplifted as you surf upon my salty waves of emotion. Naturally, whatever goes up nearly always has to find an unsubtle means of plummeting back down to Earth again, and I was no exception to that painful rule. Rocketing skywards and then thundering way back down became my way of life, causing all kinds of crazy mayhem along the way. I can honestly say, hand on heart, that I truly now know for sure what Heaven and hell is really like. Heaven is an intense state of mind combined with our present physical world, only magnified beyond belief to a full flowing manic-depressive. So many times have I been shot back and forth throughout my turbulent life, through too many barrels that were not always brimming over with laughs. So many times my manic shuttle ignored my pleas to ease up a touch on the accelerator, upping the stakes instead to hastily race my cluttered mind far away to somewhere beyond belief and totally out of control. It is only when you begin to slip and lose touch—not only with common reality, but also with the unreality that briefly became crystal clear to me, somewhere between Hill End Psychiatric Hospital and the Planet Mars—that you yank out hair in depressing clumps and start to panic from deep within.

I have been unconventional one minute, boringly straight the next, an artistically frustrated would be Bohemian, a disintegrating shell of many previous skins, the keenest seeker without the treasured map, and the taker to boost the giver. When anything goes, everything fits with belief of the unbelievable, backed up to the hilt by special mentally festering wretches in full public view, reluctantly teetering toward paralysis of the mind, wobbling on what were once diamond shod feet—a bipolar affected or a manic-depressive human being, call us what you will, are all of these things to the extreme and a whole lot more besides. Somebody who suffers from larger than life mood swings can never be accused of being boring. A complete pain in the backside yes, and at the most inopportune of times maybe, but *never* ever boring, even when they are plummeting the loneliest gloomiest depths of unrelenting doom and undeserved despair. Bipolar affective disorder does not let up. This illness will continue to pursue its mission of touching millions of unsuspecting souls from all four corners of the Earth, so I think it's better to go prepared.

Allow me to share with you my own experiences as a fully paid up member of the bipolar affective disorder society (BADS). I shall be covering many intriguing issues as clearly, concisely and as soberly as possible. By using varying angles of thought I hope that I will succeed in putting across something of relevance and value for everybody. It is so important to look at bipolar affective disorder not only from the beholders vantage point, but also from the often painful view of the caregivers who also have to contend with the unpredictable upheaval and grief that such a tricky illness such as this, or any kind of mentally related illness can slyly pose. A whole new perspective of mental illness will open up if only you will allow it to. On offer is a front row seat. Given time that seat will enable you the reader to swing open new doors that were once stuck shut with a gooey stigma. Paint new optimism from a pallet of invigorating colour. Soak up drops of glorious sunshine and bathe in a ray of hope. All matters mentally related can be lifted up and socially accepted for what they really are, and for what they deserve to be. Sketchy impressions, thoughtlessly massed produced without due care and attention inside blind ignorant heads will be disposed of forever.

Triggers are not only found on weapons, they are also found within the pressurised and demanding lifestyles that man in his infinite wisdom has selfishly created, all at the expense of the vulnerable. That selfishness is now backfiring big time. Much of what you are about to digest is immensely personal, exactly as you would expect from a book of this nature. There have been moments during writing in which I have had serious second thoughts about laying myself bare for all to indulge, but then my rational side took over the proceedings and insisted that this project had to be an all or nothing affair. I chose *all*. Awaiting you are the jagged edges and slippery corners that always play starring roles in the loathsome lows. Alongside the horrendous lows is an immortal cocktail of stretched out senses and addictive highs. It sure is better out than in, especially for somebody like myself who unwillingly stores too much scantily clad observation and coded data inside his head. Getting a load off and on to paper is hugely therapeutic and highly recommended.

Professionals in the world of psychology are mental locksmiths who possess the intelligence required to unravel the key to peace and tranquillity of the mind. Perhaps a mind-map that suggests personalised instructions on how the invisible and intolerable can be zapped may be drawn up one day. It all sounds a bit like a Flash-Gordon episode right now I know, but it doesn't do any harm to have a positive dream in the right direction. Part of my job is to describe what it is like to be manic-depressive, or bipolar (I will be using both descriptions throughout.) I have been glued to depression, gagged with double sided duct tape, and strung up with steel rope while the little devils kept jab-jab-jabbing twenty-four hours a day, seven days a week. On the reverse side of that well worn coin I know what it feels like to control the whole system of things, to have the angels visit me on a whim of fancy, persistently tug-tug-tugging on my frayed shirtsleeves every single minute, night and day, demanding that I drop whatever I was doing and come out to play with them immediately. Occasionally I came across a medical professional who proclaimed to know more about how it feels to be me than I do myself! This is a *very* rare occurrence indeed, but it emphasises my point that we cannot expect the experts to know absolutely everything, even though the qualified professionals that I have been fortunate enough to lock heads with were never far short of the mark. They are wonderful people indeed. What if the coin lands on its edge? Does that mean all is fine and dandy and that is that? Hardly, because all I would be doing is teetering on the precarious edge of life, waiting for the next topple or flip. Why not widen the coins edge, build a sturdier base and recruit a strong support system? In theory this plan is fine, but putting it out into the big wide world is a whole new ball of wax.

All we have to do is work together to enable each and every one of us to lighten our loads and ease the burden. Not in a trillion years would I wish upon another human being a single one of the vast amount of mentally related conditions on offer. The problem is that any strain of mental illness could pounce upon any one of us at the unlikeliest of times, and I mean *anybody!*

My intention is to take the liberty of becoming your mental gardener, planting just a small seed of thought and better understanding inside your head. This seedling will have the potential to benefit everybody, even the nasty pieces of work who think nothing of taking advantage of the mentally ill's present but fixable lot in life. Manic depression for the uninitiated can be an awfully deep and daunting sea to swallow up in one sitting. Just start by taking a sip and then slowly work your way up, then down, then up and so on. Digesting the nitty-gritty a little at a time should sharpen up your receptive powers and tolerance levels.

Manic-depressive people are not mad people, they are just temporarily on a different planet (sometimes affectionately referred to as Planet Janet.) When they come back down or back up, depending on which way they were pulled to begin with, a marked change may be noticeable in that the mind traveller now seems a little calmer and a little more reassured. An awful lot of new life-lessons are absorbed too, helping to make the beholder more at peace with themselves and also with others around them. A little extra smart solid knowledge picked up along the way and used very wisely never hurt a soul. Prescribed medication and self discipline regarding alcohol consumption is all that I need to keep both my feet on the ground. Regular blood tests are needed to check the therapeutic levels of my prescribed medications, and to check that no damage is being caused to my internal organs, especially the pancreas and liver.

Are you ready to set off on an expedition into the deep mind of a manic-depressive person, to explore what up until now you have only made assumptions about? I shall be introducing you to a cast of colourful characters that I know you will love and some you will loathe. These lovable oddballs are real life individuals, all of whom have played their part in shaping many aspects of my truly amazing life (so far.) Most of their names have been altered to protect their privacy.

The further we dare ourselves to venture the more we tend to gain, but that doesn't necessarily mean that we are about to set sail on a comfortable journey. This project is about an exploration of the mind, *my* mind. The deeper you delve, the more revealing it will be. Don't worry about getting lost in the dark as I will always be there with a light to guide you through to the end. If a little open minded time is spared to strip back the juicy layers of life that confronts us all, in that brief moment I am confident that we as a race can and will be unified as a common spirit for the good. We can be blessed with a way of life that is far richer than plastic, paper and rock could ever buy. This high interest account of bipolar affective disorder or manic-depression will astonish, enlighten, educate and enthral. You will be pleasantly blown away by the true story of how one young English cookie crumbled, and then with the help of many went about rebuilding his life, again and again. Welcome aboard, have a safe and pleasant trip!

1

Lift Off

My formative years were spent in a typical boyhood style. Even from an early age I sensed that there was a slight difference between myself and other children, but I just could not put my finger on what exactly, so I carried on regardless, not wanting for anything in a safe and secure loving environment.

Just before I had reached twenty-five unexplainable moody years of age, filled to overflowing with unpredictability, I was offered a modest single bedroom apartment to rent from the Dacorum Borough Council. I prefer to see it as a maisonette, nicely located in a peaceful little village on the edge of Hemel Hempstead, Hertfordshire. This was back in 1989, and fortunately for me—though perhaps not for quite a few others—I am still residing there in the sought after and secluded Vicarage Lane. The quaint village of Bovingdon or "Bovvy" as many of the Hemel residents call it, used to be up until the early 1900's a hamlet, situated within the larger parish of nearby Hemel Hempstead. Bovingdon means "Above the downs," making it rather an appropriate place for a severe mood swinger to reside. So, Bovingdon has its independence, it has its history, it has its pretty little leafy country lanes and then it has me.

With the help of my reliable Brother-In-Law Philip and my ever generous Father, in I moved. My sole possessions amounted to a few sticks of old furniture that I had managed to rustle together, my vinyl record collection, a reasonable assortment of clothes and my old faithful rubber plant. If I had been presented with a million pounds I wouldn't have been any happier. The problem was that I had become *too* happy. My Mondays to Fridays were spent driving a Mercedes diesel van as if it were a formula one racing car, merchandising all over England's gorgeous Dorset, Devon and Cornish south western counties, delivering hefty bags and boxes of sweets and nuts to holiday parks and garden centres. By Friday afternoon the empty van felt so much lighter, so I would put the pedal-to-the-metal in order to get back to one of Bovingdon's five old rustic pubs. There I would be in my absolute element, trying my level best to urinate the fairly meagre but hard earned wages that I had not long collected right up the porcelain wall. This routine went on and on as if it were one great big party that had no beginning and positively no end in sight. Little did I know then, but my whole life was about to be shot apart. The triggers were being cocked all around me. It was just a matter of time before something from within went off and blew those who were the closest to me away. Misjudgement of my moods, mismanagement of my finances, and a total disregard of my general well being were all contributory factors in creating the monstrous collapse that was waiting to happen. This was the start of something big, something overwhelming that I had yet to feel the full impact of. Unbeknown to me due to the mask of alcohol and my environment, strange changes were blatantly taking place inside my brain. Soon my whole life existence and any perspective that I had left of it would be turned upside down and pulled inside out. A weighty chain of merciless torment had begun to swing menacingly. This looming nightmare would cleverly disguise itself, and then without any warning it would delight in taking a slippery grip of my entire soul with one hand, and thoroughly mix up whatever remained of my pitiful grasp of reality with the other. This would undoubtedly prove to be the opening ceremony of a disorder or an illness that I was going to have to, somewhat reluctantly at first, keep in check and then rapidly secure a firm grip on by means of taking the necessary and correct dosage of prescribed medication for the rest of my life. I have since learnt that this is such a small price to pay for prevention, and it's absolutely no hardship in comparison to what so many uncomplaining people have to go through day in and day out in order to retain a decent quality of life, or in the most extreme cases, to remain alive. There are still those who disregard the chiselled rules at their own cost, and to the dismay of far too many innocent others who often have to pick up the broken pieces. It would be quite a long time before I would be officially recognised and then diagnosed as being yet another fully paid up member, along with so many other colourful and highly intuitive people, of the bipolar affective disorder/manic depression society.

Brain chemistry: neurotransmitters, dopamine, serotonin, noradrenaline and so on—all of these may be over the top of your head to begin with, so instead of bombarding you with medical jargon now, I will bring them gently into play as we journey on. All will become clear to you in pretty much the same order as it did for me, except of course in a compacted form. This is not meant to be a medical encyclopaedia, but an easy to read insight of manic depression straight from the horse's mouth. The professionals who are qualified in these matters can compile the medical reference books. Everything that I have written and perhaps suggested are strictly my views only, and apply to only me. Please do *not* take everything I say as being the gospel that will work for you. Each and every one of us are made up of different complexities and so have different requirements. A few helpful tips from an experienced campaigner never goes amiss, but in order to properly glean all of the specialised medical help and information you must seek the advice of a top quality professional, and there are plenty out there ready and more than willing to be of assistance.

It would be easy for me to churn out a barrage of medical facts and figures, but I will limit (partly due to inability) any medical references to when and where I feel they would be of relevance to you when reading this book. Also I shall cut out the fancy talk, and instead stick with plain good old fashioned English that we can all understand without too much trouble. We will look into the mind of a manic me, a totally pissed off suicidal me, and we shall also try to catch a glimpse of the "normal" me somewhere in the middle of the two previous extremes. Are you keeping up? Good.

All I want is for you to take a little in so that I can get a lot out. It is very important indeed to realise that despite taking the full impact on the chin, sometimes literally, we BAD folk are not the only ones who suffer, not by a long way. I have said it before but I will keep on saying it because it is *very* important indeed to be aware that it is always those who are the closest, your nearest and dearest, that suffer also. They bear the brunt of sorting out the practical things as well as having to deal with their own emotions. They have a life and a schedule to maintain as well as caring for another. They have to stay strong despite being vulnerable to a depression of their own. This is how it is for my mother Shirley. My father Ken then worries about the knock-on effects that the strain and worry has on her health, which in turn affects him. So the cycle goes on and on, often behind closed doors where nobody else has a clue as to what anguish is actually unravelling, and what steely springs are becoming so tightly coiled. Keeping one's cool under the same roof as a clinically diagnosed manic-depressed person can often prove to be too much to bear, so some steam is released in the sensitive surroundings of home which can then upset the seriously ill and overly sensitive person. This accumulation of pressure has the effect of making everybody who feels cornered and concerned even more glum, and on it jolly well goes until at long last that day of awakening decides to arrive, carrying with it much less heavy baggage than it had done all those dreadful days before. Equal stress and worry is soaked up and expelled when a happy manic is off gallivanting around town, spending money he simply does not have. In my case it especially meant drinking far too much alcohol, which in this scenario only fuels the manic more and more until they are drinking the evil spirits as if they were tumblers of water.

How about a thought for those people who have nobody with whom they can confide, and no strong shoulder to cry on. When I was experiencing one of my down episodes I could clearly remember thinking to myself how terrible it would be if I didn't have the people around me that I do. They are special people that I used to take for granted. They are going to be there to help me out of my latest scrape no matter what. Without them I would probably be pushing up the daisies a little prematurely. Fortunately for myself and thousands of others in the United Kingdom there is the support of community psychiatric health and crisis teams who provide key-workers, with whom contact can be made at any time if one happens to be feeling high, low or drifting slightly off centre. There is no need for anybody to be totally alone through that trying time of need.

Before we devour the meat of manic depression I had better explain to you some of the effects that Mister Booze, or indeed any abused substance has upon the consumer. Believe me, I have knocked back enough of the strong stuff in my time to know what I'm talking about. Most of us know that alcohol is in fact a depressant, and that if it is drunk more and more when feeling low it will provide a brief boost into a false happy land, but it will not hold you there. The only outcome is that you will be dumped even deeper in the brown stuff. So what do you do? I simply drank more and more, foolishly trying to keep my head above the depths of depression, and in doing so I became a depressed binge drinker. Now I can clearly see how I drank from the age of fifteen to combat my minor mood swings and screen my insecurities, long before I was actually diagnosed as being a manic-depressive/bipolar affected person. Many sufferers of this treatable mental condition turn to alcohol in a vain attempt to mask and change their mood, when of course they should refrain as it can nullify the desired effect of the proper medication administered by the experts. If the chemical laboratory inside my brain begins to enter, or is already in a deep manic state, then the irresponsible consumption of liquor will only serve to aggravate the bubbling condition. Alcohol is a depressant that if taken on that slide into hell, just to gain a little relief, will ultimately become disadvantageous and only add to the downswing in mood, never mind the damage it is causing the innocent liver and the thinning wallet.

Oh yes, it was alcohol that became my main trigger of choice. Bipolar disorder is always laying dormant, ready to blow either way, especially when triggered by a controllable outside force. My judgment was poor, causing me to shoot myself in the foot, which in turn would send me catapulting into one of two hazardous directions. The best place to land was of course on Planet Manic. Being high on the back of mania is the best feeling there is, the best fun, the best of everything and a whole lot more besides. It is a place where every sensation and emotion are tirelessly breeding new sensations and emotions, whose sole purpose in life is to work devotedly at raising the beholder up to a paradise tantalisingly close to where mankind is really intended to be, an existence that perhaps we may all have been sharing as normality today if Adam hadn't managed to go and cock things up for us all by munching on that blessed big apple.

The Greek word *ania*, meaning to produce great mental anguish, and *manos*, meaning relaxed or loose, go together to form the word *mania*. There are several other etymologies proposed by the Roman physician Caelius Aurelianus, but I think this one fits the bill. Fully blown episodes of mania contain an unlimited amount of enticing options. I felt that I was capable of anything, superhuman in fact. Most precariously of all was my belief, with ever growing conviction, that I had become or always had been totally invincible—bloody dangerous stuff! Grandiose feelings even elevated me up there with Christ himself. Half measures are never enough, my glass had to be filled to overflowing. Every minute of the day had to be lived in excess and to the extreme. Every thought fuels another thought that blocks out or postpones the inevitable burn out and crash. The longer mania goes on for the more severe the crash, not only the initial fall from grace but the depth of the depression that will inevitably follow. It doesn't take a clever Dick with a degree in mathematics or physics to figure out the opposite reaction to an abnormally upbeat action. Scaling the crumbling tumbling wall so that I could stake my place on the other side always proved to be my undoing. If my carefully prescribed medication had not been taken and monitored properly, and the shackles and chains suddenly broke free, there is the strong possibility that I could leap into another lengthy flight of the foolish. This has never been the case with the professionals I have dealt with over the years. There were many times when all of the due care and attention from doctors, psychiatrists, family and friends went down the toilet because I rebelled against being labelled as a sufferer of bipolar affective disorder. Subsequent episodes of mania and depression often saw me refusing to go along with sound, highly qualified advice. Lessons did *not* want to be learnt. I allowed myself to go completely nuts, ignoring all of the previous warnings and pitfalls. Why not make the merry mistake of celebrating my release from the hellish grip of a clinical bipolar depression? I honestly felt as if I had the God given right to make up for every second of lost time, to kick the depression in the head and pull out the rotten teeth that had gripped my limp soul for far too long. My eager head would be pushed back into oblivion as I sped upward at an increasing rate of knots, managing only the briefest glimpse during the ascent upon the dubious area that we are told to believe is normal. If the world today is normal then I give up. That alone is enough to send an intelligent law abiding person to the funny-farm, or to the not so funny pharmacy for a supply of pills just in case. Wham! There I would be, sorry and full of regret, back to the paralysis of a depressed unfulfilled mind. Moderation and patience to get to where I selfishly want to be have never been my strongest points. Breaking free from a bout of depression and getting a bit carried away with the relief is probably tolerable for the first time or even the second, but ripping the backside out of it and seriously abusing the trust put in me again and again certainly is not. The sordid details will reveal themselves as we move deeper and deeper into uncharted territory.

Delusions of grandeur manifest themselves in so many different ways. It could be Jesus Christ one day and even God on another. I tried these roles when I was flying at my highest level, both of them were great fun despite the terribly long hours and immense responsibility. The pay check never did arrive, but it was payment in itself to control the world by means of invisible buttons and psychic power. I could take my "work" with me to a pub or a concert, and then wash the intoxicating atmosphere down with a pint or shot too many—wonderful!

Those of you who are manic-depressive illness or bipolar affective disorder sufferers will probably be able to see where I am coming from here, and be more than able to relate and connect with my account of living and coping with manic depression than perhaps an outsider is able to. I am fully aware and respectful of the fact that we all have our own stories and that none of us are walking the same path. What I have to say depicts *my* life. If my experiences are of use, or just an enjoyable insight into the world of manic depression/bipolar affective disorder, then all is well and good with me. Those of you "non-members" who may well be affected in some way or another by manic depression, will have a tighter grip on a much improved understanding of what takes place within the mind of a manic-depressive. What is it exactly that drives them to tick either way 24/7?

Expect some nausea to jump out and gag you as you read through some of the fluffy candy covered pages. That is what manic depression can be like, but at least you can escape by putting down the book. Myself and millions of others around the world simply cannot switch off the mind mayhem without assistance, and we will never have that golden luxury unless we obey and then act responsibly upon the advice and expertise of the medical profession. Let's not forget about our own generous helpings of commonsense, for bipolar sufferers are on the whole pretty intelligent people; too intelligent for their own good at times. A sane, level playing field to inhabit has been marked out for us, and I am going to play ball from now on in order to have and maintain a stress free lifestyle, with both feet planted firmly on new ground.

As we are all aware, a deep relaxing sleep and a nutritious balanced diet are the mainstay's of a healthy and productive life. This is not too hard to obtain if given some thought. Achieving this can be a nightmare in itself, yet it comes as such a welcome relief. A general practitioner, psychologist or a psychiatric health support worker will have the knowledge and advice needed to get the ball rolling forward. Sleep deprivation is to be avoided at all costs as it pushes the mania along and also increases the hallucinatory factor. The trouble is that even the first excitable rumblings of mania beg to stay out a little longer because there is so much to see and do. Everything is seen in a different light, and the rising manic wants to absorb every last ounce of it.

My experience has told me that when I begin to skyrocket or submerge, my sleep pattern, or rather lack of sleep, served to magnify the mood in question, pushing it up or pulling it down. Not for a single minute would I be irresponsible enough to suggest that we all go out and experiment, but when I was already heading skyward with little or no sleep the higher I went, not to mention the hallucinatory effects that go hand in hand with manic insomnia. I found that at the onset of a depression I usually lacked sleep, but I made up for it as time went on. This form of sleep deprivation was caused by the niggling worries and doubts that I was nurturing in my over active mind, expanding tiny seeds of negativity until they hurt like mad. It can be a bit like a computer that has gone completely wrong, sending random pieces of unasked for and unneeded data all at once, so much so that it is impossible to give each item rational due care and attention, instead sending them back without being dealt with properly. The body is tired and so is the mind, but the mind never gives up, it just goes on fighting sleep. With me it didn't take too long for my mind to arrive at the stage where it would wear itself out and I could sleep soundly again. At first, sleep is the only means of escape, but when events hot up the whole story can suddenly turn very smelly indeed.

It is a drastic way to find out, but if you really want to know who your friends are then have an episode of mania or depression. To my disappointment I soon discovered that one counting hand sufficed, which is not at all surprising considering how awkward and unapproachable I had made myself. My family have often been pushed perilously close to the edge, but they did *not* topple over. Some of the people that I spent time with in a psychiatric hospital weren't as fortunate. There was a depressed chap in the hospital who had to deal with the separation of his parents, followed by the stress related death of his heartbroken father. This isn't exactly the kind of news that will lift sagging spirits, but the man in question, whom you shall meet later, made a full recovery. The complete blame for this type of occurrence should not be put upon the shoulders of a temporarily out of order human being. The fact of the matter is that none of this would have happened had the poor chap in question not succumbed to the torture chambers of depression. Yes folks, we manic-depressive/bipolar people certainly aren't overly selfish, we openly invite you all into to our topsy-turvy world of unpredictability whether you like it or not.

In the idyllic setting of Potten End (another small Hertfordshire village on the edge of Hemel Hempstead) there is tucked away a family run engineering company that specialises in the manufacture of rubber printing rollers. Along I went for an interview. "Production operative" became the latest addition to a long list of job titles that I had been collecting up until my twenty-fifth year. Fortunately, I was interviewed for the post by Mrs. Slater, wife of the boss. Her workaholic husband, who joined us toward the tale end of the interview had, I later discovered, been the unfortunate carrier of a recent dark dogged depression. All that I could detect as we went about the usual guided tour of the shop floor—smiling a little sadly at the prying production workers eyes along the way—was a strong feeling of camaraderie. Six months earlier Mr. Slater very nearly succeeded in a suicide attempt due to a severe bout of clinical depression, leaving his teenage son, daughter and loving wife to muddle through the emotion. They managed by the skin of their teeth to keep the fledgling business afloat, as he underwent the slow and painful journey back to a fully functional life. A heavily bearded Mr. Slater made me feel very much at home in my new surroundings, without dwelling upon or mentioning at all the mini depression that I had been lumbered with in the months leading up to my interview. Taking the open and honest stance certainly worked in my favour on that occasion. Honesty, despite the consequences, has always been the route that I prefer to follow. Knowing where you and those around you stand, even if it isn't always appetising, is still so refreshing. Most employers preach equal opportunity and no discrimination, but the truth is that they don't always practice it. This did not apply in 1990.

Having spent four years at Rolls Royce Ltd, first as a craft apprentice and then as a rooky sheet metal worker, probably tipped the scales in my favour. "So when can you start young man?" asked Mr. Slater. "Now," I replied a little cockily. After what seemed like only a few minutes of knowing them both, we found ourselves huddled up in the cupboard size office discussing an extremely personal and sensitive subject. Sometimes adversity shared is not only halved but it brings people together, people worth knowing that might otherwise pass you by. Without any shame or fear of repercussions we chatted openly about mental health issues for a duration far longer than the job interview itself. When

I had squeezed my big I've-just-got-a-new-job grin into my little red Volkswagen polo car, there was only one destination on my expanding narrow mind. "Why the hell did I get my knickers in such a twist over an interview?" I thought to myself as I negotiated Boxted Road at my usual illegal speed. David Bowie's voice crashed out of my modest speaker system as I headed straight for the Top Of The World public house in Warners End, just three convenient miles from my maisonette in Bovingdon. The aptly named "Toppers" public house was full to the rafters with thirsty customers, most of whom were regulars and also close friends of my uncle Ron, a hard working and highly skilled roofer. Three years earlier I had worked for Ron as a labourer trying to learn the trade, but my milder inexplicable moods got the better of me again and that was the end of that. Any excuse, or indeed *no* excuse at all to sink a few too many jars of silly-water (beer) always appeared to be the only law that everybody abided by, and why not? If you work hard then why not play hard? So long as nobody gets hurt along the way then where's the problem?

Despite my over enthusiasm it had been agreed that I commence my employment at Transia rollers in a weeks time. For the first few hours of each new day leading up to my latest job commencement I was firmly focused. Come the afternoons I would be stewing my buzzing brain again in a regular flow of alcohol. It could be wine, rum, sherry or cider; anything that did the magical trick. Somewhere in the fog I still found a way of coping with the routines of every day and a whole lot more. Not only that, but I didn't feel particularly drunk, even if I had knocked back enough of the demon brew to fell ten elephants—dangerous stuff indeed! God knows what this self abusive behaviour has done to my poor liver over the years. If I had kept this level of self abuse up I would have been a dead certainty for cirrhosis of the liver, with *no* way back, *no* second chance.

Feeling light-headed and light-footed were pleasant early symptoms of what was yet to come. From pub to pub I would float. It was as if I had been put on automatic pilot. Getting from A to B posed no problems, but it did send a shiver down my spine when no matter how hard I tried I could not recollect the middle part of the journey, especially when I was "dream driving." My mixed up mind wanted to live somewhere else, do so many things, to make my own indelible mark after finding the right form of expression. I was nowhere and everywhere. Transia rollers, where I was due to start work, now struck me as being an obstacle in my quest to find whatever it was that I yearned so much for. Something wonderful was happening, but being a newcomer to this gorgeous feeling meant that I couldn't actually reel it in tangle free and grasp it with all my might. When you have that first sweet taste of mania you are hooked for good. Nothing else compares to that heavenly spirit lifting nectar. All that I had been experiencing during the run up to my forthcoming career in rubber roller manufacturing was hypomania. Hypomania sounds like the pinnacle of the manic episode but in fact it describes, poorly in my opinion, the milder form of a manic episode. During the first half of 1990 it was just a case of dipping my big toe into the heady waters, but the storm in my fragile teacup, or should I say pint glass, had already begun to brew. Giving one-hundred percent in a new job has never posed a problem for me. Trying to please everybody too soon has always been a fault of mine, but one that I am still proud of. Why turn up every day to a fairly mundane job and spend most of your valuable time working out ways to shirk off? Throwing myself into the deep end is the only way that I know how to operate, and I will never change, not for anyone. Of course mistakes that should never have been made are made, maybe wasting more time than I hoped to save by trying to be Mister Billy-Whiz. Being in a hypomanic state definitely assisted me in the excessive production of fresh rubber wrapped rollers that would sit for ages on racks waiting to be cooked. "For Christ's sake mate, slow up a bit will you, you're making us look bad," came the cries from a few of my fellow workers. Somehow or another I had to find a way of releasing the pent up manic energy that was constantly building up inside of me. Being hypomanic did of course have its plus points, the main one being that it helped to make what was really a dirty dead end job seem like immense fun. Nobody working at Transia had a previous version to compare me with, and so they figured that this was the way in which the new recruit operated all of the time. Experiencing hypomania or fully blown mania in unfamiliar territory and in the company of none the wiser strangers, can be a very dangerous situation indeed. Having at least one sober associate close by is strongly advisable, but when the world and everything in it starts to talk to you in a hedonistic tongue, there is no one on Planet Earth who can keep up with it all, though not through lack of trying I can assure you. Off the leash and manic means only one thing— trouble waiting impatiently to happen.

A pattern was developing that would remain loyal throughout future manic episodes. Money earned went straight down my scrawny neck. The more I allowed myself to become used to the punishment I was inflicting upon myself with the bottle and jar, the more of the darn stuff I needed to satisfy the level of intoxication that I was rapidly becoming addicted to. I was addicted to the high aspect of manic depression rather than to the actual drink itself, that I can see today. On top of everything else I was becoming higher and higher and still feeling reasonably sober as a result, and so I kept on pushing myself, upping the stakes. Less and less sleep was needed, or so it felt. Lack of sleep, excessive drinking and a yet to be discovered chemical imbalance going on inside my brain were becoming a little too friendly with each other, compatible in a camouflaged manner. Despite my self gratifying excesses, there still appeared to be a little cash left over to blow away where and whenever the urge grabbed hold of me. Living all by myself in my new abode was still a huge novelty, in fact everything that I saw or touched felt new and alive, with far more substance and depth than ever before. Dull became bright, and badness took full circular outings that would return home to me as extremely good alternatives to the common belief of what is right and wrong. I could laugh in the face of evil for it was included in the equation to make good, a bit like a forgiving of all we allow to determine our destiny. All around me were meaningful explanations, a constant karma. Simplification and the relaxing of rules that bind us to where we need not be took precedence over almost everything else that was happening in my life at that time.

During the early stages of my childhood I felt a sense of cruel isolation. I was unable to put across my thoughts for fear of being ridiculed. That would be followed by the freedom of the opposite, a virgin glow that wrapped itself around my five or six year old body like a magical cloak, empowering me with extra knowledge and physical sensations, some of which were of a curious sexual nature. I could easily complete all the tasks set before me in record time, but I purposely held back so that I could stay where I felt safe, cocooned by familiar older faces that would never let me down. Sports, art, English and mathematics became the means by which I could excel and release the goodness that I felt. As quick as it takes you to turn one of these pages I could be blighted with a blankness, a sudden gut twisting introverted chasm of thought that I had no option other than to bottle up and carry around inside my tummy and mind. It was all or nothing. Very rarely would I stumble across a happy medium that would see me through. I was far too young to obey, comprehend or alter what was going on. Making the big mistake of not speaking up was a mistake I knew not, because I knew no other way. To little me this had to be accepted as my version of normality and then just get on with it as usual. These early experiences weren't a patch on what a fully grown bipolar affected adult goes through, but it was a huge deal to a curious mixed up kid like me.

At the ripe old age of eleven I began the first of five years at Hemel Hempstead's Cavendish School (named after Henry Cavendish, an English physicist and chemist who measured the density of Planet Earth in 1798.) Academically I excelled, but my behaviour did not. The usual schoolboy pranks were the flavour of every month,—making explosions in science and pursuing the girls in the hope of some extra curricular biology—but I did sometimes push my luck beyond the acceptable secondary school boundaries. This was something that three enjoyable weeks spent in Aberdovey, Wales, as a fifteen year old member of an Outward-Bound group attempted to quench. The Outward-Bound organisation's goal is to help develop teamwork and trust. Their motto "To serve, to strive and not to yield" never did sit too comfortably with me back then, but now I realise that it is what Jesus himself wants. Being good and giving to others first and foremost is in God's view a victory, not a string of gold medals at the expense of others less able. If that attitude can rub off on another soul then all the better.

"A big fish in a small pond," is how John Scott my physical education master at Cavendish once described me in one of his yearly reports. Little did Mr. Scott or any of my friends know then that there was an awful lot of time when I felt out of my depth, alone and frustrated, withdrawn and sad for something that I loved so deeply, and yet that special something, a confident clarity, kept on two-timing me. On one occasion I let out my anger at the inconsistency of my moods by placing my fist in an unsuspecting friends face. Luckily for me my friends really *were* friends and they allowed me to get away with far more than my outbursts deserved. When I was fifteen years young I began to steal small quantities of my father's unready home brew. This stuff was potent despite it tasting like dishwater. Tap water would be poured into the barrel to cover up my thieving activities, but of course my father was wise to it. Sneakiness was a skill I had yet to master.

Julie, my first true (puppy) love also came into my life when I was fifteen. She is a very artistic, flamboyant and extraordinarily gifted individual, and I think that we stood out a little from the average crowd. My school sporting days moved over and made way for my new virginal obsession. Romeo soon removed the virgin aspect and then the obsession was well and truly born. She tattooed my heart and I carved out her initials on my left arm using a scalpel blade that I had "borrowed" from West Hertfordshire Hospital, when I spent two fascinating weeks assisting in the radiography department as part of my work experience.

Cheap social club beer and a game of snooker following a days apprenticing became a habit for me right from the outset of my brief four years at Rolls Royce Ltd. The Rolls Royce aero (helicopter) engine site was based in Leavesden, Hertfordshire, and has now been converted into impressive film studios where they have made the recent *Harry Potter* and *James Bond* films. I miss that social club so much. Not long after I commenced employment at Rolls Royce a wild youthful party at my parent's house took place (they had jetted off to Spain for a relaxing fortnight), resulting in their house being unintentionally trashed. Soon after this destructive outcome in the name of fun, Julie, Jules or Ju and myself parted.

The fire that I have for her will never be properly extinguished; a common trait of many other Romeos and their first taste of the emotions that the opposite sex can send jangling. This particular Romeo drank plenty of poison over the years but survived somehow. Further splits with girlfriends always sent me into alcoholic oblivion and depression. Rejection was not welcome in my vocabulary. It was a dent in my pride that I couldn't seem to take as well as the other lads my age, but then again these are feelings that are not usually shared among pimply teenage males. Just take a look at movies such as *Grease* to see what I mean. One day the green-eyed-monster riddled its distorted summary of realism into my life, causing me to put too many undeserving young ladies through so much grief. My unpredictable worse scenario imagination would run away with itself, destroying all of the previous goodness that had been built up. Since my teenage years came to a close I have found that being happy is more of a struggle. Happiness has never flowed as freely as I imagined it should. Learning how to put on the happy smiling face when it was required became less of a wrench with time and practice, and I knew even then that my happiest most heavenly time had already been used up with Julie, quite a profound statement considering that I was still only a pup in love at the time. Having fun became an unfunny effort. Drink filled the voids as well as the landlords pockets. A special lady changed all of that just over a decade later …

Now I was beginning to feel the first rumblings of an extraordinary happiness, a happiness that had not seen the light of day since Ju and I were camping out on Boxmoor Common or cycling around town on a beaten up old tandem bicycle or best of all making magical puppy love in her home, the Moorhouse, to the sounds of Oscar Peterson's tinkling piano and Bowie's classic *Hunky Dory* album.

I had a new job to hold down. Asking Keith Steadman to hold down a job and stay in one place is like asking Michael Schumacker to drive around in a Mister Whippy van selling ice-creams for a living—it just isn't going to happen! Transia were very good to me, almost *too* kind. I took to splurging out on expensive clothes that I often wore to *The Living Room*, a nightclub in Hemel's Marlowes town centre. These very same clothes would often end up being worn into an oily grimy workplace. I had usually driven well over the drink drive limit back from the club and then stayed up all night, playing vinyl LP's that hadn't had an airing in years. If I felt so inclined I would make a few early hour telephone calls to old schoolmates and the odd acquaintance from various bars that I had been frequenting at the time. Why should I bother changing outfits? So into work I would walk wearing my new gaudy loose silk shirt, charcoal baggy trousers, bottomed off with a sharp new pair of black Italian shoes with a flap over golden buckle. As time progressed and the mania increased it would be almost impossible to catch me in the same outfit for more than a few hours, even minutes. Everything needed constant change in order to keep up with my racing mind. Dress for the part yes, but this unrehearsed "part" was ricocheting around my crazed head only, leaving the others bewildered and none the wiser.

What a sight I must have been despite donning an overall coat. The self proclaimed king of nightlife standing in front of a loaded spinning lathe, wearing a delightful full faced visor, a pair of sliced up leather gauntlets and shoes so shiny that you needed goggles to protect your eyes from the glare. All that I got from the other men were a few cheeky comments that my hypomanic receptors would misconstrue into what I wanted to hear, and that was it. When I think back I feel pretty awful about the way in which I let the Slaters down. Mrs. Slater, using her feminine intuition had indeed noticed my erratic behaviour, so she made a point of keeping a kind beady eye on me. The way my mind was operating away from the workplace was a whole new story; a different orbit was opening up entirely. It was a short matter of time before the imaginary characters that were incubating deep within decided to rear their ugly sides.

I thought that the feelings I was experiencing could be covered up. After all, I did have the past to draw from, such as my ups and downs as a child as well as throughout my pubescent years, not to mention the twists and turns of emotion already endured during the first half of my twenties. Who was I trying to kid? Certainly those who were the closest to me could and would sniff out something unappetising from my behavioural menu with the accuracy of a bloodhound. This could be achieved over the telephone by sensing changes in tone, by my outlandish choice of clothing and hairdo, or by the irrational and slightly surreal opinions and attitudes I may put forward during the course of a conversation. Revealing a nonchalant, blasé view of important routine financial matters is always a dead giveaway of incoming mania. Madcap money making schemes and many other flash-in-the-pan five minute wonders would all contribute to the final unofficial conclusion that Keith is gradually turning slightly bonkers, and you would have been hard pushed to find somebody who didn't agree with such an astute assumption. A proper diagnosis takes time to achieve though, and that valuable time is of the essence.

It is not so much the slurring of one's speech that lets the cat out of the bag, but the speed of delivery. The content often leaves an awful lot to be desired as well. Oh yes, booze certainly performed one of the leading roles in a roller coasting show that has bumped and spanned its way back and forth in full view of a safely hidden non paying public gallery. Alcohol is not the demon force here or anywhere. The irresponsible partaker, in possession of an illness riddled with addictive formats, is the devilish element. Why? Because I believe that good/evil God/devil exists in us all, and that an accused bottle of the easily picked on hard stuff is totally innocent.

On I went, doing the Monday to Friday forty hours plus any overtime that became available. My productivity soared as I shot up higher and higher, and that is without losing any of the quality. My heightening mania must be held accountable for the electrocution that happened late one afternoon. Thinking that I could handle anything electrical—especially as I had spent a couple of years at Saint Albans and Dacorum colleges studying for my City and Guilds certificates in electrical engineering—I unwisely decided to try my hand at repairing one of the hot irons that were used for trimming excess rubber. All of a sudden I was connected to the national grid. That may not sound odd to you, but when you consider that I was laughing at the same time as being fried alive you can appreciate the absurdity of it all. You never know, a few more volts of do-it-your-self E.C.T (Electro Convulsive Therapy) through my pumped up body might have changed the course of history, and those around me would have had a far more peaceful life, though not quite as interesting.

Greg, a precision grinder, sold me an Olympus 35mm camera along with all of the fancy lenses. Fifty pounds sterling sealed the deal. After work I drove down to a little photography shop in the Old High Street section of Hemel Hempstead. There I purchased a shiny new aluminium camera case, just like the professionals carry around with them. Having always fancied myself as being a bit of a handy snapper, I set off to aggravate the regulars in some of Hemel Hempstead's most frequented pubs. It was a good job that I was nimble on my toes, otherwise my telescopic would have been shoved many times by hordes of angry drinkers where the Sun doesn't shine. At the awkward decisive age of fifteen I built a ramshackle darkroom in my parents attic, producing low quality black and white photographs of absolutely anything and everything that was going on in my life at the time. 1979 to 1990 was very well documented. Why I chose the safe door of a prestigious apprenticeship in engineering to go through rather than pursue my creative passions I will never know. My mind was a muddle then, I spread myself too thin, more often than not to please and impress other people, but to the detriment of my own future. Let's face it, at that young age the only thing your interested in is getting a part time job to finance a booming social life, not to mention the obligatory record collection and of course photography. The film, printing paper and the chemicals didn't come cheaply, nor do girlfriends when a young buck is trying so hard to impress.

Convinced that I had an exceptionally good creative eye, I clicked away in the pubs with gay abandon. With no inhibitions and loaded with film it was nothing short of a manic, highly intrusive bombardment of camera, lights and undeterred action. Sensing when it was time to cease blinding the regulars with my new adjustable angle flashgun became a fine art in itself. To pacify my mostly uninterested subjects I had to keep them sweet, and so I would later select a decent shot of them, mount it in a cheap and cheerful frame purchased from somewhere like Woolworths, and then present them with it at just the right moment, completely free of charge of course. "Sweet as a nut," as they say in the UK.

This seemingly harmless enough pastime of mine became unstuck during one unforgettable Saturday morning when I was working some overtime at Transia. The latest batch of my prints were doing the rounds on the shop floor, when it was brought to the attention of Mr. Slater that one of the photographs depicted me, at what must have been 3 or 4 a.m., sitting on my green draylon sofa, unshaven, with wild piercing manic eyes burning sickeningly into those of the observer. I held on tightly to what was only a plastic toy but looking just like the real thing, pointing it firmly into my temple. The toy automatic pistol was completely harmless in a physical sense but not in any other. It damaged all of my sanity and suggested an extremely unstable mentality. It was the message that this idiotic prank put forth that deeply concerned Mr. Slater, quite understandably so. Whatever it was that I had been trying desperately to convey did not reach its target. What is it that would possess somebody to fake his own sickening execution with an imitation firearm pressed firmly into his confused wild eyed head? That's what everybody at Transia must have been thinking. Usually I stay clear of violent films and images depicting death or the devil, yet here was I believing that everything was acceptable now, and that everyone else surely understood. The antics of a bipolar affected person are often the complete opposite of their normal behaviour, as if the beholder of this condition has been specially selected and then given a key to the universe to do all of the things they desire, and that often means the things once frowned upon or disallowed as an adolescent and also into adulthood. Becoming higher and higher with every new inhalation of the purist, most agreeable communicative electricity, meant that I really didn't care about or even realise the seriousness of my actions. At such an early stage of my mania the grim inherent dangers simply didn't register, which is a *very* dangerous position to be in. The way I did see it was that secretly the others were in on the whole peculiar situation. The "others" were those with whom I had shared a personal moment with, and in doing so had joined me in my pleasure quest. I felt as if I was some sort of chosen leader with a mission. This mission would become selfexplanatory along the way with the assistance of those who were going to latch on. All that I had to do was to allow everything in and go with the flow, wherever that may take me, and try to remember that hidden somewhere in every piece of negativity that I would inevitably encounter there would be a positive lesson to be learnt, not only for myself but for the whole human race. Why do things by halves?

Manic depression is really just a collection of topical twists and turns in which a beginning cannot reach a rational conclusion. It never knows where to stop, but it does know how to drag the latest thought through the maze only to arrive at an illogical conclusion. The further lost or gone one is in their latest mood swing the more of these careless, headless thoughts jump on the bandwagon, making the initial good or bad thought much tougher to focus on, process and then put to sleep.

"Keith, stop what you are doing and see me in my office immediately," shouted the boss over the shrill noises emanating from the machinery, "So young man, can you explain yourself?" Across his busy desk were strewn the guilty photographs. Mr. Slater's face was now redder than a baboons backside, and so I feared the worst. "Don't be too hard on him," intervened Mrs. Slater, who by now had surmised that there was something a little bit more involved here than just a drunken, badly thought out joke. A steady banter back and forth followed, including the observations of Mrs. Slater. To my amazement and relief came the news that, "On this occasion I will let it slide, but if you pull any more stunts like that young man, you will be out on your ear, do I make myself perfectly clear?" "Yes my lord," came my risky high court reply. I kept my head down over my revolving lathe for at least ten whole minutes, before my upbeat vision resumed in all of its warped glory.

London's Capital FM radio station became my late evening and early morning target. Following a satisfying drinking session in one or more of the local pubs, I would return home and begin to make relentless telephone calls to the station. Even I was surprised at the frequency of getting through to a disc jockey or their assistant. If I assembled enough sense and slowed my speech considerably, I often found myself chatting to the D.J about my obscure request live on the airwaves. I was convinced that the good people of Hemel Hempstead were listening in to an 11.30 p.m. and beyond radio show, transmitted from the Euston Tower (now located at Leicester Square) in London. Cryptic messages that I believed to be hidden in the tunes were becoming clearer. Certain keywords such as Heaven, angel, eternal, life, love and God especially stood out, lending so much added weight and deep meaning to my hypomanic imagination. Contorting my wasting frame to every single drop of musical emotion released over the airwaves became a regular occurrence. Not only did my manic movement provide me with an excellent workout, I also believed it to be a living room floorshow, put on for the masses. The temptation to take it on the road simmered on. I knew inside that if I was wide awake, up and at it, sucking in and giving back all that I saw, sensed, heard, felt and thought, that everybody else must be doing the same in some other shape or form. What took place behind the dark red door of 12A Vicarage lane was everybody's business. This was to be my first serious taste of the complex mind game element of fully blown mania. All that had taken place was still only child's play compared with what lay ahead of me. I was just warming up!

A "Mental derangement marked by great excitement and violence": craze, passion (for)—This is how the dictionary describes the word *mania*. The excitable crazed and passionate part sat true, but as for the violent part, that was a definite no-no. From the outside looking in you would be forgiven for thinking otherwise.

Seventeen year old David Slater used to work a few hours after school and during half term breaks at his father's engineering company in order to earn a little pocket money. I took an immediate shine to him, probably because he was a cocky wiseass and reminded me of myself. He seemed to me to be a very focused lad with a strong opinionated mind of his own, as well as coming across as a down to earth, straight ahead kind of guy. We were both roughly the same height, around five feet seven and of a similar scrawny build. One day, during the regimental fifteen minute tea break, we agreed upon swapping my old tropical fish aquarium, complete with all of the paraphernalia, in return for a well worn-in black leather bikers jacket. This jacket accompanied me throughout many of my forthcoming manic activities. Dave borrowed a VHS videotape of mine called *Christiane F*—a colossal mistake! We were seriously discussing the perils of the misuse of drugs, especially the lethal hardcore substances such as heroin and ecstasy, when I suggested that he took a good look at the true story of a young German girl from Berlin who got caught up in the whole sleazy heroin scene at the age of only thirteen. Loaning him this film was meant on my behalf to act as a deterrent to the drug culture and *not* as an enticement to it, but that wasn't how the suspicious Mr. Slater saw it when he discovered the damn tape in David's bedroom. The pair of us put forward a solid case in our defence until Mr. Slater's worst fears were quashed. From then on I could sense that the boss did not see me in the same light as he once did. He obviously thought of me as a threat to his business and to his family, a little bit too unpredictable for his liking, and not exactly what the doctor ordered as far as his own health was concerned. He was a fair, generous man who couldn't be criticised nor blamed for showing some wariness toward me.

As if all of that was not enough to send the poor man over the edge and straight to the funny-farm, I went out and purchased a lifelike rubber mask of Freddie Kruger, the psychopathic creature from the *Friday The Thirteenth* series of gory horror films. Once again this was an example of behaving in a completely opposite manner to my normal jovial self. Apart from what now felt like my *six* senses becoming higher and higher, I was starting to find that working in that tiny workshop all day long—for so long in fact, that when I blew my nose, all that came out was a multicoloured sludge made up from a cocktail of neoprene and other exotic varieties of rubber—was having a stifling effect on me. My head was swelling, and it was like living in a goldfish bowl. My days were numbered, so why not go out with a big bang? After all, I can now do whatever I want can't I, because I'm the chosen one in possession of fantastic new mind blowing powers. What complete and utter poppycock!

"That Steadman fellow has got to be on something," is how Mr. Slater and my fellow workmates probably thought, but all that I was high on was life, which is, the last time I heard, a perfectly legal substance. Let me get one thing straight before I continue; I do *not* do drugs, except for lithium carbonate and a few other prescribed medications that stabilise and contribute toward my regularly assessed and acceptable mood level.

One of my many schoolboy part-time jobs was as a shampoo boy and hair sweeper-upper at *Robert's,* a respectable gents hairdressers next to the market square. Annie Bates, a gorgeous feminine specimen who oozed sex appeal and was a whole year older than myself,—at the age of fourteen and a half, a twelve month gap might as well be twenty—invited me round to her parents house in Kings Langley when everybody was away for the weekend. Annie, who always smelt of something exotic and wore gold chains with little bells around her dainty ankles so that we could always hear her coming, produced a huge old fashioned copper kettle and proceeded to burn a lump of cannabis resin inside of it. When it was burning away nicely we took it in turns sucking the burning smoke up through the spout. I soon gave up on it and left the more experienced Annie to mellow and chill-out to the tinkling of her dingly-dangly golden bells. All that I got for my troubles were a pair of numb lips, not from kissing Annie but from the dope.

Who am I to judge or to say what is the right and wrong thing for somebody else to do? We are all different thank God, possessing different wants and needs, which means that what is right for one individual is not always the right way to go for the other; you certainly don't need to be Einstein to figure that one out. I enjoy a hand rolled smoke of regular over the counter tobacco and a few drinks still, that's no secret. Both are forms of drugs that can screw up the benefits of prescribed medication if they are abused, something I managed to achieve on a large scale for too long. Ideally, anybody who has a mental illness and is on medication should lay off the drink and drugs completely in order to achieve maximum results. Smoking a joint of marijuana or cannabis is to me not a great deal different than drinking a pint of beer or a vodka tonic. Like most things, if moderation isn't applied, an inevitable hefty price will be paid. Over indulgence can cause many mental problems including mania and depression, as well as bringing out any paranoid and schizophrenic tendencies that the consumer may have. For some less fortunate souls, smoking the odd joint now and then can help them to relax and warn off certain ailments. They may not even be able to physically get up off of their sore aching backsides and get to a pub or liquor store, have you ever thought of that? It appears as plain as day to me that all of the rules and regulations that are doing the rounds today are not entirely made with these people in mind, and are instead made by well to do able people who haven't got a single clue when it comes down to the real issues that matter, or about the real human beings to whom many of today's madcap rules and regulations are directed. I rest my case.

The sinister Freddie Kruger made his debut performance at the Tudor Rose pub in Chaulden, Hemel, to the dismay and utter bewilderment of the quiet drinkers. Some of them wouldn't have given it a second thought before ripping my head from off my shoulders and placing it on a wrought iron spike above the pub door, but that was only if they could get hold of me, and I was quick. Round and round went my racing mind, picking up new data to process. I was speeding without taking a speeding drug, so fast in fact that I was almost able to bite the tail end from off my mind's own thoughts.

Next stop, the Top Of The World pub. Regulars at the Toppers, all seasoned "pubaholics," took one drop-jawed look at me and laughed. It wasn't quite the reaction that I had hoped for as I went about an evenings campaign of latex faced terror, but at least I came away still intact. Some of the regulars, I discovered a few days later, had thought that Ron's nephew must have some sick kind of death wish, and would gladly assist me in achieving it. They were only kidding, weren't they? Uncle Ron didn't witness the off-the-wall entertainment that evening, preferring to remain at his countryside cottage. At closing time the final results on the shock-meter revealed that a handful of people were shaken, but nobody else had even stirred.

All hell broke loose the following morning. Complete with my ludicrous Freddie Kruger attire I set off for work. It was one of those crispy mornings with an electric blue sky. The oxygen that I took in as I sped without due care and attention charged me up and up to an even higher level of sweet mania. As I stepped out of the car my feathery legs felt as if they were about to give way, so I needed time to compose myself. As soon as my racing mind and lightweight legs got their act together I was fine. Today I was floating on air. "What a crying shame it is to be stuck indoors," I thought, "On such a beckoning day it's criminal to be stuck in here performing such unnatural tasks, all for a pittance and a few mugs of tea." Tools went down with a crash, followed by the beautiful sound of silencing my lathe forever. At that stage I couldn't have given a flying fart as to what anybody thought. My days were numbered and on *my* terms, so why not have some maniacal fun with the secretary who worked in the adjoining factory unit? From the back seat of my car I grabbed my Kruger disguise, then strode into foreign territory. Without time to even think or indeed care about the implications of what I was about to do, I had slipped everything on and had begun climbing the stairs that led to the first floor offices. Being a Saturday overtime morning there were hardly any party-poopers in the vicinity that could jeopardise my moronic fun. It is so true about actors when they say that they actually become and feel the character that they are portraying as soon as the makeup and costume goes on. Lesson No.1 is to never assume that the recipient of any scaremongering attempt will see things through the same eyes as you do. Very slowly I crept closer and closer to where I could hear the impressively fast tapping of a keyboard. I approached on my hands and knees, slinking as I went like a stalking leopard toward the semi glass partitioning that separated the poor innocent girl from the fright of her young life. The Freddie kit also came with a pair of gloves that had long imitation knife-nails that protruded from each digit. Out of sight and sound the terror commenced. Rat-a-tat-tat, Rat-a-tat-tat on the glass went I, still hidden. This continued for one long minute before I leapt up on to my featherbrained feet in full view. How she screamed, especially when I opened her office door and made straight for her, laughing and growling. She then froze—scared shitless is a crude but probably the most accurate way of describing the poor young lady. I can't remember what it was that the neighbouring company produced, but whatever it was, on that sunny Saturday morning the production line came to a grinding halt. So did my spell at Transia.

Lodged in the back of my mind was a deep sense of urgency, so I told myself to keep following the clues and directions in whatever way they chose to come at me, and don't be tempted to push fate because all good things will eventually come to those who wait. It was all very good in theory but I was growing increasingly impatient to hit the next level, to be wherever I felt I needed to be in order to keep the manic party rocking. Was it my party alone or was everybody else invited? Those early days, the build up to my first fully blown episode of mania—the likes of which I will probably never see again—were riddled with utter confusion. My voyage contained so many tricks. My manic thoughts fought with one another, leaving the judge and jury of my mind with the unenviable task of putting a stop to the fighting and then instigating an amicable merger. Taking the risk of being shot down in flames by ridicule was an area of being high and in full flight that needed to be withstood, as well as being understood fully. Who was on my quivering wavelength? Surely we all knew the golden rule of never divulging directly what one is thinking, or what is being planned to take place next. I used what I believed to be coded signals, such as an ever so slight nod of the head or an eye glance. The way in which an inanimate object is positioned within tantalising view of my prospective audience, the double meaning of an old worn out newspaper headline, or maybe even a reinterpretation of whatever the news guy tells us on television—these were all coded messages that I couldn't lose by, because my mind would change according to the desired effect. Everything and anything is caught up in the manic mind. It is continuously producing and editing, multiplying, subtracting and dividing, but the most popular equation of all involves addition, lots of it. It doesn't let up, not for a single moment. A trillion words a minute gush out of the manic mouth like a verbal Niagara Falls, only to be immediately replaced by more and more froth. As the manic thinks, then thinks some more about saving the world, or something equally important such as which Hawaiian shirt to wear on a rainy day, he can at the same time conjure up the capacity to talk about something completely different, a subject that is intellectual and inventive yet fantastically surreal. While all of this deep thinking, intellectual surrealism is taking place you could be having wild sex with a luscious bevy of lightly oiled babes, and why not? You are manic for goodness sake! If it is doable then why not let your hair down and allow nothing to get in the way of your mania in motion. The restraints are surrounding us all, pinning us up against the wall as we in our own way wriggle to break free from our designated lot in life. That *lot* is a dark grey area and very hard to define, which is why we instinctively seek the answers, hidden beyond the strict boundaries that mankind often delights in laying down, insisting that they remain safe, sound and out of reach to potential meddlers.

Manic ramblings go on and on. Each dot, dash and syllable are irresistible cues to create yet another bunch of philosophical entanglements. All that an evolving manic person can hope for is to hoist their latest scheme or dream up to the top of the greasy flagpole, take a brief sabbatical and then see who salutes it. Many manic-depressives do very well by using their manic tendencies in an acceptable, creative and productive form. The degree of one's manic depression varies considerably from one person to another, and from each episode to another. Position in life has a big say in whether the beholder can or cannot channel some of that manic creativity into a job of work, even carving out a career by treading the boards, singing songs or writing down the words. Somebody has to do it, and who better than those who possess some of the most creative minds on this planet?

Try picturing this: Twin towered Wembley Stadium on a boiling hot Saturday afternoon, 72,000 beautiful people, the greatest rock and roll band in existence, contraband booze, plenty of Marlboros to smoke, my cousin Todd and yours truly. Todd and I had downed plenty of booze even before we set foot inside the most famous stadium in the world. The aroma of hot dogs, beer, sweat, perfume and dope—all the necessary components of an outdoor stadium gig were in plentiful supply that day. The Rolling Stones were on the European leg of their *Steel-Wheels* world tour, and tonight they were performing for me. Todd is my father's late Sister Valerie's son, the same age and build as me but with a very chiselled face. Both of us have always had the tendency to be a bit excitable, with perhaps a little bit more energy than can be easily expelled, although it wasn't through a lack of us both trying. Todd works very hard indeed, and is able to turn his hand to many tasks set before him. It doesn't matter what type of work he may have been doing throughout the day or night, he always made sure afterwards that he was clean cut and smartly dressed. He is quick witted too, and he definitely knows how to stand up for himself in any situation. It could be said that he's a good bloke to have around, that's for sure!

The atmosphere of a big Wembley event is always electric. We had only been inside the Stadium for five minutes until I could feel myself rising yet another manic notch, and then another. Every word I spoke rolled off my tongue eloquently. Physical movement had never felt so fluid. I danced amid the thick intoxicating air without a care in my world. Dancing an erotic grind to the Stones with a warm plastic pint of beer in one hand, a cigarette in my mouth, whilst at the same time grasping any one of the many peachy female rears willingly on offer—it was sheer paradise. I felt razor sharp and then so smooth. Diamonds could have been cut with a single smile. We both had a ball that day, behaving like a couple of frustrated rabbits on Viagra while at the same time becoming utterly stoned, not on sociable or recreational drugs, but on the valiant efforts of Mick, Charlie, Ronnie, and of course the cool Mister Keith Richards himself who rocked and rolled over to where we were positioned during *satisfaction* and gave us all the thumbs up sign. So much intense excitement throbbing through 72,000 thrill seekers served only to decrease the time span between now and the day when I could be let loose to maniacally rule the world in my spare time, in my own way, with my clammy hands tied tightly behind my back. I thought that everybody else could do likewise, but their world would be unique and personal to only themselves. In other words, we would all fit together while at the same time being totally different and free. Maniacally controlling the universe, the past and the future took a little longer to arrange as you will discover. People were floating in pieces through the air, becoming reassembled with magnetic thought patterns and then projected out once more into a recreated life form that also held the secrets that lay behind mankind's entire existence, along with the unlimited means to be something that has not yet even been imagined. I need a deep breath.

Like a strutting peacock, I made my way back to Hemel Hempstead with my cousin Todd. The dulcet tones of *Nineteenth Nervous Breakdown* bellowed out of a huge boom-box stereo system that appeared to be even bigger than the dreadlocked character behind us upon whose shoulder it rested. British Rail swept the two of us back from Wembley's centralised station to Hemel's solid grey platform on a wave of hazy over indulgence.

Because I had convinced myself that I was partly responsible for the previous days events, and so much higher for the experience, it seemed like a perfectly reasonable idea to withdraw more of my diminishing funds from the cashpoint machine and go on a pub crawl to end all pub crawls. Negativity on the part of another pub-goer toward my efforts were then reinterpreted, so that their twisting and turning away from me meant something really rather complimentary. I kept on making up the rules to fit my current mood, and to ensure that a foot couldn't possibly be put wrong. "They must still be having trouble in accepting this whole new world that has suddenly opened up and become available to us, with me as the chosen leader and you as the crew," I would think rather smugly to myself in those very brief, status threatening situations. My imagined self-conviction of supreme brilliance sometimes even blinded me and became somewhat overwhelming, too much to handle and decipher all at once. Then my manic progression went a step further, believing that perhaps I was in fact an historical character who had gone full circle, or even a higher spiritual force still to be made crystal clear to me. To answer these questions I would have to take maniacally swayed notes of the many intricate signals and contradictory clues that were smacking me in the skull with the force of an angry bare knuckled fist.

Could it be that we, during some stage in our lives have actually revolved, evolved and been recreated? The "human-recycle" sounds rather wholesome don't you think? Could we have taken it in turns to be one another, having already lived millions of lives in differing forms, male and female, animal, plant and mineral, but perhaps in a different time zone which would probably explain "deja-voodoo" and funny looking people of all nations that spookily resemble a living thing of the past. We could be eternal images of ourselves. Could we be one entity? Is what we see ahead only us looking straight back? The state of my mind controlled all of the things that we could so far imagine and comprehend. So was it in the best interests of the people to go out and please others, in the knowledge that by doing these kind deeds they would later reap that pleasure effort themselves? Was I heading a little bit above my station? You bet I was. Remaining cool and not appearing to be too big headed, which indeed I was, proved to be an enormous challenge. Later, my own growing belief in my manic world nearly crushed me, as I ran around like a blue-arsed fly trying to be all things to everyone and failing miserably. The pressure that goes hand in hand with being high as a satellite is awful at times, but it was a very small price to pay for so much pleasure had.

My drinking continued, except that now I had begun to borrow cash to finance it. My casual approach to money stemmed from my latest manic inspired theory that when I landed safely on my feet there would be so much ready cash at my disposal I wouldn't know what to do with it all. The second theory was that money would be eliminated for good, and that we would all work together within a revamped system, where sharing ensures that none of the Earth's population goes without as they are today under the present world leadership. This particular pipe dream was going to take a lot of doing. Meanwhile I had to come up with the cash to pay back a hefty handful of £10.00 and £20.00 loans, as well as to settle one or two outstanding bar bills. Without consciously knowing what I was doing, I carried on digging deeper holes for myself. Okay, I realise that it could have been thousands that I owed, tens of thousands in fact, meaning that I would have to sell off every personal belonging or even steal to avoid a visit to the fracture clinic, but when you happen to be in a pathetically low income bracket or indeed in no bracket at all as I was, a ten-pound note here and a twenty there is an awful lot of money, as I am sure many of you are only too painfully aware. Apart from a few scalpels and a Mars bar when I was younger, I would never stoop to steal, no matter what!

By now things were really buzzing. Walking continued to be quite a feat at times because I felt as if I was strolling on the Moon. Without any warning my legs would take on a life of their own, becoming slightly numb and threatening to give out on me when I was least expecting it. This disconcerting sensation came and went, but I noticed that it would strike me the most when a new manic rush of discovery threatened to fell me, or when I was in a volatile environment that had triumphed in spraying a flammable liquid onto my fiercely burning coals. Busy multi-moving and multi-sounding, atmospherically concentrated situations stirred up to a frenzy the terrific sensation of speed, choreographing movement to the sound of the record playing on the living radio or coin fed jukebox. It always happened when I sat on a bar stool, delivering a one-way million mile a minute speech to a reluctant audience. The more I said the higher I became. I felt certain that I was speaking sense, and that my babbling on was exactly what my captive audience needed and wanted to hear. The subjects that I had chosen to embellish were nothing new to the reeled in listener. Thinking that I had hooked my audience when in fact all they were doing was politely humouring me, had caused my self-esteem to rise, and so my risk taking increased. Caution was always in place, just in case everything took an unexpected U-turn and blew up in my face.

Like a passing phase or fashion I would throw one thrill out and replace it with another. My mind was able to mould new scenarios within one setting, and a chameleon influence felt at home within me. The fluidity floating in the air merged with the latest whim of fancy into the forthcoming character or place, creating a colourful puddle of oil and water instead of something with a malleable solidity such as Plasticine. Slipping to the cigarette scorched carpets from my elevated barstool eventually became a smooth lubricated manoeuvre. There were instances when I would sit trapped on my stool trying to be cool, calm and moderately sophisticated, drinking far more than I wanted to drink because I thought my lightweight lower half might buckle if I stood up.

Telephones and answering machines helped to bail me out of my minor financial predicament. At the onset of hypomania I had purchased a selection of ridiculously cheap telephone answering machines from a man who worked for yet another engineering establishment in Potten End. Where he got them from I don't know, and I didn't particularly want to know either. Some of these Panasonic and British Telecom machines were sold easily enough at the Top Of The World and the Tudor Rose public houses for just a few beers profit, but I still had five or six left unsold. I also placed the best of my V.H.S. video tape collection in a couple of sturdy grocery carrier bags and went on another selling spree. I sold almost all of them, giving me the means by which to reimburse my creditors and cream a little from off the top. This was yet another one of my badly thought out moves that I later lived to regret.

Uncharacteristically my maisonette had begun to resemble a second hand junk shop. Items that had been stowed away in the attic for safekeeping had suddenly taken on a whole new meaning and were now adorning every available nook and cranny. Old newspapers and magazines now represented a coded means to maniacally convey to a visitor something that I couldn't verbalise. Poor quality black and white prints of many yesterdays were awakened so that they could be strategically positioned throughout the building. Julie came back into my life in an unhealthy way. I don't think somehow that she would have approved of having her portrait, taken of her on top of a lion in Trafalgar Square, on the wall above my lavatory. Squirts of fluoride toothpaste served as glue.

Paranoia visited me fairly often throughout this stage of my high rise. There is always a bad element that is so envious of the good. They will do anything to spoil the party, to knock you off your perch. It is going on today with overloaded power crazy nations kicking the hell out of each other in the name of religion and natural resource—how utterly ridiculous! There are plenty of bad angels hiding out there, all of them looking for an excuse to do no good.

Guardian angels are all well and good, but instead of that luxury I felt the overriding need to install some back up security in the form of a top-notch alarm system. Bear in mind that although my humble little home is very nice and adequate for my purposes it certainly isn't Buckingham Palace, and it is hardly the sort of premises that a burglar would put at the top of his job list. Still, it was my welfare that concerned me the most. Around came the astonished alarm salesman dressed very smartly in a sharp suit and tie, probably anticipating a healthy commission. Double glazing hadn't even been installed up until then, and there I was receiving a quote that came to well over £2000 for alarms, lights and a security camera—daylight robbery! Appearing to be rather annoyed that his time had been wasted the salesman sped off in his fancy car, but not before I had tried my best to sell him a top of the range telephone answering machine. My manic way of evaluating what had just happened was to tell myself that the word has gone out via the alarm salesman that Mr. K.A. Steadman was not a person to mess around with. Even the salesman was part of the "show," wasn't he? From that day on I made do with the cheaper option, commonly known in the UK as the neighbourhood watch scheme.

Now it appears obvious that as my leaden star lightened and rose higher and higher, I had begun to be subconsciously selective about the type of company I would spend a preset amount of time with. This of course became something that I had no control over. Manic depression/bipolar affective disorder evicts set patterns, it just keeps flowing rapidly, faster and faster, avoiding as many boulders as possible. The rapid route that the bipolar affected person is drawn toward is so variable. It will occasionally pull sane relatives and friends who are trying to recapture the threads of sanity under as well, soaking them with desperation in the rocky process.

Close family members were never blanked out completely, although I made doubly sure that I didn't stay around them for longer than I had to. This acted as a preservation mechanism. In my newfound manic mind things were changing for the betterment of all that I had ever personally believed to be upright, correct and a ton of fun. As overseer I was able to see, feel and experience these things before they had even landed at my feet. Having by my side a caring soul who knew me inside and out was *not* on. Sensing a change in my behaviour and then expressing their disapproval would upset my finely tuned apple cart. On one small hand I wanted to do all in my power to protect and prevent entry to my equation creation, and on the other hand I felt the need to share and confide. Belief in myself, that I could communicate with others, anywhere, through any convenient and appropriate means, could not replace a good old fashioned heart to heart conversation. Even then I could only lean back and sip my drink, wondering if all I exhumed of myself actually hit home, somewhere else far away and long ago. Were my sent thoughts hitting the bulls-eye, but unable to be returned because I omitted the senders address? Far too many questions scrambled around inside of me without any tangible solution. The bad thought battalions often paid me a cagey visit, temporarily exhausting some of my brightest brain cells. The little devils would then dump the second hand anxiety into my minds dark well, along with the rest of the crap, forming a debilitating sludge that would later on swamp my mind and imprison my crushed soul in a deeply depressing existence, a sickening pisser of a place where I would stew in recurring regret, burn with imagined failure and be forced to mourn my overwhelmingly addictive magical manic times. Life becomes so scary and flat when one is so far down after being so high up. Instead of being immersed forever in a splash of kaleidoscopic colour, edged with electricity and tinged with God's love, depression is a flattened cardboard box that has been left out in the rain, and each day is being blown nearer to the gutter of life and death. Just when you feel that your situation can be remotely tolerable, some hobnail booted bastard kicks you around a bit and then delivers a crushing blow by throwing you into a recycling contraption. When you're thoroughly dried out, though still dull and grey, the remodelling process can take shape, perhaps this time into something better than an empty box because now you know more about the inherent dangers. More of the sad stuff later. Just like anything else in this life of ours, one must plug away and make the most of what we have got today, and try not to dwell too much on what we have not. I guess I was becoming greedy, *not* good.

Letting a confidant into my world of secret powers—where fresh new tricks were delivered at my feet like the morning milk and news, where my finely honed memory scraped another slice of history and threw it into the future, where telepathy threatened to put the Panasonic telephone answering machine salespersons out of business for ever—would jeopardise my living dream. Losing all that I had accumulated and equated in my head, scientifically and spiritually, would indicate the coming of an end before I had the chance to live my potential for real, for now, for a new addictive sense of normality that often tried without success to spin me around and down like a hungry crocodiles lunch.

Outstanding money owed from Transia came to the grand total of £160.00, and would be "Available for collection this coming Friday, or if preferred sent in the form of a cheque on Friday," explained that mornings disappointing formal letter from Mrs. Slater. Excruciatingly, today was only Monday. What a heap of difference the next five manic days were to make, but right now, busting a gut and ready to go, it may just of well have been five years.

There have been many bizarre instances in my life when I have needed help, and out of nowhere appears a stranger to offer their assistance. These strangers say very little, but they often possess the answer to free me from my predicament. The last time this happened to was when I was driving down the steep Queensway Hill in Hemel Hempstead. It was summer, but on that particular day it was teeming down with rain. "Oh no," I thought, "not a bloody puncture!" As I pulled over I noticed a figure of a man, medium build, wearing a long pale blue raincoat. He walked over to me as I fumbled around retrieving the spare wheel and the car jack. "I will help you," he said calmly, and then he proceeded to change the wheel for me. I stood there in the downpour, not having to do a single thing. When he finished I offered him a ride to wherever it was he was going. He politely declined, turned around and began to walk up the hill. I walked to the driver's door and glanced back up the hill again to shout, "Thank you," but he had long gone. The rain suddenly stopped and out came the golden Sun. There was something peaceful about this kind, self assured man. His complexion was flawless and he had a warm glow about him. He wanted nothing from me in return, yet he was standing there waiting for me in the rain to be of assistance before disappearing into the thin Hemel air.

On another occasion, when I was about 4 years old, I suddenly woke up in the middle of the night. At the foot of my single bed stood two figures dressed in robes. They posed no threat, they just stood there and smiled sadly. I spent the rest of that night, and many more that followed, hiding underneath my electrically charged nylon sheets. I know what you are thinking quietly to yourself, that there were clothes draped over a chair or something. It would need to of been a very tall chair, and about as wide as two robed adult male figures. Imaginary friends? I do not think so somehow. By the way, just in case you were wondering, my eyesight is better than average. Were these images just tricks of the mind or were they actual "happenings" trying to relay a peaceful message? Unusual experiences such as these have been a frequent feature of my life. There have been so many occasions when I have been inexplicably saved at the last minute by the intervention of the unlikeliest of people. For instance, there was the time when a knife was about to be thrust into my back by a drunken tramp, as a small group of us were heading toward London's Hammersmith Odeon. An unknown hand behind me knocked the tramp out cold and then fled without a word. My personal guardian continued to show itself in many ways and in many forms, leaving me with a feeling of warmth and goodness as well as renewing a little of the faith I have always had in our fellow man, a faith that one can find more and more difficult to hang on to during these dog-eat-dog cutthroat coated days. It seems perfectly straightforward to me that every one of us are tested and tried to the limits, and as a consequence some of us are minding our own backs and are tending to neglect other peoples blind spots. I say, "You watch my back and I'll watch yours."

Recurring nightmares plagued me too. The worst one I ever had consisted of nothing more than a black vinyl record and an old fashioned gramophone needle. Deeper into the grooves scratched the blessed needle, gouging the vinyl as the record span on its turntable. I would waken from the grinding torment to sheer peace and relief, only to find myself back in that tortuous dream as soon as I nodded off. As I snapped out of yet another screechy nightmare session I saw the two robed figures again. They were not in the least bit frightening this time, especially after the big needle had buried itself into the thick vinyl yet again. Back I went into a sweet deep sleep. From that day on I am certain the nightmarish demons have kept their distance, knowing that I had an unbeatable force on my side. You may well be sceptical, who could blame you? Experiencing that vision at the foot of my childhood bed, whether real or imagined, has had a profound and lasting effect upon me.

Everything that had taken place throughout the previous year was beginning to make some backhanded sense. Irrelevant pieces of a turbulent tapestry that began with me becoming just a little bit too happy when I first moved to Bovingdon— hurtling around like a complete lunatic in my diesel van all week—were now slowly forming. Despite being vague and tatty there was a definite pattern trying hard to slot into place. There was the time when I had my head used as a basketball on the pavement, so much blood, closely followed by a milder bout—although still horrendous—of depression that I will describe for you soon, and the Tin-Machine rock concert in Kilburn, North London, and what about the absurd house warming party that I arranged not long after I moved to Bovingdon, and … I think we had better travel all the way back to November 1989.

Last one in, first one out—a familiar story told to so many employees just as it was abruptly told to me in the latter half of 1989, when my beloved merchandising job went up in diesel fumes. The diluted drop of Gypsy blood that I have flowing inside me had been temporarily satisfied, but having now tasted the freedom on the roads of South East England, to have it snatched away so suddenly made the pill much more bitter to swallow. When a sunny week lay invitingly ahead I would take my thirteen foot beach-caster fishing rod and my two man tent with me. If I were lucky, a little lovely named Debbie from Taunton in Somerset would join me for a couple of days on the road. Evenings on a sunset beach, cooking freshly caught mackerel with the aid of my trusty blowtorch, snuggled up to Deb and a great big jug of scrumpy cider and a loaf of crusty bread could not have been nicer. Alas, it was snatched away from me, just like that, just like so many other things that are flattened and squashed such as hopes and dreams, always snatched mercilessly away when a bipolar affected person is on their way down. That transit van had come in handy for many things apart from its intended purpose of transporting bag upon bag of sweets and nuts all over the place. Because I kept the van at weekends, anything and everything bulky and heavy that needed moving from A to B got moved. One Friday evening it took me and a friend from my Rolls Royce days, Simon Ferris, to the National Ballroom in Kilburn, North London, to see a newly formed four piece rock group called Tin-Machine. Even then I felt an exquisite sensation of excitable importance and almost perfect well being. This was an immensely pleasant feeling that would come and go depending on whether or not something or somebody spoke to me in a specially coded and meaningful way. The lead singer that night sang out my desired thoughts and emotions, moving his Adonis frame as if I inhabited it, like an uncanny remote control designed only for carefully selected bodies and minds to share at the press of a mental moment. I felt spiritually self assured that evening. *Nothing* was going to harm me or dare to obstruct my own way.

Having now lost my job and the van, I began to put out the word to see if there was any painting and decorating work on offer just to keep me ticking over financially, and to keep the wolves from the door. As luck would have it, the temporary landlord and lady of the Bell public house were under instruction by the owner brewery to get a few quotes in for painting the upstairs bedroom, lounge and kitchen. As I was friendly with the couple I got the job. Simon Ferris, or "Slime" as he was sometimes known, was also in desperate need of some ready cash and so he too hopped on board the painting wagon. Big Betty the fruity landlady drank more than she sold. If you squeezed her, and many men did, gin and tonic trickled out of her pores. She was so randy. The way she preferred to greet a man, no matter who he was, or whether or not her henpecked husband was standing nearby, was to grab hold of their wedding tackle and practically crush the unfortunates balls with her inebriated strength. I warned Simon about it, but the twerp didn't believe me. Boy oh boy, did Simon yelp. We all did very well out of that job. Sweaty Betty the landlady and her husband fiddled around a bit with the quotes to present to the brewery so that we were all financially satisfied, if not a little sore below. Again, I distinctly remember that all through that job I was really buzzing. I might be up a stepladder painting merrily away and in would come Bet with a round of cold beer for us both. Sometimes she switched on the television set and put a pornographic movie on. There we were with a pint of lager in one hand and a paintbrush in the other, catching glimpses of Helga and Harold happily screwing away for Sweden. Another of big Bet's genital juggles would closely follow this, probably to determine the effect that horny Helga might be having. No sooner had we downed our pints than another one arrived, and then another. Maybe I wobbled ever so slightly, but by the time we had finished for the day and tidied up I felt as sober as a judge, and so I kept on drinking all of the way through to the final bell and throwing out time.

Money has never driven me that far. I have realistic dreams that I hope to fulfil one day, but hording a ton of money has never been the be all and end all. If there is enough to pay your way and have a little fun money left over, then great. For me, having a couple of hundred pounds from the painting job felt like a couple of thousand. Instead of putting some money aside to pay the bills, not to mention food,—my dietary needs were dropping like a lead weight to the bottom of my priority listings—I drank it or blew huge chunks of it on impulsive ideas such as hosting a belated housewarming party at 12A Vicarage Lane.

Considering that I had only just lost the job that I loved so dearly and had not yet found another position to replace it, I was abnormally upbeat about everything. Parked in many different Gadebridge locations had been my rusting unroadworthy Vauxhall Victor estate car that I had bought earlier that same year for only £100.00. This sad excuse for an automobile was intended to be fixed up and used for the occasional decorating and gardening jobs that might come my way. This old rust-bucket was a death trap. It had hardly any brakes to speak of, although that didn't stop me. Braking the best that I could with the gears and willpower became an art form in itself. With this heap of red rusting junk parked in Bovingdon High Street I went to work in preparation for my party, buying up most of the off-license, the general grocery store, magazines from the newsagents and a selection of cigars that I never usually smoked. Inside my maisonette, feeling a little more elevated, I spread out my rushed purchases with the intention of impressing all of my invited-at-the-very-last-minute guests. *Onion picking weekly* and *Which tractor monthly?* were probably not going to do much to create awareness of my newfound intellectual prowess. Three costume changes were made that evening in full view of my cousins Leona and Tracy, who were busying themselves examining a collection of my incomprehensible poems, if you could call them poems, as well as other scribbles and sketches of mine that were stuck to the magnolia walls of my bedroom with toothpaste. Leona and Tracy are very fair and opened minded women, just like their mother, my aunt Pauline. They realise how dull and boring life would be if we all walked the same and behaved like sheep.

When the last person had left I went to pour a drink, soon noticing that all of the alcoholic beverages had been slyly removed from my premises. Two and two equalled Mother. Immediately I picked up the telephone and began dialling. The arguing that ensued should never have been. "I just don't want you getting silly," is how she put it. If only she knew the truth about how good I felt inside, and how sharp and alert I felt without taking a single drop of the stuff. Mothers worry about their sons no matter what, so it had to be made doubly sure that I didn't give her or anybody else any cause for suspicion and concern. What most males never bargain for is that Mothers can read their sons like an open book, and Shirley Steadman is one fine reader.

Had I become a drunken dreamer or a dream that enjoyed a drink? Quite a tongue twister to which both apply. It was the early rumblings of a mini rise and fall. What occurred next can only be described as a dress rehearsal complete with a safety net, not in case I fall but for *when* I fall. Very clearly I remember my uncle Paul (Mother's brother) pulling me aside before he left 12A that night. Looking me straight in the eye he said, "What the heck's going on mate? Be careful buddy or you'll end up burning yourself right out." "Alright, I'm only having a laugh Uncle," I replied, not a hundred percent truthfully, and then he left for home. All three of my mothers brothers, Mark, Paul and Ron, are very family minded. They will invariably come up with the right words to say when they are needed the most, and they have always looked out for the likes of me and my cousins quite simply because they have been there, seen it, done it and haven't been stupid enough to hang around afterwards to buy the R.O.T (rip-off T-shirt.)

In February 1990 something awful happened to me. The ill-afforded bachelor pad warming party ten weeks earlier was now a distant memory. My mood had remained upbeat but more steady, allowing me to be in full control and not to make or force the usual nonsensical decisions. Granted, I had no major high powered life changing decisions to make, but if I had of done all would have been swell, I think. Eager for some familiar company I set off down Vicarage Lane, passing the cottages and the well kept school playing fields. Smoke from the chimneypieces hung low in the chilly damp air. Children still screamed and yelled as children do in every corner of their innocent world. All bode well for a pleasant tipple in the Bell, my favourite Bovingdon pub. Inside, the log fire crackled away, hypnotising those who dare look for too long. Upstairs the paint had long since dried. No longer was Big Bet and her husband strutting around as they had moved back up North. Standing next to me was the rather tall and elegant Helen Prentice, ex-wife of Dick who had moved into the maisonette below me only a week before I had arrived on the local scene. Helen is a woman of the world, and she can be one tough cookie if she has to be. Helen and I were gossiping away when in through the solid oak door burst a young man who at a guess was around 24 or 25 years old. The pub had been enjoying the most agreeable ambiance up until this degenerated numskull made his unwelcome appearance. Up until now the chit-chattering clusters of local folk, some old and creaky, smoking their pipes and playing dominoes, and the younger crowd who were huddled together in the tiny adjacent room used for playing pool and darts, were happily contented. Then it kicked off bigtime.

"Hey you, yeah mate that's right, I'm talking to you, get out of that fucking seat you old bastard," said this uncouthly piece of degenerative scum. On and on he went bad mouthing and terrorising whoever he felt like. He would *not* let up. Why the hell didn't someone stand up to him? There was only one of him and about forty of us. This brain dead lowlife simply would not leave it alone. Did scaring the old folk make him feel big? "What is your problem pal? If I were you buster I would sling your hook," said I. All that I got in return for my trouble was a sinister smile followed by the inevitable volley of abuse. "Fuck off you fucking cunt" was about as far as this pathetic creature's vocabulary would stretch. In my ear I could feel the warmth of Helen's breath as she whispered to me, "What the hell are you playing at Keith, he is a total madman, he will do anything to you, the guy is completely off his rocker. If you've got any sense in that head of yours you'll stay well clear." Well, I was stunned, flabbergasted and dismayed, but most of all I was disappointed that this whole debacle was actually being allowed to be staged without an ounce of resistance. I was becoming more and more livid with rage. My empty pint glass remained tightly gripped as I glared across the waiting pub at this cretinous excuse for a human being. Words directed at me did not register. "This ain't over yet, and I can't hear or see any fat ladies singing," I thought determinedly. Besides, hadn't she recently returned to her native North with her hen-pecked husband?

If I had not of been quite so up and buzzing, like a mild case of sporadic hyperactivity, perhaps what happened next would never have happened at all. Saying that, there is a dangerous clause in my character that I would never ever change. Cousin Todd is the same way. There is *no* way that we can back down from standing up for what we believe is right and proper. Fair enough, it may mean that you end up getting your head kicked to a pulp, but that's the way it is. I do sometimes wish that I was a little bit taller, because standing strong by one's convictions alone can be a very painful business, as I was just about to find out.

A pub full of local regulars, and not one of them defending their rights. Nobody could persuade me that this moronic excuse for a human being was really *that* nasty, surely not. After one more pint I reluctantly left, caving in to popular advice. Initially I intended to head for the Halfway-House pub at the top end of the High Street and resume from where I had left off. I only got as far as the kebab van about thirty metres or so up from the Bell. There I stood, waiting patiently for my prey to come into sight. It was dark by now, but the street lamp next to the kebab stall kept matters well lit. God only knew how this predicament was going to be tackled. Playing it by ear, fuelled to the gills by beer and its heroic 6ft 6" big talk, appeared to be my only option. Out came the verbal terrorist. He stood smugly outside the solid oak door, lighting a cigarette before looking to his left and then to his right. It was hard to tell for sure if he had seen me, or whether it was just a greasy kebab he was after. It has to be said that my gallant bark has more often than not been my downfall. Would I bite the deepest, chew him up and spit him out? Had I bitten of more than I could handle already? The first most obvious rule in street combat is to land the first blow and make sure it counts. "A kebab may be all this idiot is after," I thought. Wrong! Closer he came, ten, eight, six paces from sheer bloody hell, four, two, SMACK! I clobbered the son of a bitch as hard as I possibly could. Nothing happened, so then we got into an arms flailing scrap that lasted all of fifteen long seconds. The bastard put me down. On the way down I smashed the back of my skull on the stone paving slabs. I was out cold. The next thing I knew, I was waking up in the arms of Graham Baker, both of us sitting slumped up against a wall, his shirt drenched in my spilt blood. In and out of consciousness I went as we awaited the arrival of an ambulance. Much of what happened from then on is rather foggy, but I do remember seeing a huge pool of blood on the ground, and a large gathering of onlookers. I cannot recall the three mile journey to West Hertfordshire Hospital, only waking up in Aragon Ward with a bloodied pillowcase and a rotten headache for company. The back of my head stung a great deal as one would expect with twenty stitches expertly inserted. My sister Barbara, 3 years older than myself, became my next of kin so as not to worry my worry-guts Mother. She wasted no time in driving from her home in nearby Bushey, Watford, to be with me. Tests were carried out using X-rays and M.R.I. scans (Magnetic Resonance Imaging) to see if any skull fractures, blood clots or brain damage had occurred. Thankfully I got off lightly, because by all accounts the moronic oaf with whom I was fighting, or at least trying to fight, didn't leave me alone once I had passed out, instead he decided to play ball with my head by smashing it into the stone pavement again and again as if he were trying to bounce a very stubborn basketball. God knows what would have happened had nobody heard the hullabaloo of the first fifteen seconds and come running up the High Street to where I was laying. Graham was the first on the scene, and it was he who scared my aggressor away. Cheers mate, I'll always owe you one.

Would I stand up to an evil spirited onslaught such as that again? Oh yes, because no matter what happens, God or some other force that I continually struggle to fathom out and come to terms with is on my side, a side that I know without doubt is that of good over evil. What happened that evening may not have looked pretty, but in an odd sort of way it has made me look at life with a larger, more rounded kind of perspective, and with a greater understanding and appreciation of not only myself, but I hope of others too. Better knowledge of one's own limitations is always a useful tool to carry around. All that you can do is try to stand up to the tests and do your level best. With the confidence and pride gained you can raise your head swan fashion in the black and white lake of critical culture and say, "Well at least I had a go, I made an effort, now tell me, what did *you* do today?" Just be true to yourself, without fear to follow through with your convictions no matter who tries to shoot you down in life. There are always going to be those pitifully inadequate somebodies cowering behind one-way mirrors with their easy targets firmly set, a bit like the bloody "sport" of fox-hunting. I say, "To hell with the lot of them."

The difference between being a freethinking individual in a democratic society or being a slave to convention, is sometimes a disappointingly close, friendless affair. Safety in sensible numbers, or should you stick your caution free neck out? The latter, or a careful combination of the two tend to reap the greater rewards if used in a healthy combination of faith, determination, persistence, total belief in yourself and of course an awful lot of patience. It can be a rather painful route to follow though, as I found out to my cost.

The depression that followed was indeed severe, but by no means as despicable as the fully blown manic depressions that were to later engulf me—attempted annihilations of every normal human function. My earlier high spirits and this coming depression were, as I touched upon earlier, to act as a trial fun-run in readiness for the gruelling marathon. I do not remember ever submitting an entry form. The concussion that I sustained lasted for at least a week, although the whole affair shook me up for a lot longer. My contented little life resumed its normal service, but I struggled desperately to maintain it. Booze temporarily masked my pain, but ultimately it only succeeded in speeding up the downslide. My recent confrontation with a paving slab combined with losing the job that had boosted my spirits to beyond a socially agreeable level, plus the gallons and gallons of alcohol and an erratic sleeping and eating pattern, had pooled together and decided that enough was definitely enough. I battled with my reasonable side and argued that this body has been abused by its owner for too long, and now we are all going to go on an indefinite strike, better still, we will teach this darn fool a lesson that he will not forget in a hurry. Let's evacuate his entire body and soul, leaving him with just a shell full of darkness and despair.

How frightening it is to be overshadowed by a deathly grey cloud, to be enveloped by a tacky depression. Energy reserves are sucked dry, and nothing is fun anymore. Lust for living is lost. My capability to think rationally and to perform basic tasks suddenly eluded me. I fell and I was out, but I still had the devil kicking me in the head and twisting my poor mind without respite. Depression is being shackled to a pulsating sin filled city within a constipated underworld of dread. Depression is believing that you are going to be trapped forever, and so you start to agonisingly reminisce about the happy times that will never be seen again. Depression is a disintegrating, mentally splintering chasm of loneliness. Depression is dread of the next minute, the next hour and the following day. Depression is so much mental and bodily fatigue that a dry peaceful land always seems too far away to even contemplate reaching. Depression is when recurrent low episodes seem to be much worse than those experienced before, despite the fact that you did manage to crawl out of a previous hell-plessness. The present depression is *always* the worst depression, and the previous lessons learnt can often tragically fly out of the wide open window. Depression is also a character builder. It is an illness that is impossible to sustain for as long as you may think. Imagine what it must be like to be so depressed that suicide sounds like it could be a pleasurable means of relief. Anybody who has not experienced terrible depression but is attempting to understand more about it in order to help with and to cope with someone else's depression, is doing an admirable thing. They could try to remember how *they* felt when a loved one died, or when a relationship broke down, the job was lost, the house has been repossessed, the dog died or to discover that yet another unnecessary war has broken out in some remote region of the world. Mix this little lot together, lock it in a dark cell and drop the tiny key somewhere in the middle of the pacific ocean; do all of these things and you may come perilously close to having some comprehension of what it feels like to be under a bipolar depression on one of those rare, even slightly better days. Depression is being so distanced from an inaccessible answer, an answer that is lost somewhere deep in a forest of fear that sprawls through the mind and soul like a blazing cancer. New magnified worries are being added and multiplied without mercy until it feels as if the blighters are causing an irreversible paralysis of the blackest of minds, and are pulling the shutters on the remaining common senses. It's an horrendous hell that is frustratingly difficult to relay to a qualified professional, or to the care-persons who themselves cannot always see the home straight—the very same people that you want to free-up and offload the burden to the most—because your communicative skills are shot to smithereens. If the depressed person is able to write down in a notebook, or speak and shout into a listening ear or into a recording device their innermost thoughts, getting them out in the open for a good airing, I guarantee that with patience, persistence and even the slightest crumb of self-belief that may still be found, it *will* help. Scoop out the detritus whenever it builds up and threatens to attract uninvited pressure—it works! If the sufferer can rise up to the occasion, then arts and crafts can help to guide the negative thoughts toward an untainted medium instead. Transferring a mental state onto paper or by any other creative means enables a caregiver to read the troubled thoughts in a way that wasn't previously available. These differently angled insights can open up doors that would have blocked the path to a sane, rational recovery. This type of outlet is a terrific form of expressive therapy, and it is extremely beneficial to all of those caught up in the bipolar web, and not just the sufferer who is often left stuck with uneducated ignorant stigma, slap-bang in the middle of it all.

Over and over again were the same nagging thoughts, "Go away, leave my mind alone, stop bombarding me with reminders of my inadequacies, failures, countless sins, the people I have hurt and let down, a bleak future, fears of rejection, fear to face my neighbours, to drive a car or to cook in case I cause a fire. How do I wash, dress, brush my receding hair, run or even walk from A to B, breathe and actually live again for Christ's sake?"

I became a prisoner in my own home, too frightened to walk past a window in case I drew attention, chain smoking until I ran out, and too scared to go for a walk so that I could get some much needed fresh air. The little food that I had in my cupboard and refrigerator remained uneaten due to nerves. I took the telephone off the hook and pulled all of the electrical plugs out of their sockets, because I had a phobia about anything electrical or flammable causing a fire that I wouldn't be able to handle. I was too scared to talk and too scared to keep going in the direction that I was. If the doorbell rang, my heart would pound away like a pneumatic drill. A carousel of dizzy thoughts span around inside of me, picking up new passengers and flinging others off without coming to a standstill. It felt as if a perfectly good blanket had been torn to shreds in order to make up a raggedy patchwork affair, held together by willpower and stitched with a blunt needle. All I could do was stumble across my words and trip over my well trodden, but now unfamiliar, uncoordinated footsteps.

Looking in my bathroom mirror is not the wisest thing to do at the best of times, especially so early in the morning when my face looks as if it needs a good ironing. It is always the negative features that are highlighted by the depressed brain. It's the same as when an item of clothing suddenly looks appalling on, usually on down day, when only a few cheerful days earlier it looked so great. Those negative features were the only features that my eyes could see. A form of psoriasis or acne rosacea had begun to spread in red blotches around my nose, eyes, ears and hairline. This always occurs to me whenever I become stressed out, and it was the last thing I needed on top of everything else. I admit it, I have always been too vain, but better vain than not at all I say. That vanity of mine turned right around and kicked me in the teeth. Was I dying from the outside in or from the inside out, or both simultaneously? Nagging images stormed their way into my weary trampled mind, bouncing thoughtlessly from core to crust, bruising any remaining pride that was desperate to survive, by deflecting the unbearable grief being fired at it with my still intact yet shattering senses. The pain of the ambush does *not* give up, nor deal a fair hand that at least would have allowed me a fighting chance.

"Never give up on yourself," "Where there's life there's hope,"—what a load of utterly distant nonexistent rubbish these pep talks often come across as to the depressed soul, although those words are so perfectly true when they spew forth from the never depressed lips of the sometimes aggravating but well intentioned caregiver. Happy days will *always* return, but only in their own good time. Reminders of what life will be like again when you are feeling well isn't such a bad thing so long as they are given out in misery friendly moderation. Cutting yourself off from the real world only serves to push you further down the drain, creating an even greater uphill slog that could have easily have been avoided. In Shitty-City it is heaps better to be above ground with the hot-Gods and cool-cats than down below with the maggoty slag and vomiting rats.

Manic-depressive illness has cost me months and months, years even of unimaginable distress, culminating in long drawn out battles, ugly affairs fought to the death that thankfully have hoisted me back up onto my own two feet, so that I can fight, or rather live another day, and also be capable of facing this world and saying to *it* and to myself, "Steadman is back where he belongs, for good this time. So bring on the world, and let us all start living together on it and in it as one big happy family." Dream on sweetly …

It had crossed my disturbed young mind as to whether or not the crack on the back of my head could be responsible for this severe downturn in my mood. At the onset I just felt distant, subdued and well below par, which is only to be expected really considering what had been taking place in my life. The weighty black curtain of Hades descended upon me so suddenly. Despite being mentally stunned into a solitary silence, treading treacle in uncharted territory for almost a week, this depression was still able to be nipped in the bud at a relatively early stage.

Do you recall playing hangman, that simple paper and pencil game? I often used to play it with my two sisters at home, and also with classmates at school. I'm pretty sure that we have all had a game or two on the back cover of a school exercise book or even on the desk itself. Do you remember how the gallows took shape piece by piece? A similar thing takes place when depressed. When you are least expecting it, having gained a modicum of peace brought about by a stay of execution, a section of the gallows jabs away at you. It is a form of self-persecution that is up against no resistance, nothing of any substance to prevent it from piercing through a quivering defence to score another portion of mentally maddening mind poison. The creaking gallows slowly begin to take an ominous shape. By the time the structure is fully erect, the tormented demon ridden soul—laying semi comatose on sweaty bed sheets that are sometimes slightly soiled because he was too afraid to make the short distance from bedroom to bathroom—would gladly put the coarse rope noose around his own neck, kick the lever and be done with it once and for all. Lets face it, twenty-five years of life is far better than none at all.

On this occasion I still had a little sense and the will to plug the telephone connector back into the socket and call Virginia, my eldest Sister. She lives in Watford, only ten miles from Bovingdon, along with her highly intelligent and very entertaining husband Phil and their two children, Joel then aged four and

Emily seven. Prior to the telephone call I had been frantically rummaging about in the cupboard beneath the kitchen sink, trying to find something nasty to swallow that would complete a rather untidy suicidal job. Thick strong Domestos bleach perhaps? It was a half hearted cry for rapid assistance. Good old Keith, Mr. Self-Sufficient, Mr. Perfectly-Able-To-Cope-Under-Pressure was silently suffering like he had never suffered before. Even so, this was just a mild bout of the darkest blues compared to the evil feasts and poisonous picnics that I was forced to swallow whole in the coming years. "Gee (as I affectionately call her), Gee, I don't feel at all well, I'm feeling very low, I've got a bottle of bleach and I want to drink it, and …" A few seconds of stony silence elapsed while my sister was probably trying to get her cool head around this Brotherly bombshell. "Calm down, calm down, just don't do anything, *we are* going to get through this okay," said my sister with firm assurance. Mollycoddling, being wrapped up in cotton wool and treated like a bawling baby even at this stage serves absolutely *no* use at all, despite the obvious temptation to do so. It is not cruel to be firm and tough. Somebody must remain in control of the situation and also keep it together themselves, which is as tough as old boots to do, especially when the caregiver is very close to the self consumed sufferer. The care person has to start in the way that they intend to continue, and you have to be warned that by doing this a pretty picture will rarely be painted, at least to begin with. The foundation, the base colour, isn't particularly pleasant any which way you look at it, but it is of paramount importance to slap it down if a successful renovation of an unwell mind is to be achieved.

"Now, what I am going to do is arrange an appointment with your general practitioner right away," said Gee calmly. "What is the name of your general practitioner Keith?" It took me a while to process the question and come up with the answer. "Dr. Hope," I mumbled, "the same doctor that Mum and Aunt Pauline go to see at Parkwood Drive, not far from the Top Of The World pub (typical)." I couldn't believe that I was actually saying this to Gee, but it was good to finally share my feelings with somebody. "Hold tight darling, I'll see you soon, oh and by the way, sort out two pillows and some clothes if you can because you are coming to stay with us for a while." True to her word Virginia was with me faster than a bullet from a gun. She made no awkward comments and made no references to my shabby, smelly appearance. Gee saw straight through all of that, besides she has helped so many other people through their times of trouble that she was able to evaluate the situation quickly and act accordingly without becoming emotionally useless. She would probably have made an excellent psychologist or social worker of some sort. All that my sister

Gee saw was her younger Brother crying out for some much needed help. She made certain that I had the best treatment available right away, no matter what. She is an angel of the highest order whom I am proud to have on my team. I love her very much indeed.

Dr. Hope had gone on his holidays so I saw Dr. Holloway instead. "Please God, let there be nobody here in the busy waiting room that might recognise me," I thought with dread. How ridiculous, there I was, a cowering shivering wreck of my former self and all I was concerned with was whether or not I was seen by somebody I knew, and even worse still, would they ask me awkward questions? These fears are very common with depression, and are more worrying and magnified to the sufferer than an outsider may think. Hiding away from small curious groups of people—most of whom were reading the National Geographic magazine or the Readers Digest—is not an option, especially in the beginning. Tough love is the hardest love to give, especially when it is so tempting to soft-soap in order to find a little artificial respite for both parties. For the long term sake and sanity of all concerned life *has* to carry on in the normal fashion.

Gee came into Dr. Holloway's consulting room with me. Describing how I felt when I felt as lousy as I did was no easy matter. I did my best to put across an accurate picture, knowing how important it was to get my description as accurate as possible because the best treatment and quality of my immediate future depended upon it. This provided added pressure that nobody else could actually see, but I could feel it slicing through me like shards of ice. Being in the worst condition to explain my mental state and having to do so as accurately as possible struck me as unfair and ironic. "What the hell am I doing here, this sort of crap only happens to other people doesn't it?" I kept thinking. I was now one of those "other" people. Not that they would want it, but already I had a greater understanding and sympathy toward others who had been mercilessly ripped to shreds by a heavy depressing recipe not of their choosing. Some good, although I didn't think so then, had come out of this horrible situation. Trying to put myself across; the way I felt, the changeable symptoms, my personal lifestyle etc was a very hard task indeed. I felt as if my life depended on getting as much accuracy out, so that my doctor could process the information and convert it into the most suitable medication and therapy for me. All that I could do was my best. Then I had to rely on the skill and expertise of the doctor to recognise specific key areas of his thorough observation and of my detailed description, then treat accordingly. Gee slipped a prescription for one months supply of anti-depressants into her handbag before we exchanged farewells and left the busy practice. Dr. Holloway also issued strict instructions to come and see him again in three weeks time, so we stopped at the appointment window on our way out. I could feel the eyes of those waiting to be seen burning into me. Varying quantities of paranoia have always accompanied the bouts of depression that I have had, making it so much harder to get out and join in, to do the things that you really want to do in order to get yourself back up onto your feet and feeling well again. Irene Croft, a lovely little softly spoken lady that I have known since I was a toddler, mouthed a concerned, "Bye Keith," from behind the glass partitioning as she entered my name into her computerised appointment book. A welcoming cool breeze greeted us as we walked toward Gee's Ford Fiesta car. Everything felt so surreal, but not a nice dreamy surreal, it was more of a grotesque living nightmare that was made far worse because I could not understand nor comprehend what was taking place. It was all so new and foreign to my stunned system. The loss of basic control hurts like hell. What was happening to me, what had I done that was so bad that I should be struck down by this wicked condition? I am certainly not perfect, not by a long way, but this? God give me strength.

At Virginia's house I cleaned myself up before the rest of the family arrived home. I especially didn't want the children to see their uncle Keith in such a self-neglected state. If you are looking and living in a mess, the mind can follow suit. The more of a mess the mind is, the worse the immediate environment of the sufferer becomes. Virginia's home is always immaculately kept but the depression kept raining in, forming a deeper pond of sticky treacle to swim through.

It is all very well and good for people without any real understanding of this debilitating illness to say, "Snap out of it," or "What have you got to worry about? Take a look at all of those poor starving human beings in places such as Africa, now *that* is something to get depressed about." Yes, there *are* terribly sad situations such as famine and conflict everywhere one looks, but that does not mean to say that a depressed person in affluent Hemel Hempstead has no right to be bitten by the "Black dog at my heels," as Sir Winston Churchill described depression. Poorly informed and ignorant of the facts are many. If it doesn't have a bandage on, encased in plaster, covered in green spots or coughing up blood then they shall be burnt at the stake or drowned in the river. What we cannot see and do not understand is a dangerous threat, so let's just destroy it if it gets too close—this is the mentality of some people who go through life sharing one malfunctioning brain cell between them. Making a depressed person feel guilty for not having anything obviously tangible to account for their condition is nothing short of barbaric, inhumane and heartless. Although I would never wish depression on another human being, the truth of the matter remains that one out of ten people will experience depression of one form or another first hand, and at *any* point during their lives. Now there's some food for thought; try chewing it over.

I tried to eat as many of my sister's homemade pies and cakes as I could, but hunger takes a nosedive when one is depressed. Words didn't come easily either. To be in the company of a quiet Keith must have been quite a novelty. Stumbling my way through words with an awkwardness similar to clambering across a rocky beach, aware of the lapping sea and gulls carrying on with their daily chores in a free spirited manner, was painful and gruelling, yet it needed to be done in order to prevent an even greater submergence of valuable spirit. Sometimes I felt as if I had said the wrong thing or that it had been taken wrongly, so I tended to become slightly introverted, shutting up my verbal shop more and more often when I really need not have done.

Ten days had slipped away in Watford. Now it made perfect sense for me to return to the more familiar surroundings of my parent's home in Gadebridge, Hemel Hempstead. Being with other people is so important for a depressed person. Even if they choose at first to spend an unhealthy amount of time cooped up in a stale bedroom, wallowing in self pity and allowing new problems and obstacles to be manufactured or the existing agonies increased, the monotony can eventually be broken. Problems are always magnified a thousand times when feeling low. When a bout of depression eases up you can actually feel rather embarrassed because you allowed an unimportant grain of irrational nonsense to breed and flourish. I guess it could be described as "mental-masochism"—not a bad name for a heavily burdened rock band.

At my parent's home things gradually improved, enabling me to escape the perilous drop into a fully blown-to-bits episode of depression. Cruising through the beautiful Hertfordshire countryside with my father helped me an awful lot. The earliest journeys saw me slouching down into the passengers seat so that I was out of view to any other life-form. To begin with, I was out of sight and out of sound. The evening walks with my mother were agonising affairs that tried and tested her patience. Those brisk short walks, the exercise and the feel-good factor that such a small accomplishment gave me when I returned to the safe haven of home, helped my cause immeasurably. The goodness installed *has* to be maintained and built upon so that the recovery process is retained and continues heading in the right direction. Try to see it as mental athletics with plenty of hurdles, disappointments and victories. Depression is the mental marathon that takes sheer willpower and an awful lot of bottle, preferably filled with water! It didn't take long before the walks were taken in broad daylight. My deep fear of being seen in broad daylight had almost fizzled out. To begin with, I couldn't for the life of me see the reasoning behind inflicting so much excess torture upon myself, by stepping out for a tense car ride or a brisk walk, so I would return from these half-hearted jaunts feeling even more sorry and wrapped up in myself than I did before I left. Slowly I began to feel pleased with my progress and began to set my own small targets: distance walked, saying, "hello," to a passer-by, venturing out in daylight more often rather than under the dark cover of night—that kind of thing. All of those early painful walks and talks, the one's that you are certain are not assisting with the victorious outcome of your personal self taught, self thought out war effort, are in fact the very walks and talks of life on which to build skyward, using regained recycled confidence, willpower, persistence and guts. However long it takes and whichever way it is done one thing is for sure, you *will* climb back up high to where the Sun *does* shine. There are no deadlines to meet, no pressure upon you and no shame, only the awaiting admiration for pulling through. There will be setbacks, but for every backward step why not aim, when you are feeling up to it, to take two steps forward. Steps will become strides, strides will become leaps, and before you know it you will be up and running again, aching to resume the rest of your life. If the return leg takes longer than a professional prediction, do not be put off. If you fall backwards into the murky depths, and you most probably will at some stage, just start over again, curse the world, curse God if you have to, I know I did. Do what ever the hell it takes to get yourself going again, and do *not* ever give up on yourself because you are priceless, you are worth far more than the all of the rocks dug out of the South African dirt. Don't you ever, *ever* forget it!

My recovery was reasonably swift in comparison to what lay ahead of me. It can take weeks, months, even years to fully shake off a stinker of a clinical depression. The chemical imbalance is always there and it can be corrected very accurately with medication, but a bipolar being can never be rid of the imbalanced symptoms or entirely shake off the effects of a severe episode of manic-depression in the same way as you can wipe out a rotten virus. Bipolar affective disorder, especially in its most extreme form, burns itself on the beholders brain—there really isn't anything else quite like it. It's like having two severe illnesses rolled into one common black ball. A decent quality and quantity of life is to be found beneath the crust, but try breaking your way up through solid ice, it's hard! An awareness of these limitations isn't such a bad thing because it will act as an inbuilt alarm system, as well as becoming a means to show compassion and understanding to another human being who may be about to enter into their own mind crushing abyss or high rising lair.

My return to Bovingdon began with a solo celebration that resulted in a tremendous hangover the following day. My immunity to strong liquor had not deserted me entirely, and it was not very long before I was foolishly back to my old ways. Well, who is going to deny me a little bit of pleasure after what I had just been through? Dr. Holloway, who recommended that I returned to Bovingdon, did make it as plain as plain can be: "Stop drinking so much," he had said, especially now that I had a course of anti-depressants to get through. I foolishly thought that because I felt a whole heap better, I automatically *knew* better regarding my intake of anything medicinal. Acting like the fool that I was, my hard earned caution was thrown to the wind, or rather I threw the remainder of my pills straight down the toilet in some sort of pathetic defiance. My friend John Carter had no idea where I was all of this time, but he understood more about my ordeal than I first gave him credit for. My other Sister Barbara kept in touch regularly by telephone and also made the occasional short journey to see me at my home. She instilled in me the importance of *never* laying down and letting depression put one over on me. I am perfectly aware of how blessed I am to be a part of such a strong and loving family, when so many less fortunate souls are struggling to survive all by themselves.

That too familiar time had come again to search for a new job. My search to find a similar merchandising position to the one that I had lost proved to be fruitless. Application forms were sent off here and there. Meanwhile I wallpapered a few walls, tidied up a handful of gardens and I even did a bit of roofing labouring for my uncle's Ron and Mark who had separate companies at that time. While sifting through the engineering section in the Hemel job centre I came upon a position for an, "Operative to assist in the stripping and rebuilding of rubber rollers for use in the printing industry."

At this stage in the proceedings I was not officially recognised as having manic depression, despite experiencing an extremely low period of depression that was then followed closely behind by the excessive spending of the little I had earned, the dressing up as Freddie Kruger, the home warming party, the dancing prancing and talking too much, the dashing from bar to bar selling all manner of things, not to mention the all night lonesome drinking sessions that went rather too well for my own good. My present state of mind had lost touch with base, insisting that I was meant to be employed somewhere else and doing something far greater than the previously petty self-imposed restrictions would ever have allowed me to. My days at Transia Rubber Rollers had come to an abrupt end.

The only raise that I enjoyed since my time there commenced, following the brief depression that you have just read about, was now manic and still rising. All that there was left for me to do was to hold tight for the next couple of days, then on Friday morning I could go and collect my final cash payment of £160.00.

With half a heart I tried, but could hardly sleep. I didn't want to sleep just in case I might miss out on something that I felt I had a duty to be a part of. Throughout the spring and summer months my little maisonette had become rather odd in appearance, though others probably preferred to use "Wacky." A few friends and even fewer relations who had visited me over those past six months have since told me that they were ever so slightly taken aback by the transformation occurring, but they put it down to a combination of frustrated creativity, typical bachelor behaviour and way too much to drink. They would be pretty much spot on with their analysis. Had somebody placed that description in front of me at the time I would have agreed. How could I explain to myself, let alone a third party, what was making me feel so damn good? If I did try to explain what was happening to me it would probably be taken away, terminated, and I would be treated as a complete lunatic who is of no use unless heavily sedated and compliant to the rules and regulations of society. With self discipline I tried hard to keep my big mouth shut, and instead I allowed my fingers and toes to continue their exploration of the unknown manic pulse. The day would come when I had to blind the world with my brilliance, but that momentous occasion would have to remain bubbling away nicely on the backburner until I was given the signal to let loose my spiritual and physical acumen upon those who were playing catch-up, and also upon the "non-believers."

Pieces of junk decorated my interior rouge tiled window ledges in a meaningful shrine like way, along with tiny pieces of torn up magazines and old photographs. Most of this fire hazard had been carefully positioned with the deft touch of a heart surgeon. Each specific item took on its own symbolic meaning, becoming capable of sending and receiving mind-messages. The reasoning and the projection of manic thoughts and actions change like the seasons and the tides, with no apology, no explanation or forgiveness for the chaos and anarchy they achieve. Most of my vinyl LP's were out of their protective sleeves and strewn all over the living room floor, becoming scratched as I walked upon them with shod feet. Album covers found their way onto my walls. My Hammond Wurlitzer organ, an enormous instrument with a broken keyboard but a fully operational rhythm section, had solidified blood red candle wax all over it as a result of my alcohol inspired candlelit solo suppers. A bunch of incense sticks burned away simultaneously, creating a heady atmosphere (out of the question when I was depressed and phobic.) Occasionally I plugged the connector jack of my antiquated set of headphones into the organ socket and then placed the headphones on my head so that one of the ear pieces sat over my mouth leaving the other to cover the scar at the rear of my skull. If I spoke or sang into the mouthpiece (now a microphone) my amplified voice would boom out of the organ speakers into the jumble of a room. Not satisfied with just the organ and my manic warbling, I positioned a red snare drum to my right and used two wooden spoons as sticks. *Boom tish de waaaah, boom tish de waaaah, boom boom*—no wonder my long suffering neighbours carry heavy grey bags beneath their eyes.

Just to be certain that there wouldn't be a single grain of doubt as far as my becoming distanced from Planet Earth was concerned, I let it slip to the barmaid in the Tudor Rose pub, in all seriousness, that I intended to bullet proof my car. My little red runabout being turned into a miniature tank no less! Never mind considering how much the work would cost, especially with the *Scarface* movie inspired machine gun turrets on the top, or where such a far fetched customisation could take place. It was the paranoia thing rearing its irrational head again. One thing that I am definitely not is violent, it just boiled down to an underlying fear of mine that somebody representing evil would attempt to take me out, not to dinner, but to kill me because I knew too much. Exactly what "much" constituted of is an unsolved mystery. Following a sudden blast of spine tingling fear would always be a manic concoction of reasons why I would forever remain protected by all things that represented good. Vulnerable one minute, dangerously invincible the next, that was me. Where all of this mental manipulation was leading to I did not know. Sometimes I would be the director of my own manic thought and carry it out to the best of my ability, then at other times I ran around town like a headless chicken trying to obey a pleasurable force. If I didn't put in some thought and pain then maybe the well of perfected ecstasy would dry up, leaving me stranded in a disappointing mustn't-grumble-better-make-do place. Everything was awakening to an invigorating new way of life. People passing, television images, radio, current and outdated literature, trees, the sky, the land, the Sun, Moon, Stars and Mars, cars and alcoholic bars. I took in as much as I could to satisfy and obey so many thought processes that were bouncing off each other and into my clogged manic mind. To help with this satisfaction and obey process I would drive around Hemel Hempstead to make unplanned random visits upon friends and relations, as well as the pubs. These people were probably hoping for a nice quiet night in following a hard days work, then manic me arrives on their doorstep. Taking on the persona of a psychic/fortune teller I would stare intensely into their baffled eyes in an effort to reassure and communicate. Those who were unfortunate enough not to have made a successful exit from the room politely endured my breathless monologue until my mania insisted that it urgently needed to annoy elsewhere. It could be said that I was becoming a serial annoyer, capable of caving innocent heads in with my tongue. When suggestive bodily movements failed to bewitch and bedazzle I might try using coded quotes and references from the Bible, or mathematical equations with a strong emphasis on *equal* and No.1. This would be followed up with unoriginal remarks such as, "I wonder who came first in the human-race?" How embarrassing was I? These were the early though harmless enough rumblings of what would later become firm delusions of grandeur. I had got it firmly into my busy head that pretty soon we were all going to enter the anything-is-possible world, and that those with whom I was coming into contact with at this point knew about it too, but they needed careful nurturing in the right direction. Those people who were in tune to all of this special knowledge were the ones having to absorb information and make perfect sense out of it, freeing myself to be the Captain Kirk figure, receiving and acting upon maniacal data in accordance to a new book of rules being hastily written by a flock of frightened secretaries. All of the unimaginable powers that have been suspended in space since who knows when will come into being, *our* being, the *human* being. It had begun to dawn on me that I may indeed have won the human-race, and in doing so I had the responsibility to lead the mission, or do whatever it took to see this whole thing through to a gloriously fulfilling conclusion. The trouble was that I had about as much idea as the next man, woman or child as to what would happen next. My colourful ideas and unreasonable reasoning continued to change like an oil slicked cloud, so I reinstated my earlier plan of going with the flow of manic thought and then play it by ear. The basics normally always work best and are usually something upon which one can rely. This was not a normal situation. Get me to the nearest head doctor, quick!

My libido rocketed to an all time high. Women, all of them, even those who had a face like a bulldog chewing a wasp suddenly became attractive, and as far as I was concerned they were all available to be singed by my overflowing lava. How I escaped with a full set of teeth intact is one of life's great mysteries. Did it really matter where and when I became sexually aroused? At a bus stop, the sports centre, in a shop, pub or a library—they all powerfully hit my erogenous zones. Wherever there happened to be female flesh and I felt horny, which was most of the time, I would get down to work. No, I didn't service myself with a five-knuckle-shuffle in front of everybody, like some severely disturbed mentally handicapped people sometimes do in the most inappropriate of places. With immense concentration, determination, and as filthy an image in my mind that I could summon up, I would tense my body and will sexual excitement to flow between us. Being discreet was indeed a problem, but at least I never removed any of my "interesting" clothing. From an onlookers point of view It must have looked as if I had a severe case of hemorrhoids. I could be sexually satisfied mentally, not physically, just by sitting on a bar stool supping a cold pint. I felt very strongly that everybody else had the ability to see and interpret the world surrounding them in the same way that I could, only they would always be a touch behind me, having to play catch-up forever. Whatever information or power somebody "in the know" took on board would be automatically generated to other equals across the universe. I felt that although the equals had the Godlike ability to see the world through rose tinted glass and were more than able to communicate through thought manipulation, the responsibility to oversee and protect their interests lay solely with me. They in turn had to protect me in order to protect themselves from those who struggled behind, otherwise known as the non-believers.

The absurd belief that I possessed special powers and that I was the big all that ends all, would come and go. If I chose to I could turn off or adjust these notions freely, so if for instance a maniacally originated wave of thought didn't go over quite as intended, I would twiddle with my mental control box and hey-presto, there would be an army of excuses to back up any flagging doubts about the validity and credence of my manic beliefs and dreams. Today, most of this seems to be so ridiculous, but this early phase of my first major manic period was to me at that unforgettable time so *very* real. I still believe to this day that some of the manic elements were for real, but inexperience prevented me from catching all that had been tossed into the air, leaving nothing that remained completely intact or reliable enough to hold up in a court of psychiatric law. Down to earth came my dream, but not until I had milked every teat in town to death. Holy cow!

Tingling with anticipation of what may happen next, I found myself moving from A to B by itchy foot or in my car. Sitting still for longer than ten minutes proved to be an impossibility. Remaining reasonably quiet when high is for me completely out of the question. Interrupting other peoples conversations with one of my rapidly spoken pearls of wisdom took up the remaining chunk of a long week waiting for my small fortune. My car had been running around Hemel Hempstead throughout the day, and also into the early hours of the morning. Food, the little that I desired, could be had at my parents house, preferably when they had gone out so that I could avoid being subjected to the third degree. I even went to pubs and drank the residuals that I found on the tables. I believed that I was being left the warm dregs purposely by kind, in-the-know folk who were preparing me for a taste of freedom. This was when I took to smoking other peoples old cigarette butts, a dirty habit that stuck throughout the not quite so wretched highs that were to follow.

Thursday, the day before I was due to collect my £160.00, shocking news of a missing child had swept the town. A three year old local lad named Tommy had been abducted. His frantic mother naturally feared the worst, that he could have been snatched away by an evil minded child molester, or slaughtered and left in one of the many farming fields that patch together the beautiful county of Hertfordshire. Tommy lived in Gadebridge, not very far away from the terraced house where I was born. Thousands of local residents offered to help with the search. I scoured wooded areas where I used to play as a little boy, but to no avail. My newfound manic abilities were worth bugger-all when I required them the most, leaving me irritated and angry but not undeterred. I felt that I had a duty to help solve the abduction mystery. I even questioned whether or not it was I who should take the burden of responsibility because this might well be the seedy, low down revenge tactics being employed by the evil non-believers. This whole drama became one of the driving forces behind what was about to take off next. The good people of Hemel Hempstead never gave up hope, sticking rigidly to the painstaking task of bringing young Tommy home safe and sound. I was eager to cruise all night long around this town of mine, with a wooden Louisville slugger baseball bat that I had brought back from New York in 1981 by my side, searching frantically for a dodgy looking character leading a fair haired, blue eyed little boy by the hand to who knows where, for a reason that didn't bear thinking about. A distinct lack of petrol soon put a stop to that idea. I needed every fume I had left to get to Transia the following day, and besides I might easily have mistaken the abductor for somebody else, whacked the poor innocent party over the head and ended up behind bars. Can you imagine being manic and trapped behind bars, having to endure the indignities and restrictions imposed? It actually happened to me as you shall discover later, but my incarceration wasn't because I clobbered an innocent bystander over the head with a baseball bat.

Yet another sleepless night ensued. Sometimes tiredness did still manage to strike me out, overwhelmingly so at times, but with dogged determination I was able to force myself through to a symbolic time or place where there was always a fresh injection of energy to be absorbed. As I said earlier, the longer one goes without any sleep the higher and more deluded that person can become. The higher and further distanced from reality one gets the less sleep is taken, and so the problems mount up and multiply. One condition feeds off the other in order to survive, forcing the mania up to the next precarious level.

At 5 a.m. I could take it no more. I always gave a huge sigh of relief at around this time, safe in the knowledge that this glorious feeling was still washing over my naked carcass. I had to get out of Bovingdon there and then. It was still too early to go to Potten End, so I threw on my tight black jeans, a gold buttoned black silk shirt, gold buckled black shoes and my recently acquired black leather bikers jacket. To cap it all I threw on a battered old trilby hat made of cheap burgundy felt that I had purchased from a Southend-On-Sea novelty shop. Through my heightened eyes I looked very striking, despite the fact that I was unshaven and unwashed. Feeling optimistic that I wouldn't run out of petrol, I set off first to Gadebridge. In the glove compartment were a pair of silver reflector shades, very Elvis looking. On went the sunshades to complete my transformation from bighead to complete dickhead. If I had worn a polka dot G-string, used banana skins for earrings, stuck two well chewed globs of chewing gum on my nipples and then cavorted down The Mall to see the Queen, I can guarantee that I would have speedily contrived a plausible reason for doing so and would have stuck firmly by it too, unaffected by the inevitable ridicule—such is the all encompassing power of a highly manic mind. Mania isn't just silly appearances and actions. Imagination is heightened, resulting in a prolific output of workable ideas. This can be associated and recognised more easily within the arts, but maybe tamed mania to some extent fires the high flyers of finance and industry as well. Perhaps they know no other feeling or mood and so to them it is second nature. That's my latest theory and I am sticking with it.

Gadebridge woods had already been thoroughly searched for clues as to Tommy's whereabouts. Even so, I had to have another look just in case. No luck there, so I turned my attention to my old senior school about a mile away. On this particular day the mania in me had decided to go for broke. With every tall step and long breath that I took, there became a uniform flow of clearer, bolder, burgeoning purpose to everything my expanding mind soaked up. A far greater significance dawned upon me and then downloaded. All that I saw showed itself as being an embodiment of all that is good and possible. Silent ghostly laughter stuck its middle finger up and whispered in the breeze that we mere mortals have not yet even begun to bite into the innumerable, immeasurable and unstoppable skin of the eternally evolving, mysteriously enticing possibilities that have forever been staring into our ignorant inverted faces. Possibilities such as these are not scientifically man made or computer generated. They are there to be used by the bright spark who manages to find the right frame of mind in which to place this new found knowledge, in preparation to display it centrally for all to see. Boosted by my one sided reasoning and an increasing amount of self-importance I drove on both sides of the road to my old haunt, The Cavendish School.

Children were still entering the school gates when I arrived. "Did I look as young as that at there age? Surely not," I thought during a rare manic timeout.

Today had so far been highly successful, so much so that it had to be a short matter of time until I was formally presented with the key to the city, or perhaps even to the universe! I felt so cool and self-assured as I parked my car in a space opposite the gymnasium. Memories of Julie came flooding back, making me feel obliged to put a tape cassette of Bowie's *Space Oddity* album on the car stereo, very loud. *Cygnet Committee*, the longest most emotive and poignant track on the album was often played at Ju's home when we were a fledgling item. By now, nearly ten years later, I had almost convinced myself that we were still an item. My manic high was now racing, setting new records with every lap. Unreality was taking over, so impatient to become my new reality.

Only a couple of sleepy eyed stragglers were left to make their way into class for registration, so I stepped out of my car, leaving the door unlocked and keys in the ignition. I headed straight for the music and drama block. Surely they would be honoured if I were to grace my old stomping ground following a nine year absence, wouldn't they? This ground level building consisted of two large rooms for group music and drama sessions and five other smaller rooms where the poor instruments took one hell of a beating and blowing. Music and drama were not subjects that I excelled in, or even participated in a great deal. Julie did, and she now teaches both subjects to dysfunctional youths. At school I could be a cocky little show-off but lacking confidence in these arty class subjects. I do wish it could have been otherwise as I would love to be a performer of some sort when functioning in a sane and proper manner. Today was my lucky day. Hold on, I *had* been performing in my maniacal way to the largest audience ever, had I not? "It sure can be confusing these days, but you must follow through with what you truly believe is meant to be, because something truly amazing is awaiting you, just go out and find it,"—these were the repetitive instructions that I kept drilling deeper and deeper into myself. No harm will come to me, no matter what. Ouch!

Today I knew that I looked ultra cool. Today I really looked like a 5 foot 7 inch blind terminator on speed who had somehow found his way into a thrift shop and then robbed the place. Today, the heroes and the zeroes were in great demand and on full display for each and every one of you lucky people. With a twist of a knob and an encouraging shoulder barge, I let myself into the music room. I allowed myself to fall back in time. The unique smell of the place immediately brought back fond memories. Surprisingly the teacher didn't pay much attention to me as I wriggled my way through the seated pupils toward a huge walk in cupboard. Housed inside were the shiny brass instruments, some screechy string instruments and my favourite of them all, the drums. I entered the cupboard and there they were, waiting to be pounded upon. *Crash boom, crash-tish boom*—Steadman had finally made it to the school reunion. When nobody questions whatever it is you may be doing when gliding high, it can be taken as a green light to go on and make an even bigger fool of yourself. In this instance I left the class completely speechless. So long as there appears to be no immediate physical threat to anybody, the flabbergasted audience can sit back and enjoy a show like no other. Audience participation is optional. If the police had been called, and I am very surprised that they were not, I may have curbed my behaviour somewhat and not proceeded in the same direction. Then again, the awesome pull of manic bred schemes, whims and dreams would undoubtedly have drawn me back on to the wacky-track, leaving me with by far the preferable conclusion that the interference of my quest had been nothing more than an unnecessary test set by those well meaning believers, all of whom were playing catch-up, and for a mad minute or two they had lost sight of who I actually was—a very modest, though some would suggest *the* oddest, leader of the manic pack. Yes, quite.

My next stop was the drama hall. I knew that it was in use because piled up outside were a heap of stinky shoes and socks. It suddenly hit me that Shakespeare's Romeo and Juliet had to be the play in rehearsal. This romantic notion would fit in with the current scheming of so many things. Only the gentlest of pressure upon the black door was needed and in I went, hoping to stage some kind of academy award winning psychodrama for the students. At first I had hesitated slightly, a reaction that bolstered my faith in what I believed to be a foolproof emergency back up system. Again, not one syllable spilt from a dramatic young huddle of bare-footed heads. The drama master gave me the once over, which wasn't quite the reaction that I was hoping for. I was becoming far too big for my buckled boots, but I had no option other than to keep playing the roles that would piece together my rolling show. Not all of those parts were a barrel of laughs, as will become apparent. Did there have to be an ending that satisfied my soul and many more besides, or could this be my version of the never ending story, a tale without a beginning or an end? An "eternal, universal and spiritually encompassed amateur soap opera" describes fairly accurately how it often felt when I was soaring. Each episode failed to conclude the resident plot, instead dragging it over vacant days into the next broadcast, losing certain aspects and picking up new parts along the way to throw into the mix.

Not a single word was exchanged inside the black curtained drama room. They may have been practicing mime for all I know. Those pesky feet of mine suddenly became itchy again, so I bid them all a psychic farewell, along with one of my best "knowing" smiles, allowing them all to be left in peace to become an apple tree rustling in the Vermont autumn wind or whatever it was they might have been doing before the "School-term-inator" interrupted their progress. Wowee! This felt so fantastically good! Having got away with two inappropriate drop-ins, a sudden increase in possibility and pleasure took place. Standing in the tarmac covered quadrangle where I used to play ball and the fool, made me realise that as children we do wrong to learn what is right. How can we appreciate what is good if we do not have at least some hands on experience of what is wrong? Not everything can be taught from books or television. If I made a mistake now, I could only be accused of contributing to the future good of mankind. No matter which way I turned, I had convinced myself that I could do *no* wrong. My higher state of mind had been hibernating, growing slowly but strongly, waiting for just the right time to emerge from the shadow of an unfulfilled, monotonous and restrictive recent past, to be reborn and reinvented. We would all in time find this part of our make-up gradually increasing with everybody helping everybody else on their merry way, until the day comes when there is a mental intelligence network of far greater quality and speed than any dot-dash-forward-slash Internet system. All of us will have the shared capability to release the lost part of a spiritual mind, that cannot help other than to exist in a place of exquisite beauty and perfection. That place is here right now. It is just that too many greedy sighted people are blind to it, and much poorer as a result. If we can share resources, knowledge and love, and also learn to shut-up whinging and whining, and be satisfied for the things that we do have in abundance, we will almost be there. Being financially rich is not always a reflection of success, used as a rough guide yes, but I feel it can sometimes act as a restriction on everybody else's God given right to freedom and a decent standard of living. The Bible preaches everlasting life in Paradise does it not? People believe in that without even experiencing what I and so many other people on my wavelength have experienced for real. I get my opinions from living my life from one extreme to the other. Not everyone can say what I am saying without getting themselves locked up in a secure mental institution. It all depends on where in our world one resides and who observes. People listen and take more notice of dimwitted numskulls with meaningless titles to their names, or to those with more money and inches around their waists than ounces of sense in their brains. I am not a sheep. I am not stupid. I have a voice worth listening to. I would like a fair share of wealth and good health. I am also a turned *on* manic-depressive man donning a silly Southend-On-Sea trilby hat, standing in the school sunshine, basking in the sheer joy of total freedom, a joy that with deep sorrow and reluctance will eventually have to become a turn *off*.

Protection from oneself is the key medical issue, but first I had to be caught. Without trying too hard I made sure that I kept one shining step beyond the rest. "Where to now?," I thought mischievously. I began to jog around the quadrangle, noticing an inquisitive row of young heads peering down from their multistorey language, mathematics and science classroom blocks. I felt a little lightheaded at times but I forced myself to remain in control. My manic gearbox felt as if it were about to hit top gear prematurely. I was on automatic pilot, but I desperately needed the self-control of a manual shift system. As bold as brass I jogged into the science block, one of my favourite places nearly a decade earlier. Caught unaware, I was suddenly surrounded by a chattering swarm of school children, some of whom were asking me if I was the person running around outside. I told them that I was indeed, which fully satisfied a few of them, but some of the others still wanted to know exactly who I was. "You'll have to guess won't you," I yelled as I started to sprint back out through the open doorway, this time in the direction of the sports fields where I had many mixed memories of the encounters that had taken place there. Chasing behind me were a crowd of about twenty kids, all boys, all with their regulation purple, black and gold frayed school ties flapping behind over their shoulders. One Rocky-Balboa style circuit around the well-worn 400 metres grass running track sufficed. I followed that by performing a few sprints and side steps on an area of grass intended for rugby where I once, with the help of Russell Clark, succeeded in clean breaking my right clavicle during a practice session. Completely satisfied that I had shown off sufficiently, I made my cocky way back to the open car ready for the getaway. Running around with a horde of screaming kids chasing me felt as if I was actually in one of the six excellent *Rocky* movies. My expanding and even wilder imagination had been allowed a free rein, giving me such a thrill. After all, this was indeed for real and not just make believe on late 1970's canned celluloid, wasn't it?

My car felt more and more as if it could drive itself just like Herbie the lovebug did. They *were* both Volkswagens. It seemed to steer even better and with greater acceleration, and that was with the "fuel empty" needle well into the red zone. I decided to double back to my maisonette to collect a few belongings, just in case I decided to dash off somewhere else after I had collected my £160.00 from Potten End. As I approached the mini roundabout at the foot of Northridge Way and prepared to turn right into Fishery Road, another emotional fist landed and then grabbed my empty stomach. Ahead of me in Saint Johns Road sat the Moorhouse. My head twisted to the left in the hope that Ju would come running. Oddly enough she did not. My obsession with her had now gone well past the normal boundaries of acceptability. There weren't any doubts in my open mind about the pair of us being meant for each other one day. It was a case of exactly when, where and how. I had no idea at that time that she was living in Manchester and had a little boy named Samuel by her husband Gary. This would be made clearer to me much later. When I was still stripping (rubber rollers) for a living I occasionally visited the Moorhouse to visit her parents, Andrew and Jean. Andrew is now a professional artist, specialising in abstract modern styles. He used to be a history teacher before winding up his employed life as the Cavendish School careers officer (Very handy!) Jean had been a midwife, a music teacher and is now an authoress. She has written about her views on combating eczema, a disease that she suffered from terribly, and also about her experiences as a midwife in London—both are well worth a read. These visits had become a little more Julie inspired, but they were dismissed as harmless enough by a very shrewd, free flowing Jean. On this particular day I chose to carry on driving toward Bovingdon. Eight weeks later I did visit the Moorhouse and everybody was there, but today I gritted my teeth and kept going. It was to be a long time before I stopped, and when I did finally stop, I sank.

"Somebody way up there must be keeping a watchful eye on me," I kept telling myself as my fume driven car made it the two miles up Box Lane to deposit me back at my maisonette. Inside I began frantically packing as many objects and items of clothing that I possibly could into as many pieces of luggage that I was able to find. Growing stronger by the minute was an overwhelming urgency to travel somewhere important, to a place that will enable this whole manic puzzle to be slotted together not only for my benefit, but for the benefit of everyone who lived yesterday, those alive today and for those born tomorrow. Answers were out there. I had been building up for an endurance test. I had to resolve the unsolved mysteries not only in my personal life, but the mysteries that have been bugging everybody from day one. Freedom suddenly felt so pressurised, and the only hope I had of combating that was to keep moving on. "Do not stop Steadman, keep going, do not give up," I kept telling myself over and over again. What I was actually doing was loading more and more pressure on myself in the irrational belief that I shouldered the responsibility for everything and everyone in existence, and in order to reap the benefits I would have to work my butt off. The better I made it for everyone else the better it would be for me. This gigantic grandiose leap took place too quickly, bringing with it a trolley full of impossible duties.

So many of my old clothes that had found their way out of the attic and back onto my body looked even cooler now than they did in recent high climbing weeks. A dollop too much of hair gel, trying out wicked new looks and certifiably bizarre old looks, some amusing and others with a far more serious intent—all of these recreations rapidly took place, helping to alleviate the short sharp blasts of anxiety and boredom that can periodically seat themselves in-between moments of being the one, the only, truly manic Mister Magnificent.

The sense of being watched by the masses, an egotistic adulation that I welcomed most of the time, did make me feel slightly uncomfortable to begin with. Slight delusions and paranoia were marvellous when I felt as if I was in control of matters, but when I felt that I was being watched by hidden telepathic cameras that relayed my every burp, fart and hiccup from here to kingdom come, I would become uncomfortable and agitated, wouldn't you? I even took to calling, "Cut," in the toilet so that my privacy and privates, what there is of them, would not be exposed on the manic "head-net" or the bipolar affected "mind-net," and especially *not* on the flourishing "telepathetic-internet." It was pretty much the same story with all of my manic discoveries, some of them just took a little more getting my head around than others, that's all.

Out there somewhere was an irresistible magnetic force pulling me toward a place where all of the answers lay in an orderly fashion for all to read. The world today is in disorder, that's no secret. In my Manic state I decided to go out and find my own future, to observe it, and then share it out between all of those who could handle it, and especially to those who deserved a first crack of the whip. So many other ideas flashed through me as I continued to pack my bags like an eager young hurricane that had decided that the time had finally come to make out or break up. High-fidelity noise, once music, threw itself loudly at my magnolia notice board walls as I hurriedly threw some V.H.S video tapes including *Scarface* the Al Pacino version, into the same brown metal framed backpack that served me so well when I backpacked around Europe. A selection of 35 mm negatives and Kodachrome colour slides also found their way in, some of which were taken on the old Wembley Stadium football pitch following an England international fixture. Along with Mel Jones and Russell Oldman, my old schoolmates, I would often sneak into the big soccer matches at Wembley without paying a penny, and on this particular occasion we decided to push our luck a bit further so we took a ball along to kick around afterwards, unheard of today because of all the strict security regulations, such a shame. Photographs that I had taken inside the local pubs, my infamous Freddie Kruger self portraits, shots through the passing years of girlfriends, friends, relations and so on. These and so many more nonessential items found their way into my busy baggage. My old green sports bag, the very same one that I used during my final year at The Cavendish School, didn't escape the overloading treatment either. In went silly hats, sunglasses, a double breasted suit, ties, jackets, a few books, pens and paper, summer and winter shoes, a six inch recently sharpened sheath knife, tripod, Olympus and Exacta camera equipment, fresh rolls of film, passport etc. You name it, I found a place and a reason for taking it on the trip to wherever. An old ripped brown vinyl suitcase bore the brunt of all the other ridiculous items that were to make the trip. At the time of packing, everything had its own special purpose or symbolic meaning. It was as if I needed a piece of everything that I am, or indeed have been, representing me in order to feel that little bit more secure. Much later on it became apparent in my distorted mind that belongings were of no real importance, and so I went from the sublime to the totally ridiculous. On that Friday morning, concealed behind double bricked walls, manic activity ruled, filling the air with so much pent up manic electricity that a spontaneous combustion of either my maisonette or myself seemed like a very viable proposition. Little lost Tommy, my piano playing Julie, my dead and alive grandparents, all of those that I had ever loved, friends and acquaintances that come and go, peoples of other nations, the relevance and the significance of one issue to another, from one thing to another, from everything to anything, the songs they are playing for me on the radio, on television, from the grooves of circular black plastic or flimsy brown tape that might not be real after all, giving the viewer from outside the biggest laugh at my expense, making me a tail-ender of the fully cycled inhumane race in which we eventually live as each other, covering all time zones, until we finally arrive back to square one again, awoken in a universe full of collected crap that we hung onto just in case it may come in useful, Phew! This is how my unstoppable manic mind works, forever asking my body to keep up with the marathon decorating job.

Raucous uncontrollable laughter followed whenever I looked at a photograph of a familiar face, and saw a strong resemblance of a character from many Moons ago staring back of me. With a little imagination and a couple of drinks anyone can come up with a bleary eyed photo-fit that bears an uncanny resemblance to another person, but in my case it was so real, some faces even appeared to move and smile at me, in a knowing way of course. My brain tried to solve and serve a thousand thoughts, some as plain as night and day, others jangling around like lottery balls waiting to be drawn, bouncing around frantically like a swarm of desperate wasps in a large jam jar that only has one life preserving hole pierced in the sticky lid to escape through, as the other gluttons for punishment are trying like mad to get in. Occasionally a wiser wasp would escape like a clear thought out into the open sky. Was I barking up the wrong tree, losing my religion and gaining spiritual freedom all at once?

A large unframed black and white photograph of Granddad Steadman with his collection of gardening trophies looked at me and demanded, "Go on Son, go get em." In went that crumpled old photo with the rest of my belongings. Satisfied that I had packed all that I could possibly need for wherever I was heading, and that my appearance fitted my mood, I loaded my little VW bullet on four wheels. With an obscured rear view I turned the key and started her up. This was it, legs turned to jelly, feet floated onto the pedals, and for insurance purposes my brief prayers were directed to those who knew. As if I needed it, the late morning air was bright and fresh, suspending a fragrance that lifts even the lowest of spirits. Reaching out my left hand I switched on the radio, "Not too loudly," I told myself, as I was so buzzed-up. Doing everything properly took precedence over everything manic, but only until I reached the foot of Box lane. Waiting at the lights next to the Swan public house was my cue to pump up the volume. What could be better than Jimi Hendrix and *All Along The Watchtower* to get the party going? My quivering feet tried their best to work in conjunction with my upper limbs, succeeding in sending me toward Bourne End. Without money I had no option other than to fly past the small petrol station and down Winkwell Lane, over the canal swing bridge, past the Three-Horseshoes pub, and then climb up through two miles of country lanes to Potten End in order to collect my hard earned £160.00 wage packet.

With the handbrake on, ignition switched off and Jimi on simmer, I casually strode over to the Transia office. Knocking only once and without waiting for a response I walked right in. "Hello Keith, come for your money love?" said Mrs. Slater. Her husband was on the shop floor, a location that suited me down to the ground because all I wanted to do was take the money and run somewhere fast. I was a bit standoffish in the hope that I could cancel out the slightest whiff of a conversation as I had far more urgent matters to attend to. Sometimes when in a heightened state it is necessary to assert a little firmness in order to get things done, and more importantly to make yourself feel as if they are being done more than adequately. Frustration at not getting something completed because of petty barricades can often cause wild rages from a manic-depressive, immediately followed by the most placid of creatures who would bend over backwards to please, ease and to create a world full of harmonious vibes. "Are you going somewhere love?" queried Mrs Slater. Typical female, noticing everything and questioning it. "Er Umm yes I am actually. I was thinking of a trip to the coast or something, maybe the Isle Of Wight or the Southwest, Cornwall perhaps," I lied through my back teeth. The way in which I had behaved during my final two weeks at Transia coupled with the late night, or rather *all* night drinking sprees that were etched across my wild wide-eyed face told her, without having to put two and two together, that I had become so high I needed to wear an oxygen tank on my back. "Are you sure? Perhaps it would be best if you had a little word with your doctor love," she cajoled in a concerned Motherly voice. "No," I replied in a firmer voice than her genuine concern for me merited. "I'm fine thank you, honest I am, thanks for having me," I blurted out as I moonwalked back to my car. As Jimi and I drove off, I strained my neck to blow Mrs. Slater a kiss through the crystal clear air. "See you later baby," were my final words. There must be some kind of way out of here …

Before I could go anywhere I needed to fuel up. "Are you sure that this stuff being poured into my tin tank is not just funny smelling water? Is anything for real anymore?" I questioned myself repeatedly. As far as I was concerned everything and anyone that felt like pouring its soul and source into my mind mattered. Imagination became solid through powers of suggestion, and everything would come alive at the right time. Fruity ash burning cash, dusty lust solid trust, spilling seed watery bleed—my over active mind played with basic words that now created a slight opening and awareness of the eternal areas of undiscovered possibility. I kept driving around and around my town, feeling for the call, the pull that would change everything. I drove past the present and past sights of living and dead relatives, and I was overcome with emotion. This filled me up from deep within with even more manic gasoline, a sort of spiritual lift like nothing else I have ever known. I cried like a baby but was unashamed, proud in fact that I had it in me to feel the way I did. It felt as if the rest of the traffic was helping me, guiding me, this was to be *my* gig, the biggest mind blowing, life altering day ever, the longest day—it was heavenly!

My brain still craved some untangling. I needed someone else now, but knew not who. I felt that I was owed, that it was me who had to work out the mysteries of the universe, dissect them and put them back. The foolish and guilt ridden days of my life up until now have always suggested more to me, hinting and then daring me to be a little bit of what we are all made of, not divided up into brown or white slices of life but neatly packaged as a whole, needing no label. Why is it so hard to be compatible Earthlings who have a healthy mutual respect for our different ways of living, believing and praying to our own refreshing version of what are essentially the same damn things? It is so simple, obvious and true, but oh no, mankind still has to go and complicate matters.

My mind was made up with the help of the traffic and the pedestrians who made gestures that I took to mean, "Go that way, no not that route, the other way." I must have already charted my course subconsciously, a route that took me toward the hectic M.25 motorway. I contrived everything that I set my eyes upon or heard to be a message or a sign. My route through the small villages of Apsley and Kings Langley to where I would pick up the anticlockwise London orbital seemed effortless. Cars in front of me were pulling over or making a left or right turn, helping me to glide through without any trouble. Oncoming vehicles seemed to be travelling at a very slow pace and were hugging their curb. Behind me was a black London taxi cab that appeared to be keeping a respectable distance, not trying to get up my backside as so many drivers irritatingly tend to delight in doing. I felt ecstatically important one second and then would momentarily forget my manic position, causing a mild panic to rip right through me. Tidal sized shockwaves lessened considerably as I drove on, or perhaps I was learning in record time how to ride them down to a functional ripple. The good sensations were now lasting for longer and longer as time flew past. Going slightly higher is like being wide awake then suddenly jolted into another sphere of alertness, then another and another.

West London's Heathrow Airport had to be the obvious setting for the launch of my lifetime. Driving at only 60 MPH on the inside lane was sufficient. Now I had been joined not by one, but by three black cabs, one in front acting as the pacemaker and the other equally distanced at my rear. The third cab remained at my right hand side in the middle lane. I removed Jimi Hendrix and slid in David Bowie, my favourite. Without a shadow of a doubt the entire human race was somehow listening to the same music as I was, and if they were not then the message that was being put across by Mr. Bowie, on my behalf, would be accessed in some other comprehensible way. I figured that if we had all lived through each other, forever as one cloudy mass of sediment that eventually settles to form a solid rock, then we would all have the right to expect another soul to be able to speak up in their mother tongue and put across their own crucial part of the puzzle on behalf of us all. The closer one gets to figuring out the meaning of life itself (or why socks are always getting lost in the wash) the greater their profile becomes. They then speak for the masses, but first and foremost for themselves. This manic business can be so confusing at times. I am thinking these things and a whole lot more as I drive in my dreamlike state anticlockwise around the M.25. It's as if I'm a rolling static ball that cannot but help picking up more material, sticky stuff that is determined to stay and possibly stain the fabric of my mind. That ball is becoming highly charged with each revolution, and so it desperately seeks to expel its energy fast before blowing up. The trouble though is that the faster the ball rolls around trying to release its energy, the more energy it is in fact soaking up. Releasing manic energy simply winds the coil up again in the process, so you have no option other than to keep going until the burn out stage arrives, and it *will*. I liken it a little bit to the space capsule coming down to earth. The closer it gets to the Earth's atmosphere the hotter it becomes, yet the craft has no choice other than to fall back down to Planet Earth as gracefully as possible. Either you survive by means of the safety net that has been built around you, or you perish through lack of care, understanding and exceptionally special technical knowledge.

Two of the highly polished cabs exited the M.25 with me, keeping up the illusion that they were going to remain as my escorts all the way to one of the terminal car parks. At a busy roundabout my angels with Cockney accents disappeared deep into London town, fluttering away as gracefully as they had appeared, leaving me with the job of finding my way into an open air ground floor car park. Honest to God in Heavens above, below and somewhere in between, I could swear that my car was chugging along on autopilot! *The Man Who Sold The World* cassette album that was playing extremely loudly, but with a disconcerting clarity considering the poor quality of my speaker system, crackled, paused and then blew into the thunderous opening bars of *All The Madmen*.

I came to a halt, not quite believing what was happening, although that didn't stop me from following my heightened senses and then seeing what occurred as a result. Next to where I had parked my car sat the only luggage trolley in sight. It seemed to have appeared out of nowhere especially for my usage, so I piled high my varied assortment of raggedy luggage—luggage that need not worry about being confused with somebody else's. I chose not to bother with a parking ticket as I thought that minor detail would be taken care of somehow. The sound of aircraft engines lifted my spirits to new heights. With slight apprehension I made for the terminal building that catered for most European destinations. On the way there I passed a car park attendant who failed to question me about my absent ticket, but I did ask him if he had ever dreamed of being a space-man when he was a little boy. Blank looks I took with a light pinch of salt.

2

Milano

In July 1981 I had my first exhilarating experience of jetting off from London's vast Heathrow Airport with the other members of Ember-Echoes, a youth football team who were due to compete in an international tournament on Long Island, New York. Today, not to put too fine a point on it, promised to be something completely different.

My fast eyes flashed from one funny looking person to another as I stood firm, trying to acclimatise myself to the pace of so many well heeled legs through a cacophony of airline announcements and multilingual tongues. Scuttling to the left, to the right, and straight down the many middles were spirit enhanced chemicals otherwise known as human beings, bagged up in tailor made Saville Row suits or Kensington frocks. The young European travellers wore their finest jeans and distressed leather ensembles. A light sprinkling of cultures—some of whom were openly flaunting their religious allegiances and others displaying their undying love for one another—were all dropping in and then dripping out of the airport pot. An awful lot of sharing was going on that wasn't restricted to small pockets of people, or so my mania insisted.

Amid all of the sleek commotion I began to search for my United Kingdom Passport, bound in a rich brown leather casing. Although I swore that it had been packed, it was nowhere to be found. Either it was buried deep within my old ripped suitcase or backpack, or it was back in Bovingdon. I would have needed to drive clockwise all the way back to Hemel Hempstead had there not of been a temporary passport booth available. As I waited to explain my dilemma to the pretty young passport official I gave my bags an extra rummage through, and there it was. Tightly clutching the passport, I made my way from the queue to a seat so that I could check the expiration date. No good. Once again I found myself queuing up at the temporary passport desk. My ten year passport had in fact been issued in 1979 when I needed it to go on a two week Danish farm holiday in Svendborg with my schoolmate Karl Charles. Following my needless animation of the situation, the passport person handed me a straightforward looking application for a one year passport. Photographs were required. To me, the whole darn procedure seemed pointless because everybody knew who I was, didn't they? I reasoned that the pretence had to be kept up for the benefit of those who have yet to emerge from the old sticky way of life into the state of an open free mind. Too many excitable individuals through the gate too soon could set the whole processing clock back to the very beginning.

The manic thoughts kept coming at me thick and fast. There was nothing in which I couldn't see and feel beautiful pleasure and enticement. One thought would flash across to another thought at the slightest hint of a misdirected manic suggestion. Suddenly I was sitting in a film set along with a thousand extra faces. The next thing I knew, a chilling rush of anxiety and doubt as to the authenticity of my living dream would smack me in the mouth, like an obese elephant doing a belly-flop onto the Maid of the Mist.

I wheeled my mountain of luggage to a nearby photograph booth and sat for the correctly sized shots. Then for the third time, I waited in the same impatient line. At last I handed back the form and photographs. "Sorry Sir, but I'm afraid I am unable use these photographs because you are wearing your hat and sunglasses," explained the polite passport person. In all of my manic fed excitement I had completely overlooked the obvious and had kept my felt Southend-On-Sea hat on, along with the gaudy silver reflector sunglasses. Far from being beaten in this latest test, I borrowed a pair of scissors from another helpful desk—a gesture that would *never* be allowed today. Frantically I submerged my feather-light touch into one hectic bag at a time until I came up with one of many envelopes packed solid with "meaningful" photographic images. Aha, bingo! I found a couple of photographs that were just the right size and lacking any disguises. I returned the scissors and then went straight to the passport desk, this time without having to wait. "Hello again Mr. Steadman, let's have a look shall we," smiled the same glossy lips. She wrongly accepted my do-it-yourself photographs and duly issued me with a temporary British passport, valid for European travel only. To me it was just a worthless piece of card, but as I was almost as high as a Lear jet by then I concluded that it would be a small order to keep the peace, until the day arrives when we all rise up together, high above the petty bickering of imbeciles and float around in a world unwrapped of its stifling red tape and dead end constraints.

Not a single soul, apart from my friend at the passport desk, knew of my plans. Come to think of it, I didn't know either until a split second after making up my manic mind. With a driven spirit intent on breaking limitations through the human race, it was a miracle that I had made it this far in one piece, avoiding the long arm of officialdom, not to mention the clenched fists of the few who had failed to escape my tiresome exuberance, arriving at their wits end in record time. It was early days yet.

Above the booking desk hung a large electronic board that displayed European destinations like an assortment of coloured candy dots. Buying an airline ticket may not sound like a thrill to you, but I felt like a celebrity, a celebrity who has his progress monitored by the masses through extra sensory perception, regular television and radio, or simply by concentrating so hard that it makes the satellite shudder. The heavy hum of terminal babble felt rather reassuring. It was as if I had protection, no matter what I chose to do. Plenty of friendly booby-traps and decoys to keep me on my toes and to rub in some much needed caution, had been set in order to wipe out any threat of complacency within my ranks. And what about the evil non-believers who were always closer than I thought, out and about not to spend two weeks eating fish and chips and drinking San Miguel's in sunny Spain, but to do me some serious harm? As you can see, I kept building one imagined thought onto another, inventing people and scenarios, casting and directing, plotting the next move, dodging all that I subconsciously felt had been launched at me from an early age.

As I poured over the fluttering destination board the city name of *Milan* jumped out and grabbed my attention. "Yes, that has got to be it," I thought, "That's got to be the place where little Tommy is." It was the mania speaking, *screaming* out even louder to me. I had to shake my head to rid these absurd racing thoughts from my mind and refocus on the job in hand. What happens now is that I think I have erased a thought that is so crazy and off-putting to the job in question, only for that original epic bent thought to be replaced by another straight thought that arrives as a small B-movie acorn, which then grows, digging its roots firmly into my subconscious, sucking up my goodness. The old original manic epic in full Technicolor decides one day to come out and be screened, to have a spurt of growth. Thinking that by this time I am far wiser and on top of it all, when in fact I am so far gone down the wacky racetrack, I allow the mania to reproduce a silent family, like a spreading vine. My good manic driven nature comes to the conclusion that everything deserves a second chance, so I go along with the reformed flow. The devious acorn turns out to be an evil disguised seed of the poison ivy, a dark seed growing out of my mind, my body and my soul.

So here was I, standing alone in this mental carousel, trying to decide where my spiritual energies would be best employed, and how the case-hardened tools that I carried around in my brain would be utilised. No matter where I chose to roam, the pulsating set, complete with its versatile and challenging players, would always accompany me. This was going to be the travelling show of all travelling shows. "One way to Milan, Italy please," I asked politely. With my ticket and passport dealt with and luggage checked in, I had time to bask in the glow of molten pleasure. My manic side still crept higher and higher with every successful step. Even the stumbles were now programmed to fall gently into my soft lap. Waiting, when there were so many things to do was not easy for me. By spending this free time observing, I learnt new tricks. By blurring my vision ever so slightly I found that I could transform extraordinary human beings by metamorphosis into animal figures; a trick that refined itself with every upward step. Every one of my five, possibly six, stretched senses stood to attention, when a concentrated sample of each component came by to spill a sample drop into my manic pleasure bank. New excesses of sensory emotion, not always pretty, left welcome living stains in my head that could be, with a little practice, generated into sound, light and action. Even today, I regularly come up against reminders of things and situations that are booted into the pretend manic fray. I may be perfectly on the level as far as lithium is concerned, but I can still pretend that things are not always quite what they seem, which in an averaged reality they indeed are not. If you can believe in the Bible's stories, then why is it so absurd for a modern person to have meaningful experiences and sensations? These modern happenings or spiritual stories are not meant to be thoroughly examined and understood intricately, but have been presented in a simple form to put across an important life lesson to the common man, a lesson that will be of benefit to all existence.

"Normal" human beings have the same built in safety mechanisms as I do, but unlike me, their chemicals do not need balancing out. They also have it in them to become a little high and a little low if their natural chemical supply sings ever so slightly out of tune. New Mothers can become high when holding their newborn baby for the very first time, as was the case with Virginia when she gave birth to Emily. Depression arrives in many forms, as does elation, and nobody is immune. Having said all of that, I will stick my neck out and state that there is *not* a single bipolar free soul on this planet who has ever visited, or come close to visiting the universe of a fully blown *manic*-depressive. Drug addicts do not come close. For one thing our "trips" (man) can last for months and months, whereas a druggy needs a regular fix and may not physically travel anywhere except briefly within his or her artificially altered mind. We manic-depressives have been in situations that the average human being will never know first hand, so our voices are well worth listening to.

By the time I was called to go to the Alitalia departure gate, I felt so high that I could probably have flown there all by myself. My heavy hand luggage consisted of a silver case full of camera equipment and my green school sports bag full of slides, photographs and unsold V.H.S tapes. How I managed to board the plane with such an excess assortment beats me. At the time it just felt like another little customised perk, an acknowledgment of my status in the scheme of things. I was forever being welcomed into a fully used, neither old nor new, but always present and available world, occupied by millions of wide open and available minds that could be tapped into or combined to produce minor and major miracles. Did I pack my knife with my larger luggage or did I have it with me in the cabin? It must be in the hold. Could I make some money in Italy using my creative photography skills? Despite the cultural differences between the pubs of Hemel Hempstead and the catwalks of Milan, I felt confident that I could attack and conquer anything that I turned my manic hands and magical mind to, absolutely *anything*! That's quite some feeling.

Getting to the plush departure lounge involved a lengthy walk along a tunnel, so I flagged down a vacant luggage buggy by tantalisingly waving my remaining £40.00 to the driver. The buggy driver had probably never made an easier £40.00 in his entire life. Before I knew it I was hurtling along the tunnel backwards, waving to the predominately Italian passengers as if I was someone of great importance, to be held in high esteem. They must have been wondering what in God's name was the matter with me, because I appeared to be more than able when I hopped off the buggy at the other end and did a few musical free dance moves. I was a roaring manic as well as being an extremely important person, increasingly so with every blink, shimmy and nod. Those few hundred yards were probably the most expensive that I will ever travel. What I didn't have a clue about was the price I would be paying for every ounce of mania yet to come. The richer that I believed so strongly I was becoming, the poorer I finally became. The rise is like nothing else, it just blew me away. The fall? Well, what can I say except that I for one have paid my bipolar union dues with a deathly disinterest. At the height of my illness, if somebody had pulled me over and shown me the price tag I would have sought help and tried to escape by dashing out away from the store of goodies, but knowing the nature of the beast and my luck, I would probably have ended up in the shop window with the rest of the well dressed dummies, or "manik"ins. When my mania was actually happening I felt more and more secure, when in reality I was walking on a knifes edge without a safety net. No other person can be expected to become your insurance policy, scraping you up when you are flat, broken and down. You have to take that responsibility yourself.

"For crying out loud, hurry up," I thought as I waited in the departure lounge, frothing at the bit. Surrounding me were mostly businessmen and business-women, a sleepy huddle of children and a well turned out mixture of all sorts. The bulk of the passengers were the expensively attired "beautiful" people. These were the people to whom I believed I belonged—there goes my hypocritical equality theory right out of the window. Still perched upon my beautiful head were the moth eaten floppy trilby and the silver shades. Need I say more, except that in God's prying eyes we are all created beautifully and treated equally, even when we are dressed up like a complete and utter twit.

Sitting head in hands for a change, eliminating the outside world from my open housed head, I gave some purer thought to my self-inflicted agenda. My first job was to find little Tommy and get him back to his worried Mummy in Hemel Hempstead. Secondly, I needed to track down my romantic manic obses-sion and then marry her, just like that. There were no solid clues, only long shot hunches that suggested that she would be in Milan. The closest connection that I could come up with was that she used to sing in a choir, and that Italy has plenty of churches. Julie wasn't even Catholic, so that ridiculous theory, that lasted for the same amount of time as it took you to read it, went hurtling out of the cathedral window. My whirring mind overcame these minor inconveniences and quickly concocted irrational reasons, though rock solid enough to me, to keep on pursuing my manic injected quest. A manic church is merely one God and a bunch of bricks with a few crosses and candles inside, along with a huge great bell on top. It would be a piece of fruit-cake! When the grand ceremony is over, viewed by the entire population of the world—so many in fact that it would make Prince Charles and Lady Diana's fairytale wedding seem like a Las Vegas quickie, followed by a chimpanzee's tea party—we shall hop into our Ferrari Testa-Rossa, paying attention not to crease Julie's silk gown, only the best that no money can buy, designed and presented as a wedding gift by the top fashion designers that Milano has to offer. These very same designers can put me in the ring with the cream of high society and the glamorous world of photography which will enable me to make money out of photographing sexy naked women. I could then lap up the cream instead of leaving it for the fat-cats to grow even fatter from, viewed and approved by Ju who would then accompany me back to our golden palace in the new Eden where, with her slender back arched into ecstasy, we would make a little one, perhaps even two or three as part of our duty to mankind. The sky will be filled with the songs of birds from every continent, feathered angels never caged or left to perish in spilt oil again, but able to fly freely into the oxygenating trees of life, the very same trees that store the freed spirits from every rotting corpse that ever bit the dust, trees that bear the juicy fruits that we all gobble prior to swallowing or spitting out the resulting seed of life down into the dust, forever being blown away and coming alive, reborn in the wild winds of Italia …

"Will all passengers please make sure they have their boarding passes ready, and wait in line," requested the announcer. I snapped out of my manic daydream and boarded the white and blue DC-9 aircraft, destined to fly me to the charismatic city in which I would live out my first glorious manic episode to the maximum, and then some. Customary niceties were exchanged with the stunning Italian air stewardesses as I jostled my slim frame through the tall suits to my aisle seat at the rear of the pristine aircraft. I stowed my old green school bag alongside an expensive collection of well-travelled attaché cases, keeping my aluminium case as a footrest. Sitting next to me was a young Italian man, dressed to the nines and smelling of money. The remainder of the passengers smelt of expensive designer fragrances. They must look upon this flight as nothing more than I would taking the No.52 bus to Watford. Everybody looked so beautiful as I soft focused on them gliding effortlessly in and out of each other along the narrow aisle, finally coming to an allocated rest in their sumptuous seats. *Clunk-Click*, I buckled up. With great skill the pilots taxied their flying metal cylinder full of human beings across the glistening tarmac surface, until the aerodynamic nose of the craft pointed down the runway. Thirty seconds elapsed before the forces thrust me back into my seat. We zipped along the tarmac faster and faster, gathering the speed to leave the dirt and dust of Planet Earth. Up went the proud Italian nose into the mid-afternoon blue sky. To this day I can't help but display a wide grin whenever I'm sitting comfortably at that lift-off angle, except when I'm in a dentist's chair waiting to be drilled upon. Even with so many well coifed heads on display, I still believed with all my heart that my mop of hair and felt hat stole the show.

Alcohol was not available on board the aircraft, not that I needed a belt of vodka or Scotch anyway as I was in my own happily deranged manic element. I ogled the stewardesses, convincing myself that perhaps they were in awe of me, fancy me even. The only life form that fancied me was myself. The dangerous truth regarding alcohol was that I had become so high that it would hardly affect me one little bit even if I went on a bender to rival all benders. Abstaining for a while didn't pose any problems. Remaining still for the hour and a half flight *had* proven to be an impossibility. An H.D.A.D (attention-deficit hyperactivity disorder) child on Ritalin would have appeared monk like next to this crazed Englishman. Impatience grabbed me by the throat and threatened to eat me up. Something in my repertoire was needed fast to alleviate my enclosed emotions.

Once I had finished making satisfactory love to the stewardesses with my intensely focused mind, I decided to get my camera equipment from under my feet. With the opened case on my lap I clicked a standard 50mm bayonet lens on to its Olympus body, popped open the back door and loaded a four hundred speed colour film. This was then topped off by my pride and joy, the multi-tilt flashgun with which I had already annoyed so many people. Every fluid move that I made felt as if I wasn't making the move at all, but was instead being controlled remotely, sometimes leaving me feeling as if I didn't require the usual amount of effort and concentration. Feeling this way is where the real danger lies, not in opening my camera case, but out on the streets when I begin to open my big fat mouth to the wrong person, or when I run and never walk for no apparent reason along the wilder side of life. Dropping my guard by being maniacally drawn in by a foolish, false sense of security can in the extreme, be fatal. Believe me, I know!

Two minutes of tripping the flashlight not so fantastic into the backs of slicked heads was enough. Again, it was incredible how I got away with being such an annoyance. Not only did I get off leniently with so much, but I actually scored a few confidence points by way of a "knowing" smile or two from the peachy-reared stewardesses, or were they sympathetic smiles? When I had finished slipping my camera equipment back into their rightful spongy slits, my attention turned to the right where I caught my first glimpse of the breathtaking Swiss Alps. Even viewed from above they looked mightily impressive. Those snow capped peaks certainly shut my racing mind up for at least one whole precise Swiss minute, in the same way that sitting alone on a pounded beach, looking out at the all encompassing ocean demands that you stop, and try to remember that little common you are only a tiny acorn that will either be left untouched to grow tall to rule the forest, or felled in an instant to be made into something useful. The waters that crash down onto rock are screaming out loud of a cyclic regeneration, letting me know in no uncertain terms that I am not such a big-shot after all, just a temporary spirit leasing a body assembled of the same old dirt. It also has a calming effect that does not suggest, but *tells* you face to face that you can overcome, continue and climb up or down to wherever you would care to be in this life, hence all of those atmospheric relaxation recordings that are used in group therapy sessions or in the privacy of one's own cosy nest.

If the flight had taken any longer than one and a half hours I would probably have had no alternative other than to pace annoyingly around the cabin, grabbing a little attention by indulging in a spot of "thought-messaging" and "mind-massaging." The idea of mutually feeding of each other to keep my mood buoyant fell a little short of the anticipated mark, so I put a rain-check on that idea. We landed safely at Milano's Linate Airport, disembarking like peas from a giant multi-ton pod. "Now I am really in business," I thought as I made my way to the baggage reclaim area. With luggage loaded onto a nearby trolley I was on my merry way. A slight feeling of uncertainty shivered its way through my entire body as I realised that here I was, actually in this foreign airport in a far away land and without a brass-farthing to rub together. Just as sudden as my anxiety descended there came many waves of reassurance that reminded me why I had felt so compelled to fly the six hundred miles out to Milano on a whim of fancy in the first place, thus eliminating any seeds of doubt that had toyed with the idea of germinating before I even had the chance to fill my lungs with warm Italian air. Having breezed through customs with the aid of my new quickie one year cardboard passport—later confiscated as it proved unsurprisingly to be illegal and totally invalid—a touch of hesitancy stirred its way into my recipe for mayhem. "Now what do I do?" I pondered, dramatising the next manic movement in my head before stepping right in it. Setting up a makeshift studio to photograph bemused passers by struck me as being a pretty good entrepreneurial idea, so that's exactly what I attempted to do. With equipment primed, I was ready to shoot. The only fly in the ointment was that in my haste I had overlooked the No.1 rule of photography; to take successful pictures there must be some film loaded in the camera! Apart from the few frames left over from the airborne shoot, I had just one boxed film left. I unrolled my long shutter release cable, screwed it onto the camera body, and then sat with my back leaning up against a huge wall that was covered in illuminated plastic advertisement boards. I shot a couple of vain portraits until the camera ran dry. Reloaded I continued, but this time I turned my lens upon the two-way body of traffic before me. A few curious looks of disbelief hit my 50mm target, but were deflected into a safe and agreeable location, somewhere deep within my over acting mind. I'm sure there were a few derogatory Italian words uttered that were aimed below my belt such as *Vaffanculo* (Fuck You). Most of them smiled back at me. The smiling people were the ones who knew of me, and also of my long awaited pilgrimage to Milano, one of the fashion capitals of the world. The contrast between my attire and the fashion conscious Italians became more and more pronounced as my stay in Milan progressed.

Needless to say, through lack of film, tact and ability, my professional career as a top international photographer took a self inflicted nose-dive, coming to rather an abrupt halt. Away into its silver casing went the equipment, and off I went to locate the exit doors. The warmth of the Italian Sun, and the unique aromatic mixture that every new city hands over as a welcoming gift embraced me with open arms, propping me up another few notches to an even greater level of mouth-watering mania. No sooner had I drawn my first fresh breaths of oxygen than I was confronted by one of many short sleeved, dark featured, cigarette smoking taxi drivers, the rest of whom were leaning proudly up against their black and white taxi cabs. Both the Italians and the French are well renowned for their love of tobacco, so as a result I did not need to overly exert myself in the search for a decent length discarded cigarette butt to puff away on. I stood still as I pondered on what I should do next, trying to stay focused on only fifty things at once instead of fifty thousand. Suddenly I was pounced upon by an unemployed taxi cab driver. His aim was directed more at my luggage pile than at me. He kept trying to get me into his idle cab. "No, I haven't got any money pal," I replied politely. If there were ever to be an Olympic event for persistence then this guy would win gold. "Bugger off will you, I have not got lire, I have no bloody money at all!" This irritating banter went on far too long for my liking. During the foreign verbal exchange I felt myself clicking up yet another manic gear. Then it occurred to me that I didn't need any money, that this Italian character would take me to any place that I desired, at any time and for free, wouldn't he? Of course, I didn't have a clue where I was heading but there I was anyway, weaving through the busy Milano traffic with my rear window wound down. My keen driver didn't have a clue that his English passenger was completely devoid of money. Very abruptly we came to a stop outside a rather fancy looking hotel. Out of the car I stepped in the belief that all of this opulence and splendour had been carefully laid on for me, that a communication had been sent by one of my knowledgeable associates back in England, or even from the airplane. I stood upon the step of the hotel with a three metre expanse of Milan paving stone separating me from my luggage, mistakenly awaiting premier service and a penthouse suite. How wrong could I be? Of course, none of this hoped for luxury had been laid on for me. Now I saw my ex-driver in the cold light of day. Trying to understand what an Italian is saying when stone cold sane and sober is hard enough, but when you encounter one in full passionate flow you might just as well give up and head home. Following a lengthy exchange of incomprehensible yelling and arm waving I managed to get through to him. None too pleased with the situation, and looking as if he was going to provide the viewing street audience with an impression of an erupting Mount Vesuvius, he accepted my offering. "Take this mate, it's worth forty or fifty quid," I said as I handed over my tripod. He must have thought that this whole farce was a setup by the Italian equivalent of candid-camera. Without understanding a single vowel or consonant that I said, he angrily threw the tripod onto the front passengers seat and sped off into the traffic. I bet that he radioed through to every other cab warning them to stay well clear of yet another crazy Englishman wearing a silly hat and sunglasses, and by the way, "does anybody out there want to buy a tripod?"

We had travelled about two miles to reach the hotel. No pot of gold sat at the end of that rainbow, but there were plenty more to chase. "It's all part of the game," I would tell myself, "There will be a huge prize, not a financial reward, but a scientific and spiritual reward waiting for me and for everyone else too if I can keep *it* together, keep going and manage to take on board the hidden clues, the advice, support and backing that is with me at all times and in so many ways." My guidance hid in the howling of the wind, the pictures in the sky, the patterns on the floors, in the words and gestures of other humans and through the tastes and feelings of life and death. Everything will help the manic flow if you open your mind to all possibility and allow it the freedom to breathe. "Just go with the flow Keith and you will be alright, do not stop believing," I kept demanding. As you can gather, the regular talking to myself had begun. This is so typical of mentally related problems, although at the onset it was mostly through deep intricate thought. A few days later I took to singing in public at the top of my voice.

I was still struggling to find what the hell it is I am meant to believe in: love, life and me? Three short yet huge words can create almost anything. Yes, others I have loved deeply. Staring me in the face has always been myself, but never have I embraced or explored myself, nor have I really ever liked myself, let alone loved. Perhaps I was about to set off on a series of challenges to explore my spirit and soul, to discover my limitations, to learn how to love myself before I can properly love another. It may sound very pompous, self centred and egotistical, but if you haven't found, or are seriously lacking in love and respect for yourself then how can somebody else honestly love and respect you?

Already I had begun to replay footage of "telepathetic" film shot by my own eyes and commentated upon by my audio thought processor. This, plus the other clips contributed by the rest of the world's fantasy press via the top news agencies such as Reuters, BBC, CNN etc, for all I knew was being beamed into every home and receptive mind from Shepherds Bush in North London to anywhere at all where there was any semblance of life, intelligent or unintelligent. If there was no life I would breathe it into that particular area so that there was. The mania was breeding and spreading through me like wildfire. Previously hidden laughter now burst out of the most unlikely situation or object. Dogs taking their masters for a walk, a tree swaying in the breeze, large posted advertisements offering me food and drink, airplanes and birds suspended in a blue washed studio sky, lit by rechargeable Suns and not so distant stars—all blatant examples of the manic mind's hilarious trickery. Further up the manic ladder I clambered, so far without any distracting questions. I took all that came my way lightly, ballooning it all into a massive gaseous lift. Little did I know that I was teetering on the edge, firing thoughts higher and higher from my revolving manic mind. Boy, did it feel *good*. Soon I would be entering a world far beyond that of the average manic-depressive. Fully blown mania with a sweet talking cherry on top kept calling out to me.

Having experienced all of the variants of manic depression since my high life experiences in Milano, I have to say that my first big helping was by far the tastiest, the most mind blowing and highly addictive natural disorder that I have ever encountered. Its potent force means that nothing else that follows can ever live up to what happened back then. I rose to a higher level by flying a prototype plane, now too expensive to put into full production. I sensed an increased yet confused intelligence. I couldn't suck up enough of that sweet yummy manic syrup. The sour jar sat depressed and sealed in the back of the cupboard.

There I was, sitting on my suitcase outside the entrance of the fancy looking hotel. Alternating thoughts kept up a rapid fire. My glossy magazine never ran dry. An impulse to do this, that or the other would strike, urging me on, followed by another and another. My poor brain's overworked filing system struggled to do its unlevelled best, creaking slightly under the unfamiliar weight. Prioritising these initial impulses took some doing at first because I was being pulled mentally in every attractive direction. I had only been in Milano for a couple of hours but my buzz rating had escalated a couple of storeys. Brief spells of unnerving calm anxiously poked me in the ribs when I looked in the wrong place. By looking in what I chose to believe were the right places I forced myself even higher, very fast. An occasional self allowance to turn the heat down and simmer for a while reduced me to a concentrated mental block, that had the room below and the space up top to soak up and let out even more manic juice. More worrying for a manic on full steam is the illusion of invincibility and immortality. This terrific feeling had gone a step too far and could not hold back, demanding instead to try and run before it had figured out the best way to jump. Too much manic back patting, that I loved, took place. Those same caressing hands were taking a very dangerous, possibly fatal grip upon me.

The hotel looked rather intimidating, but that soon changed. In I went fully laden, expecting to be taken good care of. Not a chance. Despite my repeated requests for a spare room, a room that I had promised myself would be ready and waiting for me, I got zilch. The male receptionist in the hotel foyer was adamant. My perseverance proved to be fruitless but I tried to remain polite, after all I had once worked as a hall porter myself in Folkestone, Kent. Changing my clothes took priority over securing a room. Every piece of baggage that I possessed had by now found its way into the gents toilets in the foyer. The tall porter offered no resistance. On went a different pair of older work-worn black jeans, a wide black leather belt with a brass horseshoe buckle, a dark red Paisley print cotton shirt, my swapped black leather bikers jacket and the gold buckled shoes. My knife in its sheath slid gingerly down the front right hand side of my tight jeans. The Southend-On-Sea trilby took a rest, allowing me to slick back my earlobe length hair. On went the silver reflector shades and I was ready for the lights and cameras, but most of all for the action. I emerged from the gent's toilets looking like a miniature Johnny Cash minus the guitar and a great singing voice. Walking with a sheathed knife down the side of my jeans took a little getting my head and a few other things around, but at least every Milanese I met thought that I was pleased to see them. I knew that I appeared to be slightly menacing dressed in this attire, which suited me just fine because I intended to roam the streets of Milano that night searching for little missing Tommy. When Tommy had been found I would then meet Julie. She may run out of the wind and into my arms, moving the whole zany affair toward an Earth shattering climax, shared by everybody from every race on every planet.

Very kindly the receptionist allowed me to store my belongings in a cupboard that was already full of hotel cleaning equipment. There would be no turning back. The entire night would be spent out on the streets of Milano taking things as they came to me, fast and possibly furious—I was up for anything "they" or "it" could sling at me. Something that I did make a big effort to do was keeping hold of my flimsy temporary passport. This I found easy to also slip into my front right jeans pocket and forget about. Out I stepped into the unfamiliar night with no inhibitions, only a manic view of life as my guiding light. Confidently stepping tall through the busy Milano streets, not knowing north from south nor arse from elbow, caring less and less because it is that unknown factor that creates an even greater rush of overly excited manic blood to the speeding head. To say that I hadn't got a clue whether I was coming or going pretty well wins the coconut, although mania fools you into a false sense of security and direction. A steady flow of city traffic dribbled past, leaving behind the mad rush of commuters.

Forcing my inverted chest out, my chin up and taking long bouncy strides added to the brew of self-imported importance as well as to the rigid belief in La-La land.

Believing that all along I had somehow been at the centre of the universe entitled me to take on the persona of those whom I admired a great deal from the distant past and also from the present day. Everyone that had ever been from Jesus Christ to Spike Milligan, Michelangelo to Winston Churchill and Da Vinci to David—they all figured somewhere within my scrambled equations. As I walked along the streets my mania turned me into these people. When I sang it sounded to me like my favourite singer of that Milanese moment. When I tried to be tough to my shadow I became an odd cross between Ali and Stallone. When I had to act I became everybody, especially the 3D's: De Niro, Depp and Douglas. I half expected these fine men to charge out of nowhere to join my merry gang of one. Of course there were plenty of females on my list, but my lusty manic thoughts were more about what I could do *with* the majority of them and not actually *as* them. When every area of my manic behaviour began to gel, I became a condensed human goulash. Due to the high demands that I placed upon myself, this goulash would be watered down to make a popular soup. I became a human soup kitchen. Like blood, an awful lot can be given in a good cause, temporarily weakening the body. With a few pints of cold water and some deep thought the blood is soon replenished, providing another pot of boiling goulash. Perhaps that's where the phrase "Getting in a stew" originated?

My first obsessive priority was on finding little lost Tommy, along with the other absurd hope of finding Ju. The manic notion that Tommy may be our ready made son did cross my mind, and to make this dream a reality all I had to do was find them both among millions of Italians. What Tommy's mother would have said about my little arrangement doesn't bear thinking about, and Julie may well be snuggled up to her husband back in England. It did cross my mind that it made no difference who made love to whom, because in my grandiosity I represented the men, and Ju represented the women, meaning that we were making love through other people every second of every day. Was Ju a feminine image of me? There were many similar trains of manic thought that I didn't want to ride on.

"Whoa, slow down," I can hear you cry, "Stop, wait a second." What is this big headed asshole getting off on? I was simply getting high on being high and them becoming higher still. It was as if each separate discovery that this heightened state kept on offering me on a plate for free were fusing together, resulting in an increased intensity. My thoughts were multiplying so rapidly that I had to try and slam on the airbrakes. The upgrading process happens whether you like it or not, and only too often it occurs when the body and mind is settling into the latest manic groove. It's not unlike a seventies disco, filled with the hottest hits, when suddenly a new release is played for the very first time, upping the mood as well as the rears of the pretty wallflowers. When it all comes together in the right setting, and all five spandex and sequined coated senses are rubbing up hot and close, the magic will begin to gush out, coating the illuminated dance floor in slippery sexual tension. My dance feverish floor lay all around me, not in flashing coloured squares or pretty yellow cobbles, but in solid grey stone. My mania continued to fornicate, producing new strains of thought that spurred me into a lightweight/heavyweight land, so I danced and danced for miles, trying every step and style that I could possibly think of, plus so many that I invented myself as I jumped and glided, twirled and darted over the hard cracked truth.

Cigarette butts on the pavement were scooped up and placed in a small plastic bag that I had scrounged from a litter-bin. The butts that had a few puffs worth of tobacco left in them were offered up to be lit from the expensive lighters and glowing cigarette tips belonging to the handsome folk of Milano. Aah, coffee. A rich sweet aroma from the many coffee bars hung in the air. I began to believe that I was actually drinking in the thick smells as if they were real food and drink. Great, this latest manic discovery meant that I no longer had to worry about food, not that I was overly concerned in the first place. Only a few feathered angels, the stragglers among the flock, flapped their way toward the well hidden ledges and holes to rest their delicate wings for the night. I tried to remember the lyrics to *A Nightingale Sang In Leicester Square,* the favourite song of Julie's father, but instead I had to content myself and anybody else in earshot with a whistling rendition. Darkness had well and truly fallen upon Milano. The crystal city lights sparkled over this living breathing film set, filled with frantic manic movement one minute and still placidity the next. No more messing around with cigarette butts, now was the time to explore, to search for little Tommy and the elusive Ju, to try out the latest fashionable tricks of my mind and to show my bristling foxy face to the calling streets.

First I began to run, slowly at first then building up to a sprint that took me into the pretty peopled streets. I side stepped like a rugby fly-half through the sharply dressed, brushing bags with my slipstreamed hips, determined to out perform the status symbols as if by doing so it would help my cause immensely. Naturally, the world's media were trying to get on my back—if they could keep up with me! I had to perform now. I had to keep going and never stop until I found what I was searching for. Thinking that every cough, splutter and slip that I made was being fully covered and broadcast by the world's news services, and also captured for the silver-screen, I ploughed on in every direction, pounding the ground as if my life and many other lives depended upon it. God Almighty, did I perform that night. How many miles I covered I will never know for sure, but it isn't the physical distance so much as the mental mileage I subjected myself to that provided the most manic kudos. I gave it my all on that first night, or at least I thought I had until four days later when my blistered feet split and bled on those very same Milano streets. Unsurprisingly there were no signs of little Tommy or Ju. There were plenty of doppelgangers who sent me on even more of a first night runaround. False summits came forward with cold open arms, cajoling me to scale them, only to be let down roughly, to tumble down physically and emotionally to the other side of my forever changing Heaven. My unstable first night had only just begun.

If it was visible it spoke to me, telling me which direction to pursue. I mistook rubbish lying on the floor for forms of trashy signage. Anything becomes an excuse for direction once it has been vacuumed into the minds compressor and spat out as unstoppable manic determination. A window told me that it reflects, so I would take that as meaning, "Look back," or, "Go in the opposite direction." Everything spoke to me if I allowed and needed it to. Of course I was speaking to myself, issuing the instructions that suited me down to the ground. Misleading words were taken from straightforward words on billboards, traffic signage or discarded chewing gum that stuck to the streets in letter-form or in little arrows—pretty much similar to reading the tea leaves at the bottom of a cup. For example, if I saw the word *vodka* I would see the K and A, the first two initials of my Christian names, Keith and Alan. The remaining V, O and D may be maniacally interpreted as, "Very Odd Direction," so I may then interpret that as a route to be wary of, or a route to pursue because of the unknown temptation. Therefore vodka became not only something nice to drink with a dash of lime and a couple of rocks, but as a propellant toward even more manic charged chaos. Up and down the alleys I trotted, whistling different tunes to an ever so real fictional character, or I would fly along a different avenue, kicking empty cigarette packets or the odd soft drink can into a makeshift goal. If I hit a lamp-post it might mean, "Stop and see the light, try harder now to absorb some energy by using incoming thought-messaging and energy-transference."

The manipulation of words and numbers into a living breathing puzzle book—so that I could readily take and randomly select exactly what I wanted to suit the job in hand—played a major role indeed, becoming one hell of a useful tool throughout all of my manic experiences. With twenty-six letters in the English alphabet, and with so many words in the dictionary, even when behaving and feeling sane or balanced, a manic-depressive's deep thinking and overactive mind can become a very dizzy and frustrating place to be. Failure to express a strong point right on the money can be *very* irritating for a bipolar affected person, as well as for their nearest and dearest who often have to withstand a tirade of misdirected verbal abuse. Instant manic answers and remedies often fell short of the mark, and so there is much re-evaluation going on at the same time as carrying out the latest manic movement.

From time to time I would find myself going round and round in differing circles, some long and some short. None of those circles wanted to roll with me fully, even if they were flipped up onto their sides and given an almighty push. The ultimate experience—for me it kept changing all the time and is manifested in so many different ways from one manic-depressive to another—remained hidden in my mind and in my dreams, venturing out to play only through my prayers. Achievable happiness and contentment had always been there for the taking as a by-product to hard work and clean and honest living, and now I took to kicking the arse out of it without meaning to. So there I was in this foreign country, an alien alone in a city that is home to millions of native spirits, living out a doomed dream that I struggled through Heaven and hell to love in the way that it demanded. An up to date instruction manual and rulebook were never available because everything became defunct the split second after its occurrence, imagined or not. The guiding "book" needed to be constantly rewritten, while at the same time coming up with a blueprint for the not to distant future—a hopeless task for even the fastest word processor. I felt like one of those novelty silver foil helium gas balloons that has wriggled loose from its supermarket checkout moorings, floating up to the heat filled ceiling that separates it from the sky. It remains stuck up there for all to see, still smiling down with a silly grin that makes every man woman and child laugh, but the squeaky helium is slowly seeping out. The balloon is now losing its puff, but it has managed to find its way through an open skylight. The smiling balloon, now licking its puffy lips with a taste of freedom will not stay still, nor will it be able to rise too high. This is a perfect time to perform a thorough examination, followed with any luck by the correct diagnosis and appropriate treatment. The descent to an uncertain, unstable terra firma is a gradual, unpredictable slump, making it very tricky indeed for another human being to realise the severity of what is actually taking place. When that balloon is roaming, temporarily lost of mind but striving to find the peace within it, and there isn't a kind soul to loosely tie you down until treatment can be given, that spells out one thing only—big trouble!

Sleep was not on my agenda. Far too many manic thoughts were finding their way into my disorganised mind. One minute I would be singing at the top of my voice to the sleeping angels, more commonly known as birds, and the next minute I could be heard all the way back in England screaming for further instructions. Fights continued to flare up inside my head as the mania fought with what little rationality remained. When that difference of opinion was set-tled, always in favour of the irrational, another dirty trick campaign began to ensure that every manic thought had pride of place. By not bringing sleep to the forefront of my worthless agenda, I worsened. Sleep deprivation will, and in my case most definitely *did* play a major role in how the mind operates. In extreme cases, prolonged periods without shutting off the mind, allowing it to cool down and rest adequately, can trigger an hallucinatory state. This eventually happened to me as you will discover, although to this day I still can't say with any great accuracy what was actually real and what was not. Perhaps a part of me is still madly in love with the euphoric idealism, the sweet conviction that much of what I experienced was indeed for real, though camouflaged with the help of an extremely peculiar illness. At least I have plenty of ammunition in my conversa-tional machine gun with which to bore people down over dinner.

Following hours upon hours of headless goose chasing, trying to identify what I was determined to find and then coming up with nothing, I sometimes became engulfed in an overwhelming sadness. My brown eyes bawled uncontrollably in the open streets. What did I care if passers by saw me letting it all out, as far as I was concerned we were reciprocating every innermost thought and feeling. There had to be a huge flood of sympathy, support and solidarity floating through the air and into my very soul, well wasn't there? "Tell me where it is and I'll go and get it," I insisted. Still a big fat zero. This manic saga, still in its early stages, was in severe danger of becoming a dreaded test. This was just a warm up before devouring the manic morsels that lay upon my bipolar affected table.

The 1990 model Keith Alan Steadman must have been by far the most believ-ing, trusting person who openly displayed more sheer bloody minded determina-tion to reach and then build upon an uncertain base than anyone else I can think of. Of course he was also the biggest plonker on the planet. The passion kept insisting that it danced and cut its eternal flame through my veins like molten diamond. I arrived at a place in my own mind just before all of the other leads in my telepathetic manic movie. This helps to explain why I was always alone for far too long, and why I was usually two stretched strides ahead of myself, forever landing in a distant place, a place that was also too close for comfort and too close to home, a place where I needed the support that never materialised, a place of Brothers, lovers and so many others.

"It's all in the mind," is in fact the perfect description, tuned in spiritually through the brain to the chemistry set it tries to maintain. Sometimes the original order form fails to include enough of the necessary components, so instead of it being rectified at source early on it gets passed down and down and down, on and on and on to generation after generation. A distant dyslexic named Gene must have written my original order. Scientists today think that they are very close to knowing how to locate the origin, enabling them to know who and when to check and treat in order to rectify the situation, saving so many perfectly normal human beings from untold grief, instead filling them up with joy and hope for a promising full and productive life on the level.

A police car pulled up. Two officers stepped out and walked over to me. They began to speak in their native tongue but I interrupted them rather rudely with polite sounding English, a language that we could at long last all get along with. Out came my crumpled makeshift passport. As I did so they caught a glimpse of my knife that I had placed inside my jeans. The only way I would have been provoked into using it would have been if little Tommy's abductor gave me any trouble. This was just in my mania driven mind, as I certainly am not the sort of guy that goes looking for violence, although as you have probably surmised I do have a tendency of becoming embroiled in it a little too often for my own good. Having a six-inch blade in my possession was simply asking for trouble. The two officers were subjected to the story of Tommy. Amazingly they both drove off, allowing me to keep possession of the knife. This early encounter with the Italian police force gave me a little lift. Now I believed that they were on my side, backing me up. Later on, my high regard of the Italian police took a severe downturn, but for the time being they were up there with the elite, well in tune, permanently ingrained and enjoying our maniacally concocted super-world.

My energy level increased twofold. I felt so light that I thought I would eventually need pinning down, or would I be able to fly? The scabby plastic bag that I had lifted from a rubbish bin had by this time been filled to overflowing with clues, evidence, directional data and souvenirs. Yes, it was just a useless stash of junk, but when I was in that heightened state I believed that everything possessed a valuable relevance to the "cause," and would prove to be handy when unlocking the shroud covering this manic Italian quest. So I became a junkie on the streets of Milano. Yours truly was definitely an olive short of a thin crust pizza.

Light rain fell during that first night in Milano, cooling my warm clammy frame. Energy filled my body within a matter of seconds, like a racing car taking a pit-stop at the nearby Monza Grand Prix racing circuit. Only a sprinkling of traffic existed as I moved my body along a wide expanse of street, passing a small cluster of brightly lit shops that had remained open. I distinctly heard what I believed to be a gunshot coming from a large building on the opposite side of the street. There were no vehicles running that could be held responsible for a backfire, besides it sounded different to me, like a very loud crack of a whip. There were no lion tamers to be seen, only an ill twenty-five year old Englishman trying his level best, come what may, to get from here to where he felt his destiny lay. The building from where the sound may have originated appeared to be an apartment block. Peering up with my hawkish eyes I could detect no evidence whatsoever of a sniper, perhaps my assassin. My busy mind, now on compulsory overtime, took the situation in and processed it along with all of the other existing manic thoughts, coming up with the notion that I had been shot dead by the very same person who abducted little Tommy. Paranoia tried to grab hold of me again. The way my manic mind was working I reckoned that Robin Hood, Al Capone and Flash Gordon all stood a very good chance of making their comebacks. Why was I still standing with the sound of the "gunshot" ringing in my ears? Where was my blood? Why wasn't the spot where I stood running red? When the fatal bullet struck me I must have returned faster than an e-mail to a living form in Heaven, a place where everything looks the same but really isn't. "Have I reached an even higher platform than I had done before," I pondered, "and gone through a preparation process in readiness for what I was about to receive?" Believing that I was deceased, yet alive as can be, took a little mental adjustment in order to accommodate. "Then again," I reasoned with myself, "I always had been a regenerated human being, sharing a dense body of spirit with everyone else."

So much happened so fast. This meant that I had to find any way of keeping up, even if a little justifiable elimination took place. I needed to perform the different roles that were given to me. Sometimes these roles would interact amicably, but at other times I felt as if I was being torn between too many conflicting, contradictory options, setting me up nicely to be the world's biggest hypocritical corpse. Now I knew how it must feel to be the push-me-pull-me from the *Doctor Dolittle* film, except that I had to contend with the added weight of a thousand wild screaming heads on my shoulders, every single one of them vying for the foremost position. At about 7 a.m. I managed to find my way back to the hotel to collect my luggage. My early arrival and hyperactive demeanour took the baffled night porter by surprise. The idea of leaving my belongings where they were and just having a change of costume when I felt the urge, came to a swift end as soon as we established communication. The perplexed porter could not get my luggage out of that cupboard quick enough. No amount of pleading altered his mind, so I found myself back out on the street. Possessing so many objects—following a long night of placing greater importance upon the junk that I had picked up from the damp ground—made me feel, in a material sense, as if I had it all but without a real need for any of it. I decided that this weighty burden of baggage should and would easily transform into a means by which I could continue my manic journey. Within a few minutes I had spread the entire contents of my baggage over the wet pavement. Off came my black clothing and on went a crumpled pair of light blue jeans, topped off by my another long sleeved burgundy cotton shirt. Old white and black bitumen streaked basketball boots protected my feet. Six inches of warm steel still hung close by. Changing clothes in public is great fun. Standing in the middle of Milano wearing nothing but a pair of Y-fronts and a huge smile is even better fun, but not a pastime that I would recommend in a hurry. There may well have been one or two Versace clad cigarette smiles thrown my way, but my behaviour was really a disrespectful show, unintentionally disgraceful yet hilarious and harmless to a whistling manic in full swing. How can I be accused of a display that is perfectly normal to a manic? Accused maybe, but found guilty *no*. If it is good enough for the naked singing cowboy in Times Square, Manhattan, then it is good enough for me!

So there was I at around 7.30 a.m. opening up a low-level shop on a glistening Milanese pavement. I even manufactured a "For Sale" sign. Why not go the full Monty and shout out my wares at the top of my voice to the passing punters? And so that is exactly what I did. "Video tapes, double breasted suit, alarm clock, picture frame, camera equipment, books and magazines," I yelled, "roll up, special offer, get it while you can, today only …" Of course, being English didn't exactly help sales despite the Italians having a better grasp of English than I did of Italian. I had everything bar the kitchen sink laid out beneath the early morning Italian sunshine. I ask you, who in their right mind would buy an old crumpled up suit with holes in its pockets from a wiseass Englishman who makes no sense at all? Not to mention the fact that he looks decidedly dodgy. A manic Italian might cave in to temptation, but I don't think that there were any turned on bipolar comrades wandering down my piece of street that morning. The occasional *Gran Disgruziato's* (Big disgrace), or *Scemos* (Idiot) were thrown my way by a few natives who couldn't be expected to know what was grinding furiously away inside that head of mine. Not a single item sold, what a surprise. I did manage to charm a small handful of potato crisps from a couple of children, but apart from that I had to resign myself to the fact that my days as an early-bird Milano street trader were well and truly over. Suddenly a lone policeman appeared. The duty manager had contacted the police because my sales pitch looked and sounded awful outside his posh hotel, lowering the high class tone somewhat. I explained my harmless intentions as succinctly as my English tongue would allow, but to no avail. Why did the hotel manager fail to discuss the matter with me first? The flabbergasted policeman issued me with his clear and very precise ultimatum in pidgin English. There was nothing at all angelic about being told to pack up quickly and disappear. What I had attempted to do was obviously illegal, so I reasoned that when in Roma it is probably best to shut the hell up and do as the Romans do. But this wasn't Rome, it was Milano, and didn't the Romans get up to all sorts of mischief?

They may have been laundry sacks from the hotel. Two large reinforced plastic sacks appeared, similar to those used by the postal service but much larger. All of my belongings were slung haphazardly into these two huge sacks. Still tingling deep inside of me were all of the loyal manic feelings, a delicious recipe of bubbling magical power garnished with a sprig of mayhem. Unshaven, unwashed and unbelievably able, I slung the huge bags over each shoulder and started to walk my unbalanced five feet seven away from the hotel.

Four years earlier I had left my tin-bashing position at Rolls Royce and set off on a three month solo backpacking trip around Europe. When I arrived in the Northern Italian seaport of Genova I decided upon a train journey to Milano. The *Stazione Centrale* became my first ever taste of Milano, and four years later that familiar place reeled me in again. In an odd sort of way the *Stazione Centrale* became my only friend, the only familiar stoned face that I found to be real, and did *not* play teasing games. I needed something solid, something that would stay put so that I could catch the little breath that I often thought I didn't need. It also became a reliable place to plan my next manic movement.

Plans, to a bipolar affected person in the manic phase are usually meant well and with the best intentions for one and all, but they usually fail to deliver or become irretrievably sidetracked by another manic whim of fancy. The impossible dreams are kept being made because the manic needs a full well of possibilities to draw from, and although those plans or dreams tend to end in disappointment or haven't quite reached the expected heights, they have at least been let out of the manic mind without too many regrets, allowing room for the next instalment.

So I kept on pushing myself beyond the tough limits that I could not stop setting. If I stopped I believed that I would let the entire world down and that life would no longer be worth living. The transparent pressure that I had mixed up in my mind often became unimaginably intolerable. Living a life that had not stretched me far enough both physically and mentally was I'm sure the catalyst behind much of what happened to me, only in my case the illness of manic depression pushed my frustration over the edge of the cliff. The painful impact onto the sharp depressing rocks below is determined by the height from which the actual drop was made. By keeping mobile I postponed the drop; a plunge that when it did come was going to be of harrowing proportions.

I kept walking and running, occasionally even crawling on my hands and knees when I was instructed to by my internalised regime. After a while I realised that I was heading in the wrong direction. Even know all, stubborn manic-depressives at some point need to button up their lips and swallow their pride, well at least for as long as it takes to be given some agreeable direction. A friendly tanned finger pointed, advising me to take a new route. Why I didn't think of popping into a newsagents or a book shop so that I could look at a map I don't know. As far as having my face sprawled across the front pages of newspapers and up on the big advertising boards was concerned, I had concluded that similar versions of myself were being used not only to hide my true identity from the nonbelievers, but to project my latest movements to the masses in a coded form. It really doesn't take half a brain to take any aspect of an image large or small and then relate it to you. It could be that the pasted models are depicting a car chase of some sort, or that the shipwrecked man and woman who are wearing flimsy Italian bathing suits and advertising an alcoholic beverage are telling me that, "No matter what you wear or what stage you are at you will always find your woman—probably driving her fast car." When she is found the celebrations could begin with a cool drink of something stronger than water. I would worm my way into the scene as if it was a disguised reflection of my life. By concentrating on some of these large posters I found that I could literally soak up what they had to offer. For example, by looking up at a picture of whisky or gin for long enough, my heightened senses could make it come alive so that I could actually taste it, drink it in by concentrating hard and believing with all my heart that this was actually happening. A manic mind over matter is a powerful thing. The taste was so real. When very high, so much more is accessible because of the combination between the five known heightened senses and the over active mind. An hallucinatory effect is actually what's taking place here, but hallucinatory or not it sure is good!

I do not apologise for my manic rambles, some of which veer off the beaten track. Rambling thoughts are an important component of the manic make-up and they go an awfully long way toward understanding the psyche of a bipolar affected person. Sometimes you've got to search long and hard in the thickets to find what it is that makes them, or at least a part of them tick. So if you pick up a little bruise or get a scratch when rambling off my beaten track, consider it worthwhile.

My cognitive abilities continually conjured up new surprises, although many of these surprises were somewhat distorted and in disarray. Up until this early point in my manic proceedings I had felt in total control. My extrasensory perception (ESP) felt as if it was in tiptop order, able to rev-up and break down at will, when really I had well and truly lost the plot over a month ago back in England. Whenever I felt that my ability to deal with so many demands was waning, I would dig in and grind my way through regardless, ignoring the fact that I had not eaten nor drunk adequately since flying over Switzerland. Also, I had uncharacteristically not bothered to shave or wash despite having the means to do so buried somewhere in one of the two sacks. Nor did I feel the need to defecate, which is not a surprise considering that I had not eaten. Urination took place up against any wall available, dog like. All that came out was a weak dribble. I made sure that I was out of view to prying eyes, and I also shouted "*cut*" to the European editors of my up and running telepathetic television station. The further I climbed the ladder, the further I could fall. My head had emerged from the cotton wool clouds, the same clouds that are full of biblical faces that merge into each other but remain as one. The droplets fall, spurring on new growth, passing through as they had always done to provide for our needs before rising up again. I likened my life to a prickly rose that is fed by liquid manure and sunshine, but on the same hand I realised that a thunderstorm has its own special purpose in the growing, weeding out, trimming back and recycling processes. That is how I still feel today, that I am reaching through to the stormy skies, forever surrounded by human foliage that I gladly tolerate instead of pruning back like a power mad fascist dictator. Natural gardens full of wild flowers and pretty weeds attract birds, butterflies, insects, rodents and other creatures. "Keep off on the grass" signs have always invited me to go on the grass, as well as acting as a reminder of the mental health risks that come with smoking or popping too many drugs. I am stretching higher and higher, far into the electrical blue city in space. Why do I always get pruned back so much these days?

With such a ridiculous amount of baggage on tow my progression toward *Stazione Centrale* slowed. Meaningful and miraculous things were awaiting, allowing me to relinquish the burden and to give me a much needed breather. I can clearly remember that at this time I didn't give a damn about anything other than fulfilling the many different roles that I had been collecting like second class stamps. I had to live up to my self-proclaimed brilliance. All of those material things such as clothes, food and a little money would in their own good time sort themselves out, so there was no need to worry. No need to worry? God preserve us all!

There it was in front of me at long last. A huge stone structure fronted by a huge facade and crowned by two proud looking winged horses. This impressive building, second in size only to Milano's Duomo Cathedral, was indeed my old friend the *Stazione Centrale.* The closer I came, the lighter I felt. Everything transformed into a wish-wash of peacefulness, so surreal and pretty. I felt overcome with emotion, prompting a few salty tears that I mopped up with my shirt-sleeve. Gracefully I swam through the tearstained mist to one of the grand steps, where I sat with my sacks at either side. Restrictive reminders of the shoddy past were all they had become. My old stoned friend suddenly put a cold and heavy arm around my sore shoulders. This made me very anxious. My surroundings tried to warn me of the inherent dangers of pursuing a solo career based upon one inexperienced vision. I told my old friend to go to hell.

Milano's *Stazione Centrale* is the second largest mainline station in Europe, so naturally it is extremely busy. I found some more cigarette butts and gained a light from one of what seemed to be a million worker ants scurrying from out of nowhere and heading somewhere, each with their own thoughts and feelings. Were they individual thoughts and feelings or were they universal? This was the big question that I struggled so hard to answer. With all of my manic roles bubbling away I climbed the stairway, passing the elegant art-deco wall designs until I came to the bustling ticketing hall. Once inside I positioned myself along the wall that ran parallel to the top of the stone steps. Now I was opposite the ticket booths where a swarm of modern travellers jostled for prime position. Suddenly I experienced an acceleration of the senses. An eerie quietness fell, hushing the entire hall. I could feel myself effortlessly rising as my mind was taken to a giddy height. Then something truly amazing began to take place. One hundred and eighty degrees of life spread out before me walked from their A's to their B's perfectly normally, minding their own business, when suddenly they all came to a complete standstill. Gradually they began to move in very slow motion, gliding ever so delicately across the hall. When all of this was happening I found no problem in articulating my own body in any manner or at any speed that I chose. I contorted my face and twisted my limbs, bending over backwards for an excessive love-life affair that I could not explain away merely by using words. Almost every move of mine was executed at regular speed. Regular speed to me was still breathtakingly fast for another mere mortal to read. I checked the crowded scene before me and then looked down at my lower half for evidence that this spectacle was really unfolding before my very wide eyes. Was it disconcerting? Yes, a little. Was this a figment of my imagination? Never. Without warning the whole place begun to hurtle around at a head busting speed like a movie on fast-forward.

Then everything returned to normal. I stared into a million eyes to see if any of them had gone out of focus, but they all fluttered and blinked as though nothing had happened. By chance, I discovered that by raising my head up slightly the occupants of my community spirited hall would dart around without colliding, like a colony of demented worker ants in designer clothing. When I lowered my head the very opposite happened, slowing every man, woman and child down to a snail's pace. If I had bent down and put my head between my legs everybody may have walked backwards on the ceiling, can you imagine that! I didn't actually try that move so we will never know. More of my uncontrollable manic laughter resounded around this wonderful dreamy theatre. Did my cohorts have any clue that they were doing all of these wonderful things? Were they still playing catchup, or were these "quick quick slow" Italians entirely blind to the signals that my stray manic satellite was beaming down to me? The same old questions kept nagging away. Who is living in whom, when and where? In what order are we? Am I first or last? Is there such a thing as first and last? Are we all images of ourselves? Have we been born yet, or are we born again and again? Sometimes I felt as if I had died a thousand times, but only now had I reached the right age of twenty-five, having collected and protected enough knowledge and experience to put some things right in this world. Are we all on a level pegging? Have we walked long and far enough in each other's shoes to snap together all of the world's outstanding mysteries in our cracked swollen heads, creating a Heavenly body of love and contentment? Think think think. I couldn't do much else other than think. New networks of mania came thundering at me like an express train, smashing through my skull without causing any real harm. New manic arrival did help to prop up and bolster some of my more outlandish beliefs; that *I* had been the sole instigator of life, and that *I* had indeed gone full circle, finally landing in an overgrown garden (Planet Earth) full of starving children, my children and your babies too. This latest confirmation of so many little gems was going to take some explaining, that's for sure! I was high yes, but still residing at base camp. A mountain of false summits remained.

Delusions of grandeur are magnificent in regulated and controlled conditions, but they become very dangerous when one is vulnerable, miles from home and without any real form of sustenance. None of us are placed on this planet to be any greater or any lesser than the next person. Having said that, I couldn't help myself from getting a bit too big for my smelly old boots again by wondering if I was the creator of it all, or if I was his, hers or "its" next of kin, or just a bisexual blob of green jelly upon which bacteria and other organisms grow. Everything we can comprehend is an altered image of the creator; it is just a case of where in the

pecking order we all are. Wanting it all too soon at a time when I was least prepared to take the reins began to tarnish what could, and can often be a maniacal
pleasure cruise. Steadman had to go and take his hallucinatory dreamboat, an
inflatable raft filled with hot manic air, around Cape Horn during rush hour. I
think I must have sniffed too much South American sunshine on that particular
day in my distant manic past!

There were the infrequent times when I could have given up everything for
a pint of beer and a game of pool back in England. Oh well, I made this single
bed and so I suppose it was I who deserved to lay on its lumps and bumps. Unannounced, my sad and lonely friend stabbed me in the back again. The incessant
bombardment of old and new manic thoughts, each one stored irresponsibly in
my minds broken locker, sometimes drained me to the point of collapse. Instead
of a bearable drip, the floodgates were pulled wide open, exposing my naked soul
in its most frail form for all to bear witness to. The responsibility for the past,
present and future often clung to me like discarded chewing gum on the sole of a
brand new pair of shoes. Again, I started to wonder whether or not I had actually
died or if I was still in the same earthy body that I thought I knew so well. "Am
I alive? If so, would somebody kindly inform me so that I can be put out of this
terrible misery," I thought over and over again. The worst thing about all of this
was a growing belief that everybody I knew and loved back home in England
were, in some unbeknown way, dead and buried. Boy, did I cry like never before.
I mourned my parents, my sisters, relations, neighbours, friends and even Ben,
my sister Barbara's fat black Labrador dog. Following ten minutes of utter mental
and spiritual mutilation, a self-preserving instinct kicked in that enabled a rapid
reorganisation process to take effect. The thoughts that I determined to be positive and focused in the right direction were downloaded until a normal service
resumed, cheering one sad little Englishman up a little. My tears had not, as I had
feared, consisted of embalming fluid. Doubts as to the validity of my existence
did continue to arise, but for now they were well and truly buried. My folks back
home were now alive and kicking. What had happened was that I had a surge,
an overload of anxious manic activity in my mind, bouncing around, refusing
to make any sense that had some stickability. The manic thoughts remained but
they had bounced their way to bed, leaving me with the task of ensuring that the
rest were made to slot in according to my fine and unlimited merry-go-round
specifications. My directional acumen left a lot to be desired. Manic made directions were dangerous as well as being completely useless, presenting me with
more than enough avenues to run down and get lost in. Despite the positive
intentions, the targets and goals that I set myself were just too unrealistic and

far too ambitious. As time went by my mind cleared a great deal, and I believed without a shadow of doubt that everything *was* possible, but my body put up a brave fight and screamed, "Enough is enough."

Clearly visible to everyone was the fact that I was beginning to neglect myself somewhat. I didn't look upon it as such. All I knew was that my appearance served a purpose, it sent out a message. Later, when I had no clothes left except for the torn remnants drenched in sweat and spots of blood that loyally hung around my bruised back, I still figured that this was all part of the big test, the master plan, the ultimate scheme of things, my destiny. I think I would have sacrificed myself if I knew for sure that as a result this whole world would work in harmony, and that we could all love thy neighbour and exist happily ever after in a wondrous land. In the evenings we could lay down on the grass and bet on the cows hurdling the cheesy Moon and perhaps even have an each way flutter on the flying pig races. Manic idealism comes with a hefty price tag and too much small change. Immobilised views and far out visions are all one has to go on. Nothing much changes physically apart from the brain's chemistry, but the way one looks at life mentally and spiritually following a high or a low episode is very different indeed. A bigger picture opens up and becomes available that many non-bipolar people can't access, making their vision seem so much narrower, shallower and lacking any real substance, and yet they profess to know more about everything than you do, when nine times out of ten it is the other way round. I think that many people like to feel as if they have an advantage, or one step up on somebody who has a mental illness. This is a sorry state of affairs that only goes to highlight the insecurities and prejudices of that person. It takes all sorts of differing characters to make this funny old world go round, or in my case upside down and inside out.

High on well intended bullshit, that was I. An urge to put my double breasted suit on punched into my mind. Never mind privacy. As quick as a flash I was standing with my back to the wall inside the *Stazione Centrale* wearing the same pair of yellowing Y-fronts, smelly socks and a menacing smile. This impromptu public overexposure was the one move that finally ruined any chance I may have had of becoming the British Ambassador to Italia. On went the suit, complete with a creased pale blue dress shirt and an old navy blue tie that last saw the light of day in 1986, when I spent an unfulfilling year attempting to sell Ford automobiles in exotic North London. My shiny black shoes had the unenviable task of sealing in the stench of my feet. Plenty of pigeons were also using the *Stazione* as a place to rest and also to poop, just as they do in Trafalgar Square, London. I spent hours watching them with a strange fascination, circling around the ticketing hall and coming to rest on the ledges. Pegasus One and Pegasus Two remained set in stone above the station entrance. I flew down the grey stone steps so that I could look up to these huge sculptures in the sad hope that they would come alive and fly above our heads. The feathered angels kept giving me all the inspiration I needed to bellow out yet another dreadful rendition of *A Nightingale Sang In Berkeley Square* for the delight and delectation of the general public. I was unable to see that I had become a sideshow that lacked any real talent, just a scruffy laughing stock to one and all. The title of "Bovvy village idiot" would have been a reasonably accurate description, but Milano is hardly a village, so that title awaited me back in Hemel Hempstead. Instead I took on the mantle of "city fool." I am *no* fool though. I believe that bipolar affective disorder at its extreme is in relation with a persons existing intelligence. The highs and lows will still feel as extreme to the individual, but the visible behaviour and mental capabilities in one person may not reach the outlandish standards set by another. If I was as thick-as-a-brick (and there are plenty who would agree with that), I would still become high and low, but without the severity of an intellectual and intelligent mind. Not for one second am I suggesting that I am up there with the Da Vinci's and Dali's of this world, but when flying high I *am* able to live out in the open my wildest and most imaginative dreams for all to see. Many other higher than average minds are applauded and encouraged to paint or to sing their creative dreams and beliefs in an acceptable and controlled fashion, often making a very decent and well deserved living into the bargain. The "Battling Birdbrain of Britain" accurately sums up my mental condition at this early stage of the proceedings.

With both sacks dragging, I bumped down the *Stazione* steps and made for the *Piazza Duca D'Aosta* directly opposite. This is where I resumed the nonsensical search for possible suspects in the little Tommy abduction case. My knife was safely tucked away in the bottom silk lining of my suit jacket because it had fallen through the gaping hole in one of the inside pockets. Around and around the Piazza Duca D'Aosta I went, hauling my belongings at either side. If I had the money I could probably have put all of my stuff in safe keeping at the *Stazione*, but I didn't have the money, and even if I did have it my addled mind would have refused to come up with the most obvious and sensible solutions when I needed them the most. Complicated issues of impossibility dominated my thinking, kicking any remaining marbles well into touch. Had I drawn up a phoney sponsor form and asked people to sponsor me per lap of the Piazza, to dishonestly raise money for a new magnetic resonance imaging scanner for the local hospital, I would have become a wealthy man, but I did not and I was not.

All that I had in the way of money were a few pieces of English silver and some useless coppers, completely worthless to me. If I had wanted to I could easily have found a way of reversing the telephone charges to England, but I chose not to as I thought my adventure was being captured and channelled into every living room and bar on sloppy Planet Earth.

After an unprofitable few hours of walking slightly dejectedly around the Piazza I headed back to the cold *Stazione* steps, where I surveyed the latest bag of odds and ends that I had collected. Now I had resorted to stealing "useful" items from the filthy rubbish bins. This new "evidence" was only a pile of trash, but when I was manic in Milano these findings represented a great deal more than garbage alone, so I tended to put a whole lot more worth in these things than I did in my two sacks that were full to the brim with homely possessions. Having so much baggage was like being shipwrecked on a faraway desert Island with nothing but a briefcase full of cash. Fresh water and a bite to eat would then become priceless commodities, and the paper money could be used as firelighters. Knowing my luck, a rescue party would arrive just as my life savings went up in smoke. I was a severely disturbed individual in conflict with the true values of life.

My feet felt fine, they just smelt bad. On closer inspection I did notice that they looked a bit worse for wear so I rested them for a while. Two young Italians approached me, offering a cigarette as they did so. Without any suspicion or distrust I accepted this friendly token. "A kind gesture from my European cousins," I thought. They then sat either side of me. All they wanted to do was rip me off. They must have seen me behaving abnormally in the ticketing hall or walking around the Piazza over and over again, singing and calling out maniacally to an increasing collection of players in what I felt was dramatically becoming, at an alarming pace, the biggest event in the entire history of mankind. One of the young men wore an AC Milano soccer jersey. I do not remember anything about the other one except that they both had long greasy black hair. This devious pair must have been studying my every move, how I approached so many astonished pedestrians insisting that they join me and help with my manic driven pursuit of little Tommy, as well as locating and then marrying the unobtainable Ju, uniting the world, eliminating every form of racism, feeding the starving, saving the rain forests and endangered species, preventing global warming, finding cures for acquired immune deficiency syndrome (AIDS), for cancer, leukaemia, tuberculosis, mental illness, hiccups …

It felt so good to feel happiness again after being an absentee for such a long time. At the time of elated realisation it became very hard to keep a lid on the grand belief that I had fallen on my sore feet and hit the jackpot of life. In order to keep the ball rolling and finish the job that has no ending or beginning, I had to forge ahead and sort things out. Whatever it took to earn the right to live in perfect unhindered harmony, I was more than prepared to do it—severely *ill prepared.*

One thing only lurked in the two evil greasy minds that were sitting next to me on the Stazione steps, "How can we turn this British weirdo over?" A pair of tatty old shoes appeared from their plastic carrier bag. Their plan may not be enough to merit an airing on CNN or the BBC's world service, but it held as much callous premeditation as an armed bank robbery. They were also out to humiliate me, which is probably the most heartless thing to do of all. My glazed manic eyes could see none of their dastardly plan so I went along with everything. Even the scabby shoes that they produced looked beautiful to me, representing the poor people of the world whose shoes I felt that I had to walk in so that they would rise up from a life of depravation. One of the shoes on offer had a sole that flapped about like a camels tongue. These shoes were probably smart brown brogues in a previous life but now they were rubbish, presented by two Italian rogues that not only took advantage of a seriously disturbed fellow human being, but spat in his wide eyes too. None of this abuse in motion prevented me from agreeing upon a ridiculously lopsided exchange deal. My reasoning behind such a swap was that I had to somehow teach or pass on valuable "lessons" to my ever expanding audience, so that they could fall in and become correctly positioned in order to assist themselves and others in achieving all that is good. My manic propelled aims and reasoning would always be changing to suit the present climate. Just supposing something went terribly wrong, I would invent a quick and obvious reason as to why it went wrong. I became so gullible when I used this kind of reasoning process, not only to the suggestions of street tricksters but also to myself. I was rapidly becoming many different versions of the same confused person. Each version must have been a subconscious aspiration that I had gathered and stored for later, like a squirrel and his secret horde of nuts. From an early age I have always been a bit of a gullible fellow, but on this particular day as I sat on the stone steps smoking my cigarette I excelled myself. I could have bought a "birthday suit" for a snip, then wear it out to the *Teatro Alla Scala.*

Before I knew what was happening one of the greasy Italians slowly began to unbuckle one of my fashionable and expensive new shoes, while the other greasy lowlife attended to the other. As I said earlier, I'm not really a one for violence although I do have a knack of getting caught up in it quite often, without much success. This pair of spaghetti-heads with meatballs for brains would have to be dealt with if I ever met them again. The bastards wouldn't know what hit them, but my six inches of steel would always remain closer to the warmth of home and not stained with the blood of two other human beings, who may even have more good points than bad. Despite allowing them both the benefit of the doubt, they still had an awful lot to learn when it comes to foreign relations, especially the treatment of unwell visitors from England. Thanks boys, I owe you one!

Did I have to suffer and keep on giving giving giving, before pushing myself through the labyrinth of highs and lows, soaking up other peoples suffering, dishing out dangerously huge dosages of manic ecstasy, giving the sweet kiss and taking the resulting blows? The two daylight robbers may have walked away with my expensive shoes, but they nor anybody else could ever steal my steely resolve to see this forceful thing through to the very end, no matter what! It crossed my mind that if I revamped my many ways of thinking and began to put to use the sense of increasing strength of both mind and body sensibly and sparingly, I would be able to parry the blows or indeed handle anything that any cynical soul may care to, or rather dare to fire in my direction. Nasty people such as those shoe thieves could in essence be partly responsible for the downfall or even death of another human being who is mentally ill, roaming the streets and in urgent need of specialist help. Any sailor worth his or her salt will tell you that untying knots that should remain firmly tied can lead to untold disaster. I know, I have been there, seen it and done it, but some rotten sons of bitches stole my freaking T-shirt.

When the manic rise is in full flow it feels as if you are becoming both physically and mentally stronger, and that there is *no* limit to what you believe you can and will achieve. You are in reality becoming weaker and weaker and increasingly vulnerable. The higher the manic-depressive climbs without the requisite tools to do the imaginary tasks properly, the easier it is to slip up and come crashing down, it's just a matter of time. Broad shoulders and big hearts dripping with love are not always there to catch you as they may be employed elsewhere in a completely different time zone, perhaps assisting another soul who happens to be stranded in the pouring rain with a flat tyre.

Yet another wide awake night was spent wandering the streets of Milano. My feet were now feeling rather sore; a discomfort that with a little mind-over-matter I was able to conquer. As you are probably aware, with most kinds of physical pain brought about by movement, it tends to hurt far more when you suddenly cease whatever activity you were doing. Should I gradually wind down or warm down? Do me a favour, I was far too stupid to work that one out, and far too preoccupied with manic thoughts, so I was either in pain or on the move—a very good recipe for burnout. Despite feeling like a billion lire (or Euros) my body had begun to cry out for some much needed nutrition, not to mention a good scrub-up. Water was readily available inside the *Stazione*. I continued to scrape the pavements and gutters for cigarette ends. The *Stazione Centrale* remained the base where I duly returned early in the mornings as the rich city of Italian leather and lire sprung into life. Every sensation and manic thought process that I have so far shared with you were gradually becoming so demanding and unbearably intense that something had to give way, enabling some of the relentless pressure that was pushing down so hard on me to escape. Early one morning as I dragged my two sacks across the ticketing hall to where the lines of trains stood, I broke down. Hauling an unfair workload through a mind-field of burden had begun to take its toll. Leaving the two sacks just outside on the platform, I clambered aboard an empty open carriage and collapsed onto the seats, allowing my pent-up passion to flood out. I put all of the crying babies in the world to shame that morning, and once again I couldn't give two hoots who the hell knew about it. "What on earth is going on here?" I thought over and over again. In the blink of a teary eye I suddenly felt near to perfect again, as if some of the demons that were hitchhiking in my mind had now been exorcised. A kind looking middle aged gentleman had sensed that all was not quite as it should be with the lonely figure that he had noticed getting onto the train, and so he followed me on board. The English he attempted to speak was incoherent, but his physical presence restored my faith in man*kind* and compensated for the stolen shoes. Optimistically I reasoned that the world needed rogues with brogues in order for good to prevail. Then my kaleidoscopic-thought-analyser (Brain) began to offer untried and untested reassurances that we human beings and everything else on this planet were a division of one, meaning that I am them, they are me, you are him, he is you, she is him and so on. So many familiar faces, yet none of them did I know on a personal one to one basis. If I drank beer in England, would Bruce in Australia belch on my behalf? I think not. There was something peculiar yet comforting about the man sitting opposite me in the carriage. He showed no sign of urgency, no checking of Rolex or Cartier that would indicate any hurry to catch a train or to greet an arrival. His face looked exceptionally healthy and expensively pampered, giving him the appearance of a thirty year old, although he must have been fifty something if his charming mannerisms and calming presence were anything to go by. My brief encounter with this Italian body of strength brought me back to a controlled state of manic chaos. This angelic figure, without saying so, seemed to know exactly what I was all about, where I was coming from and where I would most likely end up, or so I chose to believe. With his job of silent reassurance completed, the man departed. Seconds later I stepped back onto the platform and looked for him—he had completely vanished! A little anxiety busting peace and tranquillity had arrived on my platform yet again, right on time.

Back I went through the *Stazione* to the open air stone steps. A fine cobwebby rain had begun to fall. Umbrellas emerged as if they were built-in extensions of an upper limb. Despite the rain, yet another open air striptease performance began to take shape. Back into my old jeans and loose shirt I slipped. Despite being well aware of having other footwear available in my sacks I told myself to refuse, because what had happened earlier on these same steps was meant to be for a reason soon to be discovered. I surrendered my knife to the stone steps too. What a sad case I had become. The piazza and my skyward face glistened under the welcome patter of rain. Mania shouted at me to remove myself from the partially sheltered steps and put my body further out into the life giving moisture. Leaving behind on the stone steps the two huge sacks containing all of my belongings, I proceeded to march in a trance like state into what had now become torrential rain. Umbrella clad pedestrians had now run for cover, leaving me to dance around in my ripped up shoes with hands reaching high as if I had scored the winning goal for England against Scotland in the World Cup Final at Wembley Stadium. A no-holds barred rendition of Gene Kelly's *Singing In The Rain* concluded that morning's bizarre entertainment. One could say that I felt rather good *man!*

My two sacks sat upon the steps unattended. That sweet smelling rain helped to revive me so much. I felt as if I had no more need for my belongings. I could and should be able to get by without. Let the people distribute it all among themselves. "Roll-up roll-up, come and take a piece of me, I will show you what is really needed in order to live this life of ours!" I shouted, sung, danced and mimed for everybody to witness. For twenty minutes I stood outside the *Stazione Centrale* dripping wet, preaching in a North London accent the manic gospel according to Keith Alan Steadman, in a tongue foreign to some but easily deciphered to those who were "in the know." Without any emotion or self questioning I made for a nearby street that up until then hadn't had the dubious pleasure of my company. "Keep walking, keep walking," I kept telling myself, "You *must* go to Switzerland, everybody is behind you, rooting for you because they know that it's in their best long-term interests to do so. New clothes and food will be supplied en-route. You will be watched over because they are a magnificent part of you and you are a colossal part of them." My huge headed think-tank kept rolling on, destroying all of the conventional barriers that had stifled my life's progression, until now that is. This type of manic tangle loved to launch unannounced premieres. Then I realised that life is just one huge premier of a continuous show on the biggest ever stage. Just as I was beginning to think that things could not possibly become any more wonderfully mind-blowing, something happened to me that I would regard to be the first of many amazingly vivid happenings.

The absence of my two sacks enabled me to clock-up a couple of burden free kilometres in a very short space of time. Quite a thirst had built up, so I weighed my anchor and surveyed the area for a possible watering hole. Nothing came into view except for lots of freshly dumped puddles that lay strewn across the pavements and in the redundant road. What a sorry sight I must have made as I got down onto my grubby hands and knees and began to slurp up the fresh rainwater from out of the lowly puddles. The rain had ceased, but my clothing and hair were still a little soggy. A touch of rising damp didn't bother me in the slightest, as I was only interested in the refreshment that had fallen from the sky. Down came the warmth of the rays, creating a fresh rainy smell that shampoo and air freshener manufacturers attempt to package. Still kneeling over a puddle, I noticed a flower petal landing only a few feet away from me, then another and another. For half a minute or so these bright red petals trickled out of the sky like kamikaze butterflies, surrounding my street oasis. Yes, a tall building stood next to where I was kneeling, but as they fell I could not for the life of me spot the actual source. In my manic eyes this sweet phenomenon became a clear-cut signal of a divine nature. Signalling what exactly? Trying to be careful I gathered a dozen or so of these bright red petals and put them into my jean pocket, partially crushing them in the process. Feeling refreshed from the rainwater and for the spiritual lift that the falling petals had given me, I carried on along what I believed to be a promising route that ran all the way to the centre of England, where my blurry quest had temporarily turned its focus. This daft decision was soon quashed, beaten back and outnumbered by the pull and possibilities of an even more attractive Milano. I had no firm idea of where I was, let alone compre-hend the directions and clues that simple streetsigns threw at me. The increasing speed of thought made it very difficult to concentrate and then follow through with any kind of instruction, sensible or not. Everything became more and more confusing. Wherever my manic guidance system decided to send me I would obey. What other choice did I have when I was that far removed from reality? Road signs and billboards continued to be confusing, sending me to where I had already been. If I could have remained still and allowed my directional dilemma some rational thought, I might have inched forward. "Which way is forward?" I pondered, "If I change my mind again how the hell am I going to claw my way through the Alps wearing only a cotton shirt, blue jeans and a pair of shoes that even Charlie Chaplin wouldn't be seen dead in?"

I kept on walking, sometimes frantically running—when I remembered that telepathetic television may be on air I always upped my performance, trying to give the imagined audience my manic all—like a freshly plucked chicken that had just burnt its raw backside on the barbecue. Something caused me to stop in my tracks, a glint of a very tiny shining object. I picked it up for a closer inspection that revealed it to be a very old looking key about two inches long. One side of the key was in pristine condition whereas the other side was pitted and tarnished. There was no conceivable way that a brand new key could have been lying untouched in the middle of a walkway long enough for one side to be showing so much sign of wear and tear. Puzzled, I popped the key into a jean pocket and resumed my eventful little trek. Suddenly a rare spark of sense ignited a temporary flash of realism, telling me to about turn and face myself as I retrace my steps all the way back to the *Stazione Centrale*. This inability to see a projected thought through to anywhere near its final conclusion is typical behaviour of the manic personality. "With a bit of luck my belongings may still be sitting on the stone steps," I thought with naive optimism. No such luck existed. Immersed in deep regret, I dipped again in spirit. Second thoughts regarding my act of generous spontaneity made me feel sick to the stomach. Something new and uplifting to make sense of my momentary madness would always be arriving soon on platform V.1(Virgo-One), and delivered by the unlikeliest of porters. Being high felt great for most of the time, but the situation that I had willingly put myself into was becoming more and more ridiculous and irresponsibly dangerous by the minute. Alive or dead, I didn't overly worry about my folks back in England despite them being frantic by now, worried and concerned that I had disappeared so suddenly. Dashing off somewhere new and exciting is not such an unusual occurrence, but I usually let somebody know of my intentions beforehand. There was I in Italia, existing off the false belief that everybody back home was with me throughout every step of the way. Wasn't everybody egging me on for the sole benefit of Mister and Missus Wright and Wong from every four corners of the sweltering globe? Occasionally the morbid possibility of mass family death and destruction struck me, although this terrible sensation fortunately waned as my time trotted on.

As I briefly mentioned earlier, the lack of fluids and solids made it unnecessary for me to use the *Il Gabineto* (Toilet/bathroom) very often. Innocent Milanese felt my cleansed but still filthy paws placed upon their shoulders, as I attempted to apprehend them one by one by using a hastily thought out citizen arrest technique. Amazingly nobody lashed out at me, perhaps because they were in a temporary state of pity and disbelief. A few members of the Milanese public did yell and scream, but I was far too quick for them. Little Tommy's case had reopened with a sudden flourish. Suspecting the entire population of Milano for an abduction that had taken place in Gadebridge, Hemel Hempstead, did not border on total insanity, it *was* total insanity. From my stepped up vantage point I was able to scan the hordes, "clocking" the bronzed faces before me with my eagle eyes, and with the supple neck twisting of an old wiseass owl. Most of them looked disconcertingly familiar. The more I darted my eyes from person to person using my own slow shuttered visuals, the muddier the super-imposed mix became, bringing one and all together in the wrong format and for the wrong reason. The mad-dog had to start barking up a different tree pretty soon or run the risk of receiving some grievous bodily harm.

Where was Ju, in Verona? Where were the film crews, the reporters and photographers? Am I living? Am I mortal or immortal? Where are the Mafioso when you need them? Are they making movies in Hollywood? Could I be the biggest cheese himself? These are *not* the sort of questions to yell out to a bunch of strangers in a hurry. The absurd manic notion that I am anybody or anything that you may wish me to be, played havoc with my non-progressive exploits. Press the right buttons and see me play the parts. Appearances can often be very deceiving but they are intrinsically flexible to the manic perspective. Owning up to such grandiose delusions can be an embarrassing and daunting task, yet they are important admissions to make. It is these nuts, bolts and whirring cogs that hold the manic together and makes them tick loudly during an extended episode into unknown territory. Lack of sleep and the incorrect medication to balance one out behaves as the force that turns the winding key. Being wound up so tightly will blow a vital mental fuse, and maybe even strip an irretrievable thread of sensible thought. Delusions of grandeur, the very common element of the manic soup, throbbed through me erratically. It was only later when I had been admitted to the first of two Milanese hospitals that these delusions decided to brutally pound away at me. I couldn't comprehend the sense of it all, therefore I stood alone. Seven star hotel Heaven had yet to open its rubber swing doors and double-check me in.

Having made no arrests but feeling many collars, I took to making mad dashes from pillar to post, dodging people as if they had 10,000 volts running through them. Darting around wildly like this helped to expel some of the physical energy that mania cons you into believing you have in abundance. The more I ran around the more excitable I became, creating a replacement charge in the same way that a car alternator does. The title of "Ever Ready Steady (man)" finally fitted! Faster and faster I ran, even when my heart felt as if it was about to explode out my chest. One manic command after the other pressed to be obeyed and fed, while at the same time anticipating what may lay ahead. By now I felt so high that it sometimes scared me. The brief flashes of fright and utter terror were probably the leftovers from an electrical storm somewhere on Mars, that's how high up I was. These milliseconds of panic were soon mugged by the more secure manic thoughts that I had chosen to cling tightly onto and trust with my entire life.

Flashing around town like a golden fool took me to places new and stimulating that thrived on promoting chaotic creativity. Close to the *Stazione* sat a tall plain looking hotel with a small lawn at the front. I would be drawn to this place over and over again because of whom I believed to be residing there. Four or five visits must have been made already, each one causing more and more guests to stick their inquisitive heads out of their windows to view the performer below, who seemed quite content to be running around their neat little hotel lawn singing out of tune and dancing dementedly, while at the same time waving and blowing kisses at the tall confounded people. I could have sworn that some of the hotel's guests were a selection of my favourite celebrities and also my friends and relatives from England. My trespassing had caused some understandable concern for the hotel residents, so a few kind souls had taken it upon themselves to alert my friends, the *carabinieri* (police) who were due to arrive at my new movie location very soon, *cut!*

The belief that a hotel room was waiting, allowing me to take a brief respite from all of the locomotion in and around the *Stazione Centrale*, provided ample reason why I should attempt to get my raggedy feet through the glass door. A collective force of elderly women wrapped in shawls stood their ground, not allowing me to take a single step further. This made me angry. I felt that I had been through enough, given plenty, teased and tormented for too long with all of mankind looking on. My side of the bargain had been kept, plus interest, and now it was like reaching a disappointing summit, not a false summit but a real repellent one. This was unfit ground even to pitch my robust, level-pegged Outward-Bound tent upon. I was out on a limb (out onaliM) in Milano.

How I yelled at these people. I ranted and I raved like a trapped animal, taunted and deprived more than once too often. I muzzled myself because I knew too much to be said aloud, and not because I may bite the hands that were feeding off *me*. Beyond the short and buxom army of ladies I could see my heroes.

Famous faces from the world of music were smiling at me from their dressing rooms, or so my crystal eyeballs would have me believe. Attentions turned to the quiet arrival of two light blue and white police vans. Out stepped four rather large *carabinieri* sporting smart two-tone uniforms, secured around the middle section by a white belt that carried a set of shiny handcuffs and a sobering gun. They then proceeded to confuse me with their rapid-fire approach. I pulled out my moth eaten passport and handed it over to the officer who appeared most likely to be in charge of the proceedings. *Parles Inglese?* (Do you speak English?) he inquired. *Si* (Yes) I replied. "Donta yow maka no sound okee," instructed the leader, "or yow getta theese." This brave Italian policeman made a fist with his right hand as the other three closed in on me. If I couldn't speak up for myself I didn't stand a hope in hell of coming out of this confrontation intact. "My name is Keith Alan Steadman, and I come from ..." *Smack!*—the greasy *bastardo* (bastard) sent me sprawling to the grass. Like lightening I sprang back up onto my sore feet, my legs now slightly apart and my fists clenched tight. Now I showed defiance and rose even higher onto my blistered toes. I wished that somebody would be willing to try and explain to me what the hell I had done to warrant that kind of cowardly treatment, but nobody had an answer or even the guts to try. As these big shot bastardos continued to give me their tough guy impressions, I reminded myself that these scenes would go toward making some great movie scene footage and that the police were really just trying to liven the scene up, at my expense of course. "Two can play at that game," I thought. One of the other three *carabinieri* who stood directly behind me, tried to pull at my shirt in a way that felt as if he was checking me out, like I had just arrived from another planet. There was absolutely no way that I was prepared to stand there and take that, so I spun round to face him, *Whack!*—one of the others sent me reeling back down to the damp grass. Not satisfied they pinned me to the ground, pressing my face hard into the grass while at the same time bending my arms behind my back in the traditional restraining hold. All of this hurt, but nowhere near as much as it would have done had I not of been scaling the dizziest heights of a manic episode. They showed no sign of easing up on me as they figured out what other humiliation tactic they could use in front of a gathering crowd. As I lay face down on the sweet grass I thought it would be a good idea to eat some of it. When my lynch mob yanked me back up onto my feet and saw me chewing defiantly away—sloppy grass pulp dribbling down my stubbled chin—they resumed my undeserved punishment, Milanese style. I glared at the nasty piece of work who led this brave ring of clowns. "Take this you piece of shit," I shouted, and then proceeded to splatter his face with slimy salivating grass. *Bang!*—down I went for the third time. This time they meant business and were extremely vicious. What they would have done to me had there not been a crowd of bloodthirsty Milanese to witness the assault doesn't bear thinking about. Another more animated discussion sparked up among them, probably along the lines of, "What the fuck are we going to do with this English asshole?" The treatment that I was about to receive was unnecessarily harsh, but at that time, even though it is no excuse, many of the Italian people, let alone the *carabinieri,* were hostile toward the English, especially toward young men such as myself. The reason being that a handful of moronic so called football supporters from England had recently been involved in violent clashes with equally moronic Italian supporters. Also, I don't think that the memory of the Heysel Stadium tragedy in Belgium back in 1985—when many people were killed following violent clashes just before the European Cup Final between Liverpool and Juventus—had faded a great deal. For some people the memory of that day still sat in their minds as fresh as the grass I had just spat at the brutal bully standing before me. A small minority can ruin so much for so many, but it is not right to tar everybody else with the same brush. Most Italians are lovely friendly people, but just like everywhere else in the world there are the small minded few who think that if one small element of beer drenched, pot bellied pigs cause trouble, then the entire population of their country of origin is the same.

So there was I, having already made a good job of running myself into the Italian ground, now with my face rammed down as before and with my arms wrenched unnaturally behind my back. With gritted teeth and dogged determi-nation not to bow down or to cave in to their abusive behaviour, I endured the further indignity of having my wrists and ankles cuffed together, forming one fleshy metal knot. The combination of mania and adrenalin meant that I hardly felt the punches raining in, but the double cuffing did generate a lot of pain. Not satisfied, and probably for entertainment value, the macho *carabinieri* lifted me up by the knot. Remember that here I am, a five feet seven inch Englishman in need of some serious and urgent medical help, instead being sentenced for a crime that I did not commit. They lifted me up to their waist height and held me there for about ten seconds. A few more words were uttered. Without a countdown or any kind of warning, they dropped me face down onto the same patch of flattened grass. One of the *carabinieri* rested his foot firmly on my back. I tried to shake him off with a wiggle and then told him many times to go forth and multiply. Whether or not he understood my universally acknowledged request I'm not sure, but just by opening my mouth I earned myself a repeat performance of abuse. The second impact with the turf was more tolerable, because I was able to brace myself for the impact. With all limbs still cuffed from behind they carried me the short distance to a police van that was waiting to take me away to a cell. Before boarding they lowered me, gently this time, to the stone pavement and then released both sets of handcuffs. They cuffed my wrists again, this time in front of me. Now I was ready to be bundled unceremoniously into the van.

Despite being treated in such a despicable and degrading manner, I still held on to the belief that this had simply been another piece of the mammoth puzzle set before me. Nothing was going to get in my way and stop this man on a mission. I had come this far, and I intended to see the "job" through to its never end. All I knew then was that right now I had become bogged way down in the sticky stuff, and I didn't have a shovel to dig my way out. An axe would have struggled to hack me free of this predicament. So there I was, as high as sky and forced down low in the back of the police vehicle. I was now on the way to a very different kind of station to the one I had grown fondly accustomed to. Repeating my name and address and showing my temporary passport didn't cut much ice. They preferred it if I shut up (nothing particularly unusual there) and besides, I had grown rather attached to my already chipped front teeth. Two burly *carabinieri* escorted me to the tiny cells. One of them gripped my right shoulder very tightly along the short way. Still in handcuffs they locked me up and walked away without enlightening me as to what might happen next. Around twenty minutes later a policewoman appeared on the scene. She unlocked my cage with a slight smile and then led me to a small brightly lit room where two male officers were waiting, one of them I recognised immediately as being one of my lynch mob. Obeying their request to empty all pockets, out came my tatty passport again and the old/new key amid a scattering of darkened broken petals. All of these items had the effect of revving my manic motor, reminding me of a million manic possibilities. One of the officers began to finger the tiny gold cross that miraculously still hung from a very fine chain around my sore neck. My positive plus/cross symbol remained in its rightful place against my chest. As is routine, my grubby fingerprints were taken. I then requested to use the *gabinetto*. Both male officers escorted me to a room that housed two cubicles. They then ushered me into one of these cesspools and removed my shackles. The toilet, if you could call it that, consisted of nothing more than a lowly dirty hole, more like a heavily shit stained wooden bench. Without food I only needed to urinate, but the two creepy *carabinieri* insisted that I drop my jeans and behave as if I was going to defecate. They were both laughing like sick hyenas at my humiliation. My protestations fell on deaf ears, so they just carried on laughing at my expense.

There are some real sicko characters in this world and I had the misfortune of meeting two of them when I least needed it. Thankfully the policewoman made an appearance in the gent's cesspool and put a stop to their unfunny perverted amusement. She didn't appear to be shocked in any way by what she saw. Perhaps this was common practice among bored *carabinieri*. I finally got to squeeze out a dribble of urine before being escorted back to my cell, handcuff free this time. Three to four hours at a rough guess (my watch had long gone with the two sacks) is all that I had to endure of these sick sadistic examples of mankind's not so pretty side. Without anything tangible to pin on me following the routine checks they simply let me go, able once again to walk straight back out onto the busy streets of Milano.

Darkness had now fallen. Despite knowing that it was fairly close by, in my disorientated state I had no real idea where I was in relation to the *Stazione Centrale*, and there was no way that I was going to ask a policeman or anyone else for that matter for directions. The new location combined with recent events had thrown me slightly off kilter, creating a little confusion among my many ranks. Eventually I decided to ask a harmless looking old man who pointed me in the direction of the *Stazione Centrale*. The railway station had become my safe haven despite leaving all of my worldly possessions there for the taking and being robbed in broad daylight by the two shoe thieves. As I headed in a northerly direction, reflecting on the farcical events of the day, I came across a tramp who was sitting on a large doorstep with the customary bottle of cheap alcoholic beverage clutched tightly in his lived in hands. "*Buon giorno* (Good day), can I sit here with you?" I asked. "*Si si* (Yes yes)," said the man. "Any chance of a swig out of your bottle mate?" I asked. "Huh?" "A drink *per favore* (please)?" I replied. "Ah *si si*," said the man as he passed me the half full bottle of cheap but potent vino rosso. Boy, did it taste good. My taste buds were blown to Heaven's Heaven. I thanked my red wino friend very much before jumping back up onto my tender feet to resume the short march to the *Piazza Della Rebublica*. From the Piazza I headed up the *Via Vitore Pisani*, through the centre of the *Piazza Duca D'Aosta,* and there it was.

I began to relive the detailed steps of my journey so far. It felt like I had become a trillion different people and travelled an even further amount of miles, all within a limited amount of space, and during such a short amount of time. I even wondered in my maniacal way whether my facial features automatically altered to suit the latest role that I was undertaking. Further rationalising of the irrational concluded that just like television, newspapers and the billboards, I would *not* be able to actually see myself properly, instead only an interpretation of the real thing—that I would have to unscramble and decipher in order for any of it to make valuable sense—would be made available to me. I had become even scruffier and grubbier. Out of the window went the cleanliness and Godliness/state of mind theory, because I decided that as things stood the exterior appearance shouldn't be what we judge a person upon, it is what exists inside that counts. Take my red wino friend for instance, he is financially poor and he smelt a bit like a cat-litter tray, but apart from my train carriage angel it was he who showed me the most kindness up until that moment in Milanese time.

My left sleeve had been partially ripped from its torso during the scuffle with the *carabinieri*, so with a sharp tug I ripped it right off so that I could make a bandanna out of it. With the cotton creation adorning my scab ridden head I fancied myself more than ever, now totally convinced that I was a cross between John Rambo and the two Bruce's—Springsteen and Lee. My need to let off steam by using any God given form of bodily expression welled up again, even after such a hectic day. I had to run run run or screech out love songs to the world, some of them recognisable and others were made up as I went along. I needed to dance in the most spiritual and soulful way that my human body could handle. I felt as if I could speak to the inhabitants of this world by feeling the tension and looseness of my muscles, then transferring those deep feelings and emotions by mind-messaging. Through the medium of telepathetic television I posted my heart and my soul. By invisible class they travelled through the universe so speedily they would sometimes arrive at their destination before they were even sent, or so I thought. A thousand theories were all leading to one possible answer, one explanation, one major thing, and I had to push and push myself on and on because I believed that our whole existence depended on finding out what it was, or maybe I was searching for something that didn't even exist and never will. Living on manic Planet Janet is not all about hedonism and living life at a million miles an hour.

I swear that I could come up with lyrics and tunes with no effort at all, and I also swear that they were pretty darn good as well. We all have so much inside of us that is unused, untapped. All that we see and hear sticks to our mental hard-drive, but it often needs a reminder or a jolt of extra stimulation to let it back out into the open. A myriad of harmful drugs or the endless natural beauty and love that surrounds us are some of the most common stimulants. All of the known senses are perfectly capable of obtaining enough of their specialist boost in order to produce a lift slightly above the average description of normal. Many musicians, writers, actors, politicians and caught out athletes have produced there finest hours having just shot up, popped a pill or powdered their noses.

For some it is taboo, and for others it is acceptable. I accept that my wailing efforts may not have been a threat to the great Elvis Presley or Frank Sinatra, but I sure had a good time with my energetic attempts. Around the ticketing hall I jigged, span, twisted, rocked and rolled to the increasing beat of my own heart. My singing and flip-flopping around in wrecked shoes was just myself living out for real what most of us would like to do given half a chance. I pretended to be Jagger, Bowie and Elvis Aaron Presley, except the only difference was that this alternative "entertainer" did *not* leave the building.

Some bipolar affected people with a passion for trainspotting may go one step further and hop around Planet Earth on borrowed money—wearing nothing but their ripped anorak with the stuffing oozing out, a rainbow cardigan made by Aunt Mabel for last years Birthday pressy, and a pair of Gucci Jesus creepers with white sports socks—collecting the numbers from trains that have of course just arrived at platform twenty-five from Planet Jupiter, or maybe even from sweet sultry Janet. As you can probably gather, I often reflect upon those fortunate human beings, who in my humble opinion are naturally high from a very young age. They may not see it themselves because to them it is normality, and they know no other form of existence. On the other hand there are those poor souls who have always found it agony to even raise a smile to the outside world, only aware of biding their time at the centre of a heavy leaden world full of painful pointless drudgery. As Thoreau put it, *"They live lives of quite desperation."* Those successful bubbly characters who never burst in public (although may be prone to deflation once every so often) are blessed indeed when their enthusiasm for life can be channelled into their work or chosen purpose. Painters, musicians, comedians, actors, inventors, scientists, a few eccentric politicians, philosophers and writers—many of these human beings are more often than not a little bit different, extroverted or introverted depending on which way the wind is blowing on that particular day. Some have the ability to see and then express their new angled view of the world to an intelligent and open minded audience. That paying audience may or may not be willing to accept change for the present and long term good of us all. So many of those intelligent people that are looked up to and listened to are really as mad as mad can be, always in and out of rehabilitation centres and health farms or persecuting their own people, but most of them have managed to domesticate their mad streak and use it to carve out a successful and productive career. *Mad* really isn't a bad mad word at all, it is just one of those freely used words that is taken out of context too often so that those who regard themselves as sane—compartmentalising themselves in the safe insecure land of the self titled sensible—feel in greater control and slightly superior. It is a classic case of whether or not the lunatics are on the inside, or on the outside of the asylum. Being mad *for* something is showing a great passion, and this is how I prefer to look at it. As I mentioned earlier, without the means by which to release the pressure cooker within, a person can fly completely off the rails and do something that they will live to regret, or in the most severe and rarest of cases never emerge from the far side of the tracks. Taking one leap beyond into virginal territory is what it's all about, and that is exactly what is needed for mankind to progress. Never knock an effort maker with a valid crazy notion. Could it even be a form of jealousy? Allow a little madness into your life. We all have a little hidden if we are completely honest with ourselves, it is just that some of us haven't got the courage to let it out.

A virtuoso I may not be, but an unintentional parody of many who are, I indeed am. My impromptu three minute ballet career should have been a definite non-starter, but just like everything else I tried to be it was whipped up to a frenzy and then flogged to a pitiful death. If I was a horse, as my surname, *Stead*-man (steed/stud) suggests, I would have been carted off to the knackers yard by now to have my bones crushed and then made into glue. Throughout my impromptu performances I knew for sure what a renowned artiste would feel like when they are performing their brand new party-piece in front of an 85,000 stadium gathering, and also in front of a live worldwide audience that are sitting comfortably in front of their television sets, scrutinising and then loving the images provided. Now *that* my friend is what I would call a real global warming, manic or not. It does become a drug, a terrific rush backed up to the hilt by an immensely loyal anticlimax that has to be comforted with precaution. Blindness to public opinion sets in as the previous level has to be emulated or surpassed in order to stay hovering up there in Cloud-Cuckoo-Land. My addiction intensified with every frenzied thought and dynamic action. I may well call "*Cut!*" to my hidden telepathetic film crew, but nobody had the decency to yell "*Cut!*" to me, the manic addict. If they did I would probably have chosen not to listen.

Milano has an excellent underground rail system that I decided to use as an aid to spread out and explore new horizons. There was no chance of me doing this in the normal way, oh no. I sprinted as fast as I possibly could to the nearest ticket barrier and leapfrogged over it. Now I had landed a manic part in an action movie, with myself caught up in the chase scene. So unique were my acting skills that I was able to alternate between the pursuer and the pursued, which meant that I was chasing myself again like a dog chases its own tail during an entitled mad half an hour. The storyline of my latest ill thought out epic bent and stretched constantly to suit my current mental trend. Being a generalist has more recently struck me as being the way of life best suited to my make-up and character. Manic versatility certainly goes a long way to unblocking the monotonous restrictions imposed by an A to Z of dead end sanity streets.

Fresh environments sparked off new ideas. Just as an artiste is impulsively inspired by their immediate surroundings, my pleasure pressure shot up a notch or two when I exploded into the ground breaking depths of Milano's metro system. Passengers became alarmed at my unpredictable behaviour, but I didn't allow myself to remain in one given place long enough for anyone to act against me. My general appearance didn't exactly offer any solid reassurances, but I couldn't have cared less. Keeping the Milanese people guessing who I was and what the heck I was doing gave me some of my best kicks, but the trouble was that I had about as much enlightenment regarding my own extra curricular exertions as they did. Crouching below the platform seating, sometimes occupied, or diving onto the floor of the trains pretending to aim a pistol at my imaginary pursuer (played by myself)—whatever it took to make the "film" look as authentic as possible I would gladly do without hesitation or consideration of the inherent dangers. I flew up and down the escalators and blasted my way in and out of the many look-alike stations in which I found myself. Authenticity was of paramount importance, so I threw myself headfirst and feet-first into the starring role, but with far more potency than a Hollywood action flick or a lively West End show. From time to time I surfaced for some exhausted air and a spot of sunshine. This stimulating cocktail of light and lead persuaded me (not that I needed much persuading) to dodge the moving cars and slide across a bonnet or two as they do in the unreal "real" movies. The crowning glory was to run down the centre of a busy road with my arms raised high as if I had just won the Olympic marathon in under an hour. Rows of environmentally friendly bicycles stood outside the entrance of one of the metro stations. Some were unlocked and all were unattended. Bicycle chases were to be the next new innovative feature of my mania riddled mind movie. I mounted a ladies bicycle and began to weave in and out of the perfumed pedestrians and the slowly moving traffic, with a total disregard for direction or road signage. It felt as if I was creating chaotic art by travelling into no particular place except for where I was being pulled, like an organised disorganisation. Sitting on the handlebar was an old fashioned metallic "ding-a-ling" bell. That was it. Off I peddled with the bell "ding-a-ling-a-dinging" for all to hear, attempting to slalom in and out of the slow moving mopeds and cars. A young lady whose bicycle I had borrowed could only stand and stare in open mouthed disbelief, as this ragged wild eyed and out of tune fruitcake from England dismounted and carefully replaced her unscathed three speed up against a railing. With a grin to be wary of I sped away to once again penetrate the depths of my Italian metropolis.

Throughout my life I have kept reasonably fit and athletic thanks in main my participation in a host of sporting activities, lots of walking, a healthy balanced diet (apart from the cigarettes and drink), and not forgetting the vast collection of physical jobs that I have had trouble in holding down over the years. Putting all of that aside, I still to this day cannot get my head around the fact that I could and *did* endure and exert so much for so long, without hardly any food or water to provide nutrition and hydrate my emaciated body. The fully blown manic side of a bipolar beholder has to be seen or experienced to be believed. If we all became high at the same time it would be very interesting to say the least. Perhaps it would work out pretty much the same to how it is now with the same mix of personalities, only each personality would be heightened. The flair factor and creativity in all of us will be allowed to open up without the suburban fear of ridicule. We would definitely be understood better and possibly even teach the non-believing parties a trick or two about life's intrinsic values, such as how to love and understand more fully those whom you once turned your nose up at, or even hated for no apparent reason. That sticky slice of life's bread and jam is perhaps better left untouched, for now.

The sheer energy, the heightened senses, the unfailing belief that anything and everything is possible, the spiritual highs—these areas of mania are so over-whelmingly powerful that the transition from being manic down to what society generally regards and accepts as being normal can sometimes turn into a night-mare. The upward journey is suddenly rewound, forcing you to retrace your steps as if stepping back in time to a place that the mania originally tried to pull you away from. The rose tinted light bulbs are replaced with clearly lit substitutes that expose and exaggerate the damage caused in the quest for better things. Normal white light stings the soul. Too quick a drop into the human wasteland is like a reversal of the bends, creating too much real life pressure to stomach.

This rapid decline in spirits can be controlled properly if a qualified profes-sional specialising in psychological matters, or a general practitioner, administers an anti-psychotic drug (Lithium carbonate is also used as an anti-manic drug as well as a means of assisting the stabilisation process.) The shine has dulled and all the buffing in this wacky wide world will not be able to restore the former glori-ous flight paths through manic Heaven. All is not lost if an established dosage of lightweight lithium salts is taken and the lifeblood of the manic-depressive is reg-ularly tested. Because lithium can take at least two or three weeks to accurately kick into the human system and have any beneficial effects, an anti-psychotic drug may also be administered by a professional in combination with the lithium to speed things up a little. No manic human being in their right paradisiacal mind wants to say farewell to their Heavenly high, especially when it took so long and so much effort to get there in the first damn place. The safe level on the lithium scale is between 0.8 and 1.2 mmol/L—(millimoles per litre.) Toxicity caused from an excessive amount of lithium is always a major concern, so that has to be monitored carefully as well. The levels for toxic concern are between 1.5 and 2.0 mmol/L. Becoming well aware of the side effects possible from all of the medications that one has to take is very important indeed, because although a doctor does a suberb job in giving all of the care and attention within their power, they cannot be there all of the time. Responsibility *has* to start with the bipolar beholder if at all possible. I detest listening to people who have to blame every single thing that goes wrong with them onto something or someone else. Do *not* do it unless you want to lose all of those friends who have been so good to you in the past. Whatever treatment works wonders for one human being does *not* always have the same stunning results on another. None of us are the same, thank God! Assembling a package of treatment that is tailor made to suit each priceless individual is where the years and years of study and experience come into play. The therapists can evaluate the condition to be dealt with, and then by working in close conjunction with a team of other professionals they are able to arrive at a position from where an agreed course of treatment can be suggested and then applied.

I cannot stress strongly enough the importance of undertaking your own research regarding medication and its possible side effects. To find out almost anything regarding your condition and the treatment of it you simply must consult your most available medical professional and also read the leaflet that comes folded up tightly along with the medication. For the other issues try surfing the internet or visit your local library and see what they have to offer. Every question has an answer, but you have to get off your backside and go and find it. I know that I have said it before, but we are all unique individuals, each and every one of us are worth more than every single sparkling rock that has ever been dug from out of the dirty depths of (our?) abused planet. Therefore, we should treat ourselves as such. I am me, and me only. What I write, regarding treatments in all of their evolving shapes and colours, applies to *myself* only. One manic-depressive person is *not* the same as the next. We can react differently to a myriad of treatments. Please do *not* use my medication as gospel. I am describing *my* symptoms and personal requirements only. No matter whether you are a manic-depressive or indeed suffer from any of the other mental problems on offer, or perhaps you are a friend or relation of someone who is, always remember that there *is* a solution waiting for yourself or for a loved one to locate and put to good use. I guess that the scientists, doctors, therapists and support workers who are working on behalf of mankind's good side, can also be considered as angels—sterile angels in bright white coats, carrying a clipboard full of good intent under their wings.

Back in Milano I was becoming uncontrollably higher. My muscles and mind were buzzing at a higher frequency, tensing and letting go, unable to get a firm grip on the present, let alone on that distant land called "reality." Without a single word being exchanged between myself and the young lady whose bike I had nabbed for a Butch Cassidy joyride, I fled back into the submerged labyrinth, still screeching aloud my self composed songs. Bursting through the barricades, oblivious to any objection, ignorant of correct procedures (I made up my own) and blind to the dangers. I hurled my frame into the cauldron of incoming commuters, surfed down an upcoming escalator and threw myself onto a departing train. At the next stop I leapt out of my speeding coffin and ran as fast as my jelly legs would transport me, through the entombed crowd and over the pointless barriers until I had exhumed myself yet again. This up and down business went on for at least three more stations, rapidly increasing the feeling of invincibility. If there is ever a stage when a fully blown manic human being goes over the top and tries to do that extra something that puts their priceless life in jeopardy—attempt to fly off a building or walk through fire—then this was it. To this day, and for probably as long as my privileged existence on this version of Planet Earth stretches, I will always get a shiver running down my spine and then back up again when I recollect what happened next in Milano. From Lanza station I took the trip of my lifetime.

The *whooshing* of yet another train pulling in was all that I needed to start another countdown. What orbit this trip would catapult me into could only be discovered if I took that extra step into my personal unknown. Sweeping down the escalators as if they didn't exist had by now become a mastered art form, but not one that I would care to ever re-master. As I levelled with the train, it had already gained quite a speed. In my desperation to take this train and not the next one (due in a matter of minutes) I spotted a vertical metal handle protruding from the platform side of the rear carriage and sprinted toward it. It only took a split second to make a maniacally biased decision that very nearly finished me off for good. What I then did has been done by thousands of kids worldwide, I remembered seeing it happening on television, but it was to be a first for me. I hadn't taken the precaution of testing the gap between carriage and tunnel wall.

Undeterred I leaped at the vertical handle and held on for dear life as the train gathered speed and shot like a bullet through its warped barrel. It was a good job that there was enough room between the tunnel wall and myself otherwise I would have been dead tenderised meat. My arms began to ache after about thirty seconds, but worst of all was my weakening hand grip. On and on thundered the train for what felt like an eternity. For the first time since landing at Linate Airport I *really* started to panic. All that I could do was scream at the top of my voice. I think that the screaming gave me added strength, as if I was going into battle. If I had lost my slippery grip and fallen to the tracks it would certainly have been curtains, and the light at the end of my tunnel would have been that of the crematorium flames. Fluorescent salvation came into view and embraced me with open arms, but I still had to hang on in there and ride out the next few metres in braking speed. When the tunnel wall became platform my sweaty grip gave in to gravity, sending my body down again to the familiar solidity of a cold stone floor. I had grazed my elbows and banged my knees in the downward slide, but it was nothing to cry home about. There I stayed, just laying there slumped on my side in the foetus position. The drifting crappy wrappings of Milano's underground sat all around me, but not a single human being bothered to help. As always, I had to help myself.

Five long minutes were spent recuperating on that cold platform, when suddenly I felt a resurgence of energy that bounced me back up onto my sore and blistered feet. "Nothing is *ever* going to kill me, and if it did I shall return, just as I did earlier when I got shot in the street when out searching for Ju and little Tommy,"—this was how I distortedly saw most things at that desperate time, followed closely behind by, "Bloody hell, that's gonna look just great in the movie—*cut!*"

Closed circuit TV cameras were positioned in almost every area of every station that my darting eyes looked, so of course I played up to them. "Chances are that somebody is bound to be on my trail by now," I reasoned, but I had been too elusive for them. Nobody was going to catch me. From time to time, usually when I stopped for a rare pause, I felt intense pain in my feet. Unaware as to the extent of the damage being inflicted upon them because of my manic state, I forced myself to plough on. Another fuse was lit so off I shot, this time out and along the busy streets shouting "Hi, how are you doing?" to everybody as if we knew each other intimately, instead of the more polite, "*Buon giorno, come sta?*" We were in each others spongy minds, enabling each and every one of us to read the electricity radiating from off another thought pattern, or so I thought. Stops were made to pick up freshly discarded cigarettes, some still smouldering nicely.

Darkness fell. Electric alien transporters danced with their own reflections on the slinky streets. I drank in the tin canned drops of liquidised afterbirth that were still floating down from the mint condition masterpiece above, painted in mint condition sacrificial lambs blood and God's rich starry red soil, splashing more and more seed over snaky lady life from whom we all eat and then throw up and up. Yes, I know that mania talking often sounds ridiculous and on other occasions it can make a perfect sense. The experienced or trained observer will always have an endoscopic view of a mania affected mind because of these visionary outbursts. I know it can also be a little bit too poetic, often grotesquely odd and far too complicated to follow comfortably, but the pretty/ugly picture that I have just whipped up is only a tiny wave among an ocean of thoughts, crying out on a regular basis to be unscrambled in order to find the meaning of the latest nagging puzzle or mind-blowing observation. Rules and fools are always there to be broken down and deciphered.

My thoughts slowly became a visual reality. Again I mingled with the traffic and waved at my startled newfound family. I sung, or rather wailed like a banshee to the poor birds. I fondled pieces of shiny paper whilst trying to figure out what they could mean to me and to you. I danced a kinky dance with my spotless reflection in the highfalutin shop windows. Opulence surrounded me, but there was no need to be master of any of it, no urge to own it by handing over wads of cash. I felt richer in terms of pure freedom and happiness than probably the wealthiest person on the planet, yet I was a deteriorating ragged mess who probably ponged quite a bit by then. To put it bluntly; I was completely off my head! (but what fun I had!)

Of course I like to have enough money for a comfortable standard of living, but the many more controlled manic experiences that I have had since this one proves overwhelmingly that money isn't everything in order to achieve great happiness. I continued to have an open ball by changing the form of other human beings through the corners of my eyes. All that I had, apart from my manic buoyancy and straight ahead belief in what the hell it was I was doing, were a few articles of breaking down clothing and the manic dummy on which they hung. My seriously neglected body did not have the foggiest idea where my mind was taking it. I must have looked like death on legs, but I had the strongest pulse in the city. Where I would finally end up became the latest debate to grapple with. For once I struggled with the answer to my destination question. I simply did not have a clue where this place was that my poor feet were taking me, but as I was so determined and passionate not to let anybody down I threw even more caution to the manic wind and headed there anyway.

The following evening was spent ferreting under the ground in a rapidly increasing hallucinatory state. At each new stop I would come up for air, and then stare up at the well groomed heads on billboards that I believed were speaking to me, presenting me with more cryptic clues and misleading messages. My camera sharp peepers framed every dancing person that I looked at, causing my eyes and head to jerk in every direction to the silent beat of human movement. My brain put together the separate visual shots and turned the images into something similar to that of a flick card book or a what-the-butler-saw machine—the sort that can be found at the seaside arcades situated in-between the tattoo parlour and the fish and chip shop. That was tremendous fun! The multifaceted images that resulted from these harmless enough indulgences flowed into one grandiose gyrating form that I believed, even more strongly than before, to represent myself as us all, and of us all as myself. It was a good job that there weren't any doors to pass through as I boogied on down street after street, because my swollen head would never have made it. My nifty feet hurt terribly when I refrained from dancing, so I thought, "Oh, what the hell," and danced all night long with the one partner that I thought would never dare let me down, although in the "real" world I was doing just that.

In one of the metro stations I noticed a small room, free of staff. This room was home to a sizable bank of monitors and flexible stemmed microphones that were used to pick out at the flick of a switch, manic-depressives like myself running amok in the underground, as well as delivering the dreary passenger information. The door to this room had an invisible sign that screamed out loud to me, "Come on in and do your thing," so without thinking twice I did exactly that. In I went pressing buttons left right and centre. When I thought some of the microphones were live I began to yell into them. Through the monitors I could tell when contact had been successfully established in a particular area. I could see the people standing on the platforms looking up and around at each other in utter bewilderment. Focusing on one platform, I launched into a avalanche of nonsensical indulgence beginning with a few lines of *Going Underground* by The Jam, improvising most of the lyrics along the way, and also a little snippet of *Tunnel Of Love* by Dire Straits. Still nobody had come to evict me from the premises, so I figured I would take this golden opportunity not to save the whole wide world or to find a missing little boy who was probably found by now anyway, but to continue with my harmless fun. Not a single Italian soul approached me. Maybe I looked too scary, like a rabid wolf, or they couldn't come up with a game plan to eke me out. Or was it the lack of soap? I didn't waste any time hanging around to find out. Was I being allowed to get away with far too much for my own good? Probably.

Moped engines revving up suddenly sounded much louder and more aggressive. They growled with an urgency that kept me on my toes. In the corners of my eyes there were all sorts of unusual activities taking place; pedestrians were waving at me and dancing with each other, but when I turned round to face these people normal service resumed. Sometimes I became so frustrated because it seemed as if everybody else was holding a secretive party behind my back, still allowing me to be the leader but at a high price. That price tag meant having to be the outsider, and I didn't know if I could afford or even wanted such an existence. Too much of my mania concerned only those at a distance, the folk that I could *not* reach. What a mistake it would be if I went through my entire life, risking my health and reaching out for something that is unobtainable. I was pushing for so much more instead of being satisfied with being a flying fish in a goldfish bowl. The unachievable always remained a far fetched dream that I was always ill-prepared but ready to work my feet to the bone for, so that I could at least catch a fleeting glimpse of how the "other half" live; *not* the financially rich other half of our money obsessed society, but the other half of our precious body, mind, soul and spirit—the tools and components that can assemble a better future for us all if only we let them develop, and instead stop spending so much negative mental energy on knocking down the spiritual skyscrapers that we have striven to build, yet often struggle to fully understand. My toolkit and your toolkit are constantly growing, demanding a greater respect and an ongoing maintenance schedule. These tools are all we really have, and they are worth far *more* than the pots of gold nowhere to be found at the end of every fairytale rainbow—you can bet your sparkling rock bottom dollar on that!

On a few disconcerting occasions I looked down at my feet and had the giddy sensation of being ten or more feet tall, as if I was looking down through a pair of binoculars held the wrong way round. I always wanted to be a little bit taller, especially so that I could get a better view at concerts and football matches, but this was nothing short of ridiculous. Occasional signs and sounds of doubt were immediately turned around and positively translated into "Steadmannish" or "Steadmanic," then tucked up and put to bed in the storage bank of self-belief. It was a relentless catalogue of twirling roundabouts and seesaws, wonderment and surprise, an adult playground full of childish fantasy and make believe where the dealer deals out ESP instead of LSD, and a knowing smile seals the deal.

All of my leaping about the Milano metro system had landed me in a residential area. Streetlights shone brightly, illuminating the gaily painted houses. After only a short distance my manic thought processor struck up a familiarity between this Legoland movie set and the quaint village of Bovingdon. It didn't take long to pinpoint a familiar starting location from where I could search for my home from home. By non-identically twinning a plan view in my mind of Bovingdon with the surreal surroundings that I had inadvertently but happily gone and trodden in, a merging mental watercolour of the two places formed, rather awkwardly, but attractively none the less. By establishing the direction of where my Vicarage Lane maisonette would have been, and by using careful thought instead of sore erratic footsteps to navigate by, I slowly made my way to a small house. Any similarities that I could find with this house that reflected my own home in Bovingdon only went to confirm my manic hunch. Let's face it, how many maisonettes are there in a terraced row with a dark red front door, two windows at the front and a tiled roof? Just a few I would say! I think that there was a No.2 in the door number (mine was 12A), but on average so do·a tenth of door numbers. Up to the red door I boldly strolled and pressed the doorbell. This was to be *my* house in Italy, *my* reward. An elderly man who looked more like a sultana on legs answered the door. "*Si?*" he said in a smokers throaty voice, "*Si?*" His wife, also very sun-dried, at least attempted to break the ice by speaking to me in a questionable tone. Neither party had a clue as to what the other was striving to convey. Unable to offer her a polite reply I pointed through the doorway and gave an open mouthed nod that was meant to say, "Can I come in please? (whether you like it or not)." As bold as gold I entered their house. I must have appeared to them as if I had been through every war, sounding like an explosion and smelling like a rotting corpse. I felt great as I admired their family photographs. They must have been too shell-shocked and maybe even a little bit too frightened—it was never my intention to put the fear of God into them even though I burst in their house uninvited—to scream or shout, or even to call the cowardly *carabinieri*. My audacity and pitiful state probably spared me from another bout of aggravation with the Milanese police. As I left their house I gave them both the universal thumbs up and the V for victory sign, along with my finely honed look that clearly stated without actually having to open my big fat mouth, that we all knew that this unexpected visit made sense, and that it was all part of the big "game," so let's just keep it under our hats for now shall we. It came as no surprise that the Sundrieds, lovely couple though they were, didn't extend an invitation for me to stay for some tortellini and ice cream—was it my breath?

I continued to annoy Milano with my sideshows. The impression I must have given was that of a whisky soaked drunkard on a super quick amphetamine. Back at the Metro station I pondered my next move. By this time I had splashed an already overflowing puddle of utterly perfect nonsense over too many good people for far too long. The well of wishes was in dire need of replenishment and sustenance, instead I bowled on down the Italian avenues and alleys, full of dynamism and belief in my quest, but empty of much needed nutritious food and drink. I was in the pits alright, but there wasn't a medical mechanic in sight.

At 12.30 a.m. the Milan metro system grinds to a halt, and the late night revellers or workaholics have to find alternative means of transportation. The streets are so much quieter. My laborious efforts to locate those who were close to my heart continued, although my cause was becoming a saddening affair, more so with every poster that I spoke to and with every moonlit street that I maniacally ran, jumped, hopped, spun, whistled, shouted, sung, laughed, cried and bled down.

At 6 a.m. the metro system came bouncing back to life. Unchallenged I raced my way through the barriers and down to the trains. This morning's manic fantasy took me on an hallucinatory tour of Europe no less. Within thirty seconds I had travelled south to Genova then westward along a secret underground coastal route to Nice, then to Monaco, up to Paris, and then southeast underneath the French, Swiss and Austrian Alps. By making a right at Austria I came to rest somewhere back in Milano where I had started out. It is so amazing what a manic imagination can do, it knows *no* bounds. Ridiculing or persistent questioning of a manic persons behaviour or mental boundaries is *not* always the best course of action, although it may be well intentioned. A sudden attempted assassination of a manic dream can possibly result in anger, frustrated violence, or perhaps even outbursts of uncontrollable manic laughter. In my battered manic case there is a cast iron will to go out and attempt to prove all of the doubting, pointy fingered, non-believing, dream squashing spoilsports *wrong!*

Why didn't I come up for air at these different stations/countries? I think it boiled down to the fact that my manic quest was centred around Milano, and my subconscious feared that there might just be the remotest chance of not being quite where I hoped. This time it might prove to be too much mental effort to turn my delusion around and make it become a believable mind ride. A shocking revelation such as this might hit me so hard that I may crumble and fall by the wayside, and even roll into the ditch of depression again, a place that tastes so awful even in the sunny season. Zipping around Europe in half an hour even freaked me out. This new conviction of mine—that I had indeed tripped over such a long distance in less time than it takes to write down the English alphabet—proves clearly that the little sanity I still had tucked away was becoming very close to being lost forever, along with one tripod, two sacks of nonsense and a pair of golden buckled shoes. One minute I felt all fine and dandy with everybody and everything in amicable agreement, and the next minute I would find myself locked inside the Empire State elevator being launched higher and higher into a far out world where I had to live alone and fend for everyone. It was a bum deal with too much small print to lose, which could possibly explain why I and many other of my manic-depressive comrades kick the backside out of their manic opportunities, suffering severe burns in the process. You may as well get it why it lasts. Nobody, even in their right mind wants to miss the manic boat when it sets sail upon the high saline seas. Hoist a million manic flags and have a ball why don't you, but remember that the decks will eventually need a jolly good scrub.

Help needed to arrive by my side *very* soon. Getting right off the streets and straight to a doctor became my only option. I was blind to that option. I fought commonsense. Blinkered, I trotted on and on to who knows where, hoping that a breakthrough might be made in the little Tommy case or in the ludicrous search for my happily married childhood sweetheart. So many other unfinished dreams and obsessions were crammed tightly into my manic pack, the weight of which would eventually slow me down. Romeo I am not, but at least I tried. There were no nightingales or bluebirds on my shoulder, but hey, that didn't stop me from whistling to them in conversation as I performed my way through Milano. Suddenly a police car pulled up and two more of those annoying *carabinieri* scumbags stepped out. "Oh shit, here we go again," I thought, but this time they were compassionate toward me. A kind person must have alerted them, either that or I had been picked up by big Brother's intrusive eyes in one of the metro stations. My body needed a break before it broke. The feathered angels of redemption must have heard my whistling call. Hallelujah!

3

Hospitals

Could this really be the same police force that dealt me such a tough hand? Compassion and concern shone through this time as I was assisted into one of the awaiting cars. My captors spoke brief but clear English, informing me that I was to be, "Taken care of," whatever that meant. Despite my ghastly appearance I still couldn't work out what all the fuss was about. Content to go with the flow, I sat back in the rear of the police car and convinced myself that now I was some kind of royalty being chauffeur driven to my crystal castle on the other side of town, a place that constructs itself as you walk through it and is fortified by blunt tungsten tipped palisades. This castle is where the high minded will quietly congregate for telepathic conversations, while sipping from a fountain of red wine and nibbling away at a mountain of cold steak and kidney pies, liberally coated in the finest salad cream. My mind raced just as fast as the streets shot past my head. The car felt as if it was hovering, and the dashboard looked so much more hi-tech than anything else I could recall seeing before. What I had once looked upon to be instrumental in achieving only the mundane tasks now took on a completely new meaning. Petrol, electricity, television and radio signals—they all had to be a joke surely, like an energy placebo. The only way to turn something on and get it to work is to will it to happen. This was my latest manic theory, one that I had already mooched around with in England, but was soon to be blown to smithereens and contradicted by another half-baked manic solution, due to arrive rather too soon on platform twenty-five. My shark like senses fathomed that our destination was of course the *ospedale* (hospital), hurrah! If my amicable captors had laid one rough finger on me I would have snarled and then ripped into them, but luckily for them and for myself they kept a safe and respectful distance. These two *carabinieri* deserved some credit, although my utter disgust toward the bastards who had delighted in clobbering me earlier remains firm to this day.

The journey to the hospital was slow and gentle, stop starting through the hot-blooded traffic, unlike the previous occasion when my taxi driver seemed to think he was racing against Mario Andretti just up the road at Monza. I am pretty sure that it was the largest of the five Milanese hospitals, *Maggiore Di Milano*, that became the hospital of choice, although I am not one-hundred percent certain as I was in such a faraway mental state. Midway through the car journey I produced my tattered passport as well as offering a few personal details to the attentive officer who was sitting by my side. On arrival, a porter and a nurse were waiting for me with a wheelchair. It felt as if I had arrived at a grand hotel (It seems that I've got a thing about hotels)) and was being given the star treatment. So many people suddenly seemed to be sympathetic toward me and were more than willing to give of themselves. "Ha ha, the superstar treatment, now this is more like it," I thought to myself, "this is the reward for my efforts to date, for giving it my one and all." It was a reward maybe, but not in the sense that I believed it to be. "Free food must be part of the deal, as well as a wash and a jolly good looking after by the Italian nurses," I thought craftily, "who in their right mind is going to refuse such an offer?" Not for one second did I consider that the last thing these nurses wanted, was to deal with my dirty mind and stinky feet. It didn't take very long before my impressions became so different from how they were on admission. My initial manic visions of the hospital had been rather overblown, but those visions were as sane as a psychiatrist (well, most of them) in comparison to the events that were to follow. There I waited in the belief that I was in my right mind. Who was I trying to fool? What is a "right mind" anyway, and who on Earth decides? Answers please on a postcard and sent to "Heavenly Hospital," somewhere in Milano.

It struck me as a crying shame to be inside on such a sunny day. In I rolled, flanked by a young nurse and a male doctor. Smelling the many aromas that a hospital has to offer sent my imagination off on a wild goose chase into the past. I thought of my mother whom I had visited in hospital many times as a child when she had to endure what seemed to me like a "woman's problem" every other month. Aunt Pauline, my mother's younger Sister had not long had a severe stroke along with a host of other undeserved complications, so I thought of her and her loyal partner Harry. My grandparents were with me too. So many memories filled me up, memories of the new born babies that replace my dying friends and wrinkled relations, the broken rugby clavicles and split gym knuckles, two weeks in Hemel Hempstead's X-ray department as part of my school work experience, so many deep cuts stitched and sore, and now of course there were the fresh memories of my recent encounter with a High Street paving slab.

The two *carabinieri* explained my situation to the doctor as they saw it. When the formalities had been dealt with we were off, weaving our merry way through a maze of corridors. The thrilling but slightly uneasy sensation of climbing to an even higher unexplored plane—a place where life forms resembled my own personal impression of perfection, and inanimate objects would suddenly spark into a life of their own—took over from my street "skills," challenging every one of my five or possibly six senses to handle the new highly powered manic vehicle, being showcased for the first time within these hospital walls. We all bathed in a rare spiritual beauty and serenity, marinating in an eternal elixir made of love and understanding. What a great feeling it was to be wheeled into the bosom of that throbbing medical engine, into yet another stimulating environment. The real reasons why I ended up in Milano were waiting for me to unravel. I know that there is a lot of wasted telepathy and unused brain power inside each and every one of us. Perhaps if we practice plugging in the brain power a little more often and stop being afraid of all things spiritual, we may then be able to use what we have been given to its full potential and for the good of mankind—a bit like getting high together but in a clean and controlled way.

I was taken to a bay that contained six freshly made beds, all of which were empty. My entourage deposited me in the first bed on the left side of the bay, next to the entrance. A long white cotton gown was provided for me to slip into. I removed my tattered passport and the key I had found. Off came my shirt and jeans, leaving the pieces of petal to the mercy of the wash. You really *do not* want to know about my rancid underpants. Wearing the gown, I flopped my lean carcass on top of the cool bed linen. I laid back and stared at the ceiling. It felt like I had entered a Heaven that people already in Heaven might go to on their summer holidays. The doctor seemed rather concerned about my red raw feet, and so he might as they were in one hell of a sorry state. Every examination imaginable took place on and in my body, for which I am very grateful. It escapes me whether or not I was administered any sort of injection or had a sample of my manic blood taken, but they did wire me up to a heart monitor and set up a drip solution in order to put back some of what I had taken out of myself. A brave auxiliary nurse had the unenviable task of bagging up my clothing and sending it off for a wash; something that *I* was desperately in need of. Words of English were exchanged sparingly in direct accordance to the job in hand. The nurse cleaned up my feet and then put a dressing on the worst areas. There was no food to be had at this stage, just some water. For the very first time in quite a while I had no choice other than to rest, to be still and try to relax. My body succeeded in achieving all of these requirements, but my over active mind didn't want to play ball.

Fifteen years earlier, on a fishing weekend by the Hampshire Avon in Southern England, my uncle Terry Steadman—one of Britain's top authorities in the world of hypnotherapy and behavioural psychotherapy—taught me one of the simplest relaxation techniques. The idea is to relax limb by limb, until it feels as if you are slowly sinking into the comfortable surface that you are laying upon. So with eyes shut tight I gave it a whirl. Instead of sinking I had a sensation of hovering ever so slightly *above* the bed, not a level I cared for at that particular moment in time. I stopped concentrating on relaxation and instead began listening to my heart beating out an electric pulse. Impatiently I waited for the next attractive occurrence to rear its pretty head, hopefully shedding a little more light on my growing predicament.

After ten blissful minutes there was a loud *thud* on the bay door. In came an elderly man, pushed in a wheelchair by a hospital porter. He positioned himself at the foot of my bed. The mute porter left me alone with this prehistoric Italian gentleman. I spoke to him in English, followed by a swiftly invented gobbledegook of merging European influenced tongues—a sort of rapid Esperanto. He gave no response, which wasn't surprising because even I was unsure about what it was I had attempted to say to him. I tried to convey clearly, "*Buon Giorno,*" which earned me an acknowledging nod of his tortoise like head. It was all very bizarre. The old man appeared to be not of this world. He seemed unnaturally old, as if he had lived for thousands of years with a locked in secret. Now he remained preserved at a constant old age. Maybe he poured formaldehyde on his cornflakes every morning and only drank water. He grew to be a calming presence, despite being slightly creepy to begin with. Why put him with me though? He reacted to a few things that I said but it was impossible to know if he understood a single syllable of what I was trying to say. For almost an hour I laid back on the crisply laundered sheets with my head slightly propped up by a few pillows, trying to take the peculiar situation in. It made no sense to me, even though Iwas *very* high. Without any warning or obvious reason my uncommunicative Moses look-alike chum, sitting sombre faced at the foot of my bed, began to weep. Tears from nowhere were rolling down into his bushy grey beard. Did my feet smell that bad? A very cute nurse entered. She smiled at me sadly and then left without saying a word. "What on earth is happening here?" I wondered. Another porter arrived to collect my ancient friend and return him to the museum or mausoleum that he originated from. Little did I know then that very soon we would be reacquainted.

Doctors and nurses came and went, checking my drip and probing my body. Anticipating what may happen next was also a pointless exercise because I knew already from my early manic experiences that there was always going to be something bigger and better just around the corner, waiting to blow my mind that little bit further away from base. When the drip had expired the nurse disconnected me, leaving the tube connector and the needle driven firmly into the back of my left hand just in case any further solutions may be deemed necessary. The same porter returned with an empty wheelchair. Gingerly, with the nurse's arm on my shoulder, I swivelled my buttocks to the left and placed my bandaged feet onto the floor before coming to rest in the wheelchair. The porter pushed me through corridor after corridor, some of which had a slight incline that may well have taken us up a few floors. I can remember using an elevator at some stage too. Eventually we came to a dead end. To the left was an open bay door, to my right a closed door that I later entered when on a forbidden walkabout. I was wheeled into the bay on the left. My bed was the middle one on the left hand side. I hauled myself back up and into the pristine sheets that were held wide open by another gorgeous angel, also mysteriously wearing a sad smile. She covered my body, making me feel safe and protected. I took a good look around the room at the other patients. There were others, one on either side of me and the other three propped up in the beds opposite. This room, just like the police car dashboard, also struck me as being extremely high-tech, full of scientific medical gadgetry that I had never seen the likes of before nor since.

The same old man that had for some inexplicable reason been positioned at the foot of my previous bed, was now sitting upright in the bed directly opposite to mine. All of the others looked as if they were taking the same brand of multivitamins and cod liver oil as my new crumpled buddy. Their faces looked *so* old and craggy, full of valuable knowledge and distant experience. Their eyes, all smiling, suggested that they knew something I did not, something special, *very* special. I felt that I was in very unusual but safe company.

When my nurse and the porter left, I decided to be free of my cotton robe and instead slide naked beneath the sweet smelling sheets. I closed my eyes, keeping them closed for what must have been the first time in nearly three weeks. This attempt at getting some much needed sleep was pleasantly cut short by another two female nurses, both stunners. This delicious pair could have easily been top models who had just strutted off the sexy catwalks especially to be by my side. The privacy curtain was drawn before they turned their undivided attentions toward me. It became apparent after spotting a bowl of warm water and soap, cloths, sponges and towels that I was in for a real treat. They said very little to me as they went about their business in a professional way, allowing for a sexy smile or two which sent my hormones and a few other body parts jangling. One thing that they could never scrub clean was my mind!

Earlier in the week when I roamed the streets looking for Tommy, I thought I had been shot dead. Now I knew for sure that I had gone to Heaven, my own private Heaven on Planet Earth, full of all the things I love the most. The brunette babes began their nursing duties by lifting up my top blanket, folding it neatly, and then gently placing it on top of the cabinet by my side. They must have figured that they were dealing with somebody who is high, not from drugs but from a chemical imbalance. Now it was the turn of the white cotton sheet that was by now clinging tightly to every perspiring contour of my body. I had been feeling quite sticky, so this delightful manoeuvre would come as a godsend. One either side, my nurses carefully lifted the edges of the white cotton sheet and folded them into the centre, and then again. Still hidden by the folded section, I allowed myself to become sexually aroused. Considering that one's libido increases when manic, this sudden uprising didn't come as a shock to me or to my two horny looking angels. Both women saw what was happening but carried on folding the sheet with a curious precision, until a small folded pile of sheet sat with a pleasant pressure on my private party. One of the nurses handed me a warm soapy sponge as the other lifted the folded sheet and placed it on top of the blanket by my side. I cleansed my face and neck with the sponge then allowed them to wash me, front and back. As they attended to every square inch of my body I laid back, unable to believe my luck, admiring their shapely curves, imagining them as naked as I was and displaying just as much sexual tension. By concentrating hard I was certain that they could feel the sexual electricity sizzling through the sterile air, lubricating their sweet Italian tunnels of lust, creating an aromatic aphrodisiac that connected the three of us as one climactic menage a trois. Give me the real thing any day on a loving one to one basis, but this telepathic orgy certainly wasn't something to be sniffed at in a hurry. These hot Italian lasses are something else!

Both nurses carried on with their duties as if nothing out of the ordinary had happened, which indeed to them it had not, or had it? Raunchy thinking soon turned into torture, eating frustrating great chunks out of me. What I badly needed was a diversion, something new to divert and grab my attention away from the firm young lusty busty nurses. Distraction from excitement served itself up in the tasty form of steaming pasta. Taste buds that have been left unused for just under a manic week do tend to respond with extra sensitivity when real food is presented. My first meal in nearly seven days looked, smelt and tasted just as good, and gave me just as much satisfaction (well, nearly as much) as if I had been locked in a sauna with only my two sexy nurses for steamy company.

My feet hurt even more now because they were not on active duty. Mania dampens the pain an awful lot, especially when in full active flow, but since they were cleansed and dressed they stung and ached an awful lot. My nurse gave me a mild sedative after my pasta meal, along with strict instructions to remain on my bed and allow my beaten up feet the chance to heal. Assisted by the sedative and watched over by five old men, I closed my eyes and fell into a light sleep, waking periodically to the sight, but still no sound, of the five solemn faced men. The changing view through the tall window to my left indicated nightfall. Wideawake, the geriatric five resisted outside influences and kept their vigil over me. All of this attention translated into renewed thoughts of grandeur, that I was some sort of streetwise messiah. And what about the ritualistic folding of the perspiration dampened cotton bed sheet? My manic interpretation was to suggest that it was the "Milano shroud," following in the sore footsteps of Jesus Christ himself, amen! Could it be that I was the main-man himself, reliving the past in a new modern place and time? A bipolar affected person genuinely believes these things to be so true at the time of happening. To suddenly shatter these beliefs without due care and attention can result in unnecessary damage. Delusions of grandeur are still only delusions I know, but they especially should be treated with the greatest care and respect. To be in a delusory state is like being reborn in any way, or in any form you care to choose. To be in a delusory and hallucinatory state at the same time takes the biscuit, as you will soon discover.

What strikes a self-proclaimed sane and normal human being as being unbelievably far-fetched, can strike the travelling manic soul as being a deadly serious situation, not to be sneered at or mocked, especially if you have any compassion in your bones and value your good "normal" looks. I doubt if I would carry out such a violent deed, but somebody who has been pushed a little bit too close to the edge, and is struggling very hard to express an important train of thought just very well might! To limit the severity of the grandiose fallout, a gentle approach should be adopted, and ridicule which has the venom to crush and paralyse the toughest ox should be left safely at home. Grandiosity has always remained with me, showing itself during the nineties within a series of bipolar episodes, but always to a much lesser extent. A bipolar affected person cannot be forcibly programmed to be a figure of his or her own choosing, it just happens depending on the ingredients that are pulling a current circumstance or situation together. Sometimes, even when I am supposedly sane, I lean back on past bouts of grandiosity. This I might do in situations where I feel threatened or inadequate. In *no* way am I suggesting that I can tune into the highest of highs at a minutes notice, but from a very short distance I am able to turn "it" on and become the closest friend and confidant of my chosen character; it just takes a well rehearsed script, a head full of imagination and a bit of acting.

One of the nurses checked up on us all before replacing the daylight with a soft orange nightlight. Feeling sleepy and about to fall into a peaceful slumber, I suddenly entered into what has to be the most terrifying of all the dishes offered up to me since I began feasting at the global table of life. Semi conscious, I began to sink. Down down down to a place so awful. Unable to move, pinned down, entombed. I eventually managed to force open my eyes, but the good that I needed was not forthcoming. Only the prospect of an unrelenting mental annihilation pierced my grilled mind, leaving me half alive and definitely not kicking, stranded in a bottomless sickening nightmare. This was hell all right. I had now arrived at Satan's sinister table, strapped to my high chair, but refusing point blank to eat up his poisonous envy. How long would this tortuous subjection to the devils playground last? I can remember very clearly thinking whether or not I would ever be released from this wrongful imprisonment. Are there others stranded in purgatory, praying in vain for the arrival of a mislaid atonement? It is amazing how much one thinks in such a situation. My brush with evil seemed to last for at least one extremely long Milanese minute, although I suspect it was for far less, especially when you consider that the average dream lasts for only three seconds. When the claws lost their grip, I let out a scream that could be heard back in England. I kept this up until the main lights of the bay were switched back on by the hospital staff. I could then establish with great relief that I had indeed escaped from some kind of hell and was now back on more familiar ground, though still foreign. Two different nurses were holding my hands and cupping the back of my head as I yelled myself out. Ungratefully, I flung my helping hands off with unnecessary force, a reaction of mine whenever I feel a restriction of bodily movement (If my feet get tangled up in the bed sheets I become equally panicked and have to thrash around until I am free again), it's just one of those "me" oddities.

This type of terror ordeal was later categorised by an English psychiatric nurse as being a "subconscious nightmare." When a person reaches the highest level of mania and begins to hallucinate, these nightmares are more prevalent. When they try to strike their prey out, things can become extremely frightening, but more about them later. The nurses in Milano were very understanding and attentive toward my plight, and they took no noticeable offence at the rough removal of their caring hands. Now wide-awake and scared of falling asleep in case it happened to me again, I sat up in my bed all night long, listening to centuries of snoring and wet sounding, toe curling farts. I am fairly certain that the staff at this particular hospital—although they knew I wasn't quite right in the head, thanks to being briefed by the *carabinieri* and also from their own observations on admission—didn't fully latch on to the severity of my present mental disposition, despite my demonstrating all of the attributes required for them to make an unofficial diagnosis. They were concerned with my physical well being first and foremost, something for which I will always be most grateful for. The following morning kicked off with the presentation of a pair of second hand Italian made brown leather shoes to replace the pair given to me by the shoe thieves. I still have them today as a souvenir. That old pair were on their last legs long before I took ownership, so they were discarded along with the hospital waste.

Dramatic changes in the facial appearance of the five elderly men seemed to be taking place. Each face began to live its way through the passing years, stopping briefly at how I imagined Leonardo Da Vinci or Moses to look, and then flowing into a more up to the minute character. They smiled softly in amusement at my delight and bewilderment. This blatant change of face did not faze me, as I had grown rather accustomed to such bizarre, mentally misshapen and disfigured visual activity. I tried to find the meaning of it all, throwing these clues into the manic melting pot, but the soup remained cold and misconstrued, and the five men returned to being craggy and old. Trying to determine the exact time when the supple leathered old men would metamorphose into bright light young butterflies, or indeed when anything manic based happened was virtually impossible in this hospital. All that I could do was sit back and play my manic melody by ear. The old men had ample strings to their bows, so it wasn't very long before they struck an emotional chord with me in the form of five long gone, distantly deceased relatives. Wanting to believe them to be my old relations is probably closer to the mark. Ancient Grandfathers and Uncles materialised before my very eyes. Even female forms shone through the outer crust, smiling a familiar reassuring smile. This was a little spooky-weirdo I have to admit, but it was also a harmless and comforting spectacle that helped me to relax my mind and feel a little more at ease.

With my over active mind being constantly deprived of sleep, coupled with a perfectly normal though temporarily chemically unbalanced brain, I was a prime candidate for a major hallucinatory joyride. The apparitions, not only the old boys but those still yet to come, were always so unbelievably real. I swear to this day that what I saw, heard, felt, smelt and tasted really took place, never mind the mania. There is an awful lot more to this manic business than the experts think, I am absolutely certain of that. A certain level has to be reached before special doors can be opened, allowing the visitor to enter a reinterpreted world where everything fits like a surgeons glove. It is a world that doctors *cannot* see. They can only see the madness in the eyes of the bipolar beholder, and they can only witness the repercussions of the rising mental annihilation. *Nobody* sees what the manic-depressive sees.

I found that I was even able to hold my own in a conversation with the old boys by gesticulating, and using some made up Italian sounding words that I didn't really know the meaning of. My command of the Italian language mysteriously appeared to increase tenfold without any effort. Perhaps the stored vocabulary had been jostled to the surface by manic interference, or was it some kind of miracle? How did I manage to reply with ease to the old men? We covered some pretty heavy subjects, chopping out the bits in the middle and leaping straight into the fire with the solutions, not the questions. Simple conclusions to the meaning behind all existence—how it began, where it is going and why?—made themselves known in coded forms that the six of us succeeded in solving without exertion. It was a breeze and a blast. The wise old spirits of a zillion tears and years were being drawn out of me in climactic colour. A utopian overdose was just what I needed; the complete opposite of my ghastly subconscious nightmare.

Everything made perfect sense at last. It all slotted into place. I cried with sheer relief at the realisation that my folks back in England were alive and well, and that they were probably watching me at that very same moment in time on channel 22 as I wrote my mathematical signs on the wall; signs and squiggles that always arrived back at one little dot. That little dot is a precious speck that sometimes shrinks and sometimes expands, to be seen and not to be seen creating all there ever was, and all there ever will be. I could see it so clearly now. I honestly felt that I had figured out life itself. I figured it out by riding trains inside out, sharing red wine and my belongings, drinking in the cool rain from the dirty ground, surviving everything that was thrown at me including a few right hooks from the *caribinieri*, and I figured it out most of all from the care and attention shown by angelic souls when I needed them the most. The fact that I was still alive summed so many things up in my nutshell. This is why I always felt different since I was a child, unable to say what I really wanted to for fear of sleepless ridicule and for being regarded as an oddball outcast, shunned by everyone. Don't ask me to remember the exact details of how I did it, but I knew by the atmosphere and by the reactions of the others in the bay that I had completed equations and figured out the obvious answers. When these obvious answers were put together they explained the not so complex mysteries of our whole existence.

Profound lecturing drained out of me with ease. My mental chip calculated then converted the groans and grins of the five younger looking gentleman into, "Why didn't we think of that?" Harmonious sighing with each peaceful agreement filled our bay. The realisation of life's many mysteries created the hum of an electric charge, lifting us inch by inch with every new eye-opening revelation. At that time I could and would have interpreted anything to mean whatever I wanted it to mean. I felt like Roald Dahl's Charlie Bucket character when he won outright ownership of the chocolate factory, as if I now had total control, all the power in this universe but too much for one human being to handle single handed. The old men took it in turn to sob and wail with true Italian fervour. The mathematical equal sign (=) became all things to me: a parallelogram, horizontal, level lines, tracks, bars, ley lines (Wemb-*ley* stadium being a famous ley line landmark.) Could it be one thick, short and stocky stick laying on its back, split down the middle, creating two individuals that come together again to make one? Maybe not, but boy oh boy, Steadman's manic muscle was really cooking this time! The straightforward thoughts that I had previously been complicating were hitting me at a million miles a minute, and for almost a half an hour I was not only defending myself with two straight bats, but I was returning verbal winners straight down the edge of the tram lines, or should I say metro tracks? Hey Andy, I had another fifteen, plus some!

My clothes arrived neatly folded in a white plastic bag, and were placed in the compact cabinet by my side. Using the bathroom became a bit of a private joke, because due to my sore blistered feet I had to negotiate the short distance in the same way that Dudley Moore had to negotiate the sunburnt sand in "10," the hilarious 1989 movie he starred in with Julie Andrews. Remaining in bed following so much physical inactivity, and being under the reigns of a nurse, no matter how attractive she might be, didn't always bode too well. I had to be gently restrained and cajoled into submission on a number of occasions by the picture pretty staff. My spring was coiling up tighter with every motionless moment. Deep down I knew that I needed to rest and allow my ripped feet the chance to heal properly, not to mention the urgent replenishment of my body's lavishly spent natural goodness.

Mid-afternoon on the day following my admission, I was asked politely to slide aboard a trolley. A cotton knit blanket covered me and a couple of fresh pillows raised my head up to a comfortable position. We were obviously going for a ride, but the staff did not offer an explanation as to where they were taking me, and to be perfectly honest I couldn't have cared less. Dialogue in English was very rare indeed. The same two nurses that looked after my interests the day before escorted me and the male trolley porter through the corridors, and then down a sloping tunnel section to where the elevators were. Throughout this journey I clearly heard the familiar sounds of wood sawing, hammering, electric drilling, and the chattering of workmen. My hands mimed along to the sounds that I could hear, producing what I can only describe as a very fast mimicking sign language for the manic deaf. If I heard the hammer pounding hard and firm, my arm would pound down too as if it was holding the hammers handle. These sounds without their sights were right there in the tunnel section. Where were the workmen? The nurses appeared to understand the reason for my sudden alertness. We remained quiet until the sounds faded out, leaving behind a stony silence. Some people hear voices, but I had to be different and receive sound effects that were pulled out of a long a list of past work experiences, curious indeed.

"Bing-bong," into the elevator I rolled. "Bong-bing," and back out again, uncertain if I had gone up, down, backwards, sideways, back to front, inside-out or round the bend. It didn't really matter to me either way. My silent porter faultlessly manoeuvred the trolley through the brighter windowed corridors until we came to a double door on the right. The trolley brake was applied, then the porter left. My two nurses entered the double doors that swung back forcibly whenever a different face entered or left. An awful lot of traffic was going back and forth which struck me as being mighty odd. Those who were about to enter, a combination of patients and staff, would pause and smile at me before entering. Some simply nodded. Me being typical me gave the thumbs up sign and said something like, "Hello mate, what the hell's going on here then?" The silence that I received was not particularly golden. Still none the wiser, I kept quiet and laid back in anticipation of the next juicy instalment. A little wary? Yes, but I was still excited and pumped up for the new occasion. The same old man from my bay, the one who had sat at the foot of my bed and cried like a baby, pulled up behind me on an identical trolley with an identical blanket. Another trolley joined the queue, and then another. "It must be a bloody big room," I thought. One of my nurses reappeared, smiling at me intensely. She released the brake and began to gently manoeuvre my trolley into the overcrowded bay. This bay was exactly like mine, with six beds and one large window. It was daytime but the curtains were drawn and the lights were on. An air of great expectancy hung over the room. I got the impression that everybody present knew the significance of what was about to take place, except me. The room smelt pleasantly of freshly cut roses or of some other sweet flora, a fragrant reminder of the red petals that had fallen out of nowhere, and had probably now been reduced to mush in the hospital wash. My nurses adjusted my trolley so that I was in a sitting position before wheeling me into the centre aisle, two thirds of the way in so that I had the best seat in the house. Two beds were positioned at right angles directly in front of me. The old man came in next and was placed directly behind. The others somehow squeezed in too. My two nurses stood either side of me, with the beauty to my right placing her delicate hand upon my prominent clavicle that I had clean broken eleven years earlier. Why there were so many other people in that room is a mystery that I struggled to solve but couldn't. Why was I there? I could feel the eyes of the bay burning into me like inquisitive laser beams. My eyes were burning into somebody else.

Sitting next to the empty bed ahead of me and to the right was a middle-aged woman, dressed in a traditional Italian white lace garment. She sat transfixed to the young lady in the bed opposite. There didn't appear to be any reason for concern except that for the first time in quite a while everybody present made me feel like the one with the *most* sanity. The pretty young lady in front of me and to the left, had her head propped upright by a pile of white pillows, and her soft gaze was directed back to the strange woman opposite. What happened next, just like everything else in Milano, really took place, I swear to God. I can remember pinching myself and slowly looking around the bay, taking in this whole strange gathering as carefully and in as much detail as I possibly could. What did this all mean? Something special was about to happen, that was for sure. The young girl, who must have been Italian and in her late teens or early twenties, had both of her arms buried underneath the flimsy white bed sheets. It was easy to see her young nubile form beneath the clean sheets, a sight meant to be witnessed. Her legs were slightly parted and her eager young hands were resting suggestively in-between them. Ever so slowly the young girl began to move one of her hands in what I can only describe as a gentle masturbatory movement. My penis had never stood to attention quite so fast as this before. The woman to my right started to do the same thing while still sitting in her chair, but she went for it in a far more obvious and vigorous way. A sexy atmosphere of great importance hung in the aromatic air, as we witnessed some kind of symbolic sexual ritual. Everything and everybody in that room had an edge of otherness. I had been taken to a future that was still based in the present, a present time that was made up of many visible pasts.

On further inspection I was doubly certain that those who were watching this erotic self pleasuring sexual spectacle with me did *not* appear to be of modern day Milano, instead they were widely spread, representing the many different ages of human existence. Manic reasoning presented me with only one conclusion, a conclusion tinted with more than a hint of grandeur. What we had here was without doubt something biblical, and pretty darn important too. Virgins, a possible birth, the wise old owls and my two darling angels, Mother Mary quite contrary—all of these factors and so much more filtered steadily into my highly formed hunch, and I never fell off my trolley once!

This experience is tricky to convey because I am aware that it sounds so far fetched, but it was so clear and so very real to me that I would bet my life upon the fact that it happened. How do I go about proving a thing like that, and why should I have to? What I saw did not lend itself to a photo shoot, and no matter how hard I tried to focus in on the events in hand I could not prevent myself from performing visual calculations in my already bamboozled head, and try to come up with a rational explanation for it all. Everything slowly slotted into its rightful place. I was convinced that I was part of a four or five dimensional puzzle being put together by a level of intelligence previously unknown to mere mortals such as myself. My theories continued to fly off the runway and change faster than a supermodel's shoes.

I defy any red-blooded male not to have been turned on as much as I was then. Even some homosexuals would have risen to this occasion. Both women were bringing themselves closer and closer to an explosive orgasm. The young lady to my left turned her head and looked me straight in the eye as she slowly began to thrust her hips. "For goodness sake what's happening in here," I thought, "Whatever it is, please don't stop!" I couldn't take it any more, and simply had to let off more than just a tiny puff of steam. Flanked by my two sexy nurses, and sweetly smiled at by the pretty young mystery girl, my aching nuts could easily have exploded there and then. She had no inhibitions whatsoever. My nurses looked down to smile at me as well, so I smiled back up to them as they pressed their warm midriffs against my arms, making me even more excited. How many more versions of Heaven were there? This had to be my favourite of them all so far, and I wanted a ticket for all four seasons. The whole function felt so natural, yet so premeditated for a reason yet unknown. Suddenly all of the people in the room began to weep. The young girl had kept her eyes fixed firmly on my every move and was now arching her back in sheer ecstasy as well as bucking her pelvic region in multi-orgasmic spasms. Tiny beads of perspiration could be seen on her face and on her now fully visible pert breasts. She opened her petite mouth in unbridled pleasure as well as to suck in the heady atmosphere of that hot Milanese Hospital room. A little saliva suggestively trickled down her chin, landing on an erect nipple that she had been tweaking to assist with the reaching of yet another dreamy creamy orgasm. The middle aged lady sitting to my right got up to go and sit by her side. As the young girl continued to bring herself to more and more orgasms, the woman pulled back all of her white cotton sheets, exposing her bronzed flesh in its entirety. The woman then stroked the inside of the girls tanned thighs before cupping and caressing her delicate breasts and peaceful face. My baby-browns were on stalks. Pink wet flesh soon became visible to us all. There was absolutely no dirtiness about it whatsoever. My two nurses continued to take excellent care of me, making sure that they neatly folded the cloths that they had used to cool and cleanse my hot body before placing them into a white plastic bag. One of my nurses suddenly left. A kind of love was heavy in the air for us all to breathe in and make from it whatever we desired. A little lust was of course present but it came in a satisfied second. Voyeurism had never been so good, and certainly not so bizarre! When the exhausted young girl had finished giving it her all she closed her eyes like sleeping beauty and went straight off to sleep. The trolleys that had been positioned behind me were wheeled out, reluctantly followed by myself. My one remaining nurse became mute, putting up an invisible barrier whenever I tried to prize out of her even the tiniest snippet of information regarding what exactly was going on in that sexy room. The furthest I managed to get, and was ever likely to get when my curiosity got the better of me, was a caring smile and a "Do not worry, everything will be okay, now rest." As my father always says, "If it ain't broke Son, don't fix it."

As things evolved there were to be no more trolley-jollies. My manic mind, refreshed and as busy as ever, found plenty of new distractions within the perimeters of the hospital. I held on tight to the unflagging belief that by now I had been broadcast throughout the universe by means of thought transference, telepathetic television, and of course by all of the now antiquated equipment such as satellites, fibre optics, digital radio, internet, Morse code, the postal services, messenger pigeons and notes in green bottles. Could it have been a combination of them all? My mania had briefly levelled, but soon enough it resumed inching its tireless way back up again into a gear that I never knew existed. It definitely had no intention of letting up or showing any sign of waning.

Despite the discomfort of my feet, I could not sit still in bed all day watching the other five change by manic metamorphosis into crew members from Star-Trek or members of a biblical flock, so I began to sneak off the ward for short walks. When I returned from one of these tender walks I thought that I would be nosy and take a little peak through the twin doors that faced the entrance to my bay. I was just able to see these doors from my position in bed, but not once did I see a single soul entering or emerging. Maybe it was a locked storage facility, or perhaps there was another entrance through which staff entered and left that room. There was only one way to find out, so I pressed down the handle and opened the door. In I stepped. The fire conscious door swung shut with a heavy click. The room, about the same size as my bay, was brightly lit and smelt of disinfectant, baby powder and poo. Why couldn't I smell this from my bed? A nurse wearing a standard white apron and regular condom coloured latex gloves came over to me from out of nowhere, grabbing my arm with good intent. She then led me to yet another mystery door. Not a word needed to be spoken as our facial expressions said all that was needed to be said. When I looked in and saw what I saw it certainly *did* say it all, speaking to me very loudly and extremely clearly. My sense of smell went on a rampage, picking up all of the many cleaning agents, air fresheners and of course the smelly cocktail that knocks you sideways when entering the heavily centrally heated home of a new born baby. Smiling directly at me in full ruddy colour was a woman actually giving birth! She seemed to be abnormally relaxed about the whole unnatural/natural affair. Was she with or without an epidural anaesthesia? Either way, there was no yelling, screeching, grunting and groaning or even any heavy panting. Before me lay a bloodied woman with her legs spread-eagle, producing yet another reproductive body to support yet another soul. The whole gory scene did an excellent job of freaking me out. It was far too much to handle in one sitting so I had to make a hasty exit. Women giving birth is a miraculous thing I know, but thanks to the footage on television when least expecting it, along with the birds and the bees films and lectures that I was subjected to at school, I have developed an adversity to babies and vaginas covered in blood and slime, especially when eating my dinner. The whole thing makes me feel decidedly queasy so thanks, but no thanks. Was this birth tied in with the recent routine by the two female pleasure seekers? Did I fit in somehow? Could it be possible that all of these things were interconnected, or had my mania become so rich that I was hallucinating a daydream, wide-awake to suggestion but asleep to realities truth?

Time as we all know it, didn't seem or need to apply to me in the hospital. Time and dates were whatever my mood decided. They meant nothing to me anymore, so I laughed out loud at the fact that so much importance had been placed upon them for all this time. Everything was changing but still remaining the same, I just saw and manipulated the patents of life to suit, or so I thought. I believed that I had found the place that I had been searching for, but not the right people. I was in love with a manufactured love, assembled in my imagination factory and loosely based upon a common teenage affair, an overblown affair that had deeply scarred the very section of my brain where realism had been forced to move over or die a slow death. Sadness fell on hard ground, then rose back up into the soft clouds. From the tangled roots to the highest bud, brand new growth of the bipolar tree always followed my ever changing moods, producing new ideas and completely new perspectives on my present manic activity. Too much of a manic jamboree and the mind seizes up, resulting in a thousand different things *not* being accomplished fast.

I could feel a strong spiritual force at work. This concentrated feeling, a common fixture in the psyche of many manic people, touches everything: you, me, Planet Earth and the creatures that roam, fly and swim on it, the plants, our food, oxygen and water, the Sun, Moon and the overblown stars—nothing has been left untouched. Sensations of well-being, peacefulness and love oozed through my pumped up veins. Becoming rapidly manic is a bit like being thrown into a sleeping lions den, but instead of being thrown, the bipolar affected person happily volunteers. It is just a matter of time before the lion wakes up and wants his kilo of flesh, not that there was much left on me to give.

I feel privileged to have had a taste of what I believe is yet to come and be fully understood. Before you start shouting, "Yes, but he was so manic bless him, hallucinating all over the place, and in such a deranged state," and before you raise your judgmental finger, dismissing the events that I am opening up my heart to and trying to describe in the best way that I possibly can, you simply have to understand that I have had enough hallucinatory, deranged and fully blown to pieces manic episodes over the years to know the difference. One might say that I, and millions of other bipolar beholders are an authority on the subject. That does not alter the fact that we need the professionals to guide us back to a safer, kinder place. We can teach the professionals a thing or two though!

There have been plenty of occasions when my thought processing capabilities were in an awful muddle, mutinying and mutilating my entire being, sometimes abandoning me for long periods of time, leaving me awfully frightened, lonely and *very* confused. Not all is lost, misplaced perhaps but never ever lost. A luscious chunk of me believes adamantly that the whole Milano episode holds far more close to its heaving chest that can possibly meet our limited eyes. Never before has the phrase, "There's more to it than meets the eye," rung more true. I know that I had a chemical imbalance in my brain in 1990, but that still doesn't alter my belief that in Milano there was something more than a severe case of mania taking place. A reason, a purpose and a time when all will become apparent—enabling the pieces of my manic puzzle to finally slot into place, and for the nonsense to make perfect sense—patiently awaits you and me. I impatiently dipped my sore toes in the water, that's all. It felt really good, although still too shallow to dive in head first. What was it that drew me into a world so inexplicable? Why do so many people attend church (a practice that I occasionally partake in) and believe in so many different versions of so many absurd happenings? To me that sounds a little more wacky or mad than some of the things myself and many other honest manic-depressives have experienced for *real*. Do you believe in an old book or an existing real live person? I believe in both. Why is it that so many cannot accept the possibility that some kind of spiritual force could be intertwined with mentally related issues? Why are so many people frightened of the unknown or unexplained and yet they keep on praying for it? Why do the learned experts pump you full of strange drugs and dismiss the entire affair as a just another case of a chemical imbalance and nothing else? I think that it is a little bit of this and a little bit of that. Occasionally it is far too much of both.

While waiting to be let loose on the trendy streets of Milano, I spent most of my time sitting on my bed, watching the five old men being taken care of by the staff. I clearly saw all of them being connected to separate units of mobile high tech apparatus. The man opposite me to the right appeared to die every half an hour or so, then be bought back to life by the staff. This resuscitation routine never became boring. I wouldn't be at all surprised if his long-winded existences were still in progress. The man to my left kept having uncomfortable looking tubes inserted into his rectum and also down his throat. This entire spectacle was in open view of anybody who cared to look. When the various procedures were completed, the old men laid back and went to sleep for a short while. Just like Mister Dead and Alive sitting opposite me, the whole sickening tube/arsehole routine to my left was repeated over and over again, and there's me thinking that my feet were sore!

I seriously questioned whether or not human beings died anymore. Maybe deaths still occurred, but I was being shown the proof that it needn't be that way, hence all of these extraordinarily old men. Were these repetitive procedures designed to answer my questions? Plain, straightforward explanation was not forthcoming from any of the hospital staff, leaving me in quite a quandary. Had I found my way into a whole new universe, a shared domain that had always existed but I was blind to? Falling into the future and bending over backwards into the past left me in the present I suppose. It sure didn't seem like my idea of the present, instead it felt like I was being transported, or rather guided into a brand new dimension. Today I am under no illusion that my burning mania distorted my mind to a certain degree, and that many events appeared grander than they really were, but isn't that the same with showbiz? Most of my redesigned feelings and the freakish events that took place happened for a pleasant reason, I am certain of it, and I also sense from my experiences that the future is going to be just fine for every single one of us, so instead of talking about what might and what might *not* happen, let's get on and live *this* life to its fullest potential. None of us are poor because our unique gift of life is priceless—invest it wisely!

If the hospital staff did know more about my serious state of mind, I may not have been given a discharge quite so soon, and instead taken to the nearest psychiatric unit. If the staff did possess a higher form of intelligence they would surely know in an instant what I was all about, besides they must have been expecting me, well weren't they? I needed to get my butt out of there ultra quick, and I think they knew it. Late one morning, following a second sleepless night despite a mild sedation, I made a vow to myself that no matter what, I was going to put myself back into the spherical ring, out into the big wild world. My two gorgeous nurses didn't show any enthusiasm when I hinted at my intentions, but my stubborn mind was well and truly made up. With only the five old men as silent witnesses, I quickly dressed in my same scabby but cleaner clothes. Off came the dressings that were mummifying my feet, removing pieces of dead skin in the process. Next I slipped on my holey socks, followed by my new second-hand brown shoes. "Ooh Agh," my feet hurt tremendously. As I was so eager to get moving I chewed on another bullet that I had been storing deep in my reliable arsenal. I had to get out of a place that had been so good to me. They all knew that I had to leave didn't they? As I was about to make a run for it, a nurse walked in and caught me. She wouldn't leave until I removed all of my clothing and reverted to how things were before the rabbit in me had a chance to gather speed. The following morning I pleaded with the nurses and doctors to discharge me. They may have been powerless to keep me under their care any longer now that they had replenished me and got me back onto my feet again. Maybe they concluded that not only had they done all that they possibly could *for* me, but they had also completed everything that they needed to do *with* me.

Fully dressed, with my passport and old/new key rammed firmly into my jean pocket, I moved around the bay to each old and still living men, shaking their veined hands or patting their frail shoulder as a silent, "bye-for-now." I strongly believed that somehow we would all come face to face again. One of them might even lend me a helping hand the next time I have a flat tyre in the torrential English rain. My pretty nurses allowed me to plant soft kisses on their cheeks and then I was off and away, out into the watery sunshine. Raindrops transmuted into an abundant sprinkling of diamond dust. The alchemists must have been having a field day as all around me I saw precious metals glinting in the sunlight. Everything I set my eyes upon appeared to have come alive in its own way, sending out warmth and good vibes to anyone or anything who cared to stop for a while and catch them in their mind. It is a gift indeed to detect beauty in what used to be a dull material object, or in a persons once irritating behaviour.

Precious gems, fast cars, yachts and mansions appeal to me as they might appeal the next person, but I still laugh at the status symbolism that these expensive attachments represent. Although I wouldn't turn my nose up entirely at any of that opulence, I would sooner spend my money on slightly more important things such as feeding starving people. Remember that one starving baby is priceless. No rock jewel, stone mansion, steel car, fibreglass yacht or paint on a patch of canvas will *ever* come close to the value of a single human being. It only goes to prove how manic influenced ideas, visions and views can grab hold one minute, and then fire off conflicting attitudes and opinions the next, demonstrating in every corner just how fickle and contradictory manic depression/bipolar affective disorder can be.

I continued in the same vein as before, poking my nose into places where it wasn't wanted, roaming the densely populated streets (Milano has a population of just over 1,600,000.) Despite displaying a slight resemblance to the Artful Dodger, and still singing like a strangled tabby cat, I was at peace with my world and every little thing in it. Hardly a soul escaped an enthusiastic, "Hi there, how's it going?" Back to my old tricks I went, leaving not a scrap of crap that I came across, instead collecting it fervently for a use that would make itself apparent in its own good time. I twisted, jumped, gyrated, thrust and slid my slender frame through the hustle and the bustle, attempting to avoid the stomping of city feet. Sips of wine from reliable tramps—one or two of them were slightly smelly, but the majority were rather fragrant vagrants—and the occasional cadged cigarette never tasted so good. Did I know how to live the high life or what! High is the operative word.

One thing that can never be taken away from me is that I have performed, or rather played-up and played-out, before thousands of Italian people. After a couple more days and nights of this manic behaviour, despite feeling as if I could go on forever, the exhaustion caught up and sent me plunging into a self destructible shell. Now I was becoming an emotional time bomb that lacked a concrete foundation upon which to build my colliding manic ideas. Temporarily, I had well and truly lost the plot; not that my original plots had that much substance at their initiation. My poor fooled body was teetering on the edge of a hellish breakdown. About a month later I was told that if I had continued in this way, without sleep, food or enough fluids, the chances are that I could have collapsed in the streets and die pointlessly for the manic "cause." It was a cause that I was living for real and trying to find both at the same time. A heart attack was also a distinct possibility. Even after I had been told these sobering facts, one month on from my Milano warm-up expedition, I still floated high, interpreting it to be scaremongering by somebody who was still unaware of the magical changes being made in my manic paradise. An intelligent dunce was I.

A *carabinieri* van pulled up. Rain had been falling lightly, and it must have been very late. Somehow after another session on the metro system and lots of walking, I found myself out on the edge of the city. I must have walked for miles and miles. The *carabinieri* directed their strong spotlight in my direction, illuminating the small area of waste ground that I had gravitated toward on that sad and desperate night. A tall wall covered in colourful graffiti backed up this desolate area. There is usually a significant amount of wonky reasoning, but reasoning all the same, behind my zany behaviour, but on that pathetic occasion I cannot recall any. Dumbfounded, the contingent of *carabinieri* remained seated in their dry van. Two pairs of Italian eyes glued to the scene before them, probably wondering how they were going to tackle this problem as it certainly wasn't included in the training manual. Rolling around in a large puddle of dirty water just a few metres from the wall was a human being who still thought that he had all the answers in his pocket, ready for distribution, and that Julie was going to walk out of nowhere and salvage the old dead and buried relationship. Mania had me believe that my pain and discomfort was everybody else's gain, so that is what kept me going. My prize was always waiting around the next corner. Who in their right mind would want a dirty beast like me anyway? Maybe I thought that I would have to pay an even higher price for the good yet to come and suffer in some way for my present manic art. The only picture that I was painting for my audience was that of a whacked out lunatic who was in urgent need of a check up from the neck up. Animal shadows were made with my hands onto the brick wall behind me. The bright light positioned on top of the police van shone down as I continued with my ludicrous impressions of restless birds and dogs. Then I bounced up onto featherweight feet and launched into a one man vaudeville performance, while at the same time drowning in my own manic laughter.

When a manic person is doing all of these things they believe with all of their heart that what it is they are trying to convey is full of purpose and meaning, and what's even more important is the belief that whoever is paying attention to it is understanding and benefiting from the whole display. The bipolar affected person does not realise or rather chooses *not* to acknowledge the fact that their audience doesn't always see eye to eye with the performer. I always believed that my audience's perception was the same as mine, though perhaps slightly slower, and that I was getting my important messages through without needing to verbalise.

Some manic people become aggressive if their manic views or interpretations are not accepted by their captive audience, but I just became frustrated and a little peeved before inventing a self explanatory reason as to why they didn't latch on to my point of view the first time round, and then I would set out on a brand new slant that would hopefully hit and stick to many mental blind spots. I never took "no" for an answer because I believed that I was right in practically every avenue that I chose to run down. Coming down from a high can not only be a little embarrassing, but also deeply disappointing when you begin to realise that much of what you were saying was not being heard in the way you believed it to be, and that a large percentage of your heightened perception of life was after all only a living dream that felt *so* real because you wanted and needed it so desperately.

Who could blame the police if they had a jolly good laugh at my expense? I know that I have a laugh at the crazy things that I have done, and also at many other people who have fallen off their trolley time and time again because they keep forgetting, or secretly prefer to forget, to tighten up that pesky screw on the wheel hub of their life. The *carabinieri* did not ridicule me nor give me the heavy-handed treatment that I had experienced earlier on the lawn outside the hotel. I suspect that as I was in such an appalling condition they felt genuine sympathy toward me. A thick blanket was wrapped around my sorry body before being ushered into the front seat of their van. Such was the power of my mania that I still thought that this was the latest piece of the jigsaw puzzle. My manic file was kept busy trimming down any edges that didn't fit in to my evolving vision. At one point I became angry because I felt that my saviours had prevented me from meeting Jules. The place they took me to was a Godsend, a real lifesaver.

Gorgonzola, home of the delicious cheese, also boasts a large general hospital. This *ospedale* had the provision for psychiatric patients, so that's where we drove, dripping wet and covered in mud. There were to be no police stations this time as they knew from their records and just by looking at me that I wasn't a criminal but a very unwell individual. Inside the hospital I became very fidgety. I had to see everything, touch everything, and question the other "funny-farmers" to see if I could establish what silly seeds of thought they had been planting in their heads that day. The nurse in charge, a big lady with whom you didn't want to mess about with in a hurry, dealt with my admission and then did her best to make a preliminary assessment of my condition before deciding what the best course of action would be. I was presented with some second hand clothes to change into after I had given my grimy frame a thoroughly a good wash. All of the psychiatric units that I have ever come across seem to have an endless supply of donated clothing for people such as myself. Fashionable in the average sane person's world they were not. Wearing a silvery satin T-shirt, a red crew necked pullover and a pair of faintly checked trousers that made me look like a 1970's American tourist, and I was set. I still had my beaten up passport and the special key tucked away safely. The new stimulation that I had suddenly been presented with propelled my mania to new heights, annoying for the other confused patients and the staff, but not for me. I could *not* sit still or shut up. Knocking me out with an uppercut must have been a tempting course of treatment, possibly knocking some sense into me at the same time. To dampen my ardour, the staff had no alternative than to knock me out with the aid of a heavy sedative. Whatever it was that they injected into my thigh may fell an elephant, but it only succeeded in slowing my racing mind a little, enabling my body to always catch up. Possessing so much zeal ultimately lead to my downfall, for one long night at least. On reflection, despite all of the good that they did on my behalf in Gorgonzola, I am extremely critical of the way that they put me on a hard trolley, strapping my wrists and ankles tightly to it and then leaving me alone for the entire night in a pitch-dark room, checking on me occasionally. What next? Were they going to wheel me off to the gallows or put me on the rack? From running wild and free to being pinned down and shackled was unbearable and despicable. As I mentioned earlier, I have a terrible fear of being restrained in any way, shape or form. Manic strength and willpower alone was not enough to free myself. I tried like mad to break free, but just like handcuffs, the straps gripped even tighter. My manic belief that we are going to be, or have been a part of each other either in the past, present or future still holds strong, but I think on that particular day in history Harry Houdini must have become stuck in a barrel and missed my boat. Slipping in and out of consciousness helped me to get through this latest ordeal. How sadomasochistic people extract sexual gratification out of being tied or handcuffed to the bedstead, leather bound and whipped into a frenzy by a dominatrix wearing tight fitting bondage gear beats me, but whatever blows one's horn goes I suppose.

Back in England nobody knew where I had disappeared to. Very soon they were about to find out. As I continued to lay back on the hard trolley, a very kind Dr. Conti took it upon himself to do a little investigative work on my behalf, so he telephoned the British Embassy in Roma. With the aid of my tattered passport he passed on as much information about me as he could. Then it was the turn of the British Embassy to contact the foreign office in London. The foreign office then contacted my sister Virginia at her home in Watford, Hertfordshire. I must have put Virginia down on my passport under the "Who to contact in an emergency" section, just as I do to this day. It was a good job that I did. Not a single soul back home knew of my whereabouts. There were many who didn't even release that I had gone away at all because let's face it, who keeps tabs on everybody all of the time? Going off by myself has never been an unusual occurrence for me anyway. Nobody back home had a clue as to the extent of manic havoc that I had been wreaking in my personal Milanese Heaven and hell, but they soon would!

How any of my close relations could be prepared for the force of the bombshell that I was about to drop, I do not know. The Hiroshima in my head was about to fall out, and land in the laps of those I loved. Let us get things into perspective; I was merely suffering from just another yet to be established disturbance of the mind, some kind of mental illness that can probably be put right in time with the correct expertise, medication and a lengthy spell in a peaceful stress free environment, whereas in other parts of the world there are people dying every single second. Virginia took the full blast from the foreign office. After some careful consideration she decided to call my other Sister Barbara. Together they decided to go and break the news in person to my parents in Hemel Hempstead. I wouldn't know what it must be like to be informed that somebody very close to you is suffering from a severe personality disorder, but it does *not* take Sigmund Freud or Albert Einstein to figure out that it must come as a terrible shock, a real blow beneath the belt. Knowing almost immediately that life from now on will not be the bed of roses that it once was, has to be a tough pill to swallow. The quality of life following a bipolar episode can be just as rosy as anybody else's life so long as blood is tested, the correct medication is taken and the known triggers aren't cocked up. My family, as loyal as ever, surpassed themselves and dealt with the situation superbly well, handling the unique situation step by step and day by day in the only way that they knew how, by using power tool No. 1—pure *love*.

Pain is pain, no matter when where or how it decides to promote itself. At the onset of my illness I found ways to hide my behaviour from those whom I knew could pick up on every little thing about me. I had to be cagey and not always one hundred percent honest, something that rankled my conscience. Manic depression in its manic rising phase often involves an awful lot of play-acting in order to keep the ball inflated to the correct pressure and rolling smoothly. Not everyone can pull it off successfully, but those who *can* pull it off create a launch pad in their mind and then build a space shuttle in their garage, so that nobody else can see them flying as high as their imagination will allow. Dare I say it again, but it does help to have a reasonably high intelligence, especially one that has been in the mental closet for too long and is raring to get out—not forgetting the incorrect brain chemistry—in order to steer the mind to places unknown, at an altitude never before imagined.

Virginia and Barbara rang the doorbell of my parent's home in Gadebridge. As soon as my mother saw the pair of them together she sensed immediately that something was not quite right. My mother's intuitive gut instinct came to the fore, "It's Keith isn't it, it's Keith," blabbered Mother. The girls entered the house, sat Mum down, and then calmly explained the situation; that I was in Milan, very much alive and being taken very good care of. Apparently she went hysterical there and then, and they had to practically scrape her off the living room ceiling. After the initial shock she calmed down, probably with a glass or two of her favourite tipple, brandy-shandy (Brandy and lemonade) inside of her.

That initial shock, the very first one that sends waves throughout the sufferer's caring network, can and *does* quite naturally knock a person sideways. While everybody is still reeling with the shock of it all, a short term care-plan has to be figured out and then put into immediate operation. A long term plan can be put into operation later when the extent of the problem is fully established. It can become a logistical nightmare if one allows it to be, so level-headed apportioning is required. Adjustments may have to be made right across the board in much the same way as when dealing with a person who has a heart problem, or has been struck a blow by cancer or a maybe a stroke. Mania does have the knack of leaving in its wake a trail of destruction that somehow has to be addressed piece by piece, examined for clues with a fine toothcomb, and then rebuilt into something that may not only restore, but organise the sufferers previous disorganisation. There is of course always the strong possibility that the manic person has mismanaged and run up a huge amount of debt. For me it was a straightforward enough matter of paying back the outstanding £600.00 out of a £1000.00 bank loan. Fortunately I had the foresight to take out an insurance policy that resulted in my slate being wiped clean, but not after my sister Barbara fought the usual battle with the greedy insurance company. Imagine what it must be like to run up tens or hundreds of thousands, maybe even millions of pounds in debt as some manic people often do, and have no insurance, friends or loved ones to bail you out. Throughout the irresponsible years to come I ran up some astronomical telephone bills, mostly calls to another bipolar beholder from the United States whom I happen to love immensely—more about this special lady later. There were times when I had to sell items from my maisonette in order to pay off a private loan, or to buy an inadvisable quantity of liquor and tobacco. All said and done, there were never any exceptionally outrageous financial extravaganzas operating within my manic world, thank goodness. Extraordinary generosity, not only monetary, but by the giving of yourself and of your worldly possessions, is also common place. My body and mind had been unshackled, shared out to any takers at any cost to my health, and now I had to pay the price for such misplaced, mania motivated generosity. I only wanted peace and harmony for us all in return, that's all. Bipolar people are well known for coming up with rather extravagant money making schemes. Not all of their creativity, intellect and vision come together as hoped for, nor are their plans always very well thought through, and yet we need people like that, the straight ahead souls who may be restricted for a few months within a psychiatric unit, but will create a big *wow* when they get out. Their ideas and inventions often lead to bigger and greater things, as many of history's eccentrics, or incorrectly labelled "mad" professors have demonstrated time and time again. Ask yourself; where would we be without them?

Pacified by a little alcohol, my mother tried to take in the available news that my sister's were trying to convey. My father was still at Lucas Aerospace where he worked as a quality control inspector. Virginia wrote down the telephone numbers of the foreign office, the British Embassy in Rome, and the psychiatric department of the hospital in Gorgonzola. When my mother felt composed enough to dial the Gorgonzola number she was greeted by a member of staff and then by yours truly who, in my mother's own words, apparently yelled down the phone, "Hi Mum, are you coming round for a cup of tea?" Oh dear oh dear, that set off her waterworks. Poor Mother bawled her eyes out. I was so lost in the crazy maze, that I seriously believed she might only be a five minute walk away. "Why don't all the family come round and we could have a reunion party?" I was talking out of my backside, but I meant every single word of the nonsense that I uttered to my perplexed Mother. As things evolved. It was my father and my uncle Mark (Ma's eldest Brother) who took on the role of rescue party, hopping on the next available flight to Milano. They took a taxicab from Linate Airport to Gorgonzola, paying in lire and not with camera accessories as I had done. When they entered the psychiatric unit I casually walked up to them and said, "Hello Dad, hi Uncle, how are you doing?" "Bloody hell, are you okay Keith," replied my uncle as the pair tried to take in my appearance: gaunt, hairy and in somebody else's delightful checked trousers. They didn't know if they should laugh or cry. My rock-steady Father, a sensible and practical man, saw that I was in one piece and fixable. He had no way of knowing then about lithium or manic depression, but he figured that I would sort myself out with the right specialised help. They listened in stunned fascination to my manic mouth, offering relentless misjudged and misplaced "wisdom," and fantastic tales that double-backed upon themselves. Then I fired off a volley of jumbled up words and flailing gestures at breakneck speed. Just listening to me must have been exhausting. The hat of the psychiatric unit tour guide sat firmly upon my hot head, encouraging the other less enthusiastic patients to give a performance. When that hat slid off, I treated everybody to a make-it-up-as-you-go poem about life, death, the future, the past, money, sex and drugs—performed at maximum volume and with a throbbing rock 'n' roll heartbeat. I felt as if we were all as one, as a band of Brothers with whom I felt safe, and able to bawl out my thoughts regarding newfound highs and old hat lows. Another injection of sleep soon put the dampers on my noise. I can't say that I blamed them, besides in order for me to travel back to the United Kingdom without incident I would need to be heavily sedated.

The only part of the return journey that I remember with any clarity is of a few heavy eyed minutes aboard the British Airways airplane. I have a vague recollection of disembarking at London's Heathrow Airport and being ushered into a customs security office by a burly official. My father's passport had been processed in Ireland because of a backlog of work at Peterborough, England. My botched temporary passport which was falling apart, had been deemed illegal because of the tampered photo on it. For a short while my father was actually being held as a possible terrorist suspect, the last thing we needed. It's all well and good being vigilant, but I needed to get through as quickly as possible. Come to think of it, I suppose I looked like a prime candidate for a runny nosed drug addict, assisted by my equally dubious sidekicks. Dad and Mark were having to carry my dead weight in an upright position, with limbs dangling to the ground like an abused rag doll. Our untimely run-in with custom and security officialdom came at a very irksome stage in my repatriation process. Dad and Mark were probably thinking, "Come on for Christ's sake, the bloody sedative might wear off soon and he might go berserk again, running around the damn terminal." After a lengthy wait we were told, "Okay Gentlemen, you can go now," so we went *now!* The fun and games continued. What great contrasting footage this was going to make for my blockbusting movie debut, still being cooked up within my raw mind, a mind of our own that was never allowed to rest or take a sabbatical, not even on the parched grounds of compassion.

Waiting in the arrival hall was Mark's younger brother Ron and his fourteen year old son Timothy. All of them gathered to offer moral support, and to help out in any way if required. They were all fully aware that I was temporarily off the wall—"off the planet" is a little more accurate. Barbara, my work hard then play even harder Sister, used all of her charm and negotiating acumen to retrieve my car without having to pay the accrued fees. Insanity does have its small advantages, and between you and me it is amazing just what you can get away with by using that plea, an easy way out option that I have rarely abused, unlike some. I had no luggage to collect which made up for the lost time in the interrogation room, ensuring that those who had come to my aid were not put out of joint even further. Very soon I was sitting on the back seat of my fathers Ford Sierra heading toward the infamous M.25 motorway, known with disaffection as the world's longest car park, or as Chris Rea accurately described it in one of his best songs as the *Road To Hell*. This circle of smoking metal and incomplete tarmac was made even more unbearable for Dad and Mark by my slurred chatter, in-between the brief moments of silence. My rolling commentary consisted of aggressive demands that the other cars make way for us, and that the road workers, "pull their fingers out." These inaudible demands contrasted with speedily concocted, apologetic reasons for what had now suddenly become a huge shared joke, causing me to burst out with laughter. I became an automotive-psychopath. The heavy sedative was now beginning to wear off. Under absolutely no circumstances was I to be allowed out of anybody's guarded vision, let alone return to my maisonette, drive a car, operate machinery or fly a kite. I may not have been allowed out of their sight, but they could *not* prevent me from being delightfully out of my merry manic mind.

Mark was dropped off at his house in Boxmoor, only a stone's throw from Andrew and Jean's house. Almost every tear had been used up as my mum flung her arms around me in loving relief that her grinning son had returned safely home. There was another part of her that wanted to throttle me for putting everybody on full alert and bringing so much despair and aggravation to the family. It had been brought to my attention at the first hospital in Italy that on admission my heart beat was slightly irregular and that my breathing had struggled, hence all of the electronic paraphernalia, none of which I had taken seriously. I may have stopped breathing properly for a brief while and risked my neck on Milan's public transport, but I remained alive and that was the main thing. In fact all I wanted to do, and still do, is live my life to the full.

Witnessing a loved one who has become a distant image of their former self—still all there physically, but not all there mentally, not even fully capable of realising that something is seriously wrong with them—must be such a devastating heartbreaker. Their former self has only been mislaid, and it can just as easily be retrieved. It cannot be stressed enough that the support network must *never* forget nor lose sight of the fact that the same human being that everyone knows and loves is still alive in that temporarily off course body, and that beneath the mask of a familiar stranger lays a much wiser and brighter future. Medication and therapeutic activities to suit each and every individual's stimulative needs are a small non-negotiable price to pay, and they must be adhered to even when treading eggshells and balancing upon the finest of taut lines. There is no escaping from the fact that without belief, support, bloody hard work and love, the road back to recovery will be a very mountainous one. All of the pills and potions in the world, necessary though they are, will struggle to provide a mental reformation without the outside human touch. It can take a while for a doctor to find a compatible medication that will provide the desired results, but what's the hurry when you want a job doing well? For those of us who are blessed to have a strong and willing army around to help fight the battle, the results should come in sooner. Sad souls, some of whom may live in squalor, may think that they have hardly anyone at all during a crisis when in fact they have everybody. If they would only scrape last weeks dinner from off their shirt, smile and reach out politely, encouraging others to reach in, then their lot in life will improve. Plenty of help lines and bipolar affective disorder/mental health groups, organisations and drop in centres are available, but you can't beat the intimacy of a close friend, neighbour or relation, especially as they do not have to be associated professionally with your ailment, which allows both parties an increased chance to take a welcome break from the same exhausting subject. Too many reminders of how mentally unfit you have become can only provide a negative, stuck in the mud effect. I have said it before and now you are going to hear me shout it out again, "Do *not ever* give up on another human being, no matter how hopeless their cause may appear to be." The chances are far higher than you may think, God forbid, of you becoming just another one of the statistics. We don't give up buying lottery tickets that have far worse odds of winning than a mentally ill human being does of making an inevitable recovery. Life's rich pattern often includes at least a little temperamental mutilation, it is simply a matter of when, where and how.

Bipolar affective disorder is just another illness. "Just an illness?" I hear you cry, *yes* it is, and there is no need for the beholder or the caring party to be frightened of it. Even those with a strong disposition and a heavy heart of gold have been known to crumble into dust when it comes down to the crunch. There is no shame in that. Sometimes the most unlikely people rise to the challenge, surprising everybody including themselves by showing an aptitude when it comes to dealing with mentally ill people, unruffled by the unpredictability of a mental disturbance—a complete opposite to an operating theatre student who feints at the first sight of blood.

Compatibility with medications, environment, the medical professionals, fellow patients, neighbours and family will become vital factors in the treatment of a mentally ill person. Seemingly insignificant circumstances can and will turn out to be important players, and these players will vary a great deal from mentally ill person to person. Those who have trouble communicating and expressing themselves at the best of times are obviously going to be on a back foot from the very start, and are more likely to lash out at unsuspecting victims with pent up frustration and fury at having been landed with such a bum deal. Plenty of mentally ill patients are full of well meant and ill meant words, but that is all they are—words. Most people are unable to follow up their own bleating because they do not have the tools to do so. In my situation, by the time I had stated my intentions, my racing brain had lapped itself and was straight on to the next harmless passion, leaving the last planned escapade semi-stranded on salted ice.

Many years ago, anybody demonstrating signs of a mental illness were rounded up and sent to the nearest Victorian mental asylum. They would be packed like baked beings into a mixed ward and fed a rainbow of drugs that were not always necessary, but did a good job of placating them, as well as softening their impetuosity and brains. When there was less understanding of mental illness, people who showed any sign of becoming a public liability were put into these places by the authorities and often forgotten about. Even their own families would disown them as they also feared, or simply did not know how to handle the unknown. Later, when I became depressed and had to remain at Hill End Psychiatric Hospital, my environment was a major contributory factor in making me feel *far* worse. For many vulnerable people these places offer a safe haven where the pressure is switched *off*, and regular medication and all sorts of therapeutic activities are turned *on*. There are still too many sad and lonely people walking the streets today with seriously disturbed minds. Many of the homeless people that line the city streets are missing a piece of the puzzle, but they are not recognised and dealt with as such. Most of the old Victorian mansion type hospitals in the United Kingdom are being closed down. For some of those long term patients who had to be re-housed into the community this has been beneficial, allowing the independence that is stripped away inside an institution to resurface, prosper and grow. Integration within society and improved outpatient backup has to be a positive, though immensely challenging step forward. Psychiatric units within, or separate from general hospitals are now so much better than ever before, and should be regarded as being no different from any other medical facility, with absolutely *no* shame and *no* stigma attached.

I had never set foot inside a psychiatric hospital, or even a smaller psychiatric unit that some general hospitals provide, except of course for my brief whistle stop visit in Gorgonzola. Half a mile from the old Rolls Royce sight near Watford, now Leavesden Film Studios, stands a grand looking structure. Leavesden Hospital for the mentally ill has now been partly demolished, but despite it operating on a much smaller scale and with a much tighter budget, it is still in operation. Tight budgets and fattening wallets could possibly be the main culprits in this outcry. Everybody affectionately referred to the hospital as the "Leavesden Loony Bin," which indeed it was. None of us would have stooped so low as to seriously mock the afflicted, especially face to face. Whenever myself or a friend have been in the presence of a troubled mind, a genuine empathy would emanate. Quite often one bigmouthed idiot among a group makes a derogatory comment, and is then promptly quietened down by his embarrassed and ashamed friends. Nine times out of ten the wisecracking clot in question reacted in the way he or she did because they felt awkward, and very uncomfortable about being in the same room as a bunch of harmless enough oddballs. A basic lack of knowledge, ill education and too much ignorance can provoke a cowardly verbal attack, but the unknown does not have to frighten the uneducated if the unconventional condition in question is embraced with an open mind and a kind heart.

In 2002 I helped out on a voluntary basis with two different groups of young adults with severe learning difficulties, a consumer friendly way of describing the mentally disabled. These beautiful innocent human beings should be listened to and learnt from as they could teach a few people, myself included, a thing or two about common courtesy. These people didn't have a bad bone among them. They could be a real pain in the butt at times granted, but nothing malicious. I also worked briefly in that same year as a support worker in a care home that had been set up to accommodate five severely mentally disabled adults. This fine dwelling was set up and part financed by the Shaftesbury Society, a charitable organisation founded by the Seventh Earl Of Shaftesbury, Anthony Ashley Cooper. He was a wonderful human being who became a major force in the British reform legislation, instrumental in the passage of laws prohibiting women and children from working in the dangerous coal mines. He also reformed the care of the wretched and the insane. The Eros statue in Piccadilly Circus London is erected in honour of this giving man whom I admire tremendously.

In restaurants, at pantomimes, when swimming or just leisurely looking around the Marlowes shopping centre in Hemel Hempstead, I occasionally detected the sounds of cruel laughter. Then you come across the loudmouth in a restaurant who has had a glass too many and behaves in a prehistoric manner that questions man's faith in another. It is so tempting to go up to the twerp and tip their meal right over their pea brained head. Why reduce oneself to their level? It is all about understanding. To ignore is the only way to treat these oafs. For goodness sake people, we do not live in the dark ages.

Most of us know of a mentally troubled person, or has at least seen a movie portraying the vast scope of mental conditions such as, *One Flew Over The Cuckoo's Nest* (1975), *Rainman* (1988), *Awakenings* (1990), *Mr Jones* (1993), and not forgetting the movie yet to be made about this book, *The Bipolar Expeditionist* (200?) There are numerous TV talk shows such as *Oprah* in the United States, and *Trisha* in the United Kingdom that often devote valuable airtime to the subject. Documentaries by high profile celebrities such as the multi talented Stephen Fry are always a good draw. Massive financial investments are made by pharmaceutical companies that enable further research into the origins and remedies. A whole host of books are sitting in bookstores and on library shelves as well as being available through Amazon.com—sometimes in the cheaper downloadable "e-book" (electronic book) form. Let's not forget the never ending stream of information to be found by logging on to the world wide web. There is no excuse to be ignorant of the facts these days. Those who ridicule in a sick nasty way need their thick heads seeing to. One in two hundred of us will experience at least one episode of mania, hypo or fully blown, at some stage during our life on Planet Earth. One in ten of us will have a severe or mild bout of depression to look forward to at anytime during our short and cosy stay on this old faithful planet, and three to four percent of men and eight percent of women are currently affected by phobias. I think that the best cure for a phobia is a distraction—something else that takes the mind into a more agreeable place. By the time the new place has sunk in, the old worry has been buried in an historical rubbish dump. Agoraphobia is the most common phobia of all, and the average risk of developing a schizophrenic type illness is around eight people in one thousand. Last but not least is alcohol and drug misuse, which is held accountable for one in twenty cases of mental health problems recognised by general practitioners. So long as a full recovery is made, I believe that experiencing first hand what it's like on the other side of the funny-farm fence can be extremely beneficial. It wont feel so funny at the time, unless you become high, but it *will* be an awakening to the turbulent world of mental health.

One minute the clown is performing to pairs of eyes and ears, the next minute he is behind locked doors, drowning somewhere in a bloodshot wilderness. An ocean of love is needed, *not* a dead sea. Pillars of scientific strength hold firm in the form of a tablet. Then the buck stops with the troubled soul, there are *no* excuses. We have to be our own best friend and make some effort, if only to inspire and encourage others to join ranks and help fight the cause. Secret alcohol and drug abuse is simply another way of digging an early grave. Even those who are the closest will find that their tensile love and loyalty is tested to breaking point, sometimes a whisker away from snapping. How would you like to be the one to blame for the downfall of another? Believe me I know, because I have done it. It is nothing to be proud of, so use your brains wisely and *don't* do it! If you really couldn't care less about yourself, then at least cut some slack for the next person; your noose can be as tight as you like.

Remember that the "nut-bug" can land on you like a big pile of steaming crap from the great dumper in the sky. My question to Mr. and Mrs. Mock-The-Afflicted, and to all the other dim-witted human abusers is this: Who's going to pull *you* out of the shit during your time of need, and drive you to the nearest cleaners? My feet hurt …

4

Hill End High

My parents home became the meeting point for a handful of well wishers and my regular general practitioner, the superlative Dr. Hope. House calls, unlike many areas of the United States, are still common practice in the United Kingdom for cases of extra severity and sensitivity. The humble Dr. Hope is a very special, intelligent and kind human being. He personifies professionalism and humanity and has given the best of his expertise to many of my relations and not just myself. He has made it his business to keep abreast of the latest breakthroughs and treatments regarding mentally related disorders, but more than anything he possesses a rare gentle human touch that in itself contributes toward the healing process. Some professionals have diplomas and degrees with all of those little shiny embossed stamps pinned up on their clean white surgery walls for all to see, which is all very reassuring but they have no idea about communication, surely one of the main ingredients within the world of medicine. Since 1990 there have been one or two occasions when I have attended an appointment with a doctor due to feeling low, and have actually felt far worse on departure than when I entered the surgery/office. This has never happened with any of my regular doctors, only those with whom I have had to visit on a temporary basis. Because a mentally ill person may be depressed and unable to voice their inner feelings, they can feel trampled on by unhelpful jargon and factory line attention. Much of the best medicine does not come out of a pill bottle but out of the well practiced mouth. The right words and reassurances can so often be mightier than the quick-draw "next-please" prescription pad, that is strategically positioned ready to blow away an extra effort case. This is a *very* rare occurrence indeed, that I myself am fortunate enough not to have experienced. Nobody is stress free and perfect, though I thought I was fairly close when whizzing around Milan. Let's face it, we all have our off days and personal problems to cope with, including doctors and nurses. Dr. Hope certainly had his afternoons work cut out, not only with manic me, but with my mother as well. She has been unfortunate to suffer from high blood pressure and bronchitis, as well as enduring more than her fair share of operations for "women's troubles"—I don't mean reversing a mini into an ample sized parking space. Jackie, a lifelong friend of mine, came to visit her old friend from her parents house right next door. She spent two hours, not having to say much, just putting her safe arms around me for comfort and letting me know just how much she cared. In my eyes, and in the eyes of many other people, she is one of the nicest human beings on this planet, and I certainly missed the marriage boat with her. She is now happily married to a great guy, and is also a very busy Mum. My ship eventually docked in the petite form of an American belle. More about our extra special relationship later.

The staff at Hill End Psychiatric Hospital, situated twelve miles from Hemel Hempstead on the outskirts of St. Albans, had been contacted by the ever efficient Dr. Hope. Coincidentally, keeping up the Italian theme, St. Albans is an ancient historical Roman town situated slightly North of London. A man of Dr. Hope's calibre and experience must of had a pretty good idea as to what my problem was, but he had to leave the final diagnosis to the professionals who were either based at Hill End, or visited different clinics in a specific area on a regular round basis. The staff at Hill End were fully briefed so that they would be well prepared and expertly equipped to receive the unwell manic man from Milan. Somebody went to my maisonette in Bovingdon to fill up a bag with clothes and toiletries, as there was no way that I would be allowed to travel looking like a cross between Liberace and a used snot rag. Arrangements were hurriedly made regarding who was going to call who about what, when, where, how and why? All that I knew as I slipped out of the heavy sedation was that I would soon be in a new place and on another platform from which to weave my manic magic. A whole new audience of interesting looking characters were about to enter my manic kingdom. Had they seen me on telepathetic television? Feeling like a film star getting all of the attention, I bundled myself into the back of my father's Ford Sierra Sapphire, eagerly awaiting my next manic mission that was going to unfold in an old psychiatric hospital. A sniffling Mother strapped herself into the front passenger seat.

The idea of a relationship between mania and melancholia (depression) can be traced back to at least the 2nd century AD, but the earliest written descriptions of a relationship between the two are attributed to Aretaeus of Cappadocia. Aretaeus was an eclectic medical philosopher who lived in Alexandria between 30 and 150AD. The psychiatric conceptualisation of manic-depressive illness is traced back to the 1850's when Jules Baillarger described to the French Imperial Academy of medicine a biphasic mental illness. In 1854 Jeanne-Pierre Falret presented his description of circular insanity. This time in history was referred to as the "rebirth of bipolarity in the modern era." Emil Kraeplin (1856-1926), a German psychiatrist, studied untreated bipolar patients long before mood stabilisers were discovered. In 1902 he coined the term *manic depressive psychosis.*

I resumed my madcap conversations with the road signs, now legible. They directed my latest dream-car past the sprawling fields of waving grass. A respectful, constant speed was being kept by the rest of the traffic, adding to the grand illusion of increasing self importance. I willingly kept my guard down to allow the pleasurable distortions to hit me thick and fast. I asked my dad if little Tommy had been found. He shook his head. The car stereo played songs that I swear I had written myself and transferred to the airwaves subconsciously many moons ago. I was performing a mental hokey cokey. A thousand meanings were read into a single stimulation, trying to offer in return a million alternatives, variations of a groovy theme in full flight, wings dipped in ashes then catapulted into the Milky Way by a Greek God on two ounces of acid drops—hang on tight, here we go again!

My insatiable ambitions needed relief before they erupted and corrupted innocent others. As the car approached the entrance to Hill End Psychiatric Hospital my mind itched with the suppressed activity of so many overlapping manic thoughts. I figured that inside this huge place must be a nurse or two to lend me a caring hand, and I wasn't wrong, although not all of the hands were as gentle as I would have liked. What lay beyond the doors of this immense Victorian building? More to the point, what lay behind the human beings who were residing there? "This has to be the right direction to Paradise," I thought. It certainly was the right direction, but not necessarily to Paradise.

My cloudy dream-car sailed through the iron gates and onto a gentle winding road. We finally wound up in a large parking area directly opposite the imposing facade of the main entrance. Hill End Psychiatric Hospital now became "Hotel Hill End," although at the onset the solid old structure felt and behaved more like a palace. Silence fell inside the car as we all took in the black humoured splendour that was now to be my indefinite home. It had only taken twenty-five minutes to travel there from my parent's home, and twenty-five years to earn my entrance ticket.

Odd looking people with rubbery looking faces and curious stares were wandering through their own worlds just outside the main entrance. They sat huddled together on the wooden benches, smoking themselves even sillier. The crafty looks that they gave me were affectionate yet suspicious. How will this new addition affect the sum total? I saw men, women, some happy some sad, some far away and delightfully mad. There were the colourfully uncoordinated followers of self-expression, left refreshingly untouched by the fashion police. Not all of these people had lost their minds completely, not by a long shot. The trouble for so many was that they didn't have the option of being there or not, and even if they were deemed by the doctors to be sound of mind they often had nowhere else to go. Second-hand clothes racks with plenty of attitude, that's what some of them were like. The oddballs reigned supreme, merging into their chosen backdrop, whereas the visitors—complete with their artificial smiles for the sake of their loved deposit—stood out a mile, such was the nature of Hill End Psychiatric Hospital. A few of the soft latex faced long term characters could quite easily have been dreamt up by a clever mind working at the late great Jim Henson's animatronics creature workshop.

Accompanied by my long suffering parents I checked in at the reception, located to the right of the huge entrance hall. We then sat down on one of the heavily padded, regulation orange or green vinyl covered chairs. The time was nigh for another downer pill, washed down with a plastic beaker full of smooth cool water and observed closely by the sharpened eyes of an experienced plain clothed psychiatric nurse. All of this took place in a foyer full of reality deprived dysfunctional souls, who lacerate their way through a shabby excuse for an existence. Some of them were secretly having one hell of a good time in the process, I swear. Too many emotions wanting to be on centre stage at the same time competed with stretched senses that jangled into one orchestral warm up, causing the blood in my veins to boil blissfully. I had to give of myself and take from elsewhere simultaneously. I felt the same roving determination and waves of responsibility, telling me that I had to share and teach others so that we can all join together, creating an extra dimension with a peaceful force. The ingredients were staring us all in the face waiting to be assembled, but the dream isn't realised unless it is fully shared, understood and accepted by concocted non-believers. How could I force another free spirit to believe my fantastical whims? They have to free themselves, pick a lock or two and then meet up on the other side of this life, where we can party in the fields under the twinkling lights of Heaven—a party to *never* end all parties!

We waited for the paged member of staff assigned to my case to echo their footsteps down the main corridor. The wait was short. I couldn't stay still for long, so brisk and straight to the point formalities were called for. An attractive female member of staff greeted us. She happened to be one of the psychiatric nurses based on the ward that I was to become a part of. We then let her lead us back along the wide main corridor that had been painted a gorgeous institutional cream and pale green. We turned left, passing a busy little hospital clothes shop, then just on from there stood the big central kitchen that let out an edible aroma. On just a little bit further, around the left bend and we were there.

A small room, most probably an office in its former life, was the unglamorous setting for my first conversation with a member of the Hill End staff. Here we discussed my feelings, my motivations and my emotions. We touched upon what I had been getting up to in Milan, without digging too deep at this early introductory stage. All that she was trying to do by assessing me was to establish whether or not I harnessed any violent tendencies, what habits did I have, what were my attitudes toward a wide ranging host of subjects, what made me tick. By gathering broad pieces of a mentally dissected person in this non-threatening manner, the trained member of staff can begin to tackle the all important evaluation process that will determine the immediate all important care-plan, which in turn will assist with the production of the final diagnosis and the long term care-plan. It didn't take a genius to see that I was suffering from the acute manic phase of bipolar affective disorder, but it *would* take a skilled professional to delve deep inside my mind and fix the fault. Experience is an aid to predict the unpredictable, but there is no accounting for each individual's uniqueness. The nurse concluded by briefing me of the hospital's daily routines and activities, including a variety of beneficial therapy sessions. Key workers, along with a selection of therapists from the art and relaxation departments, would later come and discuss the options open to me in greater clarity.

Not that I needed to, but just to prove anyway that I was a currant short of a bun, I surveyed the high ceilings and then offered the amused nurse a price quote for redecoration. Mum and Dad smiled a heart aching smile although they must have been breaking up inside to see and hear (very loudly) their only son in this fragmented condition, although it had to be better than if I was laying in a Milanese gutter or in a chilled morgue. A few well chosen words persuaded me to calm down and retract my offer of repainting the entire place. I had at my disposal such an exciting abundance of new stimuli: fresh sights, sounds, smells, noises and a whole feel about the old place that belonged exclusively to us, the people with manic fed knowledge, the rubbery faced and those who were as plain as plain can be, all chosen at some place in history by a select committee on high to put right moronic man's wrongdoings. I was impatient to know it all, and to do it all.

So much fresh succulent food feeding my overworked mind resulted in a rapid lifting, from offering a relatively placid persona to offering a manic charged livewire that could not and would not rest, instead desperately wanting to please and turn everybody and everything well and truly on. All I wanted was to live and to be totally alive to life, and I was prepared to offer *any* part of me in order to have that, no matter how foolish it made me look. If trying to practice simple self-righteousness is laughable and absurd to some, then I will gladly wear a big red nose and be the willing clown in a universal circus. We are already performing in a big spinning top, juggling with fire, messing with wild life, and rising high to balance on a trapeze wire as thin as a human hair. Slacken, and it will be curtains—at least for that kind of derring-do! Heavenly falls and hellish rising eventually collide to create a mixed travelling bag full of mental carnage. This is where good housekeeping comes in useful. If your domestic standards are in a mess then that same mess will be transferred to the mind, making carnage cleanup a great deal tougher.

Anderson Ward is situated at the rear of the hospital, catering for shorter-term male and female patients from the Hemel Hempstead area. Behind the red brick hospital lay well kept lawns, further areas for parking and of course the perimeter road. Beyond the perimeter road were four matching detached derelict buildings that were once used as offices, clinics and even a nursery school for local and staff children. One of these house like structures still operated as a day nursery. Workshops for woodworking and bricklaying stood between these buildings and the main hospital. At the front of the site, not far from the main entrance, sat a half-way-house, used to recondition patients for discharge back into the community, and next to that stood the headquarters of the poorly paid social workers, who I admire tremendously for their dedication to what can often seem to be a thankless task. A modern social club for staff members and their families sat at the rear of the hospital, right next to sprawling fields where myself and a few of the other patients were to have plenty of fun on November 5th (Guy-Fawkes Night.) Myself and a few of the other thirsty patients planned to break into the social club one night and have a party to end all parties, but like so many other manic schemes it dried up and came to anything. If enough schemes are conjured up there are bound to be some that will come to fruition, and as you will soon find out, they did.

The first floor ward that was to be my home for nearly four months was divided into three large communal areas: dining room, lounge, and a smaller lounging area that housed a three-quarter size snooker table. The men's and women's sleeping quarters were at opposite ends of the ward. The main ward doors were clanked shut at around 9 p.m. with a prison like thud, and then locked with one of an overpopulated jangle of keys. Keys are one of my pet hates as I'm sure they are for most people. Over the years I have developed a phobia about keys; losing them and forgetting them. I would replay over and over again in my mind the worst scenarios. What may seem so ridiculous to some people, such as having a hang-up over keys, can be tormenting and mentally crippling to another. The ward would be locked during the daytime if a problematic patient was on the rampage, or was sad and lost. The duty staff would then have to oblige the patients request to unlock the heavyweight slab of metallic and wooden muscle if asked in a polite and civilised manner. Most of the time we had our freedom to come and go, unless under section. It takes very little time to learn that by being nice and friendly (and sometimes a shade brown nosed) one could pretty much get all that was needed to make the stay in Hotel Hill End as pleasant as possible.

The female dormitory led off from the snooker/lounge room. Another single room reserved for very unwell patients, or for new admissions, also led off from this smaller lounge. Leading off the back wall of the central main lounge was the nurses bay, the men and women's toilet blocks, and last but not least the male and female bathrooms complete with washer and dryer laundry facilities. Between meals the dining room could be used to sit and chat, listen to taped music from a bright red radio cassette player, draw pictures, knit, write, or simply sit with visitors who were then able to make a quick escape if the visit became a little trying and tense. Some of the patients chose to just sit on their own and stare out of the secured windows to the open fields, and others might smoke a tailor made cigarette or a hand roll-up (the popular, most economical option to the financially restricted.) Partaking in a little people watching never did any harm. If your name happened to be Danny Weller you would be more than content to sit on the floor adjacent to the entrances to Anderson Ward, the male dormitory and the dining room. He played punk rock music for the best part of a Hill End day, which was enough to drive anybody crazy! Danny, who had been at Hill End on and off for almost a year, is one of life's nicest. He grew up with, and attended the same Hemel Hempstead school as my cousin's Todd and Freddie. The Cousin connection put us on common ground right from the start. Heavily medicated Danny suffers from schizophrenia.

The central lounge was home to the only carpeted floor in the entire ward, and also to the only television, a colour set positioned just in front of the tall brown curtains. Orange and green vinyl armchairs provided the "comfort." Smoking was not allowed in this room, and because so many psychiatric patients smoked, the lounge was sparsely populated. We all sneaked a smoke in the lounge, just as we sometimes did in the dormitory, another no-smoking area. Not everybody, despite their good intentions, could face or even stomach visiting these places, so their useful energies were used and appreciated in another form outside of the hospital, which is just as important. Some of the patients could look rather alarming and sometimes behave in a rather frightening way, yet beneath their mask was a puppy dog wanting to play and make new friends. The unpredictability aspect I enjoyed. It kept us all on our toes and provided free entertainment. Without any warning a disgusting act could take place that was highly entertaining to some, myself included, but repulsive to others, especially new visitors. Watching the reactions of visitors to some of these displays was fun in itself. Most of the patients on Anderson Ward went about being mentally ill without too much trouble, keeping their problems locked away in their personal safe, only prized out with the help of one of the many therapy sessions on offer. The long term patients from other wards were the oddest and most institutionalised of them all. They made up the greater segment of what I described earlier as the rubbery faced. By no means did all of them fit into that category, only a specially chosen few made it.

Disgusting comes in many packages. One evening I had a visit from my uncle Ron and cousin Tim that I will never forget. I am pretty sure that Tim will never forget it either. Jadranka, a pretty young anorexic lady from Yugoslavia, only a few years older than myself, made one of her ghostly wandering appearances as Tim and I were attempting to play three-quarter sized snooker. She had been given the single room that opened straight into the small lounge. On this particular evening she was wearing a full set of second hand clothes, but there were isolated instances when she thought, "Oh, to hell with them," and set off on a very very slow, head held up high dreamy walkabout, until the staff or a patient spots her delicate naked flesh roaming free and ushers her back to her single room, where she could go about restoring her puzzled dignity. The male population, with eyes on stalks, were naturally never in any mad rush to cover her painfully thin Yugoslavian body. Her ample charms were the cause of many a concentrated groan to be heard coming from the male dormitory. Tim was finding that his plate was more than full just trying to keep up with me and my manic interpretation of the game of snooker, when Jadranka suddenly inserted a bunch of bony fingers as far down her skeletal neck as she possibly could to induce a fit of vomiting at young Tim's feet. How delightful. She then smiled at us both before gliding bare footed back into the little side room that she had originated from. This was enough to put anyone right off their lukewarm vegetable soup and corned beef sandwiches, but to Tim's credit he didn't even flinch. Because he didn't wish to upset her in any way, he didn't show a single sign of repulsion, although he probably thought to himself, "What a disgusting cow," and that would be acceptable, but he bit his lip and used his wise young head instead. It's those thoughtful things, the sparing of somebody else's pain and humiliation, being sensitive to another as Tim so unselfishly was, that truly separates the men from the boys, or should I say the humane from the inhumane.

Anderson Ward catered for people who had a good chance of making a full recovery, and for those who were able to conquer enough of their personal demons in order to cope well on the outside. On the other side of the hospital was a similar ward to Anderson except that it catered mostly for patients from the St. Albans and surrounding areas. Altogether there were ten wards at Hill End Hospital, as well as a small printing workshop where some of the patients worked for a few hours each week. There was also an old corrugated steel prefabricated Second World War Nissen hut that was now used for relaxation therapy classes, a fully equipped arts and crafts room, a sports/function hall, a well stocked library, a unisex hairdressers, a clothes shop, an operational chapel and lots and lots of rooms used as offices for consultations and a whole host of various on site medical procedures. Some doors were left unlocked but most of them were mysteriously secured. There wasn't one single room nook or cranny that some of the other lively patients and myself didn't pry our way into, or at least try our best to gain entry. It was like a great big mental chocolate factory, and I chose to be a right Charlie. Newcomers to a place such as this have to beware of would be Svengali figures who will try to suck you dry and then spit you out again as soon as your use to them, usually tobacco related, has been exhausted. Most people had harmless enough intentions, and were allowed to be themselves in what was really a live and let live community. Another person's behaviour, unless violent, ultra filthy or persistently aggravating was usually tolerated because we all knew that we were in our own way all in the same boat, and likely to have our mad half an hour at any given moment. Not everyone who spent time on Anderson Ward was mentally unhinged in the sense that is commonly associated with psychiatric hospitals. Alcoholics trying to face up to the fact that their drinking was affecting every aspect of their life, came in to try and dry out. Addictions, phobias, fears and worries about absolutely everything and anything under the Sun affects nearly everybody to some degree or another. They are all treatable with loving support, persistence, self belief and an immense amount of willpower. People with these kind of problems came and went, providing new amusement and sometimes friendships, but the mentally ill hardcore tended to take much longer.

Some of the patients had personal domestic complications that stretched much further than just their mental health problems. Domestic problems are not helped by an ongoing mental issue, and the mental issue is not helped by the domestic problem. Such obstacles can often be tackled by the often thankless efforts of a designated social worker. These unsung heroes cannot be praised nor thanked enough for what they achieve under difficult conditions and often appalling hours, and for the encouragement they bring to help negotiate the tough spells in a struggling person's life. Accommodation and finance difficulties that are hanging grey and ready to burst can only hinder a patients progress, or even become a prominent strand of the intricate web of depression. Other external problems such as strained relationships or depression over a bereavement or pregnancy can also hit some folk harder than others, especially when one's defences and immunity to life's rocks and arrows are at an all time low. Phobias, obsessive-compulsive disorders, psychological, psychotic and psychopathic personality disorders; *nothing* was too much or too big for Hill End Psychiatric Hospital to handle, not even myself and my bulging manic head.

It was carefully explained that my condition could be stabilised and then monitored, allowing me an excellent chance of living a relatively normal and fulfilling life. Alas, for many of the older and institutionalised patients, and even for a few of the younger one's, life I am sorry to say, would never be quite the same again. Even sadder is the fact that there will always be one or two souls who appear to be glad of that fact. Those of us on Anderson Ward who were in for the long haul, naturally became reasonably good friends and allies. Friendships were also formed with the longer-term patients. Some of these friendships still exist and thrive today, creating a Brother and Sisterhood that can always be relied upon in good times and bad. "A true friend walks in when the others walk out," is one of my all time favourite truisms. My grandmother Duckworth used to have a small poster pinned on her living room wall that began with, "A friend in need is a ..." and ended with a sloppy sentiment about how somebody would break their back to help their friend. My grandmother God bless her, who was always up for a laugh, doctored the sign so that it read, "A friend in need is a pain in the arse."

Those who do push their luck and abuse a valuable friendship are running the risk of ending up alone. I knew a few people like that from my days at Hotel Hill End; users, freeloaders, lazy disgusting slobs who thought about nothing except themselves. The benefit of the doubt ran its course, playing on my generous nature until I said, "Enough is enough, no more fleecing my time, my emotions and the little money that I need to keep myself afloat." These people are I hope reformed and flourishing, and only behaved in the way that they did because they were not quite right in the head at the time. If they haven't changed their ways despite being perfectly able to, then I feel sorry for the person that they choose to attach themselves to next, like a heavily medicated leech. There were the inevitable occasions when tempers flared among the male patients, usually because of somebody else's selfish, thoughtless ways. The guilty party might even receive a firm punch from another patient, but only to preserve what was left of their own highly strung sanity. This was not an advisory route to follow. I never got into serious scraps myself, although I may have been the spark that ignited a few fireworks.

A high percentage of psychiatric patients will tell you that quite often it is far more beneficial to share their most personal fears and thoughts with another trustworthy patient rather than the staff, who with all respect, do not really know what it feels like to be the patient in a place such as Hill End Psychiatric Hospital. Spilling your heart and soul to a medical professional is like talking to a well read book with eyes. The technical side of the subject is there, and a good feel of what it is like has been developed from years of experience working in that environment, but as I said earlier, only those who have actually been mentally ill really know what it is all about. Knowing that another human being knows exactly where you are coming from is worth an awful lot, even though they cannot prescribe the pills and potions and advise the appropriate therapy sessions. I must stress that the majority of the trained professionals are excellent. They listen and learn from their patients. There were just a few members of the Hill End staff who were clock watchers, and a bit quick off the mark when the end of their shift arrived, probably so that they could dash off home or head straight to their local pub for a few belts of the hard stuff, and so what, I don't blame them. It is unsurprising that the nature of psychiatric work drives many people to drink, not that I knew of any personally. It can also be the breeding ground for psychological problems of their own. Nobody is immune. Flaws are everywhere to be nitpicked, if that is your style. I prefer to appreciate a person's good points, and I am so grateful to everybody who has played their part in helping to lift me back up onto my well travelled feet a few times too often. A lot of consistency in sensitivity and skill is required, no matter whether the staff member has been on their shift for ten minutes or ten hours. An Impromptu performance by an awkward patient can take a fair bit of figuring out, not only in easing the patient down, but also to verbally loosen their tightly wound mind with a combination of carefully chosen and expertly positioned words full of personal relevance, gentle firmness and genuine compassion. As I said, some of the male patients, when coming close to breaking point, took care of unfinished business by using language that is guaranteed to be understood. There was nothing too heavy, only enough to send the right, slightly clenched message to the correct nasal address.

Physical restraint is only deployed when a patient becomes so wild and so full of fear that he or she finally explodes under the mental pressure, becoming a liability to not only themselves but also to the other patients on the mixed ward. I never witnessed such an extreme occurrence myself, although I did hear of a few disturbing instances that made pretty gruesome listening.

Hill End Psychiatric Hospital was built in 1899 and demolished in 1997. The site was sold to housing developers for only £2,000,000. There were many relations and friends of patients who could and who couldn't handle the enormity of the task that caring for a mentally ill or mentally disabled human being at home requires. The trauma of being moved to the outside world became too much for a few of the institutionalised diehard Hillenders. They passed away like a withered tree within weeks of being uprooted.

Four or five patients on Anderson Ward were repeat admissions, habitual pieces of ward furniture that knew the hospital ropes like the back of their nicotine stained hands. They appeared to know just about everybody they came into contact with, not such an impressive achievement. They had perfected the art of manipulation so that they could get as much done for them as possible without any effort or outlay on their part. That's fine to do on the odd occasion, I know I did, but for that to be your whole life? Is it not a sad state of affairs that some pathetic people are really like that, and proud of it too? Some I swear have built nothing of any value upon all of the hard work put in by their social workers, the doctors, the nurses and therapists. Most of the patients harnessed the purpose and rejuvenated interest to make a real go of it on the outside. Then there were the lazy, selfish, self centred sorts, too eager to return to the confines of the hospital where everything is done too easily for you. This minority would look for an excuse to be readmitted just for a lazy rest, expecting everybody else to wait on them hand and foot. The worst offender was a huge obese man called Lee Curry who was always in and out of the hospital. Lee was such a pig, the personification of gross. He hardly ever washed himself or his clothes, and to make it worse he had the gall to criticise everybody else. Despite having plenty of opportunities to better himself, this foul looking, foul talking human specimen continued to reek of all that is bad in a person. Let's hope that Lee and the fools that associate with him have come to their senses. I know it sounds awfully unfair, but he is one son of a bitch that I am so glad to have finally washed my hands clean of.

When I checked in to Hill End Psychiatric Hospital I had no idea how long I would be staying, nobody did. It depended upon two main things; first of all my body and its chemical structure had to be compatible and be able to tolerate the medications on offer, and secondly I would have to learn to accept my disorder or illness for what it is and learn not to fight it in a negative way. In the beginning I couldn't see the seriousness or magnitude of it all. My accidental arrival could have been greeted with open arms, or terminated just before I reached the winning post. It was not about winning and being alone, but for us all to complete the journey and to share the spoils. At first I could not and did not wish to play by the rules, unable to grasp the seriousness of the whole thing, but very soon I knew enough to keep my running nose on tap, presenting my manic self sensibly enough to the right people at the right time. I discovered that by skilfully dealing with situations I could get away with sky blue murder. Finding one's niche as a patient in a psychiatric hospital is not exactly cloaked with glamour, but back then I felt as if I was the most important person in the whole wide world. Self respect is one thing, grandiose delusions and borderline megalomania is something else altogether, presenting too many previously trustworthy daggers to stab you in the back, striking you down. There is no place to hide at the top of the tapered ladder where the icy winds blow, nowhere to fly now, only a bloody fall by a bloody fool. I made it my vocation to squeeze every last drop out of this fun palace, and to have the biggest recurring crack of all time in order to satisfy my fuss free and wide open-minded manic cravings. I loved it! Making love to my mania is the best feeling ever. An orgy of manic senses and nonsensical fantasies neatly intertwined, and then just got on with it as if every day was going to be the last.

Having completed the admission briefing, I gathered together my hasty bag of clothes and toiletry dregs and set off through the old tunnel like corridors to where Anderson Ward, my home for the next four months was tucked away. Three fun months later my manic capsule insisted, against my wishes, to come down from the starlight and see everything in the cold monochromatic light of day. My burning ambitions and dreams, the wonder, the perfection and the untainted happiness would completely disappear for the first time in my life. In only twelve weeks time my high living hell-raising would be wiped out and discarded, grey slated for a crime that I had been powerless to prevent happening. Months from now my mind will shatter over a cold concreted floor, broken into a million specks of what once was. Nobody except for a valuable clutch of family and friends will even know, or be bothered about my rapid demise. My elasticised mind was set on a collision course, heading my way like a huge comet destined to knock the stuffing out of pretty distant looking Planet Earth. There would be no three minute warning siren. I had to take it like a man, head on. There were still three pleasure filled months ahead of being happily unwell before the suicidal slide, but right now I was swinging higher and higher and loving every sweet drop of it.

For the first three nights at Hill End I had to put my head down in a small claustrophobic creamy green single suite, located right next door to the duty staff room. This location, in such close proximity to the staff, was so that a watchful eye could be kept on unpredictable newcomers such as myself, who are prone to acting in the most peculiar of ways when confronted with such different surroundings and routines. When the evening medication duties were satisfactorily completed and everybody was inside their respective dormitories, the night shift staff would sometimes lay on a lounge sofa, remaining half asleep right through to daybreak. There were of course a few times when minor disturbances took place in the early hours, but the staff reacted and handled these rare situations with the necessary professionalism.

I ditched my meagre though adequate belongings inside what I hoped would be a temporary abode, a minimal tall walled space, and then I set off on sore foot for a little look around Anderson Ward. Plenty of sunlight filtered through the escape and self harm proof windows. These windows, in the dormitories, bathrooms and living quarters were so secure that not even a stick insect on a diet could do a Steve McQueen and make a great escape. Besides, it would have been so much simpler to just walk out of the ward, passing the punky sounds of The Sex Pistols, The Cure and The Clash courtesy of cross legged Danny, through the heavy main doors, down the stone steps and then off to wherever one's manic mind desires. Being sectioned made this freedom of movement difficult for a patient as you are then not allowed off the ward unless under the appropriate supervision; a horrible restrained situation that was not going to happen to me until three months later.

My parents were still both in attendance. They discussed various issues with the head duty nurse, issues that were shared with me too but were not exactly at the summit of my manic agenda. Along came "Mrs. Dracula" to extract the first of what was going to be many blood samples. These samples would be sent to the pathology laboratory where they would determine the cause, and then suggest an ongoing remedy for settling my supersonic behaviour. Medication compatibility had to be established, which involved checks for sugar levels (diabetes) and so on. In the meantime, there was still the unanswered question regarding my actual diagnosis. Experienced psychiatric doctors and nurses know when it's raining cats and dogs. They strongly suspected, even knew what my problem was, but they *had* to be sure. They also had to have a very accurate guide from which to calculate the effective dosage of lithium carbonate salts—a very light metallic compound that was to become my main mood stabilising medication. Sedatives and anti-psychotics were not prescribed to begin with. First of all they had to know exactly what they were dealing with and not make the mistake of diving in headfirst, as that might cause added mayhem and possible major setbacks. When one human being has the professional responsibility of another human being the prognosis has to be spot on, but the actual diagnosis must be perfect. This is how a psychiatric diagnoses takes shape: To begin with, the general practitioner or psychiatrist will assemble a case history. This can be done at the patient's own home or in a consulting room at the hospital or surgery. The doctor would then:

a.   Allow the patient to tell their own story by recounting the events throughout their life.
b.   Ask the patient what their reactions were to these events.
c.   Ask for a history of the patient's family health—both physically and mental.
d.   Ask if they have noticed any changes in their mood or behaviour.
e.   Ask them how they are feeling now.

These five questions will then aid the doctor or psychiatrist to establish, 1) Where the problems may have started, 2) How well the patient is able to cope with life, 3) If there is a history of similar illness in the family, 4) How long the illness has been affecting the patient, and 5) how serious the problem is at this very moment in time.

A physical examination including psychological tests and the taking of blood samples can help to determine exactly what the problem is. Now the professional can put all of the gathered information into a pot, mix it together and then hopefully serve up the correct name of the illness. If this has been done satisfactorily the professional can then advise the administration of the appropriate course of treatment.

A diagnostic manual is a kind of servicing manual for the medical profession. This D.S.M. or Diagnostic And Statistics Manual should be referred to for assistance in achieving the correct diagnosis. There is still no substitute for years of experience and of a thorough general knowledge of all aspects of medicine gained throughout many years of practice.

Dr. Kananara—he is a man of Indian origin and a sort of psychiatric Guru within the Hertfordshire, Bedfordshire and Buckinghamshire area of the United Kingdom—spent all of five minutes with me before nonchalantly dishing out a life changing diagnosis along with handfuls of pretty pills. He was not a man with whom I would care to spend the evening in a pub with, but he sure knew his psychological stuff all right. He had a business like style of working, no frills, just a get the job done approach that surprised me somewhat given the nature of his profession. Maybe because his workload was so immense, he had no time to indulge in irrelevant conversation. He was one of a large caring team that eventually helped me to sort myself out, no mean feat, and for that I am most sincerely and eternally grateful.

Very occasionally a patient receives an inappropriate medication that may even make them worse, but this is one of the hazards during the establishing process of what is and what is not agreeable. The reaction to other previously taken drugs can be put into the equation to minimise this rare occurrence. Most side effects to prescribed medication wear off within time. What works for one does *not* always work for the other, even if the symptoms and diagnosis are identical. The medical profession's personalised medication matching service manages to get it right pretty much all of the time, that is if they can keep hold of a patient like myself for long enough in order to administer the treatment.

With a couple of hugs that nearly squeezed out my entire air supply, and a handful of ten pence pieces for the patient's pay phone, I bid farewell to my loving and ever so concerned folks. Back to their Hemel Hempstead home they not so jolly well went, where I am sure a few stiff whiskies and brandy-shandy's were had, and who could blame them? Let's face facts, this was not exactly what you might call an average day, and it was not as if I had an average common cold either.

Exploratory investigation (being nosy) was the new name of my manic game. Wearing white training shoes, white jogging bottoms and my old baggy blue and white hoop T-shirt, I set off on a whistle stop tour of the hospital. Wherever I went I discovered new secretive doors and cubby holes. Sometimes the magic lay on the outside of a closure because then my imagination would fire up and run riot with white hot possibilities as to what may lay behind the door. They say that the journey is often so much more rewarding than the arrival. I would subscribe to that. I still wonder who *they* are, any ideas?

My noisy imagination desperately needed an acceptable outlet. There were art and crafts, singing and acting, writing poems, ditties and jokes, listening to music, woodwork and chatting with the other Hill End characters. I took to wildly running around the heart, and back through the belly of the old hospital. Anything at all that would prevent me from floating up and out to sea would suffice. Bottling up ideas, theories and solutions went against all I stood for. There had to be many separate explosive combustions to keep me moving along the straight and narrow maze of creamy green tunnels and out of the mouth watering selection of far sides. The mild wild and the shy, shuffled and strode through the shortening tunnel system, allowing me a more familiar smile with every new passing. The wallflowers remained wallflowers no matter how often I said, "Hello," and proved that I posed no dark threat to their safe, red Victorian bricked cotton wool cocoon. Some of the jumbly dressed rubbery faces were understandably wary of me, and then there were the others who had boundless energy and a tendency to be overly curious, a little bit too inquisitive for my liking, "Ooh, I like your shirt, where did ya get it eh eh? What's your name then eh, eh? Got a fag have ya eh, eh?" There were so many popular hangouts at Hill End Psychiatric Hospital. Locating various huddles of patients from day to day was like discovering where the fish were hiding in the lake. Some days there were plenty to catch and chat too, and on other days there wasn't even a bite. An exercise room was also made available to the patients, usually only for a few hours a week under staff supervision. I tried that room a few times but preferred to get my exercise or rather expel my energy by darting from A to Z, being my hyperactive self. The hospital clothing shop sold everything a patient could possibly need at greatly reduced prices. I thought that the clothing shop's giveaway prices were now solid proof of how the economy was always meant to be, with the abolishment of money waiting just around the corner. Most of the high quality garments on sale were stitched up skilfully in the same room by a cheerful gaggle of plump female dressmakers. Whenever I was passing the shop I would take a peek inside to see what was new, and also to share a joke or story with the ladies.

Hilarious renditions of popular tunes could sometimes be heard permeating through the lunch or dinner filled air, becoming louder and louder as the owner of the voice approached. After only a little while at Hill End I was able to tell who was around the many echoing bends, or who may be at my rear by their signature tune, an unmistakable collection of audibility, or by their inimitable styles of walking, whistling and infectious laughter. In some rare cases detection could be made by their smell, agreeably deodorised for most or disagreeably left to natures own devices for the few who had fallen prey to self neglect. I tried to embrace everybody for who they were, besides, who the hell was I to judge? Was I the newest nut on the psychological block, fighting against the inevitable crack? From time to time and without being at all pushy, the other patients would generously offer me their own rules and advice. In a place such as Hill End Psychiatric Hospital, or in any institution for that matter, all the advice one can absorb is so vital to assist in the day-to-day survival. Little approachable and avoidable tips regarding certain helpful characters, who to ask for what, the where's, the when's and the thousand and one how's, all need to be memorised as early as possible. Let's stay well clear of the why's, because at this stage in the proceedings who the hell cares.

Good hygiene was strongly encouraged. When I was sky high I rather liked people (except for Lee the slug) to have their own pleasant natural smell, enhanced perhaps with tobacco smoke and maybe even a slight hint of distinguishing body odour and morning breath. These aromas create an animalistic familiarity that really comes into its own when one is in the middle of a high episode. It is a reassuring thing. Ideally, total cleanliness is the only way to go. When coming down from the manic high chair I became short fused through my repulsion and disgust of other peoples self neglect, despite having let myself become rather unappetising when I was roaming wild on the streets of Milan. I could remember the smell of my father's damp hair from when I was a very small boy being held at the swimming baths or on a pebble beach, a pleasant aroma that was clearly accessible if I concentrated hard enough, such is the power and effect of our memory bank's stored senses upon the present day's heightened senses. The same thing applies to the other four senses. Having these tiptop condition tools at your disposal when riddled with mania is priceless. Before long my sense of smell balanced out and I could smell things for what they really were. I could see that almost everyone was extremely well groomed and not at all smelly. Visual suggestion also plays tricks with the mind, which is why so many top talents make a pretty good living out of performing grand illusionary stunts at places such as the Las Vegas Hilton and St. Albans Civic Centre.

Walking around in the big outside world wearing what we are told to wear by the marketing men, who delight in waving their colour calendar charts at us, is utterly bizarre. Actually believing what we are brainwashed to believe by newspapers, advertisements, dictators and certain dodgy politicians is in fact more absurd than some of the reasons why many mentally ill people are, or should I say used to be, herded into hospitals like mad cattle.

Being clean and reasonably tidy, even if you are attired somewhat comically, is probably one of the most important ingredients that there is in order to create a feeling of well being and self confidence. This can lead to the growth of richer relationships between every part of your own make-up, pulling each lost part back into a new found you. As I mentioned earlier, when I was severely depressed it became such an ordeal just to undergo a simple enough chore like washing myself. This is something each and every one of us (except Lee) has been doing since we were an infant. When undergoing depression, a colossal effort to shower or clean your teeth is needed from within. The concentration needed to complete each section of a basic task is in tiny fragments. These fragments need to be put together again by other human elements, determination and guts. When these other necessary elements have also been blown to ribbons you really are in the brown stuff, especially when one's coordination has decided to desert the sinking but *never* sunk ship, and everything that is attempted only results in making you feel like a small inexperienced and vulnerable, quivering tongue tied child—and that's on a good day! If personal hygiene is allowed to slip away like liquid soap down a hair clogged plug-hole, it will make you feel and look much worse than your magnifying mind is already telling you. There won't be many people who will want to have a great deal to do with you, because the stench will be unbearable (Just ask Lee the slug.)

Despite feeling rock bottom, there is always another low level of despair in which to sink if you allow yourself to. It hurts like hell to even attempt the basics. If attempted, even if not as successfully as you may have wished, you will have succeeded because you had a go, you will have become an effort maker, and other people give more time to effort makers. Having a go, being recognised as an effort maker in order to make an improvement in your life, as well as in somebody else's life, is *highly* admirable and an achievement to be mightily proud of. Slowly, after what can and probably will seem like forever, you will find that a knock-on effect starts to set in, building you back up to a place where you always belonged, and hopefully with lots of work and commonsense you will remain. Making no effort on your part will result in the demolition of your existence, and it will not do your loved ones any favours either—definitely *not* the way to go although even the worst situations are reversible. The worst scenario of course is when you try and try but the only place you reach is suicide city. I have paid a few fleeting visits as have millions of others. Many never came back. It is a cruel dark *bitch* of a place. For goodness sake, never give up! You are a very important human being! *You* are *never ever* alone, even when you are so mentally crippled you cannot and dare not even move your body, and God forbid the horrendous thought of facing a person other than your close caring companion—if you are fortunate enough to have one. You *will* have disasters on the way out of the shaft. Your rope *will* break and you may feel a thousand times worse than you did before. You *will* think of as many ways as you can in which to kill yourself, but you *can* beat it and you *shall* recover, I promise! Never mind the estimated two to four weeks kick-in and recovery dates for severe cases, optimistically forecast by well meaning general practitioners and by the notes in medication information leaflets. The drugs prescribed will kick-in during that time, but to begin with may only be noticeable within the milder cases of mania and depression. Keep taking them of course, it is imperative to do so, but dig in deep because the severest of depressions can go on for months and months, even years. There is no miracle quick fix to this thing. The truth from somebody who knows only too well what depression is all about should count for an awful lot. Never lose sight of the fact that it is going to be hell, but you *will* be well!

My next appointment with depression, a black poetic place, was not due for three fun months. During those three months at Hill End Psychiatric Hospital I learnt where everything was located, who almost everybody was, and why he or she were there. At the end of those three months I didn't want to go anywhere except out of the hospital, nor be with another person. My heart ticked along, but that was about as good as it got. The rapid transformation from high to low left me abandoned in space, watching life from a distance but unable to participate or touch in the same way that I had grown accustomed. Coming down from a high to an acceptable level of normality would feel like a terrific body blow. Sinking to the very bottom of the shit pit and then having to start again from scratch was the cruellest card dealt, and it was that card that my demons played as their hilarious joker, the rotten bastards. Despite all of that, it was always going to be me that had the last laugh.

When I arrived at Hill End I believed that the great sensitivities I had been experiencing were going to last forever and a day. How can the feeling of being so much on top of it all be so bad? Not a great deal was actually discussed about how it wasn't normal or acceptable behaviour to be carrying on in the way that I openly did. My rapid reasoning for feeling the way I felt remained on overtime. Newly concocted scenarios and living dreams rattled my inner skull, itching to have their say. I believed it to be true that I was some sort of phenomenon that had been brought into the hospital along with a mixed bag of unlikely candidates from Hemel Hempstead—many of whom were around the same age as me—to be studied, monitored and documented, as well as being prepared for the next mind blowing stage. Everybody had their jobs to do, their own reasons and their own purpose. This operation was to be conducted in surroundings that would keep the hatch tightly bolted on too many rash plans from to many inexperienced candidates. Final clearance to surface and let loose would be given when we were all properly primed. I sure was one sick, mixed up individual, but I had never been happier.

From admission to just after Christmas 1990, Hill End Psychiatric Hospital perfectly represented the special place in which the grandiose chosen few were to be groomed, ready to lead a revamped world full of goodness, love and never before seen powers. I believed that in order to be in this privileged position, each and every one of us would need to go through our own relevant initiation test, coming out the other side a little scratched but still intact, and much wiser for the bumpy ride. The staff were there to help our healing process, for they knew that by doing so they would benefit too. They would have the job of replacing the time and energies that had been sucked out of our decimated bodies during our pioneering existence in a changing world full of unexplored wavelengths. I for one felt that it was a case of replenishing myself with all that I had willingly given up and for all of the awful pain, both physically and mentally, that I had endured, despite demonstrating honesty, hard work, care and due consideration of my fellow human beings. Sounds a bit big headed does it? I was allowed to be a little swollen headed because I was manic, besides on a good day in the land of the normal I *am* all of those things. I can also be a stinking rotten bastard when I am pushed to the limit, can't we all?

During one of my many early travels in and around the hospital I stumbled across the chapel. I made a mental note that I must attend a Sunday service or two. The same manic thoughts that I had in Milano came rushing back to me again. Humankind had gone full circle and we were really all as one. Everybody who had previously existed are now condensed within us all. Surely that explains the similarity in physical features, the metamorphosis and the deja vu coincidences in the Milanese streets and in the hospitals, doesn't it? Recycled-Life-Forms-R Us sounds about right to me.

During that first evening on Anderson Ward I was introduced to Mavis, a big bosomed warm woman about fifty years young, who was to become my key-worker. She was somebody to whom I could turn to for any reason, and somebody who was supposed to assess my progress by visual observation on the ward and by means of regular informal conversations at one of the large circular tables in the dining room. Throughout my entire stay of nearly four months, I must have sat and spoke with Mavis on only two occasions. One of those occasions took place during the fourth month when I was so depressed there was hardly anything for my trembling lips to whisper. I guess she must have observed me from afar because more could be learnt about me that way, and that information would have been documented and relayed to the psychiatric team and other ward staff.

My very first Hill End meal lasted for all of thirty seconds. Now that I had rediscovered my appetite I cast my greedy eyes over the other patient's meals, hopeful for any leftovers. There were none, but there were some shrivelled sausages or a dollop of thick custard containing sliced bananas waiting at the kitchen serving hatch on a first come first served basis. This tiny little kitchen, from where a staff member would don an apron and dish up our food, contained a large refrigerator, an equally outsized cooker, tea making facilities and a long double sink and draining board where the unbreakable institutionalised green dishes and cups were washed up. This little kitchen had to be locked and unlocked by a member of the duty staff before and after mealtimes. All of the patients were included as part of a mealtime rotation system, taking it in turns to set the tables, clear the tables and wash-up and dry the dishes and cutlery. You can imagine the mess that was sometimes created by a nervous or frustrated patient, or of course by Jadranka whose food tended to often reappear for an unannounced encore. To me, the sheer range of abnormal behaviour was all part of the fascination, and I couldn't wait for the next instalment of unpredictable fun. If I had become a promoter who could sell tickets for this psychological show I would be a millionaire by now, but the audience would sometimes have to wait a long while for a single tame performance. When the mania fades from flaming orange to dappled grey, these external displays of internal disruption rapidly become unbearably huge annoyances.

Tom, a tall and dark, rather wolfish featured fellow, with whom I would later be sharing the same curtained cubicle, knew how to expertly pick the padlock on the refrigerator when he was on dishwashing/drying duty. He had all sorts of goodies out of that fridge including the staff's chocolate bars and fruit drinks. He never got caught in the act, and nobody squealed because we would help him gobble up the bounty. Tom, as it turned out, was very good indeed with his hands, picking locks, painting in the art therapy department, and under the sheets when it was lights out. I wouldn't have minded so much, but surely he could have been a touch more discreet when I moved in, and done his seedy deed with the volume turned down a bit. Tom had a vast collection of mucky magazines hidden away in an unsafe place where even Harold, an ancient fellow whom I nicknamed "God" could often be found crouching, probably fantasising that the Virgin Mary was the centrefold, complete with a staple through her Biblical belly button. God spent most of his time reading his broken Bible that had whole chapters slipping out and onto the floor midway through his uncalled for sermons. God quoted scriptures infuriatingly often, and with a tendency to alter the meanings to suit his present needs. Tom's sticky magazines were borrowed by most of Anderson Ward's male contingent at some time or another, especially by those who were a bit on the high side of life. It was to be a few days yet before I could be moved from the isolation room next to the nurses bay and be properly introduced to the grunts, groans and lingering smells of the compact men's dormitory.

Amazingly, despite my manic behaviour of talking too much and too fast, laughing at jokes that only I could see, dancing to the made up music in my head, clocking people with meaningful jerky movements of the head and so on,

I cannot recall receiving any medication that would help me through my first night at Hill End Psychiatric Hospital. If I had of been heavily sedated then I would probably never have tried, and succeeded, to walk the 12 miles back to Hemel Hempstead. Had I been heavily sedated as I was when I returned from Milan then I wouldn't have gone anywhere, that's for sure.

Laying back on my unsupported psychiatric hospital bed, packaged in a closet sized room, my mind began to fidget. I felt the overwhelming need to get out and complete my nagging maniacally contrived duties. Crumpled clothing and softer shoes were soon reunited with my itching back and sore feet. Now I was ready to be rid of the claustrophobic cream and green room, the very *last* place that a manic person who has been used to so much freedom should be holed up in! I quietly opened the door and stepped into the dimly lit dining room, trying carefully not to awaken the night duty staff. Slowly, I crept my eager body, fully charged of nervous energy, as quietly as a cat to the first set of heavy locked dormitory doors. I teed up the situation, stepped back a few paces and then took a run up, bursting open the doors with my first attempt at a left footed Kung-Fu style kick. With no time to waste and with the strength of an ox, as well as the dogged determination of a spawning salmon, I repeated the move with ease on the next locked barricade. I jumped down the cold stone steps and then left into the creamy green passageway. This route took me straight to the main central corridor which then right turned me directly toward the hospital's grand main entrance. "This has got to look good," I thought with my movie head on and running. I proceeded to sprint the entire length of the corridor, passing the locked main function hall on my right, only slowing to open a set of floppy rubberised swing doors. These storeroom type of doors had partially obscured my makeshift one hundred metres running track. This "track" had briefly transported me back to an athletics meeting in which I represented the Cavendish School at the next Olympic games, running alongside Linford and Lewis and many more fond faces that flashed round and round my speeding head. This was rapidly becoming a quick tempo marathon without a foreseeable finish but with a thousand starting line ups. The field events would come later. The hospital library blurred to my left, followed by the final push that took me into the cigarette butt-holed main entrance hall where a night security guard usually sat in his little cubicle. I didn't hang around long enough to discover whether or not the duty guard was awake or asleep, I just shot myself through the insecure main entrance doors and out into the chilly moonlit night. St. Albans City centre was not unfamiliar territory to me because I used to attend its superb engineering college on a day release basis from Rolls Royce Ltd. Rock concerts at the civic centre and visits to nearly every public house were still fresh and fond memories. The trouble was that I hadn't got a clue where I was in relation to these useful land-marks. For some odd reason I always found it harder to find my bearings and navigate through the daze when I was high. This is probably due to an inability to stop, focus and evaluate the situation piece by piece. A lack of dedicated concentration and a shortening attention span must be held accountable for so many of the scrapes that I have put myself through during bouts of fully blown, racing away mania. Even self explanatory street signs can be guaranteed to set my head in a whirl when I'm running about town like a lost lunatic.

By pushing myself hard I finally made it to familiar open territory. The bright lights of the high street recaptured a similar feeling that I had felt strongly in Milan. It hit me like a sudden fix of a drug. I had fallen upon a colourful film set of a vibrant town, so old looking yet so new, bright and alive. Every molecule in my body breathed in a glorious spirit that took great joy in playing impossible games. These games are only won with practice and persistence, and only if one's attention span can hold out for an immeasurable stretch of time. I continued to run and run, leaving behind the Peacock public house and the White Hart Inn. My overworked heart threatened to burst through my chest, but I told my manic self that if I kept going that extra little bit and endure that extra drop of burning pain, then it will be less of a weight for mankind to carry around in the future. Whatever I did would reflect favourably upon the others, all of whom I was certain could see me, and would interpret my cheaply produced display. A tricky to grasp form of unnecessarily confused cryptic symbolism was all that I had to offer. The crazy thing was that quite often I had about as much idea why I was projecting myself in this way as the next man, woman or child. Of course, there are plenty of times when I didn't have to justify my manic behaviour to myself or to anybody else, allowing the mind, the body, and the spirit to enjoy an unparalleled party—a jolly good knees-up after twenty-five years of taking this forever precious life of ours perhaps just that little bit too seriously. I can now understand the freedom that bare bottomed naturists claim to gain under the hot Sun, or that the rock performer up on an electric stage generates to so many hungry ears through the scream, twang and blow of a gutsy voice, string and horn. Refreshing expression kills my depression.

Where were the posse? My psychiatric search party never materialised, nor did any police cars. Escaping patients were probably a common occurrence, especially the first night manic variety. Maylands Avenue, the main road running through Hemel Hempstead's industrial estate, looked me in the eye with its mouth wide open. My view from the far side of Leverstock Green roundabout sent my mind into overdrive. I felt as if cable and satellite television had been installed in my mind and every channel was switched on. I crossed the large circle—a pivotal cog for the long haul juggernauts coming off and onto the M1 motorway—and stepped onto the tarmac tongue that I knew so well. Midway along Maylands Avenue I took a left turn and trotted down the neck of Adeyfield toward the heart of Hemel Hempstead. Another gentle trot alongside the river Gade, through the majestic Gadebridge Park, over the white iron bridge and there I was, on the doorstep of my parent's house. I had no key for my maisonette in Bovingdon, otherwise I would have gone straight there. Wearing a crazed grin, and in total belief that they would be overjoyed to see me standing on the doorstep, I pressed the doorbell. Like hell they were. Well, my poor Mother nearly had kittens, and my father had me back inside Hill End (very low security) Psychiatric Hospital in less time than it takes a nightingales egg to boil. On the surface my old man looked as if he took my temporary upset in his stride, although it must have been very difficult to witness the fruit of his loins in a banana like condition, on a psychedelic stall full of soft plums and hardened coconuts.

Heavy scales needed to be adjusted with fine precision in order to evenly balance my moods and eliminate excessive one sidedness. The levelling of my mind and mood didn't happen over night, especially not during that first long distance night spent in, then out, and all about happy hotel Hill End. Nothing more than a brief explanation of the nights events were called for, enabling Hill End Psychiatric Hospital to settle back down into an orderly mess of minds that matter a great deal. Being the first one out of bed meant that I would be the first one washed, dressed and playing myself at three-quarter size snooker—a sleep deprived manic pattern that stuck for the next three months.

Vitiligo, the skin condition in which a partial or total loss of pigment causes a patch of skin to whiten albino style, has been present since I was a little boy, lessening as I aged. One such patch about the size of moth eaten postage stamp has always been present and incorrect upon the right hand side of my chin, and had now sprouted white bristles in sharp contrast to the tufty bush of beard that clung on to the rest of my drawn face. That beard, the first one that I have ever grown, looked ghastly on me even though all of us males are naturally meant to have one. My face, I have since been told, had always looked a little younger than my years, and as a consequence my stubble grew to resemble something from a joke shop. Me? Well I loved it didn't I. It was a novelty, despite suggestions from the male members of staff that I at least gave it a trim, tidy it up a little, but for the time being I was adamant about sticking with it. I stuck to my guns and continued with my unconvincing Grizzly Adams impression for another itchy week.

The many smokers on Anderson Ward, myself included, would stagger gowned and bleary eyed to one of the dining room or smaller snooker room tables at around 7 a.m. to suck in their first dose of a daily nicotine diet. The rooms gradually filled with a combination of tobacco preferences, and lungs were filled with enough high and low tar to resurface the car park just outside the main entrance. A member of the night staff would fetch the huge ring of keys and open the kitchen door. Two of the night staff would set about producing a huge pot of strong steaming tea for us early birds. I became a regular fixture, the first fixture of that early morning smoking club. My nicotine intake came from either Golden Virginia or Old Holborn tobacco, hand rolled in green, red or occasionally liquorice Rizla or Swan papers. We would all smoke whatever came our way of course, but those were my two personal preferences. The early hours of the morning were also spent reassuring myself that the heightened sensations, treats and manic tricks were still well and truly there, operating just as well, if not better than they did the previous day. I breathed a euphoric sigh of relief every morning when I knew that I was not living in a dream. I guess I *was* really full of insubstantial manic dreams and schemes, but the feeling they exuded provided me with a real and sexy fix, electrifyingly addictive and intact. When tiny seeds of doubt were shed they would sometimes plant themselves against my will, becoming a sort of mental vine, creeping everywhere they were not wanted, attempting to loosen the foundations upon which my manic trip was founded.

It didn't matter how crack-brained my activities of choice appeared to be, just so long as there was at least an element, a hint of an organised pattern streaking its way through the centre of them. My routines changed on a whim of manic fancy. Creative surges often backfired, causing all of my preset internal mechanisms to go haywire, resetting my dizzy dials to a brief demoralizing zero. I did feel a strong sense of structure, shrouded by a wall of security. I was never as all over the place as I may have appeared to an onlooker. The trouble in building with loose manic bricks alone is that they can tumble and crash, so I had to feed my busy mind with as much manic mortar as I possibly could in order to prevent my whole world from falling apart. When I was at school there used to be one ground level classroom, used mostly for mathematics, computer studies and after school detentions. The adjacent football field meant that this particular room had one smashed window after another. The school caretaker had no worries when it came to his job security, as there was always a new pane to be put in and sealed with gooey grey putty. That putty was picked off by the pupils to be used as missiles or modelling material, leaving the newly installed window wide open to further abuse. The pattern would keep on repeating itself. I had become that open and closed window, cracked then shattered, forever being willingly picked at while reinstalling my backup at the very same time. It was damn hard work but somebody had to do it.

My early morning routine, following tea, chat, roll-up and snooker, moved on to the washrooms. This steamy area became my manic recording studio because the quality of sound was second to none, or so I convinced myself. Of course I had to spend a few minutes vainly combing and brushing my hair into what I believed was a cool performing style before taking to my stage. I looked nothing like a rock or pop star, just a hairy faced blockhead with the occasional cleverly constructed lyric. The power of a manic mind in full vocal swing is something not to be underestimated or meddled with. My screeching and wailing could be heard in the lounge and dining room. My reworded interpretations of rock and pop songs were strongly laced with personal turmoil, and a deeply meaningful expression of a special belief and knowledge. They offered everything and sought it back in the same breath.

It didn't take long before my bathroom recording sessions were being played live on the regular radio airwaves as well as on worldwide telepathetic television. This was all done with an automatic efficiency by those who themselves were high up the ladder of special knowledge. It got to the stage where I thought I could pick and choose established artists to perform my songs, and that I was the only one, as I mentioned when in Milan, that was unable to catch an image of myself on television or in print, but became instantly available to anybody else in any chosen medium. I had a quick answer and a chirpy song for everything, often full of contradiction but satisfyingly fitting for that particular time or occasion. It sounds like a dictatorship doesn't it, and that I was a power obsessed megalomaniac, when the truth of the matter is that I wanted us all to remain exactly as we are. The only change I am sure we would all like to see is for us all to simply get on better with one another. It would also be nice if we ceased stripping Mother Earth naked, and instead start to give back *all* that we owe her, plus interest. My routine before breakfast had enough content to last a regular person for the entire day and a severely depressed person a whole year.

The bathroom housed three white cast iron bathtubs, divided by a plastic curtain if required. The tubs were in a locked room of their own at the far end of the washroom, and had to be opened on request by a nurse. Ursula the Scandinavian nurse declined my bubbly invitations to come inside, lock the door, and give me an all over scrub. My poor feet were used as an unattractive lure, trying to secure the sympathy vote, but Ursula was far too wise to fall for that load of old cobblers, and she most definitely was *not* a scrubber. It didn't take me very long to develop a ritualistic method of bathing. First of all I would rotate the entire length of my self abused carcass through 360 eye stinging degrees, becoming fully submerged in the sloppy process. That would be followed by another soapy rotation in the opposite direction. My movements had me believing that I was actually sending myself to every part of the world, facing mankind in every conceivable direction. As if thought messaging and telepathetic television were not enough, I would close my eyes under the bath water and see images of people young and old, sharing their different nationalities, beautiful abnormalities, refreshingly different religions, their political and cultural beliefs and so on. Yes indeed, I had my work cut out during those early morning bathtub sessions on Anderson Ward. When my periscope came up for air I resumed my singing in the same vain, until my heart was content and my lungs were close to bursting. What glorious fun I had in my manic bubble.

Although I had been formally interviewed and assessed, I still hadn't been told officially that I did in fact have a bipolar affective disorder. The assessment period and blood test results from the pathology laboratory at St. Albans City Hospital took a few observant days before a precise evaluation of my condition could be announced, along with the maiden formula to begin tackling it. When I was eventually presented with my M.D. or B.A.D. label it meant nothing to me at all, because I felt so high and miles above all of that made up medical drivel. Mine was a concocted illness, tagged on to me so that it would teach the up and coming special people all about what's to come in the not too distant future. On many occasions I turned the whole nurse/doctor/patient arrangement around so that we the patients, the first crop of a mankind's elite, were really on top of it all, and that the professionals who knew less but still so much more than they would ever dare to let on, were taking care of the fine tuning. Without question I believed that we the patients were teaching the doctors and nurses about this newfound spiritually assisted giddy level, and that we were all in disguise, myself as a manic-depressive and they as plain clothed psychiatric doctors and Scandinavian non-scrub nurses.

Allow me to take you back to the men's washroom where a large washing machine and an equally huge tumble dryer were kept. Except for weekend leave there could always be found crouching by the machines, or pacing caged tiger like around the damp bathroom, a certain Jimmy Swann. You could count on Jimmy to flood the place every single day, awash with gallons of warm water and detergent suds. Jim spent hours and hours washing over and over again his same small bundle of clothes. He obviously had a big thing about cleanliness. Why he had to open the bloody washing machine door every time and flood the place beats me, but he sure made us all laugh with his lanky gangling frame and his deep slow drawl, standing in a bubble lake with a frilly apron tied tightly around his skinny waist. Jim also had a penchant for flying out of his second floor apartment window, as his now permanently deformed right wrist bears testament. Flinging oneself out of windows is *not* recommended, even if you are fully blown away with mania or desperately suicidal. Jim suffered from schizophrenia. About a year on from Hill End I drove Jim to Stoke Mandeville Hospital in Buckinghamshire so that he could have one of many operations to fix his limp wrist. Recently a reliable source informed me that Jim had been admitted to the psychiatric ward at St. Albans City Hospital, still daft as a brush and probably covered from head to foot in soap bubbles. Jimmy never really made much of an effort to help himself, and sadly looks as if he will spend the rest of his priceless life in and out of psychiatric facilities, wasting a little bit too much of his and everybody else's valuable time. I hope I am wrong, I really do.

Four grand mini mansions stood within view from Anderson Ward's tall and tough windows. They looked very much like disused houses but were in fact the hospital's old offices and clinics, now left to rot in peace. The local wildlife that inhabited the surrounding landscape were provided with a luxurious second home, built to last on land that was once wisely used therapeutically by the inmates of an overcrowded hospital, to grow the organic fruit and vegetables that helped toward quelling the ravenous appetites of the hungry hospitalised hordes. What was left over would be sold for a pittance to the local residents, generating money that would be ploughed straight back into the system. I took quite an unnatural shine to "Keats house" (named after the poet) that stood directly opposite Anderson Ward. This derelict pile of vandalised rubble became a very special place for me to go and contemplate my manic thoughts, and to dream up even more to put in the bone-bank, accruing interest in steady readiness for withdrawal come rain or shine, night or day. The old rundown Keats building added so much pleasurable and saddening significance to my entire Hill End experience. It was a place where I would go to laugh hysterically and cry with as much passion. Too many supposedly sane people in irresponsible positions of power were at around this time planning to bomb the living daylights out of each other in the Middle East. The Gulf War of leadership incompetence was about to kick off, causing the slaughter of too many men, women and children, never mind the long-term destruction that such idiocy brings to the families of the deceased. As soon as a valuable lesson has been learned it seems that the devil lusts even more for ill feeling and mass self-destruction. Many occupants of mental institutions and visitors to their general practitioners are temporarily brought to their depressed knees, losing control through utter disillusionment, helplessness and fear of the real madmen of this world, the so called leaders that too many scared sheep follow. Those who have fought and died, are still fighting or are on standby to protect the freedom of a hard working democratic society have my utmost respect; it is the top brass who seriously need to get their combined acts together. Enough of the party political broadcasts.

Temporary derangement is available free of charge. Often it is a whole lot more than just an imbalance of chemicals or an excessive indulgence of the trigger of choice. State of society often reflects the state of mind. Even today I occasionally hanker for the Hill End high. I crave the truth of the helpless and innocent who were often the possesors of a greater freedom than the assortment of sweet and sour ruthless individuals roaming the streets, or looking after the subdivisions of Planet Earth.

Keats house became the special place where I would retreat and contemplate over the goings on inside my head and all around me. I convinced myself that this dilapidated building was soon going to be expertly converted into my new dream home by expert construction workers and decorators. I even fancied myself as an architect, so I drew up a revamped set of plans that put my three years of technical teenage drawing to shame. There were many times when I felt the magnetic pull of Keats, always resulting in an easy break-in. The upstairs had become a death trap through neglect, and also through disrespectful attention by a bunch of local youths. Large areas of missing floor meant that I had to spider around on my toes, trying to avoid gaping holes and rotten old floorboards. Night visits were made all the more difficult, although I relished the challenge. On one of the exterior window ledges sat an old stainless steel dinner knife and fork that somebody had stolen from one of the kitchens, and in a nearby bush I found a little three legged wooden stool that would have been ideal for milking purposes, but for me it became a gift from an imaginary admirer. These items I carefully placed at the foot of the big red door at the rear of the building. Inappropriate importance was given to meaningless items and my unusual actions, thanks to a very personal and symbolic culmination of a thousand eruptive emotions that were continually scalding my brain. My right index finger pressed into the layers of dirt on the door face and wrote No.11. When the wheels are rolling the manic person does anything, I mean *anything* to stay on top of the situation. They are ready and eager for the next helping of delights and delectations that the mind attempts to foresee around every corner and through every blank wall. The dagger demons are always out to trample on a good thing. Goodwill always prevails, no matter what. Belief in what is good and right will conquer an army of disbelieving party poopers, although it tests every ounce of self-will and fluctuating faith. The manic person person never gives in, despite adversity and ridicule. They have had a taster, and so they can firmly sense and confidently know what is to be found on the bright side of the door.

Not a single thing that I saw or touched declined the opportunity to delight and satisfy me. Gobbledegook messages that once stood in my way were now, to my insatiable satisfaction, solvable. The wind, the trees and the reliability of familiar ground indicated to me the right paths to follow, and those that should be avoided like the plague. I felt as if I was building up a greater rapport with Mother Earth, Heaven, and even with hell. The swirling burning tip of my smokes evoked a primitiveness within me, making me want to dance and deliver myself and my whacky manic messages in any way that I could. Flicked ash fell to the ground, and so I immediately put two and two together and thought of rebirth, and all that such a miracle entails. Everything seemed to fit perfectly, despite the often preposterous content. Telepathetic remote control had its teething troubles, but I didn't take too long to tweak my way into whatever or whoever I desired. Life was more than adequate.

What baffled me the most was the discovery of a sorry looking letter, and an old packet of green Rizla cigarette papers that clearly had 2np (Two new pence) printed on it. Naturally I looked upon the letter as being a sign from God knows who, carefully placed when I wasn't door hanging around the rear of Keats house. The ink had smudged in the damp early air and light rain. This slippery letter was placed on top of the little stool next to the big red door. All throughout my stay at Hill End Psychiatric Hospital I visited Keats house religiously, sometimes bringing gifts or offerings that I placed in a perfect position by the big red door. The doorway became a kind of shrine to whatever or whoever I had decided that day to be most in favour, or should I say most in tune with my latest manic theory or whimsical dream. Much later when I was into my fourth month at the now not quite so happy Hill End, I took a heavily burdened walk back to my dream house and saw it for what it really was; a crumbling heap of miserable shite. I had seen the old house through shiny manic eyes and through rose tinted spectacles. The tint had tainted. I felt myself progressively losing the shreds of dignity and control that still remained in my emotionally scarred and severely dented tank. I broke down and cried like a spoilt baby. My grubby offerings, some of them made to the recurring Ju and my imaginary son Samuel, had been broken and ripped, slashed and torn by local numskulls. My colour and life had washed away like the ink from my letter, never to make sense of anything again. I healed in time, but I wanted to kill the dogs who posed as guardian angels, kill the culprits and rub their noses in the shit that I was now having to wade through. Of course I knew perfectly well that if I followed up with that course of action it would only result in the deepening of my already impossible quicksand. I didn't have the strength both physically and mentally to carry out my revengeful tomfoolery, so off I went to wallow in a new phase of mind gagging. That is the trouble with depression; the mind thinks distortedly and negatively yes, but just like mania it is relentless in its hot pursuit of the two extremes, it just doesn't let up. Let me guide you through the many aspects of depression later and return now to the opening bars of my Hill End manic melody.

So much useful information needed to be crammed between my ears during those first few days, and me being me wanted to know it all yesterday. A young eighteen year old girl called Jenny took me by the hand and led me through uncharted creamy green territory to the art therapy room, so that I could have a good look around and meet a few new faces. That was followed by a short consultation with one of the two art therapists in order to organise my three times weekly indulgence. Art therapy had to be the most beneficial and fun activity that I ever got myself involved with in that now extinct place. At my disposal were as many mediums that one could possibly wish for, plus a few of my own: blood, hair, earwax, dead skin, pubic hair, snot and saliva. I seriously considered using small quantities of my faeces and urine to give my creations a certain earthiness, but I drew the line at that idea after considering the distinctive smell that would emanate from the card or paper. Warhol used to get people to urinate all over broad sheets of oxidized paper at his New York "factory" and pass off the results as "piss-painting"—taking the piss-painting is a better description, but why not? After all, who is it that lays down the rules and sets the boundaries of acceptability for artists, that if crossed are ridiculed and shunned and then years later are hailed as being brave and bold innovators? If one likes something then it is good and right, if they do not then it is wrong, but only to them. You pay your money, you make your choice. We all look at the same things with different eyes. Stick with what one thinks is right and happiness will follow. Be a feeble follower who has another to think your life for you, and you will end up full of regret with no turning back. I would prefer to go out of this world with no regrets, even if in other peoples fault finding eyes I did make a complete idiot of myself on the way.

Nail clippings also clawed their way into some of my collages. In art therapy I was given carte blanche to let it all hang out and throw it all down. What a relief it was to indulge in a concentrated period of colourful mind clearance. Sometimes the sessions were frustratingly intertwined with total chaos, full of mathematical colour and endless unfinished possibilities. I worked very fast so that I could release my mental clutter, extinguish the past demons, and fire up the future manic melting pot in one fell swoop swish and dab. I strived to make my work as universally accessible and available as possible, but by doing that I only succeeded in creating a deeper land, filled with even more fun, fear and confusion. Much of my work hit the spots of my fellow artists, but most of it went right over their heads. It was frustrating at times when my artistic messages never received the recognition that I had hoped for, but I suppose the same can be said of myself trying to make something of a fellow artists work, but that's the magic of art therapy. We all did our best, and you can't do better than that! Everything always finds its opposite and equal solutions. Simple artistic solutions were arrived at on the other side of a beautiful shambles. I discovered inside that sunlit art therapy room that life is only as complicated as one makes it, and that simplicity is usually the best way to go. Funny isn't it how the village idiot is the only one to have a permanent smile on his face.

Jenny then directed me through the hospital's very full belly, cutting across the heart and along a meandering tunnel, home to a wonderful echo. We passed the busy internal printing works that were occupied by some of the more willing longer term patients, all of whom were doing their best to help produce a selection of seasonal offerings such as Christmas cards and calendars. These would then be sold in the small hospital shop and also at a few generous locations on the outside of the hospital, so that a little money could be raised for the hospital funds to purchase a few extra straight jackets or some replacement stuffing for the padded cells—only kidding, although there were provisions for such disturbing eventualities within the hospital. I never once set foot inside the print shop, despite my insatiable appetite for all things new. The same oddly interesting people were always there doing their own thing to the best of their abilities, giving off a cheeky aura that instilled in me a strong impression that hidden beneath some of the malleable masks were super intelligent human beings, whose combined minds fought major distressing battles to be heard and understood. They were a stuck-in-the-mud minority that often sadly seemed to come across as being one big happy marriage, made in a warped heaven full of sick surprise and magical wonderment.

Never judge a freshly printed book by its smudged cover. Despite desperately wanting to believe that my super-brain intelligence theory was intact, I had to hold my small hands up and concede that although most of the longer term patients inside the hospital were extraordinary talented in a particular area, a sizeable minority were still severely lacking in the brain cell department. Maybe they were mentally handicapped from birth, or permanently disabled at a later stage in their life. But life it still is, and priceless at that.

Those of us who were residing on Anderson and Drake Wards, plus a large contingent from the other wards were mentally ill and *not* mentally disabled. We had the equivalent of a repairable broken leg compared to a paralysing broken backbone. One of the major qualities that almost every character residing at the hospital had was kindness itching to get out, and a vulnerable soul desperate to be loved. We all want to be loved, but some of us are more sensitive when the staple diet of emotion is laid on the Formica table. Aggression is sometimes nothing more than a last resort, desperate cry for love and attention. Some people are simply nasty bastards and that is all there is to it, but even they have to be respected, understood and forgiven for what they are and for what they might have done. The way in which each and every one of us is made up is out of our hands, and thank God high up above and all around us that we *are* all so different. When another Brother or Sister who is down on themselves tries to adjust and adapt from what may not have been such a pleasant image to a wholesome and agreeable person, they should be tolerated and embraced more, despite the genes saying that they are meant to remain pretty much the same as before. Acceptance of oneself goes an awfully long way to achieving personal happiness and acceptance of others, but some effort is continually needed to achieve that contentment, especially in social situations. I have wasted so much time trying to be something that I am not, instead becoming miserable with what I am. What I should have done is make the best of what I have got. So long as my heart is beating then I am the luckiest man in the world. The less we need the richer we are. Counting our blessings and *not* our inches or missed boats will bring a weak battery back to life every time, to shock and surprise ourselves into realising what a dumb waste the pessimistic alternative had been. Now that doesn't sound too bad does it? It is all about the most basic mathematics of life.

Refreshing child like honesty was in abundance, although if mixed with too much innocence it most probably will result in unscrupulous advantage taking by the well practiced in the fine art of screwing another person for all they are worth. Advantages taken consist of personal belongings, including money, right through to what can only be described as an untidy form of mild slavery, where the crackpot boss whips up the weaknesses of the vulnerable to make them do all manner of degrading tasks. I have heard some of those whips crack a little bit too loudly and for far too long, causing the animal in us all to also crack and then attempt to bite the head off the perpetrator's slim shoulders.

For no reason whatsoever, sweet smelling Jenny and myself cobbled together a few impromptu dance steps and sang a few harmless songs (common behaviour in a psychiatric facility.) A few metres on from the printing empire we twisted to the left and boogied on down the next twenty metres or so, passing the large windows of an unkempt courtyard until we arrived at an exterior door on the left. This door led us briefly outside into the cool shadowed air. Only a hop, skip and a jump brought us to yet another door. We stepped into a large cosy looking baked bean tin that had been thoughtfully decked out in brightly coloured fabrics. Cushions, rugs and blankets were strewn therapeutically across the floor, and works of art that had been commandeered from our arty first port of call adorned the galvanised curvature. Warmth emanated not only from the archaic radiators, but also from the bubbly buxom therapist who was ready and eager to sign up her latest recruit. Aromatherapy candles and oils created the required ambiance in readiness for the next group of ten patients. It was a couple of weeks later in this very same Second World War Nissen hut that I was encouraged to relax in a controlled fashion on the plush carpeted floor, before being transported mystically away by the intoxicating taped sound of rolling rapids and the Amazon jungle. After the informal introductions my new relaxation therapist handed me my schedule and then proceeded to explain very clearly the benefits of letting oneself sink into a state of total relaxation from time to time, especially when everyday things start to get on top of you. I looked upon myself as being a bit of an authority on letting myself go, especially over the top, but it soon became clear that this new definition was intended to dampen the raging fire within my uncontrollable manic existence, allowing my highly revved body the chance to slow down and breathe more easily. All said and done, Jenny and I returned to Anderson ward, taking an alternative route so that I could familiarise myself with Hotel Hill End a little more. During those early days I felt that the corridors were alike, and that they were misleading in their length. The girth of the hospital seemed to extend further than the great wall of China, but once I had made two or three sore footed exploratory sorties everything suddenly clicked into place, bringing A and Z closer together.

Jenny always carried an assortment of tiny furry toys. They went everywhere with her, poking out of every conceivable place. I found out about two months later that she was deeply traumatised because her own father had sexually abused her when she was a little girl. The poor thing had never properly overcome the terror of her ordeals, so she was really looking at a deeply scarred case of damage limitation. It was a little later when I was in art therapy, firing manic paint here, there and everywhere and behaving totally bonkers with my brushes, that she came over and opened her painful young heart. It was a brave and positive move that only weeks of building up a trust in me would allow. Manic I may have been, but sympathetic ears I still had. I knew when to shut up and listen, then attempt to offer support in any way possible. Just supplying an ear to bend and a shoulder to cry on can be all that the other person has desperately been yearning for. Treading on eggshells is pointless, and the responsibility for a backfiring well intentioned piece of asked for advice has to land in the court of the recipient. Being honest sometimes hurts, but when one has been battered emotionally that honesty must still be given if requested. When the entire tear stained laundry has been dealt with it can be put to bed and a fresh future can be looked forward to. Do *not* let another steal a part of you, they have no right. How dare they determine your life, your destiny and your happiness. Believe me, when you bounce back you will survive and live for No. 1 first and foremost, without anyone getting in your way. Each and every single one of us *shall* rise up to wherever we belong and be counted not as a problematic quirk of nature, but as the special and unique beings that we are. Not in a nasty way we have the God given right to say, "Knickers to you buddy, I come first," because if you do not look after and respect yourself first and foremost, then who the hell else in their right mind will?

Jenny was terribly upset, so by using her brief description I painted a very quick portrait of the sick beast in question. A squirt of white on black paper, a flick of the brush and a deep gut feeling is all that it took. Eerily, the finished painting resembled the Yorkshire Ripper. Our agreed game plan was to hang this creepy picture on the wall next to the mini kitchenette. Whenever she, myself or anybody else that we invited fancied having a go, the image would be spat at, slapped or have something hurled at it. Jenny often let loose her previously corked emotions until the creepy image had been annihilated. At the completion of every exorcism, Jenny would slump into my arms, all cried out. Despite having added a new self-help tool to bolster her defences and to attack her demons she still, with her young head bent downward in a way that belied her tender years, carried her toys and an undeserved burden of sadness.

After two nights of relative peace I was back up to my old manic games. I felt the urge to break out and make my way back to Hemel Hempstead again, only this time there was a marked difference in my method of movement. On this occasion I spent half of the journey trotting and walking, sideways and backwards. If a vehicle passed I would gesticulate my arms or head in any jerky spasmodic direction in the belief that a message—all of which had a perfectly feasible meaning at the time—would automatically be transmitted to the driver or passengers telling them nonsensical rubbish like, "I'm perfectly okay, thanks for checking though. Keep on driving and we can meet later perhaps for a beer."

My mania had me believe that they were tapping into my thoughts. I obviously invented their replies, but it was of course only my mania talking to itself. The conviction I had that my progression was being filmed by mental telepathetic TV and relayed by people on streets to the television sets and radios of this world still held strong. The resulting movie by comparison would make *Gone With The Wind* look like a commercial for smoke alarms or anti-flatulence pills. I must have looked like a complete fully fledged fool that the good folk of St. Albans had grown accustomed to spotting wandering around town in the dark. I made it to Hemel again. In no time at all I was driven back to Anderson Ward in time for a round the world bath and a recording session, some breakfast and a game of three-quarter snooker. Once again my feet hurt terribly, but by now I was so used to pushing myself and dealing with the inherent pain that I didn't really care. That evening I had to swallow a cocktail of pills and potions that were intended to put me on the road to a good night sleep and not on the road back to Hemel Hempstead.

The day finally arrived for me to be presented with the news that I was indeed suffering from the grand title of manic-depressive illness, or as it is more commonly known these days, bipolar affective disorder. To be perfectly honest I could have been told that I had leprosy, it didn't make the slightest dent in my manic armour. I went along with any rewritten script that I threw at myself. It all seemed to be such good fun and just another part of the major crack known only to special knowledge holders. I had become the mental health "act," and I believed that my counterparts were filling the supporting roles. I knew what manic depression was, but still believed that I was as fit as a fiddle upstairs in my head, and that the lithium and other anti-psychotic drugs that were being administered like sugar candy from the medication trolley were nothing more than harmless ineffective placebos. My job was to keep taking them without fuss in order to set a good example to the non-believing stragglers, and also to the patients who really did need them. Of course I needed my carefully prescribed drugs so desperately, but I didn't entertain that vital fact for a single second. It took me a couple of weeks to figure out and get a firm handle on who could also be on the same high frequency as myself. This task was best undertaken not by a verbal volley but by using coded bodily movements such as a flick of the wrist or a swish of the head. Secret signalling back and forth indicated accurately in my shallow pond who was in, who was without a clue, and who was still undergoing the process of being stretched to all four corners of existence. How could I lose when I dealt the hands that I needed to win? No way could I fail in my manic quest, or could I? It may well have been that I was just trying to make up for everything that I have ever wanted to believe, and then try to live those ideal fantasies out as best that I could within the confines of the hospital. Mania was my ticket that presented me with an excuse to run a peaceful and clean riot with the assistance of the other placebo junkies, all of them barking up the wrong trees, straining to hear the high frequencies that only scabby cats and scruffy dogs can truly absorb.

1200mg of lithium carbonate salts had to be taken daily to begin with. It was going to take up to three weeks of monitoring by means of visual and verbal observation and regular blood tests. It was imperative to achieve as soon as possible an acceptable healthy level of lithium in my bloodstream. Ever since the 1940's lithium has been used widespread in the treatment of manic-depressive illness. Lithium salts decrease the intensity and frequency of the episodic swings from extreme excitement to deep depression and needs to be monitored regularly. As blood lithium levels are affected by the amounts of sodium in the body it is wise not to increase or decrease the amount of salt in one's diet. Plenty of water and ideally no form of alcohol should be drunk when taking lithium. Lithium carbonate happens to be one of the cheaper drugs, which is great news if you happen to live in the United States of America where medical insurance and the cost of prescribed medication can be ridiculously expensive. The stress and worry caused by the exorbitant costs of remaining healthy in the United States probably accounts for so much depression, heart problems and so many other stress related illnesses. It does *not* make any sense at all. The insurance companies should stop bleeding people dry for very little in return—it is nothing short of criminal!

Chlorpromazine, an anti-psychotic drug that causes drowsiness was next on the menu. This drug possesses a tranquillising effect that calms down periods of mania, aggression and other abnormal and unsociable behaviour. What did succeed in shutting me up for a few hours at night? Temazepam. Temazepam is a bendzodiazepine; a common class of sleeping drug because they have very few adverse effects. This I took in a green liquid form. When I took it I would have to make sure that I was already in my pyjamas and then dash into the men's dormitory before it kicked in, collapsing me onto the bag of springs below. Within two heavy lidded minutes I would be out for the count. The chlorpromazine/temazepam combination produces extra sedation. I was so hyper, so manic, the nurses must have given me enough of the stuff to fell a Japanese Sumo wrestler, but I was still wide awake in the middle of the night. Waking up in the early hours became so frustrating because I could not get up and do anything in fear of waking the other patients and the night duty staff. As soon as I had been moved into the dormitory the rabbit in me ceased. No more gallivanting off to Hemel.

My previous rabbit hutch of a room had been adorned with a diversity of blue-tacked pictures ripped out of the magazines and newspapers that I had found abandoned on the ward. To me these pictures represented far more than pretty images, they meant something deeply personal and searching, displaying to whoever may have poked their curious nose in the room an amusing array of obsessive complexity that I was trying desperately to relay, without actually using forthright speech. Perhaps I was too scared to speak out aloud of what was really going on in my mind, as I was subconsciously trying to avoid a possible home truth that could devastate me and my new beautiful manic world. There were small shrine like clues that I left on my dresser and on the walls implying that I was some sort of superior figure (embarrassing delusions of grandeur again) in tattered blue jeans, who craved for his mate while leading his army of high lighters to a better place and beyond. In my view I had shot, canned and distributed enough beauty and relayed it by thought telepathy to every single camera, news agency and television screen on this planet, and maybe even on Jupiter and Mars as well. By cheating with the usual avenues of creativity, I believed that I had doctored my eye lined visions on to paper, some of which were slapped all over the inside of my previous little spirit sapping room. Whoever I chose to mount on my limited surface took on a great significance, even unleashing new manic theories and philosophies. I often witnessed my inquisitive fellow campers having their attentions grabbed at for at least fifteen eye opening seconds.

My plywood dormitory wardrobe and dresser were smothered with instructive cuttings that I delighted in twisting and changing to suit my mood. Naturally there were some requisite erotic artworks that reminded me that my libido was in excellent though frustrating fettle. A divide of two metres separated me from the bearded Tom. Our shared bay could be hidden from the other patients by a tall green and yellow cotton curtain that hung limply from a suspended length of curved ceiling tracking. It needn't have been there at all because Thomas, Richard and Harold would just wander in unannounced anyway. All through the manic buzz of night I had to put up with the overhead night lights—very handy if one is busting for a pee and has to shuffle their way to the single toilet near to the entrance end of the dormitory. That first week in hospital was nothing short of dynamite, a real uplifting explosion of emotion that I prayed would continue and never blow my loaded brain apart.

When a member of staff wanted to sit down and have a chat I always succeeded in turning the intention around, so that I could bore the pants off them with my accounts of Milan, and of the wondrous place that is magically evolving before our blinkered eyes, a place where we will all live one day. Mega-mouth me raced through rules and roles that I maniacally designed as I spoke in order to achieve the creative force that will be put to work, enabling the runners and riders to create the ideal life in which traditional values and basic commonsense and respect win through. Manic rambling across lush grassland took its frustrating toll. Now I needed to plough the furrows in which I could plant the solid seeds of the future.

A member of my family would make the short journey to St. Albans every single night, in fact my father visited me every single day without fail. I love that man, for not only did he play a big part in my existence but because he truly is a Steadyman. Tobacco, bottles of tonic water and bitter lemon, and occasionally a musical tape recording would be generously brought in for my consumption, but the main thing I received was the immense amount of love and support from those who are the closest. Soft-soaping would *not* do, normal treatment would. Love can come in tough packages. Some sense of reality had to be presented before I drifted further down the bipolar river without a paddle or a prayer to save me. To begin with I would offer and then insist that I gave my visiting party a little tour of Hotel Hill End, nearly always taking them to the cheap on sight clothing shop. Emotional blackmail often earned me a sweatshirt or a new pair of sneakers. I would look at them many months later when the manic dream had washed away and think to myself how awful they were, not to my normal taste at all. That is the beauty of mania; everything tastes *so* good. Come to think of it, the visitor that I had frogmarched through the clothing shop doors probably bought me something in the hope that I would stop my incessant talking, fat chance!

It had been my unwavering manic belief for a long time now that extrasensory perception (ESP) had taken a strong hold of me. By focusing on a fellow patient, concentrating as hard as I possibly could, I was able to predict what it was they were about to do or say next. I predicted what the next tune would be on the ward radio, often with stunning results, and I generally felt as if I was always a step ahead of the pack, having to ease back somewhat and wait patiently for the other coconuts to catch up. It stands to reason that if you do something over and over again for a lengthy duration then you are bound to achieve some winning results. These winning results are really only flukes, or are they? It's all down to the power of suggestion and persuasion that is used upon oneself; a form of self-hypnosis. Each and every one of us has intense thoughts, and can be thinking about absolutely any subject. The person next to you might say something that you have been thinking, or the person that you are about to call on the phone beats you to it by a matter of seconds. It happens all the time, and is usually shrugged off and put down to coincidence. This sort of thing began to happen to me often, an awful lot in fact, leaving some of the other patients and myself completely stunned when some of the predictions that I made came true before their very eyes. I do believe in the paranormal, especially mental telepathy and ESP, and that mania is a whole lot more than just a chemical imbalance. Mania acts as a natural though imbalanced launching pad into the untapped possibilities of life itself. Maybe the meaning of life can be discovered using properly monitored expeditions into a manic world, who knows? Are there that many people who really care? I think that when the mind is high it is far more receptive, but sometimes too frantic to concentrate properly on something long enough for it to make any real sense. The mind is bouncing around, leaping from one idea to another and never really hanging around long enough in order to complete the job in hand. The body is whizzing about too, trying to keep up with the motoring mind. Body and mind are like a brush that keeps returning to its pallet of colours in order to go out and paint the full picture, but more and more shades of colour are added to the pallet, running into one another, causing the brush to become so confused that it decides to take an even bigger glob of contaminated paint, far too much for the overloaded little brush to handle. The picture is messy and rushed, so the brush tries to grow but the colours are by now so utterly confusing that the sad little brush collapses onto the paint pallet, now completely black, full of depression and smeared with fear.

What was going on in my over active mind to make me want to lean down to touch the ground with one outstretched arm, whilst at the same time reach up and point to the sky with the other limb? This strange performance became another steady staple diet for my entire manic occupation. It failed to arouse much attention, nor did it rub anyone up the wrong way as it was accepted as being part and parcel of Hill End life. Some of the most outrageous demonstrations of innocent lunacy were greeted with nothing more than a chuckle and an understanding smile. Perhaps my peculiar ground/sky touching routine stemmed from my deep rooted belief that we are all related to Planet Earth, to each other and to the entire universe, or could it have something to do with the Sistine Chapel that I had visited four years earlier? Another delusion of cringingly embarrassing grandeur sounds a little closer to the mark. The old methods tucked away in my mind's overloaded and over burdened portfolio still remained the best, even if I did look like a complete buffoon. Good exercise though.

One of the older male members of Anderson Ward always seemed to be suffering from constipation. This unfortunate fellow is Stanley. Stanley must have been around 65 years old and was one of life's loners. This is unsurprising considering that he spent every waking hour stuck on the toilet trying to force one out. At meal times Stan indulged in his habit of continuously flicking a knife or fork up and over in his hand. Stan did this repeatedly in the meal queue as well as at the table, often dropping it with an irritating *clang* on to the dining room floor. Prunes were given to Stan to soften him up a bit ready for the next session of straining, hence the rather long winded nickname I coined for him of Straining-Stan-The-Prune. If Straining Stan The Prune is still around it's a good bet that his face is permanently grimaced and his wrinkled skin has developed a purplish tinge.

Many of the other male and female patients on Anderson Ward were allowed to return to their homes on Friday evening, then return to the hospital on Sunday evening in time to clock in for yet another eventful week of tears and laughter. Those who were sectioned went nowhere, staying put on a quiet and almost featureless Anderson Ward. This is what I was subjected to for the first four weeks of my stay at Hill End Psychiatric Hospital. Mutual hospitality prevailed as I roamed to neighbouring wards while the institutionalised rubbery faced residents of those wards roamed to Anderson or Drake. This is how I got to meet Ritchie Smith and his brilliant array of lost-touch and good-riddance buddies who were like human jackdaws, collecting their glittering booty and as many cigarettes as they could cadge in one fell swoop. Anderson Ward was better maintained, housing nicer furnishings than the long stay wards, creating an altogether nicer atmosphere. A lovely old boy called Doug who always wore an oversized thick woollen jacket, even when the heating on the ward was turned up high, regularly wandered with a badly made roll-up smoke dangling out of his mouth over to Anderson Ward in the hope of finding some lengthy cigarette butts in the overflowing ashtrays. Old rubber lips Doug tried cadging a tailor made cigarette or two from the visitors that the shrewd soul knew, as well as from newcomers who were still a little wet behind the ears. Vast experience told him that they would find it almost impossible to refuse his request. If they were non-smokers then a strip of chewing gum or sweets would do instead. The split second the targeted person gives in to excessive demands, they become an ongoing target. Patients that look the least likely to take their visiting prey to the cleaners are often sharper than they are given credit for, and that is how they would prefer it to stay so that they can continue to milk the situation for all it's worth, sucking every last drop of naive generosity out of their latest superking benefactor. We were allocated a small ration of our own money to spend at the small newsagent type shop situated inside the lobby. This tiny outlet pandered to all of our needs: toiletries, cigarettes, newspapers, magazines and all kinds of soft drinks and sweets. My allocation of money dwindled away fast. I really didn't need much money because all that I required was there already, or kindly brought in by one of my visitors. Allowing a manic patient like myself too much money would be asking for trouble, because in the blink of an eye I would probably be on the next intercity train to Scotland. All said and done, we took pretty good care of each other. Nobody was ever left wanting for anything so trivial as a cigarette or a stick of chewing gum. As bubblehead Jimmy Swann would say, "It all comes out in the wash."

Doug happened to attend the same art therapy classes as myself. He sat facing me, two large tables away, directly in front of Ronald. Between my high octane efforts I sometimes took a smoking stroll over to see what the others were letting out. Ronald loved to create his charcoal sketches on weighty textured paper that had been divided into manageable half sized A4 sheets. Every session he picked out one person in the room and ran off about twenty quick sketches of the highest quality, all of the same person in the same pose, just like a human printing press. Ronald didn't say a great deal other than, "Got any fags?" but oh boy, could that man express himself with a scrap of paper and a broken stick of burnt wood.

Ritchie Smith had also been sniffing too much manic sunshine. He appeared as if he had been drinking silly water from the same fountain as myself. Five feet three inch Ritchie, despite being from a different ward, took me under his ropes and into his ring, especially during my first full week inside Hill End Hospital. Side by side we jogged around the perimeter of the old Victorian institution, waving at other patients who were doing their own thing, which usually involved a cigarette. With every forthcoming mini-marathon I acknowledged more and more endangered smiles, nods and rainbow twinkles in the secretive eyes of these special men and women. Sometimes we varied our training strategy and flew around the creamy green interior of the hospital. Ritchie briefed me of the pitfalls within such a community, and he also taught me some innocent tricks and tiny scams to use on a rainy day. Learning quickly who I should be wary of and who I should get to know better came in very useful indeed, just as it is in most walks of life. Looking after myself in foreign territory when not manic or depressed has always been something that I have thrived on. I think that I am a reasonable judge of character, and I prefer to find out things in my own time and style, even if that involves getting my fingers slightly roasted along the way. Mister Smith could be described as my Hill End mentor. Ritchie is the sort of bipolar affective person who by all accounts had never quite managed to land his twirling spaceship on the big N for normal, instead missing it completely and crashing in a desert. He was either high or hyper, full of wild schemes, or he was a totally pissed off "leave me alone to die in peace" kind of guy. Not much in-between I'm afraid, though I wouldn't go as far as describing his condition as "rapid-cycling" which means that four or more bouts of depression or mania can occur within a twelve month period. Vincent Van Gogh suffered from the rapid-cycling strain of manic depression. Richard was in his early fifties and had been in and out, but increasingly inside Hill End since he was in his mid-thirties, sadly becoming institutionalised like so many of the other patients. On his good days Richard made sure that he had his stubby fingers dipped in every pie, and he knew all of the latest gossip regarding the patients and their attentive staff. Woodwork was one of Richard's loves, so by natural progression I came to be introduced to the cluttered class. It was based in a small freestanding building in-between the main hospital and another one of the derelict houses that sat next to my adopted Keats. Never before had I been surrounded by such a concentrated mixture of friendly living caricatures that were at peace with their world. Every attendee sat around the large rectangular hulk of a table, smoking and playing cards. Gallons of steaming tea was brewed in a large stainless steel pot and devoured along with a huge tinned selection of biscuits, used mostly for dunking purposes. None of the group were in any hurry to begin work on a project, instead savouring the sweet smell of tea, wood and varnish. No rules applied here and anybody was welcome to show up and have a whittle and a dunk. Richard particularly enjoyed restoring old pieces of furniture. I spent some of the following sessions repairing and repainting in bright pillar box gloss, a small ladder that I had stumbled across in the overgrown field behind Keats house. On completion I returned to Keats to lean the tacky ladder up against No.11, next to the little stool that I had already placed there for Samuel, the childish figment of my romantic imagination. As you know already, these sacred items were later smashed to pieces. Getting on well with Richard had heaps more going for it than just friendship. He was a friendly force to be reckoned with, and he knew how to manipulate the hospital staff just enough, calm down the other patients, get almost anything he needed, and most importantly of all he was respected enough by staff and patients alike to be left alone when he needed to clear his head and be hassle free. To put it in a nutshell it was a case of, "Mix it with me, and you will also be mixing it with Richard." There was never any major trouble among the patients as we all got on terrifically well with each other, but a little extra insurance couldn't do any harm, especially when I was marinated up to the gills in mania.

Little hideouts where small groups of long term patients gathered to smoke away their day, materialised in the unlikeliest of places. At first they were a little wary of the new face, and who can blame them, but they soon allowed me into their secret society. Those early weekends, when I was left behind at the hospital with the stalwarts and all, did have their advantages, all of which I took. Greater portions of food, longer soaks in my studio bathtub and a far more relaxed atmosphere than the usual Monday to Friday routine. I always had the weekend on my mind despite treating every single day as if it were the last. One by one and sometimes two by two, my fellow patients returned, full of excessive quantities of food and an abundance of exaggeration when it came to sharing their condensed weekend activities with the rest of us. We soon discovered what they had done, where they had done it and with whom they had allegedly done it with. Benefit of the doubt is free to give and satisfies one and all, so that became the weekly repeat prescription.

Alcoholics of Hemel Hempstead and the surrounding areas would normally stay at the hospital for two or three weeks so that they can give their soused body a much needed vacation, and an opportunity to dry out. It's all down to that individual whether or not they take that opportunity. Such cases had to be monitored carefully to make sure that there were no lingering psychological effects brought about by the suddenness of a system shocking abstinence. The one exception to all the rules was Mary, or "Bloody Mary" as she came to be known. Mary was nearly 70 years young and just as sprightly, if not more so than some of the younger patients on Anderson Ward. Everybody loved little delicate Mary, for she was a bundle of fun as well as being somebody with whom one could feel at ease with when discussing subjects of a more intimate and private nature. During the week, Bloody Mary made herself look as pretty as the hospital's limited means would allow, then with bag in hand she would speed walk out of the hospital grounds with only one thing on her mind. She headed straight for the nearest off license/liquor store where she would buy a bottle or two of cheap sherry, paid for with a handful of loose change. Mary had been in and out of Hill End for years and years because of drink related problems, but somehow she managed to get rat-arsed more so inside the confines of the hospital than if she was out.

Slowly but surely every Sunday evening, more and more of the familiar faces trickled back up the stone steps and into a reliable, safe and secure Anderson Ward. Some of the returnees timed their return so that they didn't miss out on the prepared evening meal, maybe because they didn't have their requisite mental tools working well enough to cook one for themselves, or a caring person to provide it for them. Back they came every Sunday without fail except for the odd one who had decided to run away for the evening. One or two of the patients preferred being on the inside where they didn't have a care in the world, just a freeloading lifestyle. The saddest thing of all is that they would often boast about it (especially Lee), and think that it's clever to be a fat lazy user and a waster of another person's highly skilled time. Alright, there may have only been a few of these dead weights dotted about the hospital, but heavy puffing slugs like them made me want to heave up my corned beef and cabbage. Users, losers and people abusers are all they were, and they know damn well who they are.

It didn't take long before Danny's punk rock music was cranked up, and for the almighty Harold to recite verse after verse from any one of his untidy yet vast collection of all things biblical. Tom was probably drooling over a new glossy girlfriend, and Stan The Prune was probably making himself as comfortable as possible on his porcelain throne before facing another few hours of eye watering inconvenience. Harold should have offered up a prayer for poor old Stan. We were all trying to force our own demons out in Hill End, some of us were successful and some of us were not. As Stan The Prune knows so painfully well, relief is temporary. Teaching oneself how to filter out the good from the bad at source is a vital and ongoing procedure, otherwise when the problem returns the dormant situation will rumble a little, inflate out of control and then *boom* explode, hurting bystanders and endangering the rescue workers who feel betrayed and let down by the promises made at the end of the last escape, or in Stan The Prune's case, the last evacuation.

Most evenings with manic flair, and also with my own snooker cue that I had asked to be brought in, I potted ball after ball on the snooker table, convinced that I could move the planetary balls by using the power of persuasive thought. This was blatant cheating but who cared. I even managed to try out some extrasensory perception before being sedated again with temazepam in readiness for a few hours of much needed but unwanted sleep. I didn't want to miss a single pocket nor a single trick before medication time and bed.

These days I take a completely different combination of medications. The only medication that remains the same is a lower dose of Lithium, the mood stabiliser. All of my medications are taken when I brush my teeth morning and night, that way it is easier to remember, especially if you fill a weekly a.m./pm. container up once a week and leave it close to your toothbrush. You have to remember that the medications and dosages that I describe apply to *me* alone. Only your psychologist, psychiatric doctor and general practitioner are qualified to prescribe a course of medication that is compatible with you or an unwell loved one. There is one more thing that you should know: *never ever* give somebody else your medication, no matter how harmless you think it may be. What is compatible with one person's system does not necessarily mean it will be for somebody else, and so instead of helping you could be harming. The worst case scenario is death so don't play God (I know that sounds a bit rich coming from me, but it's so true!) *Always* contact a professional in an emergency, it is imperative!

During my second Hill End week I underwent an "EEG" or echoencephalograph. This ultrasound facility could be found in one of the smaller extensions that jutted out of the hospital's rear. A jovial dark skinned man connected me up to an impressive looking piece of equipment. He was then able to see if my brain was shipshape, and eliminate any possibility that my encounter with a Bovingdon High Street paving slab could be related to my current condition. Living up to my high manic standards I naturally concluded that this was part of an important top secret experimental investigation, so that the scientists and the cream from the world of psychiatry could determine the origin and nature of the fidgety phenomenon now under their care. Maybe I represented a grey area. Was I a case never before seen who can sometimes be emulated, but never entirely caught up with both mentally and spiritually? Lots of little separate happenings such as having my brain tested simply boosted my unflagging and flourishing belief that I was the first of a new race, capable of using the brain's entire capacity.

I could detect the early rumblings of a threat to my manic supremacy. The devilish element that cannot accept nor grasp the nettle was out to destroy myself and my super-brain colleagues. Paranoia plays some despicably sick jokes on people, causing unprovoked alienation among previously trusted friends. Proof that I had become too big for my boots came when I noticed a marker penned piece of graffiti on one of the main corridor dividing doors that stated in no uncertain terms that, *"God Must Die."* It wasn't very easy to write that last line, in fact it is excruciatingly embarrassing, but I have to be totally up front if you are to stand any chance of comprehending this crazy big thing called bipolar disorder, where you can be king for the summer and a corpse for the fall. As you already know, when I was manic I became whatever or whomever I wanted because I believed that we were all part of each other, and I still do. Mania grabs hold and hangs on for the most extreme rides through life, and I am the one who is always motion sick at the fairground, even on the Ferris wheel! I felt confidently able to take on the personage of absolutely anybody or anything at the drop of a hat. Masculine, feminine, old, young, animal, mineral—I believed with all of my heart that I could take on the whole lot of them while standing on one leg, reciting from memory one of Shakespeare's plays, and painting a masterpiece in the dark. Perhaps the "Shaky" part flew a little too far from the angelic aviary, but I'm sure you get my point. What I badly needed was one of the patients to show me their guts and have it out with me, to tell me straight that I was in fact imagining it all, and that I wasn't at all well. Maybe in a round about way they did try to convey this message, but it failed to register. Those attempting to gently dampen my well stoked furnace were the one's yet to seize upon the powerful energy force, soon to be shared out and then used purely for the good. Convincing myself of these things kept the manic stew nice and hot. From time to time an old friendly thought would slip through the cracks in my make-up and settle uncomfortably into the not so easy chair of doubt. I never really wanted to play for too long with my old friendly thoughts, always letting out a huge sigh of relief when the manic touch-paper had been fired up again. My stalwart muses came visiting, and then retreated to Athens or Rome. They would never dream of leaving me stranded for good, so they told me the truth. They would tell me plainly that I had indeed been foolish, and that my iridescent bubble of froth could burst just as quickly as it took to inflate with warm ale air. Throughout the first two and a half months in Hill End Psychiatric Hospital I had no problem in dismissing these rare mania thieving thoughts, but later they insisted upon outstaying their welcome until I finally succumbed and fell back into a broken world full of greed and jealousy, death and destruction—an affair of the world and a state of mind that the average person regards as normal! Goodness far outweighs negativity, although it is impossible to see the good when one is mentally cascading down onto a rocky depression. A regretful blur is all there is. The entire manic period of months and months is reduced to a swift decline that sucks out every last ounce of life, or so it feels to begin with. The fall is a rapid affair. From then on it is sheer mental torture.

At Hill End I strengthened an already firm belief that when something absurd, good or even bad happens it is for a beneficial reason, and that a positive new outlook and refreshing approach will rise from the ashes to rejuvenate and improve the next block of future. Occurring accidents obviously teach us to look carefully at the circumstantial evidence, calmly re-evaluate the situation, and then make the necessary adjustments that will prevent a reoccurrence. I would take this basic rule and use it to turn around a snide comment or action that I cared little for, so that it would become palatable. Reading between the lines was not enough either. I had to turn misplaced speech and script inside out and back to front until I felt satisfied. In other words, a manic human being will take on board adjusting perceptions of practically anything positive or negative that is thrown at them, fooling and misleading themselves in order to ensure that nothing blocks the pearly path to their happy land. My ever changing views and comments tended to often be contradictory as new input swayed my already off-the-wacky-dial reasoning. I am not the kind of guy who is too stubbornly proud to admit to a changing wave of thought when the mind-tide sweeps in its foreign bodies.

At long last the day had come to attend my first art therapy session. Our softly spoken art therapist came in a pretty tasty package from God's spicy studio in India. Her name is Kashika, which in Indian means the "shiny one." I certainly took an immediate shine to her. The brilliant thing about this class was that we were encouraged to feel free to let it all out and to put it all down, so I did. Wearing a long white satin shirt that I had chosen from the apron rack I set to it, diving in without worrying about the depth of colour, immersing myself in the translation of thoughts from above then back down onto a large area of brightly coloured card that I had pinned onto a huge wooden drawing board. You name it I used it: acrylics, oils, water based poster paints, felt and ballpoint pens, crayon, pastels, pencils, glue, glitter, beads, tea leaves, clay, my hair, blood, saliva, nail clippings, pubic hair, skin, bogeys, grass, leaves, ash and earth; all of these materials were brushed, smeared, stippled, blotted, thrown from a distance, dribbled, blown and dabbed onto the paper or card, and then I might go one step beyond my existing effort and burn small sections, ripping relevant areas, chewing, scratching, crumpling up and creasing the picture until I had released as much mania as I could. Manic thoughts begged for their freedom. It was mentally draining work, which is the whole point entirely, but it often seemed as if the vacancies in my mind were being immediately exploited by greater versions along a similar theme. My naked existence found its way out and on to a vehicle that would allow those who chose to do so to hop aboard and feel me, experience me, and try to figure out what on earth I was all about. I am certain that the patients who had experience in the alternative working ways of the mind, were able to see in my creations what a plain outsider or a non-believer could not or would not allow themselves to see. My style of expression varied dramatically depending on whether that great ball of fire was finding its way through the clouds. You can call it what you will, all I know is that it worked for me and that it was such an exhilarating experience, well worth a dabble. When I got my teeth into an idea I became a patient possessed. Every single little action had a large meaning attached but not labelled in the traditional sense, allowing my work to say something slightly different to each viewer, but with a common thread running through that pulls the whole chaos together into a more compact, kinder friend. Extending my turbulence, ecstasy and sadness into an art form was a wonderful thing. The standard cannot be judged because it is so unlike another piece of work. The most important thing is to let it all spill out and have a bloody good time in the process.

Sessions of physical and mental exertion were magnificently draining and richly rewarding. Exerting so much energy into my work gave me such a lift, not that I needed to be hoisted up my greasy pole any more. Art also provided me with the feeling of well being and personal satisfaction that comes with any form of productive physical work. Yes, Steadman had become an abstract-expressionist-modernist-cubist-portraitist with a hint of go for broke mind bending surrealism thrown into the paint pot for good measure. Midway through our morning art session we downed implements and enjoyed a communal cup of stewed tea and a cigarette. Carol, a long stay patient from a different ward, would often stand behind me during tea break, or when I was maniacally arty-farting away at my desk. She allowed me to share her tailor made cigarettes, in fact the entire class, full of would be Michelangelo's or Pollock's, shared everything, creating a tightly knitted and trusting group of refreshingly different examples of God inspired creativity. To conclude each revealing art session we gave ourselves fifteen minutes to drink more stewed tea and to savour another reflective smoke. All seven or eight of us sat around the record player taking it in turns to choose that particular day's 33 rpm long player from a terrific selection of donated albums. Following my first week of art therapy it became well known and accepted that I had a tendency to become a little bit over exuberant when the music started. I especially enjoyed getting carried away to the sound of the late great Mick Ronson's album, *Slaughter On 10th Avenue.* Even sweet Kashika and the occasional occupational therapist student found my peacock displays on top of the splattered tables highly amusing. I danced and contorted to the feel of the room, in fact I became the mood of the room. There was nothing at all sad about this clown.

Nick, a very tall longer stay patient with a lanky golden mane of hair—I believed that in a past life, Nick was related to the big cat family—would clap along out of time and then for no apparent reason roar with contagious laughter.

Why? because he was happy, as simple as that. That was the good thing about Hill End Psychiatric Hospital, there didn't have to be a reason or a point to everything. We all took our turns to interpret fresh thinking patterns as being semi-serious or highly amusing, igniting spontaneous uncontrollable laughter. Private silent and invisible humour was as commonplace inside the confines of the hospital as the explosive sort that touches everyone. What a great lift a good laugh brings, and I for one had plenty of them. I nicknamed Nick "Mane-man," but I think I was the only one who understood the tame joke. I'm not kidding when I tell you that a vast majority of the paintings I produced were as good if not better than some of the work by modern artists who have their work exhibited at the Tate Modern on London's South Bank, or at the Museum of Modern Art (MOMA) in New York. Might it be that the mania was blinding me with colourful paint and pastels? At least I never resorted to eating the paint in the same way as a deeply troubled and lonely Van Gogh felt compelled to do. In 1996 I saw a superb movie in Greenport, Long Island, New York about the late Jean Michel Basquiat, a tragic young dreadlocked Haitian street artist who made good with the backing of Andy Warhol. In the film, a bedroom scene, I saw leaning up against the wall a few modern paintings that looked just like my own attempts. Obviously those paintings were not mine, but I still felt as if I had been robbed of the same opportunity as Mr. J.M Basquiat had. Then again, I don't see any reason why I can't get off my backside and make it happen for myself, just like he did. What became of all the works of art when Hill End was raised to the ground? We were told in 1990 that they would always be kept somewhere safe, but I'll be buggered if I know where that "safe" place is. I still like to think that my "works of heart" went the full fifteen rounds and made it up onto the big silver screen, even though in my heart of hearts I know that it isn't true. One day, you never know.

Kashika would wiggle around the art therapy room, stopping to discuss each of our works. I required an all day explanation session to do justice to my marathon artistic endeavours. We discussed my inspirations and aspirations, the distant past and foreseeable future, what and who drove me so fast, and what caused me to keep crashing the same uninsurable vehicle in so many different areas of time and space. I tried desperately hard to get her to accurately read my mind that I had laid out neat and naked for her on a wooden desk, sometimes with success and other times without, but I always gave it my best shot. Kashika's trained eye sometimes shone down and spread some light over a dark region, making it come to life in a blaze of glory. No matter how much effort went into these therapy sessions I often got the feeling that only the surface had been skimmed, and that my point of view had failed to perform soulfully enough on an open mike stage. These minor frustrations soon drifted into nowhere. Back on Anderson Ward I occasionally set up a makeshift art studio using one of the circular dining room tables. From here I contented myself by doodling and pencil sketching willing sitters.

Carol from my art class was of average build for a woman, but she had an abnormally swollen belly. Later I discovered that her condition was brought about partly by an adverse reaction to her medication. At first glance I thought she looked heavily pregnant, either that or she had swallowed a basketball. Carol, who was existing in a far away chain-smoking land by herself, would stroke her bump and make soft, "*Wooohee-Woohee-Whooee*," sounds as if she really believed that there was a little Carol or Carl growing inside. An informant explained to me that she actually believed herself that she was in the family way, despite the fact that her drug riddled protrusion had been prominent for at least two years. Maybe she will give birth to an elephant one day and name it Dumbo junior. Sorry Carol, I'm only kidding. There were a handful of male Hill End regulars who saw fit to take an unfair advantage of Carol by taking her to a quiet out of the way place for a cumbersome portion of slap and tickle. I secretly thought that she enjoyed these dippy diversions just as much as the next woman, even though she had no real say in the matter. Carol didn't say much other than, "*Whoooee*" "*Umm*" "Fag" and "Fuck off," but she managed to get by somehow. It was a shame to see somebody who was a few years older than myself being taken advantage of in such a cheap degrading way. Those who got their jollies off in the hands of Carol must have been pretty sick, but then again we *were* in a hospital full of mentally ill people, so I suppose this kind of behaviour is par for the course. How many holes in one were scored during a Hill End week I shudder to think.

Stress and anxiety relaxation therapy was a real blast. A motley crew of around ten began by sitting on plastic chairs in a huddled horseshoe, spilling in turn a mind full of old and new concocted and shockingly real hang-ups. "Today I floated out of bed and felt the electricity flow from my feet up to my head, and then a triple winged silver dove cooing on the window ledge transformed itself into a …"—it took an awful lot of persuasion to shut up Steadman's relentless manic banter. Before we go any further inside the Nissen hut I think it is important to explain in more detail another broad facet of my mania that is on duty 24/ 7, and affects to varying degrees just about everything. "What could be more obvious," I can hear you cry. I am referring to the gymnastics of my tongue, the pen trickery of my right hand, and the literary juggling of my eyeballs. Words are cheap and have no known boundaries. Musical lyricists, comedians, scriptwriters, newspaper reporters and columnists, novelists and the average man, woman or child in the street are capable of verbal chemistry. "Tongue-foolery" can be committed with lightening ease. The sheer speed that I delivered some of my sentences would guarantee a plethora of hands to fly up in the air telling me to slow down. Despite the annoying speed, I was taken aback by my broad vocabulary and crisp sentence structure. As a result I often struggled to keep my reasonably cool persona intact. Undeterred I spoke and strode, on and on, acting the many parts while at the same time taking care not to let out my own amazement. Playing around with words is something we all do to a certain degree or another. For example; *dog* spelt backwards is of course *God*, which automatically extends a greater manic importance to man's best friend. In 1974 David Bowie released through RCA an innovative album called *Diamond Dogs* which to me and many others translated into *Diamond Gods* by *Bow-Wowie*. Then it became *Diamond Hard Gods* from South London, which then resulted in *Diamond-Geezer*—an imaginary male character that I loved to paint in my art therapy sessions, and on and on it went. Everything is connected whether somebody has bipolar affective disorder or not. My method incorporated snippets of European language, but maintained a predominant explosion of mangled English. Here is another simple example of how the manic thought engine churns out a chain of relation: Give me a Chinese proverb and I would then spout out a spiced up oriental reply painted on pure silk and then spun into a worldwide web across twelve months of big wig fat cats rats reversal verse universal one doggy star light up down out in side way to go, and so on. It's not unlike modern rap really. Sometimes the rapidity of these two or three simultaneous meaning thinking sentences drove me wild, but I was helpless to stop it. Sometimes dear Julie came into my equation as Jules equals joules electric bright spark dark bark dog bow how good gold old sold glistening fools jewellery Jew wish five star point diamond mutt fat gutted cut head butt fart arty start stick stuck suck lucky wand blonde long goner heart attacking catty cats milky silky knockers blocker hotter trotter pony tails whales meat beef eat Keith teeth grief belief—do you get the basic barmy idea now? I guess it's nothing much more than a simple rhyme, but when you're high and it's coming your way at a 100 mph it sounds so unique and inventive. Being high magnifies one's perception of anything that is taken as reasonably normal by a mentally stable person. Straightforward word structures did it for me the most, with painting and sketching coming in a close second. In 1990 I took a lifetime of useful and useless stored data and scrambled it all into an awkward to swallow alphabetical omelette. Without the required oiling and usage much of it stuck in untidy clumps inside my brain, while the rest was generously dished out without asking anyone if they were hungry. I was so up and at them that even rotten eggs tasted sweet, leaving me with a craving for a constant flow of food to feed my dynamic manic thought engine.

Some of the most personal and revealing accounts of depression, phobia, alcoholism, mania, schizophrenia, anxiety and a whole host of other psychological related mountains poured from even the most timid of patients. The Nissen hut's calming surroundings and soft background music, coupled with an expert therapist and the built up trust among familiar faces were the qualities required in order to peel a nagging load from off one's tired shoulders. Unloading and openly sharing what is playing over and over again on your mind with the other group members makes one realise that they are not the only person on this planet with a particular temporary problem, and that by opening up and discussing it with like minded people and listening to their similar reassuring stories and solid sound advice, the original impenetrable mountain will become a hopeful hillock. It is not always so easy when some of the group members drop out of a session in tears, others in anger. At least it is a means of release that can continue if that person is brave enough and sensible enough to return to the canned horseshoe. Many sessions can slide by without even a whisper from a few, but when they *are* prompted into opening up and then discover to their astonishment that they really enjoy the feeling of spitting out the gunk of their lives, there is no stopping them, no painful straining to look back at what cannot be changed, only relief at finding their real true selves in today, and not too far into the distance. A weight off assists one's sleep pattern which then has the beneficial knock on effect to aid the repair process and also the general enjoyment of life. Following the group discussion we would all rise up and choose our preferred warm blanket and soft rubber mat from the cupboard. These we placed side by side on the carpeted floor. Something about lying horizontally next to a female always tends to bring out the sexual tension in me, which I guess is pretty normal. Giggling usually accompanied the act of lying back on our mats and wrapping the comfort blanket around our tense bodies. Making every word count, the therapist slowly ran us through the basic toe to head relaxation procedure. "Tighten your calf muscles and then relax," she would whisper rather sexily. When it came to buttock clenching time the sound of schoolyard sniggering could be clearly heard among the throng. Finally we arrived at our heads. With eyes shut tight and the mind's drainage tap open we were often able to enter a state of pure relaxation. Sometimes the sedimentary flow worked beautifully, and at other times the sludge was so heavy and thick it had to be eased out with the help of our skilled therapist. Refinement would then need to be applied on an individual basis. Sinking so relaxed into the floor or a bed is fine, but I went a step further and hovered slightly above the other patients. Of course I hadn't moved a muscle, but that didn't prevent an inbuilt manic simulator from taking over the reins for a few pleasurable minutes. Audio tape cassettes of tropical thunderstorms, bird songs and the mighty oceans took hold of our imaginations, transporting us to these faraway places until the tape was turned off with a loud intrusive *clidink*. During one of the sessions I became so engrossed in the whole atmosphere of suggestive escapism that I dozed off, only to be awoken half an hour later to a Nissen hut full of laughter, as I had apparently been snoring rather too loudly—even my snoring was manic!

Relaxation classes proved to be a tremendously beneficial therapy, helping me to feel so much calmer for many hours following a successful session.

Tom in the bed next to me had received his discharge papers, and was planning on a long trip to the United States of America to spend some of the small fortune that the shrewd fellow had acquired through a smart property deal, and good luck to him. No sooner had he gone than a bolt of lightening hit Hill End Psychiatric Hospital in the form of Ian Brown. Ian, of stockier build than myself, sported cropped mousy hair, blue eyes and plenty of gym muscle. Some may say that he was quite the "panty-peeler." He was also as manic as they come which made it so interesting for me to observe him, although I couldn't see all of the obvious similarities during those early stages. He skipped the isolation room that I was subjected to on my admission, and was instead put in the empty bed next to me! Two manic young men in close proximity struck me as odd even then, despite still believing that I was really perfectly well and had to just play along with the hospital system for a while. He had his pride and joy, a top of the range mountain bike locked up just outside the ward in the corridor. If he could have slept with his bike I am sure he would have done. One day he allowed me to peddle it around the hospital, not outside and around the perimeter road but on the inside. Weaving through the creamy green corridors of Cuckoo-Land, trying to avoid the other patients was hilarious, an experience that at the time I thought could be repeated whenever I wanted for ever and ever. Not long before Ian's arrival I had requested without any objection that my old Ferguson record turntable, a pair of wooden speakers and a selection of LP's were collected from my maisonette and brought into the hospital. I positioned it on a small laminated table at the foot of Ian's bed, right next to the only available 240 volt plug socket. The turntable wouldn't work at the first attempt, so manic Ian dived in with a dinner fork he had found from somewhere and proceeded to ram this metallic implement directly into the live socket causing a loud *bang*, a few sparks and fine wisps of electrical smoke. Ian was still alive and fully charged, ready to enter the early stages of what was to become a duet of manic laughter. The prongs on the fork had melted somewhat, but we still put it back with the rest of the cutlery, finding it highly amusing when one of us noticed it set out on one of the dining room tables and actually being used by somebody. Ian and I had one of those immediate bonding relationships in which one can almost read the others mind and predict what's coming next, a special blend that brought forth plenty of priceless moments filled with belly aching laughter. Sometimes I would be crying with laughter without even knowing why, sheer and utter bliss! I fixed the guilty record player wire, then we played our 33 and 45 rpm vinyl discs at a pretty high volume until our hearts were content and our drums were deadbeat.

Early one morning as I came out of the bathroom, I spotted a transparent plastic jug that contained what I believed to be orange squash. I fetched a plastic beaker from the dining room and poured myself some. It took a few large swigs before I realised that this "orange squash" with a warm froth floating on top of it was in fact somebody's urine. Why it was left there and by whom I will never know. To this day it remains a mystery as to who the provider was, and to be perfectly honest I don't want to know, would you? Yuk! My teeth were brushed a hundred times and I drank water until it was coming out of my ears, in the hope that by doing so it would flush the urine out of my contaminated system. Since that unfortunate day, whenever I here the phrase, "Taking the piss," I automatically return to that repulsive incident.

Very early one Hill End morning as I was taking my usual bath, I noticed a slight figure in the corner of my right eye. The heavy door that separated the bathing area from the washbasins and washing machine had been left half open, and as I swung round to my right I could see, edging closer and closer, a black hairy triangle on two painfully thin legs. The owner of these lower parts and also of the bones above was of course Jadranka, the bewildered young lady from Yugoslavia. I never did get round to finding out much about her story and how she came to be in England, perhaps she had done something similar to myself and flown away on a wing and a prayer. No, Jadranka had different, much sadder symptoms. As she could speak hardly a word of English it left myself and the other patients on Anderson Ward none the wiser. The staff have to treat a patient's details as confidential, so there was no use trying to squeeze any information out of them. Information about a patient only becomes available if the patient themselves are willing to talk. I understand that she successfully righted her mental turbulence before returning home safely, only to have been snagged up in the mindless Balkan War. Jadranka used to always maintain a twinkle of fun in her eyes, and she forever tried to grab hold of my tiny gold cross/plus symbol that had remained a permanent fixture around my scrawny neck throughout the entire Milan escapade. This was to be no different. We both fought over the cross as naked as the day we were born, foamy water sloshing everywhere. She even tried to climb in with me, so naturally I was tempted to make room for her at the plug end. In my heart of hearts I knew that this was not on at all, and I certainly wasn't about to take advantage and turn her already delicate situation into an even tougher one, so I became firm, shouting while laughing at the same time just get her out of my face. I wished that she could have remained in my face a little longer, but it was only right to preserve what remained of her fragile dignity. A female member of staff came and completed the job of removing her, but not before I had satisfied myself with a good fleshy eyeful. Danny Weller, the likable schizophrenic punk rock fan, did manage to go the distance with a confused and curvy, already married Cynthia. The romantic setting of a large walk in broom cupboard hosted their moments of polished passion. Cynthia had a split personality disorder in which her throw-caution-to-the-wind half obviously revelled in going footloose and fancy free among the pledge and toilet rolls with a runny nosed, yet lovable punk. The medication Danny had to take caused his red nose to run like a yellowy green river, yet another example of the small prices we psychiatric crowd have to cough up for a full and productive existence. The odd couple occasionally snuck out of the hospital grounds along with Bloody Mary and a posse of other patients for some forbidden alcoholic fruit at the "Camp," a charming public house only five minutes walk from the hospital's main entrance. It is hard to believe that such a high proportion of Hillenders displaying every mental problem that there is, and with all manner of medication jangling around inside of them, would go marching out for a few drinks, but they did on a regular basis! What better therapy than to be in fresh surroundings with regular members of the outside world. If a patient is not sectioned (a compulsory restriction to a ward under the mental health act) then there was no stopping them. I went along to the Camp following my restrictive first month, but amazingly enough I never touched a single drop of alcohol. Smelling the drinks was still enough for me because of the still existent hallucinatory effects. Tonic water with ice hit my spot as it tasted, with concentration, like a weak vodka tonic. Water, the fluid upon which the effectiveness of my lithium intake depended, became a bosom buddy. Everywhere that I ventured inside Hill End hospital so did a cup of water and a roll up cigarette. My water, with a manic belief that rarely felt as if it was failing or waning, became whatever drink I wanted. I wonder if the almighty would mind too much if some of us pretend to turn water into wine? God only knows.

The last time I saw Danny Weller was in the summer of 2003, when he invited a small crowd to his Hemel Hempstead home to enjoy a barbecue. His face had remained a safe distance from the fist of Cynthia's husband for many years now. Cynthia probably never let on, and if she did then an unbelievably understanding husband must have blamed her broom cupboard bonk on her other personality (it's amazing what you can get away with.) Why are criminals let off the hook so lightly when they plead some kind of concocted insanity? They blame everything on their childhood. I know a man whose parents didn't want to know him so they put him in an orphanage as a baby. He has become one of the most decent human specimens that ever roamed this planet. It can take a great deal of sane thinking to commit most crimes, so don't give me all that insanity plea bullshit. If they have the intelligence to commit the crime then they must also have the savvy to earn a decent honest living. A genuine case is fine, but the way I see it is that any unfair advantage by those with or without a history of mental hurdles is *wrong* and way out of line. To sum things up, the jury's verdict is that Cynthia is *innocent* of all charges and can now sweep the past behind her.

T-Rex, The Clash, The Jam, Bowie, Lennon, Dire Straits, The Sex Pistols, The Stones, Lou Reed, Elton, Clapton, The Who, Sade, Grace Jones, Donna Summer, The Pet Shop Boys, The Beatles, Tina Turner, Miguel Bose and Iggy Pop—all of these and heaps more had their fair share of airtime in the men's dormitory. The radio played the more up to date music. Nineteenth Nervous Breakdown by the Rolling Stones became a huge Hill End hit among a few of us, but wasted on the rest. Toward the end of my residency, Danny purchased my wooden cased Ferguson record player for £20.00. He wanted to install it into his tiny Hemel apartment when he was also fully discharged. My discharge day was still a distant pinprick in the clouds.

Guy Fawkes Night on November 5th was rapidly approaching. Some of our efforts during the art therapy sessions were directed toward this theme, and were subsequently sticky taped onto the creamy green corridor walls and also inside the different wards. The aim of doing this was to raise a greater awareness, then ignite an interest in the event within some of the more sluggish uneventful patients, as well as with the regular collection of participants and their visitors. Paintings and collages of firework displays by a manic person can be, how shall I put it, extraordinarily interesting to say the very least. The donning of dungarees and a full face visor is highly recommended if you ever happen to encounter a happy manic firework display artist standing up and dancing his art onto the paper canvas, painting an electrifying performance like no other. On completion— there is no completion really, which is why the manic is always so restless—the body that became the tool slumps into a chair exhausted, takes a cigarette and a sip, looks at his watch but ignores what it says before diving straight back into the thrill of an explosive sky. There is so much that the hectic mind begs and craves to spill and spray but never enough time, hence the display of frantic fast forwarding that can very soon wear down an observer. A bipolar participant is never barred from an event because in their mind they simply invite themselves, believing that they have the God given right to gatecrash life for an eternity. To miss out on this or even take half measures just isn't in the manual.

Late October and early November evenings were mostly spent in the company of Danny. We spent most of our time on an expanse of roughly cut field that was situated behind Keats and next to the Hill End Hospital staff social club. Plenty of firewood, mostly from old pallets, lay strewn all over this bumpy field and also in the overgrown patches of nettles and thorn bushes that surrounded it. Our brief was to assemble two decent sized, well packed stacks ready for igniting on the evening of November 5th when many members of staff and their families and friends would be in attendance. The patients, who had to remain outside the clubhouse along with their guests, would also be present and occasionally incorrect. At around this time Danny, Ian and myself dreamed up a plan that failed to hatch. It involved breaking in to the social clubhouse so that we could have a free party to end all free parties. We cased the clubhouse just like they do in the movies but never went ahead with our mission possible. It was a crying shame because we had told ourselves that whatever we do will be put down to us three having a spanner short of a tool kit, making our insanity pleas valid. I suppose that the whole event would have been highly amusing for some, but we would be abusing our positions and would also be jeopardising any trust and faith that the busy staff ever had in us to begin with. As well as having developed our own standards, we still shared a few of the same morals associated with normal civilised behaviour.

Hours upon hours were happily spent beavering about in the sogginess until our combustible piles were of an adequate size and shape. I always returned to a warm Anderson Ward covered in muck and scratches from head to toe, but I couldn't care less. I would have a quick wash, and then slip into fresh attire before sliding into the mood or character of choice, until it was that time again to be sedated in readiness to hit the manic sack. During the run up to Guy Fawkes night two new faces joined our ranks in the svelte form of 25 year old Irish Lisa, and 19 year old Elvin Lewis. Elvin, whose parents originated from the West Indies, fitted in very well to begin with, then suddenly he changed into a dangerous piece of work, intent on setting fire to everything, putting already stressed out patients and the staff's lives at a needless mindless risk. He also took to stealing clothes from the other patient's wardrobes. Elvin either had a death wish or was a deeply disturbed young man, not that it prevented one of the male patients from giving him a good hiding. The body odour that came from Elvin would have made a skunk cry, an inescapable fact not lost on me when I retrieved the pyjamas that he had brazenly taken from beneath my pillow. They went straight into the rubbish bin. We discovered later that he had indeed been expelled from another psychiatric hospital in the London area for exactly the same kind of behaviour. All that the authorities succeeded in doing was to pass the problem on like a game of pass the human parcel, instead of getting tough enough to address the disturbed young man's problem and then beat it. Elvin couldn't help the way he expressed his troubled mind just as I couldn't help prancing around like a demented donkey in a silly hat, or riding on the wrong side of a speeding underground train, but for the time being we were lumbered with each other and had to just get on and make the most of a forced acquaintance. Prison or a secure unit was suggested by many as the right and proper place for a pyromaniac pyjama pincher, instead we were stuck with this stinking nuisance until the powers that be said otherwise and moved him on. Hill End Psychiatric Hospital had an assortment of staff from many nationalities in many different shades of the same colour. To my knowledge, racism never reared its small minded, ill educated and ugly head. There is something about mental or any other illnesses that nearly always unites people. The tendencies that one may previously have had of superiority are discarded, thrown in the trash can where they belong. When Elvin was still around we wanted to take it in turns to punch him, but that has nothing to do with the beautiful colour of his skin, the shade that millions of paler skinned people yearn for. Racism as a whole is old hat, and it is only the morons without a life and who live in the past that still practice it. Come on, it's 2008 and we live in a modern world of freedom and equal rights.

Lisa turned out to be a welcome addition to the ward. She got on exceptionally well with a maternal Bloody Mary, and was so obviously hot for Ian that steam could be seen coming out of the big gaping hole that had formed in the gusset area of her only pair of tatty tight black ski-pants, visible only when she sat with her legs anywhere from five minutes to one, to a quarter to three, any time of the day or night. Those well ventilated ski-pants were the only item of clothing that I ever saw Lisa wearing. Lisa knew my cousin Todd very well indeed because of an affair they had when they were carefree teenagers. Through chatting to Lisa in the forthcoming weeks, and despite her sizzling feelings for chunky Ian, I could sense that six or seven years later she still carried a lighted torch for Todd, although not nearly as obsessive as my blowtorch was for Julie. My guess is that she lost her virginity to Todd, but anything more than that really has nothing to do with me whatsoever, so I shall shut up.

My nose began to play tricks as it had done in the pub. Now the tea smelt unbearably strong. The tea aroma reminded me of a baby's diaper, full to the brim and as hot as a vindaloo. Imaginary baby related things were tending to become a bit of a regular occurrence with me, beginning with the first Milanese hospital. A sort of fatherly thing, a natural instinct in an unnatural situation may have had a rather big something to do with it. For instance, there was my concern for the welfare of the still missing little Tommy and also for tormented young Jenny. Lets not forget about imaginary Samuel either. Despite all of this, I still drank the tea.

At first Lisa was understandably suspicious of everyone, including Ian, so she put up a flimsy barrier that she really wanted to be broken by the right person. Whatever happened in Mallorca, from where she had just come, remained a mystery, but it must have been pretty traumatic judging by the way she moved and spoke. Her meadow green eyes flashed this way and that in a feeble attempt to ward off the return of the very same evil that must have chosen her to play mental pinball with. It became apparent very early on that Lisa was one hell of a user. Without any shame or remorse she could lure somebody in so that she could bleed them dry, satisfying her selfish needs. Survival is one thing, but not to the detriment of another troubled person. Lisa was unwell and only did what her disturbed brain told her to do, so she had to be excused in the same way as the rest of us were on a regular basis. Squeezing money and cigarettes out of the male patients by becoming a little bit suggestive was Lisa's specialty, and she had got it down to a tee. One could call her a human Venus flytrap, although I preferred to think of her as a bit of a prick-teaser. At the end of the day we were all under that same old Victorian roof, and we were also under the same old head banging God who never misses a single trick. Things have a knack of balancing out by themselves. Forcing the issue quite often leads to breakage.

A painfully thin human specimen called Vincent joined us on Anderson Ward just before fireworks night. The poor fellow was unmistakably dead on his trembling legs. He made the rest of us look decidedly fat, he was that wasted. Vinnie reminded me of the toys that travel across the floor and then flip over and head off in the opposite direction when they collide with an obstacle. Poor nervous Vinnie was in an awful state when he arrived. Everyone felt deeply for him and wanted to help him, even though they were struggling to cope with their own mental predicaments. On arrival Vinnie would shuffle and shake his skinny body forward, crashing into whatever lay in his path, then turn himself around to continue his shuffling forward in a new direction. His vision was obscured because he always held his head so low. I had never seen such a sad pathetic figure on legs except of course for the starving in Africa and in other poverty stricken countries across super modern Planet Earth. Vinnie must have endured some wicked headaches in the years leading up to his admittance, if the endless torrent of head butting the solid ward walls and doors were anything to go by. My hands are up, I am guilty of positioning Vinnie on a collision course with the pungent tea trolley and directing him into the ladies dormitory. Slowly but surely his nervousness subsided and his depression finally lifted. His recovery was miraculous. We were all so delighted for this trooper who had apparently been existing in the unimaginable nightmare of never being depression free since he was a small child. He never once moaned or showed any signs of self pity before or after his mind was set free. Vinnie then concerned himself with the welfare of the other patients, bowling us over with his considerate personality and thoughtful nature, not to mention his natural quick wit.

There was definitely a lot of camaraderie between the patients on Anderson Ward. An understanding like no other existed because although we were all completely different, thank God, we were in fact all made of the same stuff, not to everybody's taste but the same right stuff. Patients are always in the same boat, which meant that we had to row together in time in order to keep travelling forward in a reasonably straight line. As soon as there is a disruption within the crew the boat drifts in circles, having to be righted before smashing into one of the many rocks waiting to wreck all of the hard work that has been put in. Teamwork is required to rebuild the crew's damaged moral, and also to fix the individual troubled oar so that the cutter can slice through life's cake of good hope that little bit easier. Everybody has a ship that *will* come in. Some of us do not realise that it actually docked many years ago, and they will continue not to realise even if an angel lands upon their shoulder and gently slaps them in the face with a firm anchor on life. Good health is so valuable, it cannot be measured in a monetary way. Illness is caused through greed, striving for more and more, never content. Most of us are so well off but are blind to it. Experiencing a mentally related problem and coming through intact sure makes one feel humble and so very grateful, not only for what we have already received, but also for what we are about to. Amen.

A "Been there done it, got the T-shirt, know exactly where you're coming from," mentality was indeed prevalent among most of the psychiatric patients that I have had the privilege of being ill in the company of. Understanding other patients to the best of one's limited ability is like living in today's society where there is no alternative other than to be in the pudding bowl, mixing it with all of the other fruitcakes. Go on, take a bite or lick the wooden spoon, why don't you? It will be an eye opening education that will do you and those close by no harm at all.

The devoted professionals have researched, studied, observed, monitored and cared on behalf of people like myself for many years. These humane beings are out of the top medical drawer. My collection of hats go off to all of those giving people who dedicate a huge chunk of their own complex lives—in a research laboratory or practicing on the front line—to making their fellow human's lives as comfortable, productive and independent as possible. The families of these people are equally important because of the support that they provide in the home environment. Since 1990 I have been blessed to have had a marvellous supportive team working alongside me during those unpredictable times of need; times that I owe to myself and those around me to eliminate. My general practitioners since 1990, Dr. Hope, Dr. Goodwin, Dr. Holloway and Dr. Perkins, and my consultant psychiatrist Dr. Bridle and her team, do have that extra special touch that separates them from the rest. Perhaps one of the best people of all to hang onto and develop a friendship with is another ex-patient, someone who really knows what's what and can easily connect with the ups and downs of mental illness in a way that no medical book or manual can ever do. Having a soul mate in civilian life, a battling friend that has survived a similar journey is worth so much, especially when one looks around in broad daylight and discovers that their loyal few remaining friends can be counted on one hand. A fully recovered psychiatric patient would probably make the best psychiatric worker as far as the listening and practical advice giving is concerned, but with equal opportunities being what they aren't it can be harder to find a decent job that you may think. I had the good *and* the bad experiences when hunting for work, as you will soon discover. Judging a person on what they once *were* and on how they have become labelled since, instead of what they are *now* and on what they have to offer, is a practice that should have gone down with the ark, but instead it is still thriving.

A couple of days before the grand fireworks display, a belated Halloween fancy dress party was held in one of the hospital's smaller function rooms. Invited to this ghoulish event were a group of twenty mongrel adults from a nearby social facility. Our welcome guests came dressed spookily as a witch or a ghost, but I had other ideas. With a big black marker pen I wrote *Crocky* (a combination of Cocky and Rocky) across the back of my white towelling bathrobe. Then I slicked my hair with some borrowed Brylcream to make it look sweaty. Makeup, courtesy of the ladies, was carefully applied around my left eye and on a cheekbone to capture the just-been-in-the-wars bruiser look. Off came my monstrosity of a beard and on went the bandages (due to a lack of gloves), wrapped around my hands expertly by Bible bashing Harold who had in fact once been a corner man within the tough amateur world of pugilism. I wore an old Harlem Globetrotters vest that Ritchie had found for me, a borrowed pair of baggy white shorts and scuffed up old tennis shoes with the extra long laces crisscrossing up my lower legs to give a booted effect, but they soon fell down around my ankles whenever I attempted to walk. God was not in my corner that evening but the diminutive Ritchie Smith was. We jogged out of Anderson Ward and down the stone steps, trying all the time not go arse over tit because of the loose laces. Then we made our way through the creamy green corridors with my bandaged hands resting on Ritchie's rather low, yet very broad shoulders. We whistled the Rocky theme tune, believing that it would add a touch of authenticity. A slight detour was made to show off a bit, and to give some of the other patients a good laugh. Our laughter must have been heard echoing through the corridors, becoming louder and louder to the partygoers as we made our final approach. The entrance had to be in grand style, so I threw a few jabs and upper cuts at every balloon in sight. The dance floor suddenly became my ring to perform in. Richard found a plastic chair that became my corner. I would spar with one of the mongrel men or women or face a wall and shadow box along to *In The Navy* or *Hi Ho Silver* Lining. Those mongrel people were great fun, entering into the spirit of the evening wholeheartedly. Nobody bothered to ask why I had come to a Halloween party dressed up as Crocky. It didn't really matter did it, besides I was a harmless enough manic-depressive doing unasked for time in the local mental hospital, so I was entitled.

Fortunately, I happened to be among the privileged few who had a regular flow of visitors. I looked forward very much to such visits because apart from spending valuable time with my loved ones, most of them would bring in some goodies. Money in large amounts, as I previously mentioned, was considered unnecessary and in my case very dangerous. The last thing anybody needed at that time was a quick repeat of the Milan adventure. Even if I only had enough to travel the short distance to Watford or Brent Cross, the damage incurred could be just as severe. The pittance allowed was hardly enough to catch a bus into St. Albans town centre, but that was fine by me. I never wanted for anything much except of course to be with my unobtainable teenage sweetheart, who of course was now far from being a teenager, and somebody else's sweetheart. Forget the material things, what touched me the most was the fact that somebody had very kindly taken their time out, usually after a long busy day at work, to drive the awkward distance, come rain, wind or shine to a place than can often prove to be rather disturbing, just to see little old me. Receiving such an abundance of love and support was something that I had become very aware of, so sometimes I tried to include a few of the other patients who had hardly anyone to visit them. Those close to me were quite happy and at ease with being shared, in fact their curiosity had probably got the better of them. Anyway, how could four, five or even more visitors all have a decent part of me at once? My sisters regularly brought in bin bags full of good quality clothing and footwear, allowing the females on the ward to have a field day. Lisa picked up a few tops and some shoes but she still wore those stinky old ventilated ski-pants day in and day out. One evening my uncle Ron made the trip from his cottage in Bourne End. Ron's wife Jane also came along. Jane worked as a care assistant at a residential home for people with severe learning disabilities. Although the patients on Anderson Ward were not mentally disabled—unlike some of the long stay patients on the other wards—we were still more than capable of pulling some outrageous stunts. Aunt Jane had seen it all before, so any absurd or filthy shocking behaviour was water of a ducks back to her. One of the hardest things for a visitor to do is not reveal any inner disgust that they may be feeling toward a patient, whether it be a burns victim at Mount Vernon Hospital or an old mentally disabled patient rocking through boredom, dribbling and smelling of faeces and urine. My visitors chose quite an eventful evening to visit. Monica, who had been on the ward long before my arrival, was severely depressed, so much so that she made up her lacerated mind to do something about it fast. She became impatient and disillusioned with the current ineffectiveness of her medications, and also with the well intentioned words of encouragement from the concerned lips of the professionals and her fellow patients. With no way out in sight, Monica lashed out, smashing a glass bottle that she had found. In front of everybody in the lounge she went ahead and sank an edge into her soft pulsing wrist. This was obviously a last ditch scream through a loudhailer for help, otherwise she would have gone somewhere quiet to slice her life away, curled up in the same position as she had been minutes before entering this trying world. Not much blood spurted out, but her feelings had been made known, the job was done and the show was over. Hitting the rock bottom of your pit is horrific. You must take the pain and *not* attempt anything stupid because the day will inevitably arrive when you have accumulated enough self-will and belief to start climbing out. Remember that anyone who is worth their salt will be throwing you out a lifeline. When you get that first non-slip grip you will be on your way back to where the Sun *does* shine. A cry for help can and sometimes will go terribly wrong, but you have got to persist and hang on in there. Your crematorium curtain call is a long way off. It is *never* curtains when it comes to bipolar affective disorder, or any of the other mentally related illnesses.

A white paper chefs hat came into my possession. I filled the top brim with two ounces of hand rolling tobacco and a couple of packets of Rizla rolling papers, thoughtfully brought in for me by my uncle Ron. On the side of the stolen hat I wrote in big bold capitals, "ROLL UP, ROLL UP," so that anyone who fancied a free smoke could help themselves. This really was a case of being off my head! As you can imagine the word soon got out that something for nothing was available on Anderson Ward, and because this something for nothing happened to be the peoples favourite indulgence I became inundated with eligible freeloaders.

My sister Barbara and her partner Roberta were regular visitors to the hospital. The pair of them are naturally very sociable, understanding and open minded people, and they soon become very popular with the other patients. Being taken out to a nice restaurant in St. Albans City Centre was a treat of theirs that I especially looked forward to. Being manic with a waiter at your beck and call is an experience that any self respecting manic-depressive must try at least once before heading on down from way up above. Virginia, my other beautiful Sister, visited as often as Babs. She didn't stand for any of my nonsense, which was a good thing because that approach brought me down a few rungs from my pedestal. She also possessed the rare knack of directing the atmosphere from conversational calm to a collection of the latest loud and lively anecdotes and jokes. You could say that she thrives on controlling human traffic jams, a difficult duty that requires a high level of intelligence and understanding, qualities that Gee has an in abundance.

Having already spent a month of weekends at Hill End, the powers that be (consultant psychiatrists) recommended that I could come home for weekend visits, but not to my maisonette in Bovingdon. I had to be in the company of responsible human beings. And so it passed that I would spend my coming weekends back at my Parent's house. With my weekend rations of dispensed medication taken care of and my car keys hidden—despite being under the delusive conclusion that cars did not really need petrol engines to run after all—I was set to return to Hemel Hempstead, the scene of some very mixed memories. I think that the keys, minus my own door key, must have been snatched from my parent's house just before my admission, but I'm not positive. Everything on the outside of the hospital was so surreal and disorientating, making my return on Sunday evening a comfortable one. This situation reversed itself long before I was in any serious danger of becoming part of Hill End's institutionalised crowd. During one of my weekend breaks my folks and I were invited over to Barbara and Roberta's modest little terraced house in Bushey. Midway through what was up until then a delightful evening in a familiar but still oddly surreal setting, it all became too much for me to handle. Music was playing in one room, the television in another, and the buzz of conversation came at me from every angle, bouncing of every wall and ceiling that I had decorated in a previous life. The overwhelming cacophony of sound grew and grew until a shrill fist punched my knotted senses. With my head cupped in my hands I hastily left the room without uttering a single word, then made for the upstairs spare room where I knew a single bed with freshly laundered sheets would be waiting. It was dark and still. Peace and solitude for the first time in ages were now mine to savour. The orchestra ceased warming up inside my head, allowing me to cut off completely and allow for a deep sleep. "Are you all right in there?" came a concerned female voice from the other side of the bedroom door. "I was until you came and ruined it," I felt like saying. They only meant well. How could I realistically expect them to read my mind?

November 5th 1990, Guy Fawkes night. The large crowd that had gathered on that bitterly cold evening were in for a real treat. Danny and myself had the responsibility of lighting the bonfires and to keep them burning well. The neck aching heavens were displaying a full compliment of distant stars, filled with not so distant wishes. We succeeded in getting the bonfires to rip and roar without too many snags. So far all had gone according to plan, but then I decided to vary it a little. From the burning embers of one of the fires I grabbed a hefty smouldering stick and then began to run around the display field, leaping like the flames themselves from bonfire to bonfire, waving the glowing tip above my head for all to see. I would follow that up by giving the bonfires an almighty whack with my smouldering club, sending thousands of glowing embers up into the crisp night air. This almost primitive ritualistic tribal dance was presented live to the amused and bemused audience of about five hundred. Performing moves that I had no control over or comprehension of became a slightly disconcerting breeze. My strong expressional body just let go to the loud music. I became the fire and the fire became me, and I suddenly understood and appreciated how fire and the burning Sun came to be worshipped by so many through the ages. That night I became a fire dancer, which is quite a leap from the shy school drama days of my youth. Even if the gathered crowd were laughing at me, saying things like, "There goes that crazy bloke again on his day off from the padded cell," I didn't care one little bit, because once again I had allowed every new emotion into my body, allowing myself to feel a whole new dimension and to see and feel another world. That world is here in a ghostly form, it has always been here. Only if you let yourself well and truly go can you experience it and become a part of it. Those who ridicule and put down people who feel the same way as me are just blind to it all. Open up your mind and let it all in. Do you want a future that is better than today? Do you want to have freedom? If the answer is yes then do something about it—it is not going to be handed to you on a silver platter.

I became the fire. I had built it, given it life and danced among its flames. Although I looked alarming, covered in smoke and ash, I knew then and still believe today that I had hit upon a new area of perception that I was revelling in. Very conscious indeed was I of this superhuman aura that seemed to cloak me. I can clearly remember standing exhausted in that smoky field with the appearance of a very keen chimney sweep, telling myself that something here is exquisitely abnormal. Strong cravings to recapture not only my Guy Fawkes night display but so many of the other high experiences, still grab hold of me to this day. There may be a long wait before the reunion, or should I say the United Mental Union (UMU), when our thoughts will successfully intertwine and our entire brain mass will work to its intended full capacity, instead of hanging around idle inside our skulls. Shoot down in flames what you do not understand, destroy what frightens—these are the solutions and the directions used by far too many, upon too many. You can try, but nothing and nobody is ever going to change my vision of hope for a much greater future.

I launched into my hastily put together fireworks routine, exploding and whooshing, fizzling and booming—generally jumping about the field like a cretinous crackerjack. So high had I become that I grabbed another small log and returned to each bonfire to beat the hell out of them, making quite sure that the crowd would go home fully satisfied and that I got my manic monies worth. When I looked in the bathroom mirror later that night I thought that Al Jolson was staring back at me. Dancing has always been an activity that I regarded myself as being pretty good at, so I went to bed confident and contented that I had performed adequately, and that everybody was happy with my evenings efforts. My charged manic mind continued to play its tricks by insisting yet again that tonight's manic activities had been beamed live to every television set on Planet Earth. Those closest to me on the ward could not admit to seeing my fire dancing or any of my other being-wonderful-doing-absolutely-anything-bonkers routines, or they would run the risk of bursting the big delicate bubble, causing untold toil and trouble.

Julie's father had discovered through the grapevine that I had not been myself of late, not quite the same old Keith that they had come to happily tolerate when completely out of the blue he knocks on the big black door of the Moorhouse. Andrew invited me along for yet another night of fiery fun, with a little culture sprinkled in for good measure. Special permission had been bestowed for me to be driven to Hemel Hempstead so that I could attend the festivities, and further my hot pursuit of a career in fire dancing. The stipulation was that I had to return to Hill End no later than 10 p.m. (or my carriage would probably turn into a banana.) I set off for the party wearing a well worn black sports jacket,—I favoured it because all of the junk that I gave so much credence to could fit inside its many pockets—tight blue jeans and a pair of light brown high heeled imitation cowboy boots that Barbara had bought for me. A kind member of staff drove me the 12 miles there. Before entering the fray I went to see my uncle Mark and his family who lived just up the slope from the Moorhouse. While I was there I noticed an old black bowler hat perched among the Aladdin's cave of antiques that Mark loved to collect. Without hesitation he allowed me to borrow it for what was to be an extremely interesting couple of hours. When I had finished my obligatory mug of tea, I placed the bowler hat on my slicked back head and set off down the short slope. An infectious bonfire had already been lit in the back garden. The popping and crackle of the old branches stirred in agreeably with the social banter. I could hear familiar high pitched shrieks that excited my nervous buttons for I knew that she would be there, and I knew that tonight was the night to make some radical changes by popping a few long awaited questions. As I passed the side garden gate I resisted the strong urge to mosey on in, instead continuing all of the way round to the front of the house so that I could arrive in the proper fashion—the only fashion that I managed to get right that evening!

Knock knock knock. Andrew opened the heavy slab of a door for me. "Ah, Keith, it's so good that you could make it. Julie, Linda and Jean are somewhere out in the back garden, but first of all get yourself a drink and a bite to eat." I told him that I didn't drink alcohol anymore, hoping to score a few Brownie points, but that didn't cut much ice. I could see in his eyes that he was well away with his wobbly home made wine and potent home brewed ale. My opening lines leaned toward Ju, nothing much new there, but they mostly fell on deaf ears as there was a lot more hosting for him to take care of. I had become besotted and consumed by my unrealistic obsession with Ju. Up until this time I thought I was primed to do absolutely anything that might bring her to me, to notice me, and now I was apprehensive, scared stiff that it may never happen, fearful of rejection. Could I take the brunt of such an unwanted truth? The only guarantee that I had that evening was of being noticed by a bunch of tiddly modern art and classical music aficionados.

Confidently I glided past the music room on the left, through the crowded kitchen to my right, into the art studio, through the backdoor and out onto the beautifully landscaped garden. There I stood in the core of the flickering party, feeling taller than ever. I expected to engage eyes with Julie at any second, praying that I didn't foul everything up. My choice of evening wear had already taken good care of that, but at the time I was confident that I was the coolest creature, if not the smartest, that had ever stepped out of line. My general appearance and mannerisms did possess the certain quirkiness that I knew she used to love, so surely that would act in my favour, wouldn't it? Most of the casually dressed guests were heavily into one art form or another, making get-togethers such as this work as a tool to open up awareness of their latest music recital or art show. Most of the guests were heavily into the deceivingly strong homebrew that caused their laughter to remain in tune, but suddenly rise through their well rehearsed scales. I heard Julie's distinctive laughter lay down a solo track, a cut above the rest.

This is the part where I get to be with her at long last. This is the time when all of the running around trying to solve the clues and mysteries would fall into place. Prolonging the social congress for the sake of dramatic art suddenly made perfect sense. Earlier I had planned to assemble some sort of display that showed how much I loved her, made from various bits and bobs that were stuffed in my jacket pockets. My compulsion insisted that I follow through with this strategy, so I did an about turn, slinking sideways back through the alcohol refill room and up the winding staircase. My route led to the site of many a teenage fumble in irregular rhythm to Oscar Peterson's piano playing. On the lacy single bed I constructed a shrine made from a few of my poems, flower petals, ribbons, glitter from the art therapy class and a few locks of my hair. Nothing ventured nothing gained. I made my way back down to the fire licked garden. It didn't take too long for Jean to stumble across my little shrine, initially causing the ex-London midwife to quite understandably flip her tiddly lid. Meanwhile I had decided to carry on where I had left off at Hill End's bonfire and fireworks spectacular. Wielding a huge glowing tipped stick, I set about reliving the old magic, not only from a few wild days earlier but from my final heart throbbing year at Cavendish School. *Cruddunch* spoke my striking stick, *Phwhackhoosh* replied the burning cinders as they flew into the gasping group of flame faced frolickers. So there I was again, at the epicentre; I would probably have been better off at the *sports* centre only a mile away. Striving toward something only half baked and never explained in full, tends to become an open emotional drain that floods the latest scene. My slow burning fuse of passion was soon to burn out and be no more, but I had to keep on going the many distances, keep on travelling to the end of my time just to be certain. Playing the madman is fine if that is what it takes to be granted a position from where all that I feel can be said, heard and done. I resisted making eye contact with Julie, instead concentrating on becoming more and more daring, jumping in and then quickly out of the huge fire, avoiding premature cremation only by a cat's whisker. "She must be in awe of me," I thought. "Why is he making such an embarrassment of himself," she must have been thinking, "wearing cowboy boots and a bowler hat too!" I finally looked deep into her pretty eyes. She smiled back her playful smile, this time singed with a sorry sadness and an ever so slightly moist pink cheek. This performance had well and truly flummoxed her, but I'm sure that with the help of her drama background her true emotions were hidden. She insisted that I, "Go and have a little chat with my dad." Andrew had by now retreated to his downstairs study to take a break from the festivities. I thought that he was in there expecting me to arrive and ask him for his youngest daughter's hand in matrimony. Now I can laugh at the farcicality of the whole situation. There was indeed a miniscule part of my brain that told me how crazy I must have looked and behaved, but it was overshadowed by the strong belief that my grail was waiting to be swept from off her feet.

I knocked and he called me in. There stood I, covered from head to foot in ash and garden debris, wearing an ill fitting black jacket, cowboy boots and a bowler hat that made me look like a cross between Charlie Chaplin and Billy the Kid, rather than a sensible and mature suitor for his precious already married Julie. Without hesitation I boldly asked permission for his daughter's hand in marriage. "No," came the prompt reply. Donald Duck would have stood more of a chance than I did on that pitiful, though highly amusing November 1990 evening. Of course I was heartbroken, blown to pieces. The small fact that she was already married to Gary (who wasn't present that night) and had a little boy didn't exactly do a great deal to boost my deflated cause. Not long after my chat with Andrew my transport arrived to whisk me back to Hill End Psychiatric Hospital. I was so upset. Manic magic had backfired and died on me that night. Back on Anderson Ward I slumped to my bed, still covered in ash. When I became slightly more composed I reached out and pulled the tall curtain around the entirety of my sorrow, so that I could bawl out my grief in as much privacy as can be expected in such a place. I could be heard sobbing, but the others considerately left me well alone to expel the deflated emotion from my charred heart, and then to begin pumping it up again with a fresh outlook. Despite being stunned and shocked there was still the relief of finality, and at last I now knew for sure exactly where I stood, which was definitely *not* next to Ju. The ordeal was necessary as it freed up much needed mental space, allowing me to move on to fresh new business that wasn't always clouded by thoughts of fantasy. It is funny now, but at the time it felt as if my world had collapsed all around me. I needed firm reassurances that the my magic was flowing as powerfully as ever, and that everybody was still rowing on my side. It didn't take long to reason with a conveniently constructed explanation that satisfied and slotted right in, reshaping and repositioning any ill-bred blocks that I had become suspicious of. For a while I was content to be left alone in quiet seclusion. I figured that since I had invested so much love and guts into my fantasised quest, I surely didn't deserve such a hard kick in the bollocks! My temper became fragile for a while, unfairly snapping and barking at people. For a few days my resilience waned and my mind asked so many questions, yet I couldn't give a toss for the answers. For a little while I became devoid of emotion, cold and cynical of outsiders that seemed to be hell bent on piercing my safe and progressive manic world. Like a geriatric jackdaw I discovered that what might be shiny and alive today can easily flip over onto its back and become dog-shit brown tomorrow, not unlike my Milanese key.

Try telling somebody on a manic high that an actual illness (chemical imbalance) is the reason behind their distorted thinking, and they will *not* want to hear it. The denial is made because the latest high peak—it does *not* matter how many times it has previously been reached and then fallen down from—is this time the *real* one, the ultimate, and the previous highs were just warm ups, nothing more than training runs to be learnt from and incessantly picked at. Just like a drinker returns to the pub following a forgotten hangover, the manic-depressive person will be tempted to continue with their accent, oxygen and advice free. Believe me, when your foot hits that first manic rung there is no stopping!

Now that I no longer needed to remain loyal to a manic machined dream, all women became fair game. Helen Crowhurst, a pretty little flirtatious trainee nurse from nearby Harpenden, joined Anderson Ward just after my flashy Jumping-Jack display at the Moorhouse. A couple of the boys and myself would often sit round a dining room table talking and laughing with her, drawing pictures and playing games, but we had the most fun singing absolutely anything that came into our minds, sometimes blowing ourselves away to a Sun blessed psychiatric city. Elaine and myself sang together one evening, accompanied by Lewis Hopper on his jumbo 12 steel string acoustic guitar. Lewis, a 46-year-old exRoyal Marine from Hemel Hempstead suffered from crippling bouts of depression, but he sure could play a mean guitar when he put his disturbed mind to it. Our trio performed in the very same room that I had performed my version of "Raging Rocky." We had an audience of around thirty of the older patients, all of whom enthusiastically tapped their fingers and clapped their hands out of time to old classics such as *You've Got A Friend* by James Taylor and *Yesterday* by the Beatles. We performed twelve songs altogether, and fairly well too. The three of us had so much fun providing that evenings entertainment, even though there wasn't a single groupie among them.

A week later in the hospital's large main hall—a vast area that was nearly always locked except for an occasional badminton session—a most extraordinary talent evening and dance was held. Along I went, spruced up and with only one curvaceous thing, or should I say person, on my mucky manic mind. Many others from Anderson Ward made the short journey to the rear of the central function hall. We all sat huddled together on hard plastic chairs around two small wobbly tables. Mischievous Bloody Mary appeared with a big grin and a wink that had some of us falling about with laughter. She was clutching a plastic bag full of booze that she had slipped out to purchase from the local off-license. Some of our gang wasted no time in getting drunk in a very short amount of time; an easy feat when the body has been deprived of any serious quantities of alcohol for a long period of time. The heavy medication that some of us were on didn't help either. I abstained yet again because I was still of the belief that a water full existence and a booze free glass would go toward the manic trust fund that I had set up somewhere between my ears, something that was not easy to do considering my fondness for a hard drink on ice, coupled with a burning manic lust for all things hedonistic. The talent show was, well how can I put it, it was *so* crappy it was brilliant! Can you imagine a bunch of nutty but nice, fun loving human beings dancing and singing for all their worth in the belief that they have got real talent? One of the serious female singers managed to get more laughs than another patient who was trying and failing miserably to be a stand up comic. It has to be said and never forgotten that many of these would be rocking and rolling, joke telling, singers and impressionists have more brain cells in their heads than your average Mr or Mrs. Clever Dick walking down the high street. They have been dealt some confusing cards that's all, usually at a time in their life when they didn't even want to play the game, but were forced.

Helen was there with her fellow student girlfriends. She kept peeking at me, so naturally I did likewise. The guys and gals from Anderson Ward knew of our mutual attraction, so they gave us both plenty of unsubtle encouragement. I was pleased to see that Helen was pouring vast amounts of red wine down her slender off duty neck and was beginning to loosen up. The gaps between one eager performer and the next galloped by with the help of a scratched disc and its jockey, giving cause for even more hilarity. A little mutual nod and a flick of the head to the twirling wooden floor was all it took to get Helen and myself up and into a fast dance. After a couple of fast dances the strobes and spots were turned off, so that the badminton court we were treading could take a cool dive into darker and more intimate territory. Helen kicked off her heels, bringing her down to only two inches above my five feet seven. My trousers firmly pressed, tight pencil skirt, silky stockings, crisp shirt, clingy blouse and a sexy white lace push up brassiere were all that separated throbbing hot loins and heaving chests. We must have looked as if we were performing a slow, centre stage knee trembler—now that's what I call entertainment!

Trouble was stirring in places other than just my baggy boxers. A party-pooping attempt came in the dampening form of a Moroccan male nurse. We often referred to the Moroccan members of staff as Martians. The Martian in question came over between dances and had a swift word with Helen. I soon discovered that the fun assassin was trying to tell her that if she carried on with me in the same vain she would be running the risk of waving goodbye to any future career in nursing. Elaine had true spunk coming out of her multi pierced ears, so she told the interfering killjoy in no uncertain terms to shove his fat head up his equally enormous arse. When it was my turn I trimmed back the eloquence and told the prick to, "fuck off out of it, otherwise I'll knock your teeth down your throat,"—no messing about! This guy was twice my size, but one has to stand up for what one believes in.

When a couple get to this stage it is a very risky move to try and part them. To cut a long story short, Helen and myself left the bopping multitude so that we could find a quiet corner in which to canoodle. This lasted for only twenty minutes until one of Helen's girlfriends located us, probably by the soft groaning emitted by a pair of sexually aroused human beings. We were in and out of each others clothing (among other things) with warm tender hands, displaying a beautiful and natural abandon, sharing the one universally understood language without having the need to utter a single word of commonsense. This must have been the longest amount of waking time that my mouth hadn't been in verbal operation since my admittance, perhaps except for art therapy. For that twenty minutes we forgot who was the patient and who was the nurse, all that mattered was that we were two human beings doing what human beings were supposed to do. Helen's girlfriend was indeed the bringer of bad tidings, relaying the threat from the Martian that he was about to throw in his wet blanket and squeal on Helen. It was in fact plain jealousy. The green eyed Moroccan monster could not get what Helen did not want to give, and so he decided that nobody else could. We returned to the main hall slower than when we left. The gyrating lights had upped their tempo and the music had risen a couple of decibels, or so it seemed in comparison to our brief interlude. Helen continued to make a different form of whoopee with her bottle of red wine, as I just sat watching her with a big pussycat-who-has-just-got-the-cream smile on my face. Frustration at not scoring a home run was evident in both of us, but who knows what the future may bring? Every time I caught the boiling eyes of the jealous Martian I gave him a middle finger salute, followed up promptly with a blown kiss—a gesture that the great oaf didn't like one single bit. Much later when I had been released from Hill End and was suffering in the evil arms of a debilitating depression, Helen would drive from Harpenden to Hemel Hempstead to hug me, and walk with me out in the open streets where I had become so scared to be seen, even in the bitchy blackness of the most silent of nights. Eventually Helen ceased flying over to be with me, enabling us both to move on and up with the rest of our long and priceless, truly amazing lives.

My blood still had to be tested in the pathology laboratory at St. Albans City Hospital virtually every week, until the correct lithium levels were found. I must have had more pricks in me than a pair of hedgehogs making love. Achieving the correct lithium levels proved to be a far trickier proposition than was originally anticipated, and my rattling mania certainly didn't want to subside by its own accord. To this day I still undergo regular blood tests to determine my lithium level. The condition of my thyroid gland and the ability of my liver to success-fully undertake its janitorial role, are also frequently checked by a busy haematol-ogist. That testing frequency has to be increased if I have a relapse and have shot way up, or have sunk to new depths. Now that I have ceased to drink heavily I should see a marked difference in my mood pattern. A lot of all medication is nullified by an excessive alcohol intake, that is if the drunk actually bothers to take their important dosages when they are in a stupor of artificial escapism. Drinking excessively because I am up, or if I am down is *not* on. When I am in the land of the normal I dare not become wrecked because of the possible trigger effect that it can bring. To preserve and invest in my prolonged and healthy existence, I must avoid the spirited highs and lows that can be bought over the counter. My normal self is rather outlandish, creative, neat and fussy, and I think that I come in an acceptable shade of unpredictability. The problem can be that if I smile too much at a clown, or I become a bit down in the mouth because the England football team have been knocked out of the World Cup Finals, it can easily be mistaken for the early tremors of a bipolar episode. That has to be for me, and for many other sufferers the most frustrating thing, knowing that my normal behaviour can be misinterpreted or misconstrued as manic or ultra glum when it really is not. Sometimes I sense that my company are trying to pick a fault, jumping on the bandwagon, pointing their unqualified fingers and thinking that, "He's off his trolley again." Knowing full well that the person with whom I am sharing valuable time is overlooking all that I have to say, and instead is hell bent on finding some sort of technical fault, is so damn annoying.

If I question them they get on the defensive and accuse me of everything under the Sun, using my illness as their weapon. Why do some people delight in using me against myself? Is it so that they can be made to feel big in the company of whom they have decided is mentally deficient? Everyone will say, "Oh no, don't be so silly and paranoid," but a few people do exactly that, and I should know because I am constantly with my manic depression, and will be for the rest of my life. Ignorant folk can only get me down if I let them, so I do *not* let them. Be careful with those false accusations because one day it could be *you*! Even a close member of my family once interrupted me in a small crowd and said, "Don't take any notice of him, he's mad!" *Mad* is a small word that hits home big. It is a serious description not to be used lightly, yet I have to admit that I have been a culprit on many an occasion. I hate it when the person I am with isn't paying a blind bit of notice to a word that I am saying, because all that they can or want to think of me as is Keith Alan Steadman, you know him, the manic-depressive chap who becomes a bit too lively from time to time, or you don't see him for months on end, and when you do see him he looks as miserable as sin and tries to avoid everybody. That is what really bugs me. It is not through self pity or feeling hard done by that puts the wind up my sails, oh no, it is simply down to the inhumane treatment that just a few people lavish at my expense in order to maintain their own wishy-washy world made out of transparent tissue paper and hot air, a flimsy hell hole bored in their heads that makes my temporary manic environment refreshingly sane by comparison. I liken it to Sir Winston Churchill's famous remark when a woman once accused him of being roaring drunk to which he replied, "Yes Madam, and you are ugly, but in the morning I shall be sober." I can recover from episodes and lead a perfectly normal existence, but can you change for the better?

I really shouldn't have to, but the attitudes of a few are contributory factors to why I sometimes choose to keep more about myself to myself instead of the healthy alternative of being uncomplicated, accessible and forthright. Maybe I am often too honest for most people to stomach and should instead concentrate on being an ever so slightly toned down version of myself, whoever the hell *myself* really is. The word *normal* is a tricky one to define. Rules, laws and guidelines are there to be adhered to, so there is a valid low barrier separating right/wrong and normal/abnormal behaviour. *Normal* doesn't really exist, nor does it have a defining line to measure it against any of the objects, situations, circumstances or emotions that it inevitably encounters on a daily basis. Something recognised as bad by one person is regarded as perfectly normal by another. Please tell me who has the God given right to insist that their brainwashed beliefs, out of thousands of choices are correct, and that mine and yours are not as true? The prime example is within religion; just look at the conflict it has caused for entire nations and for single families. Variations upon a similar theme are all that religions really are, with a small percentage of their fanatical members performing every hypocritical act under the Sun in order to dominate the market. If you were born into X religion you would be an X follower, and if you were born into a Y religion you would be a Y follower (similar to supporting a football club), which just goes to prove how ridiculous it is to insist that whatever you have been brainwashed with is the perfect No.1. It is *so* small minded it is unreal, and they have the nerve to put *me* in the nut-house, what a joke! I try to see everything from a global perspective, through the tuned in eyes of an open minded generalist, not too stubborn or proud to change my opinion and beliefs, instead of being brainwashed into the safe ways of somebody else's misinterpreted ideals. The world needs interesting people such as manic-depressive/bipolar "sufferers." We are on the whole good and caring people who have their peculiarities (show me a person who does not), but we know how to utilise our bipolar toolkits in order to make some of the most conscientious and generous contributions toward today's speeding society. By looking at my topsy-turvy life so far it appears that I have lived it according to my draught free plan, building the engine as I go, leaving me with the uncertain prospect of being a tuned up old man without anyone left to play with, or anywhere fresh to go. Whoever said that this life was going to be a smooth ride needs their head examining!

After many weeks of searching, little Tommy was at last found safe and well. At long last he was reunited with his relieved mummy and daddy. A young man in his mid-twenties—he had a complex psychological problem, but was harmless enough—had snatched young Tommy and taken him to his nearby apartment, situated just behind Hemel Hempstead's picturesque Old Town High Street. No harm came to him. He had eaten well and was kept reasonably clean. Although he must have occasionally kicked up a few tantrums because he missed his family, the whole affair probably seemed to be quite an adventure for him. No, he was not abused. So, the little Tommy story was wrapped up with a happy ending. Let's hope and pray that there will be no long lasting psychological effects; I'm sure there won't be, unlike Jenny.

Even though I was jubilant about young Tommy's safe return, it did put a whopping dent in my judgment. Any future career as a detective went straight down the toilet right there and then. On reflection, it was an accumulation of events such as Ju being happily married and the safe homecoming of Tommy that accentuated my descent. I freefell and got snagged on a loosely screwed hook. This poorly directed scene saw me hanging around at the same time and in the same place as the previous day, only down one peg. Packages of black and white slowly stacked up, compressing the base into a case hardened tool, capable of gouging slowly into the once impregnable soul and structure of what could and should have been my perfectly simple and straightforward world, but was now being cold heartedly stolen by a familiar poor boy who still had it all, yet he could not see the wood for the trees. That rich poor boy was me.

My therapy groups were proving very beneficial. I was particularly delighted at seeing a good selection of my work hanging on the lofty art room walls. In the woodwork room there were some old and slightly damaged wooden picture frames leaning against a bench. Ritchie helped me to retrieve some of them so that I could mount some of my favourite artwork. For obvious reasons glass was not permitted to enter the picture, not in a place like Hill End Psychiatric Hospital. Many of my colourful expressions stayed put upon the art therapy walls long after I had parted company with the old hospital, just as pretty Kashika had promised. The final solution, the utter destruction of my art must have happened at around the time of demolition, but so what, they had served their purpose in helping me get a load off, by putting a load onto a blank surface.

Charles, who must have been in his late sixties, spent most of his art therapy session sitting quietly at his table composing hilarious letters of complaint. These he would seal with the authoritative thump of somebody who meant business. He convinced himself that his handwritten letters brought about major worldwide changes. Charlie then gave these to his reliable daughter to post. His carefully penned correspondence found its way to such luminaries as Her Majesty the Queen, the British Prime Minister, the Director General of the BBC, and even the Pontificating Pope in Rome. Charlie told me in all seriousness about the correspondence that he once had with Downing Street in London. Apparently he had purchased a brand new pair of shoes with laces that he thought were far too long, so he complained by letter to the then Conservative Prime Minister Mrs. Thatcher that there was far too much spare lace hanging around. He argued that there must be miles upon miles of spare lace dangling from, or double tied upon the feet of the Great British public. To their credit Downing Street replied, stating politely that shoelaces were not really within their area of expertise, and that they were rather busy with slightly more important issues such as running the country. Yes, Charlie was one of those likable fruitcakes, always wrapped up in his own make believe casing, but not hurting a single soul in the process. Charles became very good friends with the equally cranky God/Harold, and for all I know he may have written to the Pope or even Jesus Christ himself, complaining about the lack of crusty bread, red wine and fresh cod served up at Hill End mealtimes.

Sometimes it took every ounce of willpower to prevent myself from drowning in inspiration. I wanted to express and digest all that was occurring deep inside and way out, but there was simply too much to handle. My back burner simmered far too many ideas and new discoveries that hadn't been allowed the airtime that I thought they deserved, so they vaporised, lost in the mists of time. The next instalment would roll in and take up a temporary residence upon the silver emulsion throne of thrills and spills. Itchy frustration put its boot in harder and harder. I often felt so close yet so damn far. Close to what exactly? A million pipe dreams, but nothing on which to base a stable foundation from where I could structure a future worth being a valid part of. I needed the place and space where dreams will merge with sense and become realistic, achievable and fun—am I describing normality?

Hell bound in a dire strait jacket, surrounded by paradise, a bent key to freedom hangs around the necks of God the judge, God the ruler, past lovers and Brothers, Sisters, Fathers and Mothers, those we mourn and the innocent newborn. It is enough to drive any human being into the pits, only to find that the fire resistant team are standing as still as sandstone by their uneconomical fuel lines. To get me through the lulls, when my stomach experiences anxious dips into foreign waters—a nervousness in the pit of one's stomach, that is not unlike the feeling one gets when zooming over a humped back bridge—I kept telling myself that it was all part of the great test. When the dust settles, my final destination will become so much clearer and self explanatory. I would desperately attempt to conjure up an old buddy, a much needed ally to help guide me through those early signs of descent, anything that would fire me up so that I could still strike the big brass bell in the sky.

My old man kept up his visits without fail. I could set my new watch by him. The pain of seeing your own flesh and blood, your own son cooped up inside a psychiatric hospital must have been immense. Don't get me wrong, there is absolutely *no* shame whatsoever in being a patient in a psychiatric hospital, as it is just a different area of medicine, that's all. Although I asserted my individuality and natural independence to remain as de-institutionalised as I possibly could within an institution, my dad bled inside, who wouldn't? Never a one for self pity, he would quite willingly give up his whole self just to have seen me clamber back onto the human racetrack. A great man, the best there is!

Being driven through the Hertfordshire countryside did me the world of good. The change of scenery, getting away from all of the enjoyable mayhem for even the shortest of rides continued to prove so very therapeutic. It was now late November and I was well into my third month as a psychiatric patient in Hill End Psychiatric Hospital. Late November and all through festive December is the traditional time for truckloads of depressed men and women to be rounded up and admitted. "Bring out your depressed, bring out your depressed," I can hear them cry, just as it was during many an historical plague. Seasonal affective disorder (SAD) is often the culprit, but although it can strike down its vulnerable victims at anytime, it is far more prevalent throughout the winter months when there is a distinct lack of sunshine around to stimulate the happy juices inside the brain. SAD can lead to far worse things, but one has to try and avoid getting this strain of depression confused with severe clinical manic depression because it is the same as putting a common cold in the same ring as a severe bout of malaria. I know very well that absolutely any type of depression is debilitating and distressing for all parties concerned, and I do not wish to undermine the severity of an explainable case of the winter blues. I am sorry to say, though wiser for the experiences, that I have been down that glorious shit-pit and crawled on my bare hands and knees along the rough rocky road, fearful that I will never get up in time when the tarmac gang arrive to smooth over the cracks, leaving me flattened and depressed like one of the characters in a Tom and Jerry or Roadrunner cartoon. Perhaps I could whistle a loony tune to keep my spirits up and also to ward off the steamroller driver. What the hell did we do to deserve it? Were we meant to suffer in preparation for what might lay ahead? There are so many searching and demanding questions but never enough satisfactory answers to go round.

Space in Hill End was at a premium. Newcomers to the St. Albans mind factory would somehow be accommodated even if it meant that some of the patients already residing on Anderson Ward were transferred to a spare bed on a long-term ward for a short while. Some of the patients with whom I had built up a rapport recovered sufficiently to be let back out into the big wide world, the real asylum, a place solely responsible for adding the *in* to *sane*. Nearly all of the patients on Anderson Ward had a musty dusty place waiting in Hemel Hempstead that they could return to, so one by one they did, slipping away to fight another mammoth day. Most of the patients made a successful return home, and some returned in much the same way that a captured escapee from a prison of war camp returns, with beaten head held low, spirit broken, demoralised, bleeding and bruised, except that the bruises and scars have become both spiritual and mental. Lisa was the noticeable exception. All that she had in the material world were the clothes and gusset hole that she stood up in, plus one hell of a fiery Irish spirit. She used to work in Mallorca, picking up a decent wage. Perhaps she had done the same as I did in Milan and decided in her confused state of mind to leave all of her worldly goods behind, wipe the slate clean and start all over again. It was spirit that saved her bacon. Lisa left Hill End still feeling rather confused, but lady luck must have been shining down on her because in no time at all she managed to locate and secure a grubby little bed-sitting room. Her new rented accommodation comprised of one room and a communal bathroom, and it was only half a mile away from the hospital. On paper this looked like a terrific arrangement, presenting Lisa with the best of both worlds. She would return during the day to share time with her closest hospital friends: Bloody Mary, Ritchie Smith, a chunky male nurse on Drake ward, and of course Ian for whom she still openly displayed her affection. As far as I could tell, Ian did not appear to reciprocate, instead he concentrated first and foremost on his manic principle of self satisfaction. This pleasure principal covered a large and extremely loud area of what I sensed to be a much quieter and introverted private life. Lisa and myself enjoyed checking out the second hand clothes that the hospital kept tucked away in one of its many mysterious rooms. We had some colourful laughs trying on the zipped up and buttoned down garments of yesteryear. Time and time again I was drawn back by the irresistible lure of far out fashion. I liked it to be ever so bright, tight and so shiny that if I wore any of the items out in the firework field at night, the saucy visitors above would probably think that I was one of their kind and attempt to pick me up. Women's clothing—well, it is only fabric after all—floppy hats, chiffon and bangles—they all found their way onto my depleted flesh, and then onto every ward on the site. Harold/God's daughter had cut my hair floppy on top, with a tapered back and sides. This rather dashing, cleaner cut look topped off my glam transformation very nicely, or so I had myself believe.

The staff often shook their heads and grinned at my harmless manic antics, that included variations of the same dance routines and song recitals. I swear that inside of me there is a budding performer desperately struggling to get out. There is a side of Keith yet to be unveiled that has nothing at all to do with frequenting gay bars and clubs; not that I have anything against them you understand, it's just that I prefer high pitched curves to baritone beefcake in a dress.

Every evening just before bedtime, the ardent smokers among us gathered in the three-quarter snooker room for a smoke and a chat. On this particular evening, myself and a few of the others had changed into our pyjamas and nighties. The sniggering started, coming mostly from the directly opposite sex. Then the men decided to join in, leaving me completely bewildered. For the next five minutes I squirmed uncomfortably in my vinyl chair, sipping my sweet tea and puffing on the last cigarette of the day. Eventually it dawned on me that my privates had been anything but. My modest manhood had been given a jolly good airing through the baggy flap of my pyjama bottoms. The following day I became known as Wee Willy Winkle. I blamed my poor showing on the stabilising medication prescribed to psychotic cases such as myself—drugs that bring down far more than just mania!

Another amusing member of our tea or soup swilling throng was a large sweaty lady from Hemel Hempstead called Doris. Big Doris could be calm and amusing one minute, and then for no apparent reason she would let out a terrifying scream, and I mean *loud*. Watching the reaction of a newcomer to these outbursts gave us all a good laugh. She would also slap the top of her head with both of her chubby hands at the same time, she sometimes even used the tea tray on her head. Barmy Doris would stop this peculiar activity as suddenly as she had started, then reach for her warm tea and sit quietly with a silly great grin spread across her hairy hormonal face, what a fun character she was. We always laughed *together*, very rarely did we ever laugh *at* a fellow patient.

Frightening doesn't even begin to describe an experience that I had one night when settling into my bed. I was feeling drowsy from my medicinal right hook so I decided to hit the sack, and that's when it happened. An invisible force or maybe an evil spirit took away my control of every bodily function. My torso, limbs and head were pinned with a tremendous force down into the mattress. I attempted to shout for help and to lift my limbs, but no words would come out. The invisible grip grew stronger and stronger. My eyesight remained loyal, so I looked up and around for a patient or a nurse who could offer discouragement to this terrible force, but there was nobody to bail me out of this sinister experience. Worse still were the heavy thuds on my chest, the sort of sickly electric thudding punch that one might expect from a cardiac crash trolley. Blow after blow kept raining down, but I was unable to do anything about it, then as sudden as it began my ordeal ceased. I got up, not at all drowsy now, and made a beeline to the nurse's station. None of them had gone to sleep yet. "What is it Keith? I thought you had gone to bed," said one of them. I did my best to explain in detail exactly what had happened to me. "Subconscious nightmare," said a nurse. Suffice to say that the official cause, or rather the convenient cause that went into my medical records was a mile off the mark, but why argue, what else could they have logged? I knew what had happened. I didn't want to keep the staff up any longer than was necessary, so I tiptoed barefoot back to the men's dorm. Nothing else happened that night, although I did surface much earlier than the rest to have a quiet shuffle around. I still stuck with my rigid morning routine despite harnessing a little fear of another invisible assault. When I returned to my awakened dormitory to get dressed, another patient threw a national tabloid newspaper onto my bed. I pawed though the pages until I came across a piece about an inmate of another old Victorian mental hospital who had, "Stabbed male nurse in frenzied knife attack." A deranged knife wielding lunatic from a hospital in the Manchester area, had managed to lay his no good hands upon a knife from the kitchen, and then take out his pent up anger by ventilating the innocent body of a nurse. The nurse survived. We all have some disillusionment, anger and a little confusion in our lives, but we have to deal with it in a controlled manner, leaving characters like this, even if they are mentally ill, to be quite rightly labelled and treated as nasty pieces of evil. As I touched upon earlier, mental illness is *no* excuse for murder or attempted murder. To commit any serious crime the perpetrator needs to be extremely clever, calculating and quick thinking. Mentally ill people who are severely disturbed have a million other anti-social activities available to them, so why pick murder and sex offences and then conveniently blame it on the insanity that their mental illness allegedly provided? I have worked with severely mentally handicapped adults who follow their natural sexual or aggressive instincts, and occasionally perform the unthinkable in the most inappropriate of places—I think you can guess the rest. What freaked me out the most was that the stabbing incident had taken place earlier that previous evening, as I was experiencing my first encounter with the phenomenon of the subconscious nightmare. Being naturally high and susceptible to any hint of suggestion, I automatically put two and two together and came up with the theory that I had received the attack simultaneously; a telepathic stab in the devils dark during the fluorescent light of day. I stretched my raging imagination even further, wondering if my old knife might be up to no good in the tanned hands of Milan.

Paranormal incidents have to be experienced to be believed. They need not be feared just because they lack an airtight explanation, and are often unable to be heard or to be seen. Have an open mind, allow space and reserve judgment. My connection with intended death certainly wasn't a pleasant one, although I have to admit that I am glad it happened because it proved to me, and possibly to a few other of my fellow patients, that there is another dimension to our existence, a dimension that we use all of the time and that has lived an agoraphobic life within us. Society needs to let it out and breathe, without having to worry about the threat of ridicule and recrimination by narrow minded scaredy-cats who will be the first to take advantage of what they once put down, abused and wrote off entirely without thoroughly researching the evidence. A couple of years later I had a repeat experience. Irresponsibly I had become very high again due to excessive drinking and erratic administering of my prescribed medications. I was in my lonely Bovingdon bed about to read a library book, when out of nowhere I felt the pressure. Whatever was intent on bugging me had secured a firm vice like grip on my body. Once again I could feel the invisible hands on my legs and on my shoulders. This time I was all by myself, no nurses or patients to come to my aid. To say that I was terrified would be a huge understatement, though *mortified* sums it up nicely. When the pressure eventually relaxed and I thought that I could move again, I could not. The sheer terror of what had just happened in my blue walled bedroom had transformed me into a block of ice.

Going to the bathroom during the night was a definite no-no. I would have been quite happy to defecate in my bed instead of venturing out and into another close encounter with some sort of angry poltergeist. Scary though that experience was, it pales in comparison to the Milanese hospital bed fright when I had to endure the awful sensation of sinking, as well as being paralysed and gagged. The fear and terror that came with the belief that this was finally it—screaming and pleading that my body and soul had been reduced by wrongful dismissal to an everlasting strife in the devil's den—is an experience that I pray never happens again. Thankfully this unseen force or presence has left me alone. I believe that we all have a strong element of good and bad in us. We ourselves possess both Almighty God and the degenerate devil. Their volatile relationship has a tendency to unexpectedly explode like the Heavenly thunder and lightening storms, especially throughout the happy and sad extremities of mental illness. This of course can happen to anybody who possesses a mentality, which of course applies to us all, but those of us who are regarded as mentally ill *do* appear to show far more susceptibility, displaying a greater perception of what is often much too much spiritual and mental regurgitation. Is it that the majority of mentally ill people simply have difficulty in processing what a "well" person can, or do we "ill" human beings have no other choice than to cram far too much into our busy minds? There is always more to be expelled from a mentally ill mind, especially a manic one, than the time of day provides, along with a restrictive choice of satisfactory outlets with which to adequately do so. I have had my fair share of battles, and I expect some more to follow. If allowed, the good in us will always prevail. Could it possibly be that when a person is way up on an episodic high, they become finely tuned into the supernatural world? My answer is a resounding, "*Yes*." When I was high in Hill End I was able to shout out the answers to the television's latest quiz show before the questions were even asked.

Some of my answers were not always smack-bang on the nose, but they sure gave the nurses food for thought as they studied me while slowly, shaking their heads in disbelief. I found that these fun things happened spontaneously. I couldn't always turn it on with the flick of my psychic switch, but when it *was* turned on it came gushing out. Profiteering from such a gift doesn't seem to work, although it wasn't through a lack of trying. The horses that I picked ran more like donkeys from a sanctuary. Indoors I am picking winners all over the place but as soon as I get inside the betting office my winning streak comes to an abrupt end—I think they call it Sod's Law, and the pesky judge stinks to high Heaven!

Susan, my current partner from Queens, New York, sails with me across the bipolar seas. She has often called me long distance at exactly the same time as I was about to pick up the handset to call her. This has happened more times than I can remember. "We all do that," I can hear you cry, but with such frequency and Swiss influenced accuracy? All men and boys know to their cost that females have an intuition that senses what was once thought to be a private mood, or they can tell what secretive thoughts are rattling through one's head, especially if those thoughts are of a mischievous nature. How many times have you switched the radio on and the relevance of the music is far more than just uncanny, as if a scripted message is being put out especially for you by arguably the world's best and most respected broadcasting corporation, the British (BBC)? Occasionally the fit is that of a sleek Italian glove, far too precise an occurrence to be a psychological or spiritual fluke. When I desperately needed comfort and hope, the painfully sore fit of my broken down Italian shoes had to suffice. This belief provides me with a feeling of well being and security that I can carry around wherever I go. I believe that myself and many others are being encouraged and supported by every player from every participating side, all of whom can see the promising light that is forever being distributed among every known, and unknown facet of our extraordinary existence. Without a shadow of doubt there are oceans full of psychic power, and too many unprepared minds. Minds that are flopping about like unfulfilled discs or bright leather hippie hats need to be hardened and upgraded to see the clues, using those clues wisely so that everything fits tightly and loosely at the same time. One day, every single one of us will be able to afford the high cost of seeing the bigger picture in an even higher definition, and laugh at how we made such hard work of absolutely nothing, designed by all of us for all of you.

Crafted visual images that represent the beautiful mess of a magnificently gifted, yet over burdened mind are explicitly revealing to anybody, but especially to the natural instinct and trained receptiveness of the therapist in question, allowing them to click the turnstile and come inside to see the group of shows on offer. Myself and the other patients hauled a sack-full of psychotic slants, delusions, hang-ups and letdowns around the creamy green corridors of our Hill End residency. That sack was tied up so tightly in safety knots that when release became necessary, some of the weaker patients struggled and fumbled with their fingers and thoughts to find their personnel code, the numerical tool that was able to unlock a jammed up mind. It would take a sterile and steady verbal thought insertion by the right person to open the lid on a closed down life. Occasionally I had great difficulty in offloading lodged emotions and excessive quantities of important niggling thoughts. It was not unknown for me to raise the roof on the rare occasions when my verbal, sketched or thought projections fell down flat on too many deaf ears. The others had equally important projects and plans to work their way in or out of. When that top coat of yacht varnish begins to peel in the saline heat, and the required and correct method in which to put across a descriptive explanation of the latest strained brainwave keeps flipping over and over in the air like one of Stan The Prune's dinner forks, and when I frantically scrape without much joy inside my battered but never beaten soul, I do tend to become a little wild.

The prominent underlying characteristics among mentally troubled human beings are able to be pieced together by the experienced professionals to create an understandable picture of where that person is coming from, and where that person is heading. Establishing where that person is at the present time—a vital location to pinpoint so that a calamitous route can be avoided—is the most important thing. In the worst scenario a fatal crash can be averted.

In 1997 the terrific idea of pouring the patients of Hill End Psychiatric Hospital all over an ill equipped community materialised. This was done to make way for yet another new housing estate, causing a lot of upset among existing and ex-patients alike. Through thick and thin, Hill End acted as a place that could be trusted and relied upon, then suddenly it was gone. Many years on from what turned out for me to be a severely depressing discharge, I still felt a deep sense of loss. A milder form of mourning over my lost papers, paintings and sculptures draped over me, but it was for the rubbery faces that I had grown to understand and love that a heavy cloak of grey came to rest upon my shoulders. The importance of art therapy to myself and to plenty of others was huge. It isn't until it is taken away that you realise just how big a part it had in your life, even if you had been discharged a few years prior to demolition. We knew it was there as a form of security. Any kind of security is so important for a mentally ill person, as it can act as a base from which to reconstruct a healthy peace free mind, and also a meaningful and productive future. From time to time I stumble across one of the many ex-Hillenders and delight in the improved human being standing there before me. It would be nice to think that they may feel the same way toward me. All of them, with a few exceptions, scrape by on their meagre incomes, but most of them seem to be reasonably happy and contented with their present lot in life. You have to understand that these people know the meaning of their lives. They may not be ecstatic, but at least they aren't at such bad odds with their existence as they may have been before. A stress free lifestyle is what it is all about, a lesson that too many intelligent high-flyers fail to learn. *Nobody* is immune to a stress related mental illness, commonly referred to as a "breakdown." None of us need to be thrown onto the scrap heap and then crushed. It can never be overstated that true success is not measured in money,—a few extra quid does help to provide a quality of life that I wouldn't argue with—it is measured in peace of mind, contentment and good health. If you manage to achieve them all then good for you. How can we enjoy good financial fortune when we are boxed up and six feet below the world stage? Don't tolerate whatever it may be that is stressing you out. Deal with the root cause before it trips you up and drags you through the trapdoor.

Christmas 1990 was rapidly approaching. John Major had become the new British Prime Minister, and there was a big dust-up brewing in the sandy Persian Gulf between Iraq and Kuwait. The coalition forces were arrayed ready to try and fix the situation if an Iraqi withdrawal was not made by January 15th 1991. The American military leader Norman was indeed "Storming." Much of this conflict was being shown live on the ward's television set, upsetting and confusing myself and some of the other patients even more. There were times when I thought the conflict was one big performance laid on especially for a worldwide audience of billions. It was of course a deadly serious real life affair for so many brave service men and women. The hospital's art therapy department was called upon to provide the seasonal paintings and decorations that were to adorn the wards and corridors. Every mental illness on the block enjoyed a fair representation. I wore the waning manic Santa hat throughout the run-up to Jesus Christ's misplaced Birthday. In customary pumped up style I flew around the hospital as the other patients proceeded to make or break Christmas. The hospital's print shop produced small packs of ten flimsy Christmas cards, and for all I know Stanley The Prune may have been busily assembling paper chains made out of toilet paper as he sat upon his favourite throne. As many people as possible were encouraged to make some sort of contribution. One of these flimsy cards was sent to New York Susie, the Bayside beauty. I wished Susan and her family a huge, "Happy," and apologised profusely for not contacting her earlier as I had promised. Before my trip to Milan I had in fact written to Susan using the address that I had found on a letter from 1981, the same year that I stayed at her Smithtown house on Long Island, New York. We had also spoken at length on the telephone which resulted in a promise to jet over the pond to visit her soon, but instead I took a trip in a manic skyrocket that flew me to Milan, giving Sue and the good people of the United States a very lucky break. I made up for it later though!

As a postscript on the white and black Jesus-in-a-crib paper card I wrote eight straightforward words, that in time were to alter both of our lives for the better: "By the way, I am a manic-depressive."

In 1981 I had no idea at all that she was a bipolar affected person. I didn't even know what manic depression was despite the two obvious clues in the title, and let's face it, when you are a young English soccer playing alien in America you really don't get involved too much with the host parents and their mental health issues, preferring instead to spend time with her son Jack who is my age, and his two younger Sisters Dawn and Leigh. Susan's powerfully built husband Patrick played a major role in organising and training the kickers team. Patrick, a very social person, was also a highly respected school principal. This intelligent fellow was also extremely generous in providing whatever it took to make my team mate Ashley and myself feel comfortable throughout our entire stay. Why would Sue wish to share with a sixteen year old a personal condition such as manic depression? If somebody that I hardly knew started talking incessantly about a bad case of gout or their irritable bowel syndrome, following a 3600 mile flight for a sixteen day stay, I would have serious doubts about their state of mind, wouldn't you? When Sue received her flimsy paper Christmas card she immediately telephoned her son Jack, who was then studying for his doctorate degree at the Rockefeller University in Manhattan. Jack told her that no matter where I was at with the illness, no matter what crazy chapter I was up to in this particular book of life, it need not affect any future friendship or the present communication. Sue knew that, but when that backing comes from a supportive son it adds extra muscle. Today Jack works as a research scientist for one of the worlds leading pharmaceutical companies. His research into the causes and cures of mentally related illnesses continues, along with a host of other complicated projects that are way beyond my comprehension. Research into manic depression is his original passion because of his mothers ties, now *that* is love! He is on the brink, along with other research scientists around the world, of groundbreaking breakthroughs. Early genealogical detection of a disorder and the treatment of existing disorders are the targets upon which the scientists strive to score bull's-eye after bull's-eye. Computerised analysis of biological data (bioinformatics) is another speciality of Jacks. Studying the nucleotide sequences of DNA and other nucleic acids will continue to produce results that can only lead to a brighter future for so many. I take my hat off to Jack, his colleagues, and to the animals that give up their present life so that man can continue with his never ending pursuit of an almost perfectly healthy world.

Susan replied immediately, relaying huge chunks of support, understanding and love, but most importantly of all she promised to help me through this chemical blip, no matter what. This news wasn't at all bad considering that it came from a person that I had been in contact with just a few times since a hot July/August of 1981. I know of no other soul who is more true to their word than Susie. Selflessly, Sue has remained firm by my side ever since that flimsy paper Jesus Christ card landed on her little lap. As I have already explained, angels always seem to have a perfectly timed knack of appearing at the most testing times of my life, and Susan Carol Rose Steck Corradi proved to be no exception. Sue gradually became my best friend, my soul-mate and my partner. The card that Sue sent to me took pride of place in my bay, carefully perched on my cluttered dressing table at the foot of my bed. "Bayside" suddenly took on new mania driven meanings.

Light grey thoughts were beginning to well up, threatening to cloud over my overactive thought patterns. The million headless journeys, trips that were being portrayed to the naked senses through my choice in clothing, clutter, art, speech and movement were now lost more than ever before. Too many straight paths were being twisted, and collisions were happening at every green light. Now I found myself always arriving at the same unwelcoming terminal, no matter what form of vehicle I had decided to use. The deadly process of wiping out my God given Sun with a visor made of slate had begun in earnest.

5

Hill End Low

Now was the time to put a halt to the fun, cease dancing and pay off the band. Every aspect of my existence saw its vitality and shine commit mass desertion. The widely recognised and accepted form of reality wanted to come home and hibernate following its extended vacation. Reality had of course always been living at home, it was a sane brain and clear mind that had gone temporarily

A.W.O.L. Polish and rub I might, but to no avail. It appeared that the genie had run out of smoke and was now sticking up two fingers, telling me to leave because the pot was empty and the lamp had gone out. That week leading up to Christmas 1990 wasn't too terrible, it was just that every activity took more of an effort. What I had grown accustomed to being lightweight now became heavier and destabilising. Interesting pursuits rapidly lost their honed edge, and the life-blood atmosphere that I thought was going to last forever and a day fell on hard cold stone and dried up, failing miserably to live up to its past high standards. My life was rapidly losing its taste at a time when I craved it more than ever. I tried to fight my way through the bricked up walls that I used to fly over, but when I knew that my turn had burned out like one of the rockets I danced with under the moon-fire sky, I crumbled. The friendly warm touch of yesterday became the cold stranger of today. There was no sign of an end, only evil laughing signposts that directed me to a dreaded door that when creaked open revealed nothing more than a starless darkness. I had to confront the frightening vision of myself digging a deep muddy hole, or was it to be my grave? Twelve years later when I was in the middle of yet another high episode I actually jumped into a grave that was still being dug. I was returning from a public house in Bovingdon following a drinking session. As I cut through St. Lawrence's Churchyard I came across the head and shoulders of a man in a hole. He welcomed my offer of assistance, so I began lowering myself into the grave. Then I dug for all my worth, allowing the gravedigger enough time to have a drink from his thermos and a smoke. So I got myself a bit dirty, but who cares about trivialities like that when you're as high as a snorting astronaut? Now I felt like a once favoured toy, who had been brushed to the back of the cupboard by the wings of a worn out angel.

As Christmas 1990 approached, an instinctive will to keep my drowning faculties above water fought to stay within my custody. My previous dalliance with depression kept prodding away at me with small reminders. The will to die finally secured its ticket to ride my mind, making it perfectly clear that it wanted to ride by itself, cleansing me of the good, wiping the floor with happier times, removing my life and rubbing my nose in the smelly stuff at the same time. The turnaround period took a matter of days, and I did *not* know what had hit me. It felt as if a rehearsal for a nuclear war was being staged between my ears. Severe depression, or any other strain of mental illness that is helped along by the madness and lunacy of war, has got to be one of the most debilitating experiences known to mankind. Mental pain sucks big time, no matter where, when or how, and it lasts for what can often seem like an eternity.

My medication kicked in, finally bringing me plummeting down in the same way as a space capsule re-enters the Earth's atmosphere, heating up and then slowing down ready for a mechanically and mentally tolerable splashdown. Get the speed and direction wrong and the whole thing will disintegrate before everyone else's eyes. This undesirable explosion of emotion, anticipation and high spirits—the sort that can and will take place on the way up, and on the way back down again—creates a far bigger mess the more it has been fuelled, and my overfilled tank was bursting at its stitch welded seams. Too much or too little of anything will affect a part of you in one way or another. Re-growth is fine, but wouldn't it be better to grow naturally, and keep in prime condition what you have already accumulated? Blowing up or burning out is in the nature of some beasts who strive that little bit too far to find their beauty. We need people like that in this world. We do not need to destroy and ridicule them just because some of us are blind to a very special knowledge that will determine all of our futures, a knowledge that is often accessed through kicked down doors and agonising minds.

My grip on unreality slipped further and further, but not with the same hard bump as a little old wrinkly woman who was leaving the hospital's chapel. One hour of Sunday service singing, praying, praising and thanking God Almighty didn't do her much good, at least not on that Sunday. For all of her biblical troubles, the only almighty that she received was an almighty crack on the temple region of her bewigged skull, as a result of slipping on the concrete wheelchair ramp. Good old God. Perhaps the almighty is also a manic-depressive, and thought that he could do with a cheap laugh at the poor dear's expense. Ritchie and myself calmed her down before scooping her up and helping her to the nearest ward where she could be patched up and examined properly. Nobody died on that December day, so we were able to share a good laugh at the irony of the situation. Richard and I visited her every day without fail until she had the dressing removed from her pastry thin skin. She was still the many shades of purple and blue that older people tend to display following even the slightest of knocks. It would not have surprised me one little bit if her tumble turned out to be the highlight of her humdrum year. There was more for the elderly patients to do than I had first thought. On the rare occasions that I wandered into a ward that was filled mostly with elderly patients, I saw them watching the television and assembling jigsaw puzzles, some of which were thick wooden cut types that had a slightly insulting childish theme to them. They appeared to be happy in an unhappy sort of way. Who knows what goes on in another person's mind? What you have not had, you do not miss, right? Wrong! We all instinctively have natural cravings, urges and dreams. I always want other people to feel as happy as I do, or did, even if it is at my own cost. There are some that cannot improve. Their minds deteriorate with age, leaving those who care for them with a job that is unrewarding in the sense that there isn't much chance of improving their quality of life, or to nurture the patients depleted abilities. The reward is knowing that they are providing a pleasant environment in which to exist. It could quite easily be themselves or one of their relations sitting there one day. Millions of people who have a loved one, you may even be that loved one, who suffers from the cruelty of Alzheimer's disease know exactly what I mean.

Alas, my optimism and twenty four carat positivism was being replaced by unending pessimism and defeatism, making it triple hard to face my old comrades. I always wanted others to see the best of me, the quick witted, daring and reasonably intelligent active chap who made things happen. I wanted to be liked, admired and loved, but I had maniacally forced the issue, creating an artificial image within an expectant dream that I could not possibly live up to. That alone is enough to make one depressed. My dream had gone full term, and now I wanted to abort (a procedure that I usually don't care for.) Rejection, dismissal and disapproval of myself were key factors in my downfall. I felt sad, used, tried, tested and abused with only my strangled soul and a sore heart to see me through the melee. This was going to be a rough ride and I was unprepared.

Along with the upsurge of worn out and broken delusions, aspirations and fantasies came a rapid deterioration in my physical appearance. My hair became dry and unwilling to go where it was told, little scabby sores appeared on my head that I would nervously pick at, and I twiddled my hair around into tight knots that were then nervously yanked out in clumps. Red stinging blotches broke out on my face, and I lost even more weight, all of which contributed that little bit more to what I hoped would be a temporary, though still a desperately real, membership to the lowly life. Vitality and energy went completely out of the barricaded window. Sometimes I sought a freezing cold solace among the overgrown weeds surrounding the derelict shell of Keats house. John Keats, the British poet who died in 1821 happened to also be a manic-depressive. I looked at this gutted building and saw it not as my romantic future home surrounded by beautiful scenery and diverse wildlife, but as a huge pile of stinking crap that was destined to be raised to the ground by heartless bulldozers, reduced to nothing more than a pile of dust and rubble. I didn't ask for that much, or perhaps I did. I just thought that my manic trip would take me to a special place, and that the harder I tried the greater my reward would be. I felt as if I had built with my own bare hands a brick tower of strength, and had written just one hard copy of a lifetimes worth of manuscript, only to see the entire lot dissolve in my stomach's acid pit.

Bipolar affective disorder has played a major card in helping me to reach the conclusion that I may not be cut out for a settled family life, not that it has to be an obstacle for other bipolar people. It doesn't mean that I don't often wish that I could feel as if I was able to cope with that responsibility. Manic-depressive people function and adapt perfectly well for most of the time. Millions across the globe have happy families and everything that such a privilege brings, and they are welcome to it, but I'm afraid that I am not one of them, not in this lifetime. I have to admit that occasionally I do become envious when I see a young family together, diapers and all, but the emotion usually vanishes just as quickly as it lands on my lap. Since the age of twenty-five I have never quite felt the same way about myself or about anything else for that matter. Following any illness, especially depression, one soon evaluates what is worth prioritising in their lives and what really isn't worth getting one's knickers in a twist over. I see things in a completely different way now, with a much bigger and brighter light. A larger scope, if one cares to look into it, captures man from afar and sees life in an expanding picture, often full of time consuming and pointless petty bickering. I see the consequences and meanings of this life. I see many dedicated people who selflessly teach their lesson in so many interesting ways to so many open-minded fellow human beings. The clues are there, we are there, but some of us need to go a little bit further to make sure that we can all arrive safely. All one has to do is look twice, listen harder and taste the goodness while trying not to dwell upon the everyday bad things, or the past times that cannot be changed, only learnt from. There is more to the saying, "Wake up and smell the coffee," than meets the eye. Bold sweeping statements such as "Heaven is already here on Planet Earth," and that our "Spirits and souls are recycled," should be left to those who have earned their God given right to speak such words, and *not* be persecuted for doing so. You know who you are, so just hang on in there. Your slice of life's cake will probably crumble, but that is a *good* thing as it enables you to take one crumb at a time as a bird takes its seed. Let it fill you with joy and nourishment before passing it on through every form of love to the next person. Share without a care within an immeasurable circle and your life will be full. Nearing Christmas 1990 my life felt empty, not a crumb of hope bothered to offer itself up. My stomach and mind groaned, unable to tolerate the negative manner in which they were now being force fed platefuls of pessimism with mouldy bread, vinegar wine and rotting fish flavour ice-cream for dessert. Never before had I felt so down. Why the drastic reversal?

With my energy levels running low, simply trying to emulate previous activities and process what should be simple thoughts, became a terrible strain. I fought hard but I fought wrong, in fact I was fighting against myself, beating myself black and blue with a slugger full of denial and desperation. What goes up must come down, and I had been up there with the best of them. Commonsense and medical facts stated the obvious; that I was overdue a dive into the deep from off the top board, but nobody offered me the most important piece of information regarding the plug—it had been pulled out. Gradually the doctors took me off the anti-psychotic drugs and put me onto a dose of anti-depressants, but first I had to trip then fall off the top board, smashing all of me to a pulp before anything was done to help. Stan The Prune got more attention than I did. Spiralling down and down to Shit-City, where the Sun stays in bed and nothing is pretty, could and should have been prevented, or at least made more bearable. I am grateful for what those doctors and nurses did for me in Hill End, except for their failure to monitor me properly throughout the high/ low changeover period. Where was my key-worker? Where the hell was she hiding when I needed her the most? My general practitioner was always one hundred percent focused on the job in hand, even at the end of a long demanding day when he looked as if he could do with a little snooze. Dr. Hope actually listened and understood. He prescribed methodically and appropriately not only my medication but also a few perfectly chosen words that made me feel optimistic and good about myself. It's a pity that a person's stable mental diet of long lasting confidence cannot be bottled and available over the counter for free. I guess that is something each and every one of us has to manufacture from within. Later, Dr. Goodwin became my general practitioner, demonstrating as much medical skill and compassion as the now retired Dr. Hope did. I suppose the rapidity from high to low happened so fast it caught everybody by surprise, it certainly did me, and I am sure that the staff did all that they possibly could for me during those awful early stages, and maybe I didn't realise. I had put myself into that deep dark position to begin with, so the buck had to stop with me. Because of my delightful and despicable experiences, I have accumulated valuable knowledge that I can now wrap up and take into an older, wiser age. I wish that I hadn't learnt the self taught lesson on depression in the way that I did. My classroom was ever so lonely. The heavy hours dragged on and on without a single break. It is a place you do *not* want to visit!

Nearly all of my fellow patients had made plans to enjoy an extended stay with their relations and friends throughout the Christmas and New Year celebratory period. Some of the merry throng returned for three or four days in-between. Of course there were the poor souls who were simply too ill to go anywhere, and there were those who had nowhere to go even if they had wanted to. Jadranka had now returned to Yugoslavia where she could look forward to witnessing grown men fighting each other over land that should and could be used fairly between everybody. Man is so dense when it comes to war. When will the so called brains who lead nations learn to get on with each other for Heaven's sake? What became of Jadranka I do not know. Part of me missed the familiarity of those who had been given the green light to be discharged back into an unforgiving and hectic world, that for some is often moving way too fast. Is the asylum on the inside or on the outside? I keep asking myself that same question. Every which way one looks only goes to prove that we are all living in and on a mental institution, commonly known as Planet Earth.

There are so many positives in the world, but right now I am giving you the depressing angle. Just take a good look at the antics displayed on some of the late night alternative perverted TV stations, supposedly in the name of fun and entertainment. These pea brained, talent free morons are sicker, warped and far more insane than any of the human beings that I shared time with in Hill End Psychiatric Hospital. People shooting each other, blowing each others brains out, destructive computer games, fighting toys, TV shows that take advantage of someone's misfortune, movies loaded with violence and explicit sex, people pumping their precious bodies full of strange exotic cocktails of drugs, trying to escape from an unbalanced society full of far too much personal wealth and far too much poverty, obscene greed on every street corner, religious nuts who are really only hiding behind a safety mask and are full of contradiction, never helping out another soul if they can possibly help it, but would be the first to complain if nobody came to their aid during their hour of need. All of this and so much more besides is destroying the fabric of society. Come on, we have to have some solid morals, otherwise anarchy might just set in and takeover. The whole lot of us are at some point completely crazy, nuts and wacko, and should all be put into a Victorian mansion close to home for what would be an eye-opening stay. The true asylum is outside my window and inside your head whether you like it or not, and that does not have to be a bad thing if we can all get it together, does it?

Out strode the old and in came the new. Christmas sure is full of surprises. Untrue to past form, I tried to avoid mixing with the newcomers as I was quietly sinking more and more into myself, becoming more and more reclusive. The exact opposite of all the symptoms associated with a high episode were slowly having a sickening effect. I wanted to join in and be the instigator of fun as I had effortlessly done so before, but the growing gloom kept forcing me back. The new patients were taking over, replacing the original crowd that I had come to love. New faces contributed to the removal of the magic in which I had bathed. Art therapy became terribly depressing as I could now make a clear comparison of how I felt before, and the mood that was slowly suffocating me now. Slight strokes of self-consciousness and paranoia brushed past, rendering me incapable of work. Blank sheets of paper only felt the pressure of my troubled head, not that of a brush. Unable to live up to my reputation as an arty exhibitionist meant that I was letting the others and my therapist Kashika down, but there was absolutely nothing that I could do about it, adding to my irrational but deadly serious collection of silly things to worry myself sick over. Of course, none of my fears and anxieties were warranted, but just as the high times were so real, so were the lows. A magnification reversal was taking place. My rare spoken sentences were short and final. The angle of the slide into hell increased a couple of degrees every day, making it increasingly difficult to keep a safe hold. Urgent connections that once fell together were unable to be made, like a congested telephone switchboard that contains only distant feint memories of past interactions. Somewhere squashed in-between the high and low episodes is the normal area, or so you would think, but I'll be damned if I could find it and pin it down. I knew that I had passed that sandwiched point ages ago, and now it felt as if I was heading toward wrongful damnation. The transformation happened in the blink of a brown eye.

My manic-depressive dimmer mechanism lowered itself until I was left in a mental limbo. Although I felt rotten, it was still a walk in the park compared to what lay ahead. Every single one of the friends that I had made inside the hospital were sensitive and sympathetic toward my plight, probably because they had either been there themselves or had seen it manifesting in other patients. You would have to be deaf, dumb and blind not to notice the severity of my turnaround. The transition from the live wired Billy-Whiz to the death on legs human being that I was becoming, came about so quickly that I think it even surprised my fellow patients, relations and the psychiatric staff alike. I like to think that I was regarded as being an acceptable and reasonably considerate manic (if there is such a thing), not too annoying, just full of zany fun and cartloads of energy. Both the patients and staff were a little upset and shocked at the ferocity of my decline. Danny Weller knew exactly when to leave me to my own devices, and when it was best to try and lift my sagging spirits. He had tact, an important quality that comes naturally for some, or learnt the hard way by others. The patients are far more understanding than one may first think. As I said earlier, some of the best advice and therapy without a doubt comes from within the patient body. The medication has to be left to the fact filled experts, not that their pill pushing talents appeared to be helping me during that exceptionally rotten time of my life, a time that nobody deserves. The regular blood tests that were still being performed showed amazingly that my lithium level was still not quite right. 1200mg of the white crystalline salt, otherwise known as lithium carbonate, went into my bloodstream without fail every single day. Maybe my body and mind were so tired, so wiped out, that I crashed naturally. Something had to give, and this something was far too powerful to be affected by a few level headed happy pills. I have a hunch that in my particular case the anti-psychotics—necessary though they are to perform exactly what it says on the label—did assist my rapid decline, because they were not stopped in time. Nobody is to blame for my body's inconsistency, that is entirely down to me. It is impossible for me to predict the exact time of my mood reversals, so how can anybody else be expected to know? Only praise do I have for all of those dedicated staff at Hill End, my general practitioners and the tremendous psychiatric back up team based at St Paul's Community Mental Health Centre in Hemel Hempstead. It was just one of those inevitable things that could not be helped. What goes up must come crashing back down again. It isn't that unlike a paratrooper floating down for a mission over enemy lines, knowing that it is how and where you land that will determine your chances of success over the enemy.

Before the bulk of us went our separate ways for the holidays we gathered to enjoy a special Hill End Christmas dinner. Normally I would bolt my food down and then be queuing first for an extra sausage or a dollop of custard. I could eat an immense quantity of food when I was high and then burn away the calories just by rushing around everywhere, expending a warehouse full of energy by being over exuberant. Food ceased to be glorious, and eating became a chore instead of a pleasure. Constipated Stan The Prune managed to put more turkey and stuffing past his lips than I did. The happy dinnertime chatter dried up for me. Every single thing that I did or touched took a colossal effort. Weariness replaced the manic rocket fuel. Forget about rising above the ground, I now wanted to sink below it, to fade and fertilise a golden russet tree full of budding new life.

"Everything goes full circle. The plot is not lost forever, it has just parted company for a while ..."—try telling that to any poor soul, especially at the onset of a depression, and they will never believe you. Despite the cast iron guarantee that a full recovery will be made, it still won't make much of an impression in the depressives foil armour. Nothing much works to begin with, but constant love, loyalty and patience will eventually crack the code, release the burden and win the first day of what will be a promising future. The speed in which the clouds cover a depressed person is sickening beyond belief, but the old heated spirit and burnt out strength have only evaporated into a darkening cloud which will eventually burst like a soap bubble, showering you with renewed spirit and revitalised vigour that will have us all singing and dancing again like Gene Kelly or Ginger Rodgers. If you can beat hell, and you will, you can compete and succeed at any chosen level on any future stage.

My paddle had snapped into two, the outboard motor had fallen into the salty water and the wretched rudder of my leaking vessel had set its own course to the edge of disturbing life. The world was flat after all, and I thought I would fall off at any minute. Maidens of the sea were nowhere to be seen, leaving this drowning sailor without a rescue party. Desert islands had deserted, and sharks patrolled my washed up mind.

Maniacally painted pictures of a high flying Santa, the three wise men and a painfully thin J.C, now looked pitifully atrocious, as if they had been created by a class of five year old children. I wanted to rip them down and tear them to shreds. I had already gone berserk in the art room, trashing a few of the pictures and sculptures that I had made, but I could not muster the gusto to get off my backside and tear into Santa and Jesus. Everything had now become too much trouble and had absolutely no point to it. My "There doesn't have to be a point to everything," attitude escaped from the descending cage without a trace. For the first time I took notice of the ongoing developments in the boiling hot Gulf, and of the new British Prime Minister John Major, but I soon lost interest. This was just too many shades of shit hitting the fan at the same time. My gorgeous manic world where everybody shared the golden unspoken rules, interpreting them fairly to suit an individual's needs, was far more preferable.

My phobic fears rose to the surface, mostly involving the loss of personal belongings, especially keys. I invented imaginary scenarios in which I would be stranded somewhere, unable to enter a place or ignite a car. Heaven knows what would happen if somebody else found them and then robbed me. How would I handle situations such as these when I'm feeling so awful? I tormented myself with these unrealistic fears until I could take it no further, or until a replacement worry arrived. The sort of things that I would needlessly fret over revolved around the normal basic daily routines and chores. When the mind becomes so knotted with small crippling fears, it becomes very hard to focus on a simple task at that very moment in time, a task such as brewing a pot of tea, preparing a bite to eat, getting dressed or maintaining a decent level of environmentally friendly personal hygiene. All of these are simple functions for most normal, sane, level headed people to perform, but to a person who is temporarily empty of zip, spirit and energy, these tasks are steep mountains to climb. The nightmare will wear itself out eventually, but try telling that to the poor blighter whose turn it is to experience the cut throat world of deep depression. Placing everything in the correct order to complete a task can take every single ounce of retrieved concentration, and it becomes both physically and mentally draining, not only for the sufferer but for those who are the closest and are having to endure these painstaking repetitions. The care person has also got to be sensible and fully aware of their own mental and physical limits. Nobody is immune. The memory appears to go on strike, so the depressed person asks the same simple questions over and over again to the annoyance of the listener. Quite often it is those who are regarded as being a rock, a stalwart in adversity, who suffers the most. When the guards are dropped and the punches rain in, anybody can be pummelled into the dirt. If the basic day to day activities that have been perfected over the course of a lifetime suddenly prove to be a tortuous ordeal, then just imagine how it must be like to have to deal with the bills or go food shopping. The fear of bumping into a familiar face doesn't even bear thinking about. What if they ask me awkward questions like, "So, what have you been doing lately?" or "Are you working at the moment?" and "Do you still see him or her, or go to this or that place?" I used to be afraid of conversation in case I said the wrong thing or put myself across gawkily, leaving me with even more to fret over, even though the person I had been talking with had probably forgotten about the one sided conversation there and then. What made me think I was so important, that everyone spoke about me behind my back, I don't know. Another depressing element is the feeling of being conspicuous, believing that every aspect of my appearance is at fault. Do I think any the less of another person who stands out from the crowd because of a disfigurement or a limited ability? Of course not, in fact I admire them all the more for proudly showing their unique true colours and talents to the whole wide world.

The severely depressed person always believes that they have it worse than anybody else, and that despite being in this mess before and pulling through, they will not on this occasion ever escape from an eternal hell. Nothing and nobody can quick fix this terrible state of isolation, desperation and paranoia. Pills, potions, checkups from the neck-up by a consultant psychiatrist, visits to the regular doctor, sessions with social workers and the community psychiatric team/key workers and any other type of therapeutic activity can and does give many people a great amount of relief, although at the time of treatment this can be very hard to believe. The first few pills are always the biggest and trickiest to get down, but you will soon get used to it. The hurdles will eventually lower as the bed of grass gets higher. If the pills are not taken correctly or the hurdle is hit hard, a rebuilding process has to take place. Setbacks are nothing to be afraid of, they are just an aggravating waste of hard earned time, that's all. Patience, perseverance and tolerance from all concerned parties is the key. Never ever lose sight of the old self that is, and always will be beneath the temporary mask of gloomy doom. Most importantly of all is to allow a regular overdose of unconditional love to enter your body and soul whenever it becomes available. Being told to, "Snap out of it," is perhaps the dopiest, most thoughtless and insensitive remark one can ever make, yet there are plenty of insensitive people who will still mindlessly dish out this kind of utter drivel, so please stop it now! Never give up! Reassemble your structure day by day, then tighten up the nuts and bolts until you strangle the depressing enemy to death. Out of the deep blue will come the realisation that you are now home and dry. Do discover your temporary limitations and build upon them. A little dab will always do you.

As many as twenty percent of women and ten percent of men will suffer from an episode of depression at some point in their lives, and at any given time five to ten percent of women and three percent of men are depressed. These statistics alone are enough to make one feel rather cheesed off and depressed. Circumstances such as the climate we live in, our occupation, our family genes, relationship difficulties and so on, vary considerably from person to patient, but the underlying mental torment and gut wrenching fear of facing up to every single one of the 1,440 minutes that constitute a brand new day remains universally unified. In my prayers I asked the spirit form that God might happen to be masquerading under on that particular day, ridiculous questions such as, "Could I possibly swap this heavy depressing cargo with any other terrible disease?" It must have been God's day off; he seemed to be taking an awful lot of time off lately. The illness that I had been landed with gave no indication of letting go. My main request was soon amended to, "Please let me die, I want out,"—that's how awful this depressive illness very quickly becomes, and it was still only in its early stages. Depression can be and sometimes *is* a killer, although in this modern day and age it need not be, so long as up to date medication and therapeutic techniques are applied by highly qualified professionals.

Back on Anderson Ward I somehow managed to shuffle my cowering frame about so that I could get things done slowly, somehow, eventually. The effort required to function was so tiring. My body was probably trying to rest following a prolonged dalliance with mania. Had the wonderful floating feeling that I had become attached to deserted me for good? Life from here on in will always play second fiddle to the high standards I once enjoyed, unless of course I re-launched myself one day just like the NASA Space Shuttle that keeps going back for more and more of the same. On January 28th 1996 the Challenger Space Shuttle and all of the passengers aboard, God rest their souls, perished due to a faulty o-ring, and on September 28th the Discovery made its maiden voyage. There is no other option other than for life to go on, not necessarily always up, but definitely *on*. Steadman had re-entered Earth's heavy atmosphere in Virgo-one (V-1), only to discover that he was now carrying not only his, but the entire world's troubles on his broken shoulders. There was still a long mental drudge ahead before he finally caved in, his backbone partially crumbled and his skinny little legs collapsed under the mental strain. The accumulated weight that had built up throughout that entire past year had finally had enough, and was now moving in for the killer punch, the final blow to end the show.

My band's asking rate was now too high, preventing me from dancing even if I had wanted to. I had never done anything so terrible that deserved such a no-show from my invisible Gods and smooth skinned angels. It was a huge let down, but it made me realise that I have to believe in myself, because we are all our very own No.1 priorities. God sure does have a warped sense of humour. For Heaven's sake, God Almighty could have at least loaned me a parachute for the descent instead of a faulty bungee rope, instead the devil laughed long and hard as I plunged into a hellhole. Could the small crater full of rainwater, that I had been found rolling around in when I was on my last Italian legs, have been made by my fall from grace? My past became confused with the present and the future.

I tried to read the future into the past and the present, trying so hard to make things fit and make sense. Large square blocks do not fit through small circular holes. My present state of mind struggled to accept the absurdity of my previous manic convictions. Too many questions jabbed at me, struggling for the solution that would lift the lid of my tomb. Answers I had none.

My personal trainer Ritchie Smith had also trodden in the quicksand, which explained his notable absence from the creamy green corridors and the cold grounds outside. It appeared that Ritchie also preferred to share his hell with as few people as possible, an unhealthy path to follow but quite understandable. On Ritchie's ward the patients had their own individual split cell rooms. As far as hospital rooms go they were rather nice, but not when you are feeling so despicably down on yourself. Lisa made regular visits to be with Ritchie in a well meant attempt to cheer him up. A few of the new admissions and some of the existing patients had a tendency to slump in mood as the twenty-fifth drew closer, and natural sunlight was at a premium. My personal collapse had the effect of making the happy patients on the ward even happier, which made me feel even more isolated. Add all of this together and we are left with a depressed wreckage, that is continually breaking down with the crashing beat of every new wave.

A cast of hundreds, who demonstrated the full gamut of psychiatric possibility, were still on constant standby to satisfy the nosey punter's fascination with the mentally interesting. We were all understudies to those of us who fell off the world's greased stage for an unlimited block of valuable time. Toilet facilities were opposite the hospital shop, so this open area became one of the most popular haunts for the patients. I made an effort to walk into the areas I least wanted to, in an attempt at reversing the irreversible. Hauling myself to the main entrance hall was exceptionally difficult, trying to avoid eye contact with another human being, trying to pick up any scraps of the old manic buzz. Life was now sorrowful and hollow. Happiness had been bored out of my skull. Beneath my feet lay the cigarette butt-holes and gummy remains of what was once a plush red premier carpet. That scraggy old carpet, the rubbery-faced regulars puffing away, memories of when I would content myself by staring in wonderment at the miracle of life; all of these things and too much more had suddenly lost their fascination and flavour, and were now becoming more and more irritating and unimportant to me. My surroundings were dying a slow death with me. No matter where I dragged myself inside that huge Victorian pile of bricks, I would encounter over and over again a situation or even an inanimate object against which I would calculate an unfavourable mania/depression comparison. Nothing tasted as sweet as the old manic candy. Manic stardom sure isn't all it is cracked up to be, the self built fame-game becomes pointless because it breeds nothing but high diving agony. The ability to enjoy a pleasurable plate of scrumptious life peters out like a clockwork toy. All that I achieved during the search for my old self was to further my grief. Persecuting myself by searching desperately for the high times only managed to knock me back even further, but what the hell was I supposed to do, sit back and be swallowed up without a fight? Shuffling through those creamy green corridors, soaking up the harsh reality of my unreal set of circumstances, simply added to the cruel and vicious battering that my depressed mind was already taking.

When I became panicky, I trudged back with my head held low to the relative safety of Anderson Ward. Hours upon hours of reading and then re-reading between the unread lines of a book didn't arouse any interest. Books and articles with a happy theme made me feel sadder, left out and discarded. Learning about the clever and worthwhile things that other people can do, made me feel incompetent and non-productive, no bloody use at all. My personal world had to survive this distressful explosion and start all over again. I was the lost, bubble free bottle of soda that had flipped its lid and blown its top. Had the past months really been in vain, and had the universal thought transference thing been nothing more than a cruel trick played upon my mind only? Unannounced anger kicked in hard. I asked myself, "How could I have been allowed to take the mania so far, unaware that waiting for me back at base was a foul tasting dollop of depression for dessert." Nobody told me in plain English that I was high, and that I had been behaving like a baloney filled hero. Perhaps the truth was that I only listened to what I wanted to hear and that I adjusted negativity so that it became a far more palatable plus. There was no warning, no cushion for the blows I received at this time. I lost sight of what was right and what was wrong, who to listen to and who to obey. How could I trust the psychiatric doctors and their pills and potions if my current pissed off position was anything to measure their expertise by? In my sadness—too frightened to converse let alone question a professionals decision regarding my course of treatment—I would swallow whatever pill they pushed under my nose without knowing and without caring what the hell it was. Nothing sank in and took root except for a devilish gremlin, ready and waiting for the long haul through my poisoned Heaven and into a mentally crippling hell. The anti-depressants that were administered had no effect at all to begin with, so my pit of shit just seemed to get deeper and deeper. As I looked up for some light relief, all that I could see were the faces that had played significant roles in my highly underrated travelling show, some sadly sympathetic and others just pathetic with an evil grin, smugly contented that they had fooled me and had achieved their sick mission of dragging me down to their lifeless level, where the losers are heroes and success is a dirty word. Food, the little that I took, tasted for the first time as grotesque as it now looked. Smelly people annoyed and disgusted me, and I shouted at a well scrubbed Jim as he set about washing yet another load of perfectly clean smalls. My collection of newspaper cuttings, photographs and drawings meant nothing to me anymore, serving only as a painful reminder of my manic foolishness, so they were ripped down and disposed of with a mixture of dejection and contempt. The staff who spoke esoterically around me really got up my nose, because I wanted to know where things stood in plain English, and instead I was confused and misled (unintentionally) by the mishmash of treatments and tests, leaving me worried that the best treatment for me had been overlooked. There was I, severely depressed and stranded in the asylum, not the nicest predicament to find oneself in believe me, and it was to get much much worse.

The manic antics of Ian and a few of the others now infuriated me, snapping my short patient stick in too many hurtful places, but then the realisation struck me that up until a very short while ago it was me playing up loudly like a jumping Jack flash in the pan. Lisa, Helen and some of the new faces occasionally asked me how I was doing, but through their own dark experiences they knew when to keep a wide berth. Leslie Turner, a 40 year old alcoholic who also hailed from Bovingdon, was very considerate toward me, displaying so much patient love and understanding. Just prior to my horrible depression she allowed me to make a pencil sketch of her, using a dining room table as our studio. The unspoken bond, the shared spirit and camaraderie on that ward back in 1990 was something to behold. Two weeks before Christmas when I was feeling fine, I had been allowed to spend one night alone at my maisonette in Bovingdon, on the proviso that I was driven there at around 8 p.m. without any money for alcohol,—I could have got some money fairly easily if I had set my mind to it—and collected promptly at 8 a.m. Leslie was also on leave. We secretly arranged to meet at my place at 8.30 p.m. A special brew of love was made all night long without the need to remove any clothing. It was a necessary time alone for the pair of us, without terms and conditions. A contract of committal was the last thing that either of us needed, so was vodka, whisky, rum, gin, beer and cider. Good people are not always able to exterminate their demons, instead they swallow more and more of the strong stuff in the vain hope that it will help to extinguish the raging ring of fire that they had been dancing through for too long. Thirteen years later poor Leslie died, her liver was riddled with cirrhosis. I hadn't kept in touch with her. God bless you Leslie.

Harold's daughter gave me another neat trim in an effort to put a smile back on my face, making a terrific job of it too, but her father kept on bugging me and my fellow patients with his latest revelations and theories in relation to the good book itself, something that I could not and did not want to stomach at the time, so I drew great pleasure from the fact that one morning he had cut his face to shreds with one of my disposable wet razors, stolen when my back was turned. He did an appalling job on himself, with blood everywhere. So much for Harold and his ten commandments (could the other nine still be intact?) It was rather cruel of me to have laughed at the silly old duffer's expense because he had his mental problems just like the rest of us, but one has to laugh if something is as deserving and as funny as his lacerated face. We nearly peed ourselves with laughter when daft old Harold made his late entrance into the dining room for breakfast. His face was covered with lots of tissue paper pieces. That incident helped me to forget myself for a few minutes, which only goes to show that laughter really is one of the best medicines, if not the complete cure.

I smoked more and more in the hope that I could catch up and savour a couple of dizzy seconds in roll-up Heaven. It almost felt as if I had built up an immunity to nicotine. The anti-depressant medication that I had been prescribed actually took away the taste of the tobacco, leaving me to puff away on hot air. The heightened senses associated with mania were virtually now all gone, dampening any remaining pleasure spots that I once had. Getting off to sleep was not the problem, it was returning to sleep after waking up in the middle of the extended nights that proved troublesome. I have always found during periods of depression that the two or three hours leading up to bedtime are the calmest of all, though still rotten to the core. Being depressed and achieving very little throughout the day can be surprisingly tiring. The mind is being distanced further and further from normal activity, only to have oodles of time to dwell upon, and then confuse and believe the magnified phobias and impossible scenarios that appear to be so real. *Never* laugh at the absurdity or size of a depressed person's overblown problems. It is the temporary inability of handling a situation, and coping in the manner to which one had grown accustomed to that is so frightening. Fearing the permanent loss of essential faculties is a major player in depression. The fear of losing the basic human tools erodes the scraps of hope that were hung onto by chewed fingernails. Why does depression refuse to clock out?

Grey thoughts tramped through my body, bleeding pain into the snarled bed sheets throughout the night. My mind's destructive buttons was always pushed well in, my knobs were fully turned, and my levers were pulled all the way down, providing me with the rotten sensation of being subjected to a terminal five minute warning every two sickening seconds. I tried praying to God to please let me go, to be my latest killer, to close the lids of my eyes and also the lid of the cardboard coffin, glued together with sticky stigma, wrapped in brown paper, tied up in black ribbon and topped off with a sweet maraschino cherry.

Maddening, saddening, repetitive hogwash flooded my nights, until it was officially time to rise and step into another daily horror story, where the hungry cast and the Styrofoam set are disconcertingly real. Depression certainly isn't pretty. It is capable of sending the most violent and disturbing thoughts through one's head. I used to feel like a prize fighter who had taken a terrible beating. My already out of joint nose gets sent first class to a different part of my face, and my mind is blown to pieces, yet there I was still taking the punches left right and centre, never allowed out of the ring except in a body bag. At one stage I couldn't stop thinking about the dreadful Nazi Holocaust atrocities. Gruesome scenarios kept playing over and over in my battered mind. Seven years later Sue and I actually visited the Holocaust museum in Washington D.C, a chilling experience that oddly enough helped me to better handle my inner disbelief and disgust. The stories of those who somehow survived were truly inspirational. This was a place where grown men were not afraid to cry. All of those sweet talkers who were meant to remain loyal in my corner had now turned their backs and were walking out on me, ashamed of being associated any longer with their one time friend who is now a mentally ill embarrassment, weighing in at far too little but way too much for them to handle. Being unsure whether or not you have become a good for nothing burden, an insane drain on those around you, is one of those things that never gets airtime, although deep down you know that the present condition is affecting too many people in a way that all of them could do without.

Sometimes I rocked my body gently in bed. By doing this I found that I could salvage a small amount of comfort. No matter what one does, it seems that it won't make one long lasting iota of difference, and then one begins to wonder if the depression will ever lift, will this awful feeling ever go away to bug a mass murderer or a child molester instead, and get off my aching back once and for all. A bouncing back cat I was not. I had one life, not nine, and that single fading life had already been exhausted. "Nobody has ever had it as bad as I'm having it now," is a common moaning groaning thought that serves no purpose, except to get on the fraying nerves of whoever is caring and loving enough to dig in for the cause. The plight of our starving fellow humans is considerably worse, but try convincing a clinically depressed person of that when they are in the deep throes of despair. Pointless gripes serve no purpose that I can think of, other than to coil up one's insides more and more before imagining and then multiplying the non-existent wrath of undeserving allies. Getting a whole load off by using aggressive and disrespectful behaviour is fine and dandy, so long as you haven't got any objection to having loads more steaming heaps piled on as a consequence. Fear of fear can be much worse than breeding the fear itself. Power is crushed into fine powder when an arm reaches out for relief and grasps a venomous snake instead, realising in the process that its skin is rougher and tougher than the slippery myth. One becomes more and more wary of attempting self help due to the underlying fear of more exaggerated failure. Rebounding from failure, perseverance and persistence are the ultimate providers of inevitable success. Small victories will follow. Major failure enables private lessons to be written, lessons that can be learnt from. We all have our unique back catalogues, full to the brim with thriving worries, fears, doubts, regrets, phobias, guilt trips and rejection, but the pain still remains the same. It doesn't make a jot of difference if you were the Sultan of Brunei or my old friend the Red Wino of Milan, who very kindly let me whet my whistle, because when the crap hits whirring blades we are all covered as equals, splattered with the same awful pain.

The way things were progressing along hell's highway, it wouldn't be very long before the termination of my life dominated almost every thought. Physically there is little left in the tank to actually do anything about these madcap suicidal schemes, besides it is too easy a way out of what still will be a full and productive life. When I was rampantly manic I was always moving from A to Z or Z to A too fast for anybody to have sharply focused their sights on me. Now I wished that their sights could be focused on me—telescopic sights on a rifle or crossbow. There were always plenty of caring eyes and gentle voices reminding me to, "Never lose faith and never lose sight of the old Keith," for which I am grateful, although I didn't think much of it during that late dismal December time. I realise today just how important those random pep talks were to keep me believing, even when it felt as if nothing was going my way. These uphill mind repairs, performed properly and practiced somewhat reluctantly take time, a commodity I had plenty of. Repairing a mental problem is similar in principle to the steps of physiotherapy. Gently does it to begin with, but if pushed too far the problem will return and the whole procedure will have to be restarted. Re-mastering the basic human skills can be a tough proposition, although it is always worth reminding oneself that the tools are still there, it's just that the brain's box has recently been turned upside down and shaken. Rust can always be removed with the finest sands of time.

Anderson Ward became an even quieter place in which to become even more mentally ill. My early morning screeching sessions in the bathroom were now conspicuous by their absence. Now I was the last one to rise, unwashed and anxious. Mornings are always the worst. The same basic tasks had to be fulfilled all over again. Sometimes I wished that I could bawl my pain out, but not even that small request could be obeyed. Ian did an admirable job of taking over the reins as chief of manic entertainment. His high pitched warbling sounded like Barry Gibb on helium. My rock steady father became friendly with most of the male patients, especially punk rock fanatic Danny. Dad must have been hurting so badly, but he always kept his feelings to himself so as not to upset anybody any further. He arrived on Christmas Eve so that he could bring me home for three days. A dribble of transparent soup slid down my tobacco scorched throat before I said a few goodbyes to my fellow patients. Carrying a weighty bag, I exited the two sets of ward doors, much heavier now than when I had high kicked my way through them before and escaped to nowhere. How does a man escape from himself? He cannot, even if he plies himself with every variety of drug there is. We left the main building through the rear instead. The floppy rubber doors that had separated me from the fresh air decided to rub my nose in it by slapping me back in the face, probably in retaliation for the times that I had kicked at it. Rain often pours when one is feeling blue, but with depression it is relentless.

As we drove toward the main gates I could see stubby Ritchie wandering alone. He looked so down and distraught, as if he believed that this time his depression was one mountain too many. As we neared the front gates I could see the same happy huddle of rubbery faces hanging out together in a silvery plume of smoke, exactly as they were when I first arrived. Some strange comfort came from knowing that some of the magical past still remained intact. The disused church, now in use as a drama workshop, loomed to our right as we slowly drove through the iron gates of Hill End Psychiatric (Insecure) Hospital For Mental And Nervous Disorders—the official long winded title. The soggy weather summed up my troubles perfectly. It was dull, block drained and lifeless. Why does the season to be jolly always have to be grim on the outside? Perhaps that is why we use the excuse of "celebrating" Jesus Christ's out of date birthday in December, so we can brighten things up a bit?

"You'll be all right mate," said my dad, and he meant it. At the same time he had the sense not to instil unnecessary pressure, by predicting a get well date that would be damaging if it could not be lived up to. Recovery will happen but it takes as long as it takes, and that is all there is to it. Anybody who makes false predictions so that the sufferer feels a little temporary warmth is as foolish as a pearl diver who looks the part, but dives in without checking the waters depth first—ouch! Artificial feel good factors can destroy so much hard work. Without any desire on my part for their company, the mental heavyweights—who had been doing a roaring trade from their round the clock mental market stall—came along for the white knuckle ride. I reckon that the tricky traders just wanted to see me foul up every opportunity I had of recovery. The stall needed constant replenishment because of all the free crap that they kept on throwing at me. I couldn't give it away if I tried, unlike Milan.

"A change of scenery, getting out of that old place for a while, it'll do you the world of good Son," my dad continued. This made me wonder how long I might be incarcerated in what had now become a dump of a place. Try telling me that I had a temporary bout of the winter blues and I would have spat in your blind eyes. If I remained for much longer at Hill End I knew that I would become progressively worse, maybe ending up as a permanent fixture surrounded by burly Moroccan Martians—no way Pedro! My instinct told me that a return to hospital would be unbearable, the last place on this planet that I should be put, a place where I knew I would rot and whither. Worrying about this possibility made me so unbearably ill. There was no other option other than to save my family and myself any further grief, and finish myself off once and for all. What a waste of a reasonably good body. What is the use of a body if the soul that has to live in it is broken beyond repair? For an optimistic, outgoing type of human being to be contemplating his own demise is really saying something, and that something was a loud, "*Help!*" Expressing the pain and inner turmoil is not an easy thing for anybody to do. Writing it down helps a great deal, and it may come in handy for the next episode, God forbid. A magic fairy isn't going to fly by and sprinkle magical green healing fairy dust all over the situation and set your world to rights at the swipe of a wand, but putting one's troubles onto a scrap of paper does help a little. I am fortunate in that I can express myself reasonably well through a few words, whereas another ill person may play a musical instrument or attempt to bury themselves in an old hobby, using that hobby as a therapeutic weapon of mass depressive destruction. At first I used to drive my mother completely up the wall with my repetitive hard done by stories, *not* a good idea. Once or twice is enough for a strong point or feeling to be let out into the open, but *not* every single minute of every day. The bombarded person, who also has deep feelings and emotions, may well be driven around half a dozen bends and up and over the wall into a psychiatric unit themselves. Tell me who, in any state of mind, wants to have that sorry and disgraceful accolade resting on their conscience? Even severely depressed human beings have to be considerate toward others, especially those who are trying their best to help in whatever way they can. The world does *not* revolve around one selfish person.

Suicidal thoughts dominated my Christmas, but had I the guts to go through with the deadly deed? Out of all the places that I could have been put in my clinically depressed and suicidal condition, an old dingy Victorian building full of so many unwanted distractions and memories was not one of them. Why not ship me off to a place where the Sun shines brightly, under some sort of supervision of course. Suicidal people supposedly need to go to hospital for their own safety and treatment. In my case the tables were turned because the dreaded thought of returning only served to heighten my terminal tendencies. It seems to be that when it comes to mental health issues the patient is the last, or has absolutely no say whatsoever regarding the best and most appropriate course of treatment—how utterly ridiculous! It is at these times that the patient should be listened to and taken notice of the most, instead of being pushed around and treated like an imbecilic second class citizen, thick as a slab and opinion free. Mental health mathematics has never been simpler, and yet so many get the basics wrong. It does nothing for one's confidence you know. We are talking life and death here for goodness sake!

When darkness fell in at my parents home in Hemel Hempstead, I would refuse to switch on the electric light or close the curtains. Drawing attention to the fact that I was staying there simply would not do. Neighbours have their own lives to lead and they certainly wouldn't be wasting their time thinking about my bedroom light or me. Fumbling around in the dark can hurt, especially if I stubbed my toes on a chair or clonked my head on the wardrobe. Hour upon hour I spent curled up on the floor or on top of the single bed, squashing myself into the corners of the encroaching walls. These behavioural patterns became abnormally routine and caused my brief snippets of reality to decrease, weakening my feeble grip on the edge of this life, slipping slowly down and almost out. "Grub up," came the shout from downstairs. When I had made absolutely certain that the house contained nobody other than my folks, I would slowly tiptoe through the gloom, out on to the landing area, turn right and then delicately step down the carpeted stairs, making sure that I held on tightly to the wooden banister rail, because by now my legs had weakened considerably due to lack of exercise. This mumbling fumbling unkempt excuse for a human being, but a human being none the less, would take his place at the action packed table, scrunching up his eyes at the brightness of a sixty watt light-bulb, and then spend what felt like forever forcing slim pickings of food that he really didn't want down his throat. "I must eat more vegetables, I must drink juice," I kept telling myself halfheartedly. We made some forced small talk before I crawled back upstairs to resume my exile. It wasn't very long before my mind was focusing purely on nothing else other than ending it all, so what little I ate didn't really matter much to me anymore. Should I starve myself to death by going on a hunger strike?

Thinking in this morbid way actually gave me my only solace, my only scrap of peace and relief. Deadening thoughts replaced my imaginary solo space journeys as a means of getting off to sleep. Never before had I felt so far away, alone and utterly helpless. What I didn't realise until much later was that my experiences were to teach me a lot about myself. Instead of feeling so far away and unreachable, I would become closer and more understanding of my own complexities and idiosyncrasies. I would come to realise that there are so many similar people and that no matter what, we will *never* be alone. Help is *always* at hand. Because of my own experiences I would like to think that from this day forward, not only will I be able to help myself, but I will also be in a position to be of some assistance to others. If we can keep on passing that experienced attitude to the next person, then I think we will all be heading in the right direction.

Concerned friends and relations sent their kind messages of support and love. This made me feel even worse, because that meant that they were very well aware of my current plight and whereabouts. When I was high I wanted to shake hands with the world, but when low I shirked them all. We all want to look good and be on tiptop form when in the presence of others, so when the complete opposite happens it adds to the reclusion, and that reclusion makes the condition worse. The more educated that society is about mental illness—the kind of illness that cannot be immediately seen with the naked eye—the less of a taboo there will be, and the stigma will eventually be prized away like a limpet from a rock. Educating youngsters at school about science, history or mathematics is fine, but don't you think that a little more time should be spent educating them about real life issues such as mental illness? They will undoubtedly encounter a whole gamut of mental health issues at some stage of their journey along life's highway, so why not prepare them a bit more for the unexpected. A little bit of real life preparation for an unpredictable future never goes amiss. In the long run it could save so much heartache for everybody affected by a mentally related problem, and there wouldn't be such a drain on the national health budget. The economy would improve as less hours are taken off sick from work. There is so much to be had in return for some further education and awareness of the many dormant mental seeds, waiting to develop into something that doesn't always come out smelling of roses, but of the stuff that helps them grow. It may also help us to be just that little bit more understanding toward each other, perhaps enabling us all to communicate and generally get along better than ever before. Well, it's got to be worth a try.

Plans began to formulate inside my head of how best to do away with myself. Thinking in terminal permanence was rather easy. My ghastly thoughts were clear, clinical and precise. The plan I chose had to go into effect when both of my parents went to do the food shopping. Meanwhile, patience and pain were the key words. Christmas 1990 was quite obviously a non-starter for me, not that I have anything against the whole tinsel and pulling crackers scene, far from it, but there were other more pressing things on my mind. When I felt fine then so was Christmas, but when I was depressed everything seemed to be so overwhelmingly pointless and grey. Hypocrites who stuffed themselves silly with far too much food while millions starved, and the trivial inconveniences such as bad hair days or the price of a gallon of petrol just made me want to puke over the planet. I hate to admit it but I did feel awfully sorry for myself and also terribly let down by my spiritual maker whose days of leading me up the garden path were, as far as I was concerned, also numbered. The life and soul of the party had left the building.

In 1997 I designed my own Santa Claus costume. That December I flew across the Atlantic to visit Susan on Long Island, New York. I had been asked to play the part of Santa Claus 1997. This involved standing up in the back of a truck, heavily loaded with sacks filled with toys to distribute among the screaming children. If anybody had told me at the end of 1990 that I would become Santa Steadman—not only for Long Islands youngest but also for my cousin Bernice's two sweet little girls, and much later for six severely mentally handicapped and partially disabled adults that I briefly worked with in 2002/2003—I myself would have called the men and women in white coats to come and take me away to the Santa sanatorium. In late December 1990 Santa could have brought me the world wrapped up in fish and chip paper and tied together with a shoestring budget, but I would have immediately seen the black light, the darker side of the gloom, and then worry myself sick about planet maintenance and global warming.

My folks decided quite rightly *not* to over pamper me because that would make it much harder to resume a normal life. Personal hygiene became a sore point, but firm insistence won the day and gave me another little victory. Small and tedious personal battles went toward winning the war and toppling the depressing governing body forever and ever. To live under the same roof as a manic-depressive person is fine when they are well, and have been responsibly maintaining themselves, but when they are either high or low it can understandably be more than enough to drive the sanest individual round the bend. My family just about held it together, rallying around to help me in every way they knew how. They also supported each other to the hilt, ensuring that nobody came too close to their own personal breaking point. Creating another lovable, stressed out head case in the family was never on the cards, as everybody kept a watchful eye on each other. The home straight of my personal human race would soon appear around the next bend. My batteries had run dry and recharging my juices struck me as a pointless exercise, simply not worth the effort. Even the smallest of unappetising pleasures such as dreaming my life away, vomiting, picking on scabby sores and scratching the psoriasis rashes that were spreading over me like a plague failed to free my mind, even for just a short while. I had permanently switched off the radio and the portable television set in the spare room of my parent's three bedroom home. Turned on all the time was a high pitched fluctuating drone that the ears either produce or can pick up. What is that noise? During my manic episode I thought that it was a combination of radio signals and electrical impulses floating around and through us, coming and going from the brain, or was it the quiet hum of the next door neighbour's prehistoric central heating system? Out of interest, did you know that one percent of the crackling and hissing noise that you can hear when turning the radio dial from station to station, is in fact the echo from the Big Bang some 10 to 20 billion years ago!

Should I try to electrocute myself? It didn't work when I accidentally pumped a few volts of juice through myself when I was working at Transia. What about placing a plastic bag without child safe holes punctured in the bottom over my head, secured by tight elastic bands? I know, why don't I get wrecked on alcohol right next to the railway line, and then head-butt the intercity express as it hurtles toward London, or shall I try to find a pistol so that I can blow my mind out against the walls that I had papered earlier that very same year? I stuck with my original plan of self destruction, the most common and the easiest of all. Overdosing on as many tablets that I could lay my hands on appeared to be the easy way out, the cowardly way out. Even if I had the energy and the money, where would I go to find a suitable weapon? Before any of you start to accuse me of giving out bad ideas, you have to remember that I haven't listed anything that most people do not already know, unless they have had their depressed heads buried in the sand (maybe that would work.)

Food shopping day arrived. My folks drove off in their white Ford Sapphire that I had sold them, and then the drums began to roll. I took all sorts of odd shaped and brightly coloured pills and capsules that I found tucked away in the bathroom medicine cabinet. I poured the ghastly contents of crusty topped bottles down my throat too, all washed down with plenty of whisky and lemonade. I then laid down on my single bed, in the very same small place, looking at the very same spot when as a child I saw two ghostly figures standing. No note or taped message, just little old me curled up in green pyjamas and mental pain. Where would my capsules take me? I was already dead but then I nearly died. When my father was out shopping he had sensed that something was not quite right. What exactly was the matter he could not say, but he had a strong feeling that things were not as they should be with me, so he dropped the shopping and came straight back home to find his only son laying on his old single bed, unconscious. When I woke up and realised that I was still alive—after having my stomach pumped out at Hemel Hempstead General Hospital—I could have died all over again. I begged them not to send me back to Hill End Psychiatric Hospital. Nobody took the slightest bit of notice, except my parents, but the powers that be slapped a section order on me which meant that my folks and I were totally helpless, without a say in the whole despicable matter. The horror that I felt inside was the worst yet. I had woken up in a clean hospital bed in a bay of six men, all of whom were total strangers and a lot older than myself. "Please don't ever do that again mate," whispered my tearful father who had stayed by my side throughout the whole self inflicted ordeal. He had returned from the supermarket to find my lifeless body curled up unconscious, and had then carried and dragged my dead weight out to the car before driving at breakneck speed to the emergency department. What a rotten thing to do, to put him and my mum through so much grief, a terrible thing indeed, but I went through with it because I felt so stinking lousy and couldn't see any way out. My father gave me life twice. At the time of fading out I felt at peace. There was none of the looking down at myself that other people have experienced, probably because I wasn't as close to death as they were. As I lay waiting for the pills to take a sedative effect, I became overcome with sadness and guilt about the horrific ordeal that awaited those who were left to pick up and dispose of my remains. Years later when working as a porter, I had to move plenty of dead bodies to the morgue at the very same Hemel Hempstead Hospital, and as I'm sure you can imagine, it ain't the nicest job in the world. I was a decent enough guy that took on and fought a demon too many, or was it too many demons in one feel swoop? I had let everybody down because they were also fighting my depression and I lost my bottle, threw in the towel and deserted. Didn't they used to shoot deserters? Not where I was going. Instead they allowed my agony to linger in full view of a bunch of reasonably friendly defectives, how delightful.

My condition became so much worse than before. Most of my time was spent sweating like a maggot underneath the heavy sheets, unimaginably frightened out of my wits. "Surely, God my old friend, it can't get any worse than this can it?,"

I would wonder. "Oh yes," came the cold hard truth. Looking back, I wonder to myself whether or not all of my trials and tribulations were some sort of Karma, and that by enduring the pain and being pulled out of the worse scenario by my father, I would be prepared for what was to come next. The future will see us squeezing out the bad stuff. Valuable knowledge will come from releasing the bad between us, which is the reason why we must help each other out in the best way that we can. By doing this we are also helping ourselves.

Dead man rolling. The patient opposite me was placed onto a trolley by the hard working porters who then proceeded to wheel him to the morgue. How ironic can it get? There am I praying to die but cannot, and the man opposite who wants to live manages to die. Comedy doesn't come much darker than that. What a year it had been: first I get electrocuted, then I have my skull bounced on a paving slab, then I ride inside-out on the Milan subway system, then I crawl on my hands and knees exhausted and starving, and now I swallow an entire pharmacy and fail. All of that, and so much more besides. Perhaps I will come back one day (if I ever get to die) as an everlasting pussycat that laps up embalming fluid instead of full cream milk.

The pump tube that had been rammed down into my stomach had made my throat red raw. Also, when I was unconscious, a gash six inches above my right ankle had to be made in order to insert another emergency tube. That gash left a horrible patch of skin that still refuses to heal up properly. All said and done, it really is such a triviality considering what might easily have been. My faeces scared the hell out of me at first when I saw that it had turned green, a result of the solution that had to be used during the pumping process. I begged my family, the doctors, the nurses and the professionals of psychiatry *not* to send me back to Hill End Psychiatric Hospital. The thought of returning to Hill End played a major card in my decision to swallow the contents of the medicine cabinet in the first place! Did they listen? Like hell they did. My folks understood, but it was the professionals who ignored my pleading and reasoning, not allowing me to have any say in the matter that affected *me* the most. How does it feel to be listened to the least when you are supposedly the main concern? Bloody awful, sickening. I was deemed to be in no fit state to have a valid say in the mentally ill patient shipping process. To be fair, there were not any options available for most of the staff, most of whom didn't have the final word on decisions such as this. Just like politicians and war, the top brass in all walks of life often tend to blow plenty of hot air, laying down the deadly rules, but you rarely see them near the battlefield, unless of course your name is Sir Winston Churchill or "Norm."

I did try to make a dash for freedom, wearing nothing but my white open back hospital gown, but I was apprehended by an army of nurses who appeared

from out of nowhere. Every aspect of my existence had disintegrated beyond recognition. I needed the greatest mental engineering know how to put me right.
Only I could attempt to recreate this pathetic little wonder of the world, one
wondrous speck of drifting dust among billions. My faeces returned to a more
acceptable shade, but the mess I was in had now become deeper, darker and so
putrid that it made me feel decidedly nauseous. Sectioning laws were not very
flexible. You were either free or you weren't free, *no* in-between—what an inhumane way to treat people! Why not send me to Whipsnade Zoo to be with the
other caged animals? Why can't they feed me to the lions and tigers limb by
limb, or strap me down and bundle me off to Rampton Secure Hospital For
The Criminally Insane and be done with it? Being sectioned meant that not
only did I have *no* option other than to return to the hospital, but I was also
not allowed off the damn ward without adequate supervision. Merry Christmas
Mister Keith!

"It's time that we should be making a move," said Mother, who incidentally
used to be a student nurse at Hemel Hempstead Hospital and also at nearby
St. Paul's Hospital, before reluctantly giving it all up to marry for the first time,
move to Germany and have two little girls, Virginia and Barbara. At Hill End
Psychiatric Hospital my bag was searched just in case I had hidden anything that
could be used to inflict serious harm upon myself, an indignity that I thought
was reserved for other people, not for me. Oh no, that was not to be the case,
no special treatment this time. It appeared to me as if I was being punished
more and more for the way I felt. The worse my depression got, the worse my
treatment and situation became. Being penalised for depression, being trapped
and guarded in a bad place only created an even deeper hole for me to sink
into. I can understand that a watchful eye had to be kept on me just in case I
might try to commit some sort of hara-kiri with a melted dinner fork, but this
antiquated treatment was way over the top. The guilt, the shame and the deep
regret that pinned me to the thunder and threw me to the earth, struck a blow
that even my old friend Cocky Crocky would have struggled to recover from,
let alone go the full fifteen. Sarcastically I thought, "Oh what a fool I must
have been not to have foreseen how this setup was going to make me feel so
much better, so delightfully happy again," do me a favour! The usual Christmas
carols would suddenly spring into life and become flavour of the day among
the others. Troubled patients wore brightly coloured strips of what looked like
cheap quality bog paper on their dizzy heads as hats. I was waiting for Stan The
Prune to dance around the ward with his stained trousers down to his ankles
and a toilet seat around his neck. In disbelief I observed sad patients who really

believed that there might be something for them to celebrate at this time of the year. For them there probably was.

The small screen beamed out *Miracle On 34th Street*, and hey, let's not forget Jude in the *Wizard Of Oz*. All of this nostalgic cheerfulness pissed me off big-time. I still saw the bigger picture, and I still picked out some of the Almighty's many little jokes and riddles. Despite opening the deep doors of my mind, just as I could when I was flying high, I couldn't do a thing with the puzzles that confronted me on the other side.

Why were most of the other funny-farmers full of so much festive cheer and turkey, when a minority group of half a dozen fellow killjoys, including myself, were wrapped up so damn tight in swaddling blankets of sadness and deep sorrow? Why were decent caring souls put on the rack? I wanted to do something that would work. I wanted to know what other routes there were out of my mind and out of this hospital. I prayed for forgiveness for every bad thought that I had since I was a small child (that alone was going to take up a fair bit of God's time), and then I put in a desperate prayer for a ticket out of my mental chambers of torture. Nothing happened, so I accused God of being a two faced phoney, along with a long list of derogatory words that at that time I believed to be justifiable. When the BBC's *Songs Of Praise* religious TV show came on I stole one of Jenny's fluffy teddy bears and launched it directly at the screen. I felt even worse than I did before. "What in this loopy old world can I do now," I thought. Usually I am all for God, Jesus and my fellow human beings, but when I am depressed I sometimes have the capability of turning the tables and cowardly finding something or someone else to partly blame for my ill deserved downfall. God does not escape my wrath at times like these, so please forgive me. I make no apologies for sounding like a moaning Minnie because it's all part of the illness that has to be allowed to roam free, until it finds a not so great but acceptable way of escape. I am just giving you a taste of depression. It is pretty awful don't you think? A severely depressed person would happily lick a sewer wall if it meant gaining some sweet relief from the anguish, and then probably die from dysentery or something equally foul. I remained barred from my life, now a non event, and yet the dull spark deep in my heart would still shock me into believing that I was still the impatient understudy, whose head was kept warm in the closet, somewhere in the wings, waiting to be called upon in an hour of need. The long running show may well have to go on, but I felt more and more like cutting short the set list, ringing my own bell and calling the shots. Where is the nearest bottle of something strong? Where is the nearest railway line? Hate set in, a bad word. I felt conned and let down, misinformed and ill advised. Hatred of others and a deep hatred of myself came to the fore, but I was too young and still that little bit too wise to be doused in hateful evil spirit, and then placed on the burning stake to fry tonight in my own bitterly wicked juice.

One of the most unproductive pastimes, I discovered to my detriment, is to look through album upon old album of past photographs. My father has always been prolific when it came to filling still albums and shooting cine/camcorder footage. All of his work has now been filed away neatly in his personal computer and on discs. He excelled at capturing in Kodachrome my early years in honest detail. There I am enjoying myself, happy as a sand boy holidaying on the pebbled Sussex coastline, or on the diverse Isle of Wight in Hampshire. Shots of school sports days, shots at goal with my left winged foot (I'm left footed but right handed) when playing for the Ember-Echoes prior to our 1981 trip to Long Island, New York, to compete in an international football tournament. There were photographs of a camping trip to Barmouth in the Snowdonia region of Wales that particularly sent a chill right down my spine. Our huge green and chocolate brown tent looked out across a vast expanse of sandy beach that was lapped up by the Irish Sea. Behind us were glorious green mountains. Every single photograph that featured me portrayed such a sad and scared little ten-year old lad who didn't have a clue what it was that had swooped down from out of the blue to infiltrate his young mind.

This had been the first time in my young life that I had experienced depression. It tagged on to a severe bout of glandular fever, keeping me away from Gade Valley Junior School for six long months. A lovely lady called Mrs. Brown gave me some home tuition during this period in order for me to remain up to date with my education, as well as getting me out and into different surroundings. At her home I made sausage rolls, did a little maths, read a variety of books, and best of all was making up silly stories that I would read aloud to my captive audience, made up of Mrs. Brown, her two year old son and a little dog.

Frustration and fear is my valid excuse for trashing my bedroom cell, I even punched my small ten-year old fist through the single paned bedroom window, leaving me with minor cuts, and my old man with a bill from the glazier. Fits of rage were the result of too much silence and inactivity on my part, not to mention the bafflement at not understanding what was happening to my young mind. I was an exceptionally bright and mischievous child who held back sometimes because I was perfectly aware that nobody likes a snotty nosed, know it all kid. I could not work out, nor compare with anything else that I had been exposed to, what was eating me up so bad. It was a scary lesson for a typical "Jack

The Lad" to have to go through. Everything that could be done in order to make my return to the land of the living as comfortable and reassuring as possible was provided, make no mistake about it. My uncle Terry Steadman recommended a top hypnotist/behavioural psychotherapist colleague of his who operated from his home in Wembley, Middlesex, only a stones throw from the old Empire Stadium. Along I went, but I could not loosen up enough to make the sessions work as they were intended. Most of my depression was phobia based. For example, if I touched anything at all that was white I had to blow the part of my hand that made contact, because I had it in my head that it was contaminated with something nasty. I had to at least attempt to do everything unnaturally perfect to avoid upsetting anybody, because I was already on a guilt trip for all of the perfectly normal naughty things that children do, and I had done the lot! When I looked at an inanimate object or another human being, I would project a mental image of violence and death onto that person, unable to leave the scene until the final vision was non-violent, non-morbid. The distant deaths of close family haunted me throughout my depression's entire unwelcome stay, so I mourned them prematurely. Normal games with the opposite sex of, "I'll show you mine if you show me yours," appeared to me as being terribly evil, so I kept on and on praying to the God on duty for forgiveness. There were lots more phobias, hang ups and imaginary fears jostling for the inside lane through my brain. It was a crippling experience for a young rascal to stumble into, and it was equally distressing for my family to hold both my hands as we waded through the treacle together. Those old photographs captured the moment, make no mistake about it, sending shivers through my entire body. It has to be said that ninety-nine percent of those old photographs depict a level of happiness that could never be bettered.

Casting my mind all the way back to my eleventh year, so that I could remind myself how I pulled hard and successfully through that maiden voyage, didn't make the slightest bit of difference to how I was feeling, instead it made my rudder shudder. Dragging open old doors and picture albums when shoulder high in misery did not work for me, although it may for you. Learn from the past but never allow yourself to wallow too deeply in it. *Now* is what counts the most. Wait until you feel much better before tormenting yourself with images of how you do and do not want to look and feel again. Why not scrap the past completely and concentrate on starting a fresh life, a complete life makeover that rids and replenishes the entire being, cleansing the mind and satisfying the soul. What often seems at first to be a dead end with absolutely no way out in sight, can often be the start of a brand new life, full of many new opportunities, it just takes a while to get the new key to your life polished on both sides and cut as cleanly and as precisely as possible. Keep reaching out for the hand that will help to pull you through. You are *never* ever alone and you *will* make it, I *promise!*

Breezing into the bathroom on Anderson Ward every morning had become a thing of the past. My plot was well and truly lost by now. Activities that I had practiced throughout my life appeared to be absent: 1. Get into the bathroom, 2. Undo buckle and lower garments, 3. Clean up, 4. Pull chain, 5. Wash hands thoroughly, 6. Leave. It sounds silly doesn't it, but anybody who has ever been in a similar situation will know painfully well exactly what I am driving at. Many of us wish to be younger than we really are, but not to feel like a baby or a small child who both urgently have to learn life's basic skills from scratch. Depression is all about being unable to function despite desperately wanting to. A depressed person has no use for riches, all that they require for their troubles out of this brief planetary existence is a chance to retry their God given life, that's all. All of my life skills, the way that I talk and walk, the things that I do without thinking about but go ahead and do anyway, the way in which I conduct myself in general; all of these attributes are in storage for a while. The problem is that I couldn't always afford to pay the mental bills to retrieve them, so I was being cut off more and more from the existence to which I had grown accustomed, an existence that was becoming tougher by the second to return to. The more that is taken away from a person makes it tougher to rectify the situation that was responsible for the problem in the first place. Supposing an artist was in a great amount of debt, would the powers that be take away the paints, canvasses and sable brushes as punishment until the debt was settled? How the hell is the artist now going to paint anything worth selling to pay off those debts? Yes, recovery is not made easier when everything is being taken away, especially freedom to go where you want to go.

Save all of the valuable plus points, the positives, the good things achieved that particular day, get tough and shout out *"Bollocks"* to the inevitable daily disasters, wash properly, eat and exercise to the best of your ability, force yourself to smile, read and write, attempt a favourite hobby or board game, watch TV, listen to the radio, take walks in peaceful stress free surroundings, try to keep communication going with friends and family even if it's only a brief "Hello" or "Goodbye"—try doing these things and your circumstances will slowly but surely become more stable and then begin to improve. When improvement kicks in, try not to run too far before you can jump, even though it is such a tempting prospect. Try to concentrate on getting the basics in place first, and when that is done you can get out there and show the world that you are back to stay, and fearful of *nothing.*

Trying to convince myself that a full recovery was on the cards continued to be a futile exercise, instead I felt that I had well and truly gone and lost my shining marbles forever, and was now destined to exist in a life of unhappiness. Danny, Bloody Mary and a few of the others from the old school knew only too well what a sickening thing it is to be strung up against the toughest odds imaginable. They had also been there, and they pulled through to the other side. Knowing this had no effect because I was doing too good a job of convincing myself that I was the exception to the rule. I was the one having it a whole lot worse than anybody else ever had—a common belief among depressed people, but it is still utter nonsense. My shoulders often felt a soft pat, offered from the hearts of so many kind souls. I was blind to it then, but now I can see how their simple gestures of silent solidarity and belief helped to cement the cracks, and balance the violent swinging flaws in my structure.

A simple courtesy costs nothing. On a good day a kind gesture can provide the giver and the recipient with a much needed boost, restoring faith in our Brothers and Sisters. I wondered how my fellow patients manage to survive their personal battles relatively intact. It is all about painstaking endurance, drawing on their reserves of inner strength and hard earned experience, plus a reliable and trustworthy circle of true family (if they have any) and loyal friends. Finding yourself alone among billions of the different faced same race, surrounded by life but nobody to phone, must be an awful way to exist. Add a physical disability to a lonely mental problem and you'll be forgiven for thinking that you have the right to have a good moan, but where is that ever going to get you, apart from being alienated even further?

Not all of us are loud and gregarious. Human nature produces the type of human being who, through no fault of their own, find contact with other beings extremely difficult. Their social skills might be limited, so they suffer in silence. The more an instrument is played the more proficient one becomes. Manic people can be lonely too because nobody can keep up and pin them down. They can also be so bloody annoying nobody wants to have anything to do with them, let alone sit down and attempt to chat at a million miles an hour. It makes no difference if you have good social skills or not, are manic or depressed, lonely or somewhere in the middle, you need not look any further as there are groups and recognised organisations in the United Kingdom such as the Manic Depression Fellowship, who offer support not only for victims but for their relations and caring friends as well. Everyone can learn about the illness and can also learn from other group members how to deal with particular problematic situations. Difficulties big or small, ideas and solutions galore can be bounced off each other, bringing enlightenment to a niggling worry. I had better not forget the sixty year old Mind organisation that caters for all manner of mental health problems. If you are really struggling then there are compassionate non judgmental volunteers only a phone call away such as the Samaritans and Saneline. All calls are in the strictest confidence. All areas of mental illness are catered for within these organisations except for the Manic Depression Fellowship. The equivalent organisations are available in the United States as well as in many other countries around the globe. Always remember that you are not alone and that you are truly wonderful, a marvel of modern creation!

A preoccupation with gloomy irrationalities can in time be buried for good as the sufferer gradually regains confidence, concentration and motivation. Setbacks will happen, threatening to overturn the makeover of your brand new life. With firm foundations and a solid set of well drawn up plans, the building process can restart with a vengeance. Those around you will become the solid bricks, just as you have a responsibility to become the same to them. Digging deep within your soul to set the foundation will be the toughest and most important job, because the foundations have to support the rest of your long life. Try building a skyscraper when you have only just been let out of the sewer, and you will fall flat on your face. The only way is up. All of your experiences will be mixed with tears of sadness, and cemented together with tears of joy, providing you with enough mortar to bond an exciting new structure.

Those who help out in our hours of need deserve *not* to be taken for granted, a mistake that I have made many times to my detriment. Performing a favour among friends does not mean that a gesture is expected to be reciprocated, but it doesn't hurt to make the effort either does it. True friends who walk in when the other walk out will do almost anything within their capabilities to pull their buddy out of a hole, but if that helping hand over does it and jeopardises their own health by helping that sunken person then they are foolish, extremely admirable but still a bit foolish. When somebody politely refuses their assistance for a while they must *not* be criticised, questioned or insulted, instead one should try to understand and respect their decision. Maybe there is something that you can do for them. Never lose sight of the fact that just because you are having a tough time of it, you are *not* the most important person on the planet, the one who needs the most attention. It never hurts to remind oneself from time to time that everybody has their own weaknesses and strengths, and that you are still only a tiny, though very important body among a galaxy of living breathing stars.

A tricky part of bipolar affective disorder is learning one's own personal acceptability tolerances. Within what acceptable limits of sadness does a funeral fit? What sociably acceptable limits of excitement fits in with a night out at a nightclub or going to a concert? There are no exact tables, only commonsense that comes with experience. As you are aware, regular blood testing is imperative if one is to know for sure what is chemically taking place inside the body. How irritating it is when those who always describe themselves as, "Concerned, that's all," suggest that, "Perhaps you are going a little bit high or a little bit low," when in fact all that I might have been doing was singing along to a song on the radio while using the cushions on the sofa as my pretend drum kit. Animated and verbal improvisation has always been a part of my make-up, but irritatingly these days it is often misinterpreted as—in the picky eyes of somebody else who is trying their best to care—the first rumblings of hypomania, diagnosed by a clueless Dr. Richard Head or Dr. Rachel sole. Inactivity and silence for more than a minute suddenly becomes depression in their eyes, it's as if they sometimes wish something would go wrong with me just so that they can say, "I told you so, look at me, see how clever I am to get it right." It is a case of everybody getting used to a situation and adapting. Over caution is to be expected, and it is better I suppose than having nobody at all to keep a lookout. Fortunately these occurrences are now very few and far between. It is being responsible for one's own actions, and remaining healthy that contributes hugely to the level of confidence that others have in you. It has to be stressed just how difficult it is to be around a person with a mental illness for long periods of time. Nipping in the bud a problem that hasn't even materialised, hurriedly concocted in the imagination of an overly caring person, goes with the territory I'm afraid, especially soon after the first episodic swings. I would rather deal with that attention than have nobody at all to keep an eye out for me. Anyway, the over reactions do ease up as time goes by, and those whom you know well become better qualified in their judgement. Worst of all is having too many opinions, qualified or not, coming out of too many heads about too many things regarding the state of my mental health. My opinion, the expert view on myself, is occasionally dismissed when I know far more about what's what than they do. Just because I have no official letters after my name, my input was often output faster than a sneaky cigarette at medical school. People react differently to stressful situations, it is just that learning all of these differences can sometimes be a real pain in the butt. I am grateful for all of the generous help and advice that I have been given from everybody, especially during the times when sharing afternoon tea and chewing the fat with Hannibal Lecter would appear to be heaps more appetising than holding court with yours truly.

The monitoring of my bouncy moods became easier as the years flew by. Reading the tell tale signs has now become second nature, but at the onset it felt like everybody was taking it in turns to find something new to pin on my forehead. Yes, it was annoying to feel as if I was being labelled every five minutes by those who I thought should know better, but I am grateful that they did. I try to stay on my leash and not bite when a well intentioned remark or poorly thought out piece of advice comes my way. How can I be angry at some kind body who is only trying to be helpful? I would rather have a few lookouts on my side of the moat than have nobody at all. An Englishman's home is his castle, but wouldn't it be awfully lonely if I had to live in it all by myself, coping single handed with the ups and downs of the drawbridge, and phoning out every night for a banquet for one.

Anderson Ward radiated a different air of expectancy, this time brought about by the next fun time on the calendar, New Years Eve. Although the patients on Anderson Ward were a bit thin on the ground, there was still a definite buzz of excitement. I tried to absorb the atmosphere that some of the other jovial patients were becoming intoxicated on, but I couldn't even get a sniff. Tobacco still tasted foul if at all, another displeasing loss of pleasure. My back catalogues of obese anxiety and anorexic hope were thrown wide open, gaining new entries by the second.

The natives on Ritchie's ward were as restless as usual, so some of them set up camp on Anderson Ward where the seasonal decor outshone their own, and the pickings were richer. Cigarettes, tea, biscuits—they were all scavenged in good spirits, just as I used to do on the other wards when I felt as if I could waltz with clouds and swing on the Moon. Food glorious food sent its aromatic message up and into the hairy nosed visitors who would then hurry, with lips quivering, home to their own ward for a fair share of the slim pickings. Our own stainless steel trolley came clanking to a halt at the foot of the stairs that lead up to Anderson Ward. From here the food was carried on its last leg to our small kitchen. The hospital chef must have failed to read the brief telling him that there had been a huge migration of people throughout Christmas and the new year, as he and his team had gone ahead and prepared enough food to feed a third world country and still have leftovers. While the others shovelled their food mountains down, I struggled to come to terms with just a few fork ends of flaked mash potato and soggy vegetables. Our Scandinavian dish of a nurse approached me after dinner and explained that she and the other members of staff had decided among themselves that it would be in my best interest if I were to take the solitary room again. This room, more like a cell, was the very same room that I had been allocated when I had made my manic entrance onto Anderson Ward nearly four months earlier. I felt let down by every place and by every person considering all that I had given of myself. My bipolar heart had been beating in the right place, even if my head had been severed and was rolling around like a crystal marble, in and out of every human sense and emotion. I might have been teetering on my last spindly legs and feeling like shit, but I knew that somehow my God would show up and help me smash in the face of depression, once and for all!

My disorder had succeeded in doing an excellent job of shutting up Steadman. The imbalance of chemicals had reduced me to a distant relic of the happy young man that I once was. I felt terribly aggrieved. Every aspect of my existence struck me hard as a diabolical mess, a stew made with vomit and a pickle. Just a short while ago I was the puppeteer, able to pull all the right strings and the most amazing things happened. I had the best seat in the house of extremes. Now my own strings had been cut, leaving me slumping in shock and shivering with fear and dread of what tomorrow might bring. The bout of the century was now on between myself and myself. Instead of fifteen three minute rounds, I had twenty-four sixty minute rounds seven days a week for many more months than I needed to have done, had it not been for missing the rapid drop from mania to depression. Maybe I am being too harsh, trying to blame somebody else for my own chemistry and also for my own shortcomings. I imagine that the professionals expected a huge dip in my mood following such a high, but all they could do was treat me with medication as best as they could. Nothing was going to prevent the natural opposite of what goes rocketing up and up. Conflicts and chemistry had brought on this severe bout of depression, but it was still only handbags at ten paces.

Helen had flown over to a different ward two weeks before Christmas, but the gorgeous creature still found time within her busy schedule to flutter over to Anderson Ward for a quick visit. Not a great deal was said during these visits, but it was her physical presence and not the words that mattered so much. I was well aware that my misery might rub off, so I tried to stay well clear of the other patients. Hiding away is the wrong thing to do, yet I was one of the worst offenders. There was an awful lot to learn from the crash course that I had accidentally enrolled myself in. I had to learn why my body was reacting in the way that it was, and how lithium—a medicine that so far had not exactly given me any cause for throwing parties—was in fact *not* a placebo as my manic personality had proclaimed, but an essential chemical requirement that will help me to become stabilised. When one is desperate for some sort of hope to cling on to they will try hard to listen, and might even be strong willed enough to believe (correctly) that a reparable chemical imbalance is the main cause of the present condition. All of the self explanatory medical facts are still hard to believe and accept when one has just emerged from mania, and is on a severe downer. A substance consumed or an extreme emotional event often fires the pistol that starts a mad dash into any sort of decline. By having something tangible to work toward and hang onto, the affected person can at least attempt to get a grip. A solid scientific reason why depression has struck, explained thoroughly and clearly, can and *must* be instilled in a depressed mind, instead of believing that, "Oh no, this is how it is going to be for the rest of my life." For some this approach will go in one ear and out the other, so other positives have to be applied, sometimes very discreetly. If any form of trigger catches you with your lithium levels down to your ankles, you will be in for a ride that may look like heaps of fun from the queue, but will actually rip you into two opposing halves of what should really be one balanced sane person. The assembly line is not always fun and games, which is exactly what I was about to find out.

My manic version of Hotel Hill End had now inconsiderately closed for urgent repairs, yet it still held its miserable doors wide open for sad late bookings. How could I expect this place to be instrumental in getting me up and running again? The drums rolled, so I dreamt of choppy times ahead, as well as those with a happier beat. The black nights always won the early duels, wedging a rod of white hot steel down my throat and out of my rectum at breakfast time, then slowly removing it just before the next long night of confusion, fright and uncertainty. Life sure pulls out all the stops so that we are kept on out toes. Life in all its generosity allows us far more chances to win through to the other side than perhaps we deserve. God's gift of life *never* gives up on *us*, no matter who we are or what we have become, so let's never ever give up on *it*.

From my bed I could see the corners of the pictures that I had put up on admission and then ripped off excitedly when I had to relocate. This was my solitary cooler, a place that I reluctantly entered to begin with. I tried so many different anti-depressants throughout the following months, giving each one a chance of coming up trumps. The side effects of these medications, despite subsiding a little after two or three weeks, only succeeded in making me feel despondent. Pills and potions do work wonderfully well at the very first try for most depressed patients, and they can be lifesavers, but for me they took a bit of persevering with. Ever since the latter part of 2002—a deplorable time, when I experienced yet another terrible depressive episode in New York—I have been directed along the most agreeable route as far as anti-depressants are concerned. Albert T. Claridge M.D, Diplomat Of The American Board Of Psychiatry And Neurology saved my bacon, by skilfully assembling a course of medication for me that did *not* have the same disagreeable effects as some of the others. Slight weight gain and the occasional skin rash are now the only side effects that I ever get from medication, but even they can be controlled by means of a healthy balanced diet, drinking plenty of water and getting regular outdoor exercise. The prescription medications are constantly being improved upon, which is something to be extremely optimistic about. The best anti-depressant is prevention and self preservation. Putting into practice professional advice and also using one's own commonsense is imperative if one wishes to park in a depression free mind zone.

Not once did a member of staff, except for Helen on one of her fleeting visits, take me to one side, sit me down and discuss my depression, or even attempt to construct a realistic set of goals that I could realistically achieve. I had to help myself to everything that had been laid out on a platter before me, but it came with a hefty price tag. If anybody was a prime candidate for electroconvulsive therapy (ECT), then it had to be me. The facility for conducting, what used to be frowned upon as a barbaric practice, existed behind one of the hospital's locked doors. The way I felt, the electric chair would have been more agreeable. ECT has come a long way since the Frankenstein days, and is now a more humane, subtle and swift procedure. I would have agreed to a good old fashioned lobotomy had it been offered. Locking a person in a psychiatric ward and then sectioning them, not to mention being stuck inside that stupid little isolation room, would drive almost anybody *into* depression. Okay, the powers that be will argue that I had to be there for my own protection, fair enough, but why in an environment that can even provoke a two minute, "Cannot stop long, must dash," token duty visitor to slash their own wrists? I wonder who the wise qualified ass is who woke up one bright and breezy morning in their country retreat and thought, "Ah, I know what we will do for all of those depressed patients, we will stop them from doing anything, going anywhere, give them no say whatsoever as far as their course of treatment is concerned, search their belongings, strip them of their dignity and oh yes, why don't we put them in a little cell of a room all by themselves for good measure? Ah yes, that will make them feel oh so much better." What utter *bollocks*! The staff did a pretty good job under the given circumstances I suppose, but there were times when I wished I had stolen a rocket from the firework display, so that I could ram it up the same professional orifice that my expertly thought out care-plan came from. Blowing up the staff would have left me far worse off, but it was the thought that counted toward a rare smile. I suppose they tried to help me and I just didn't see it. Was I so irresponsive that they ceased trying to penetrate my world? Enough of feeling sorry for myself; an unattractive form of behaviour that travels nowhere fast.

The eve of 1991 came and left just like every other day. Normally I love this time of the year, and I am always up for a party, but now I saw the festivities as nothing more than a great big fuss about nothing. Why don't we kiss and cuddle and smile all year round? Why do we wait until late December before we exchange pleasantries to strangers without fear of a dirty look or a sock on the jaw? A hymn and a prayer are seen as the requisite yearly spiritual instalment made at unfamiliar alters, in uncomfortable clothes by a bunch of out of tune hypocrites. When feeling very low I saw too much as being fickle and stiffly staged, as well as lacking sincerity and genuine love. Patience and subtleness have never been my strongest points, and I do not suffer fools who do not make an effort to better themselves, just as I am not suffered when playing the part of one. The sheer frustration of being unable to enjoy even the simplest of pleasures, and instead having to endure a mental anguish that disables the entire mechanism of the magnificent human machine, can loosen an uncharacteristic tongue. I cannot stress strongly enough how the venomous satisfaction spat out will quickly turn sour in the heat of the moment. Hurt an innocent person for one's own selfish relief is completely wrong. Do *not* drag other people down to your temporary low level. Depressed people still need to display good manners and show plenty of respect to their fellow human beings. You may feel like a shoddy piece of work now, but try to imagine that you are saving up for the renovation, and the longer you have to save the better the job will be. Have a grumble yes, get it off your chest, but do *not* bite the hands and the hearts of those who are trying their level best to hold you up where you have always belonged.

Relaxation therapy classes were still available on a twice weekly basis. Try relaxing from head to toe when the weight of twenty-five chaotic years are pressing down on your shoulders. "In for a penny in for a pound," as my dear Nan Duckworth would say, so I agreed to be escorted by a borrowed Martian to the Nissen hut. On this occasion I thought that I was wasting everybody else's time, and that relaxation therapy was definitely going to be of no positive value. All that I could focus on was the rain as it rattled like machine gun fire onto the roof of the hut, and the constant rush of negativity that filled my head to bursting. I could not see how such an excruciatingly painful hour sitting in a semicircle on huge brightly coloured cushions, along with a friendly enough assortment of troubled patients, could do me or anybody else in my predicament any long lasting favours. Hard though I found it, I continued to attend the sessions, coming away from them with the wrong conclusion that the whole therapeutic ordeal had been far more damaging than if I hadn't bothered to get up off my rear to join the stupid group in the first place. Now I am older, a little wiser and certainly uglier enough to see that the stimulation of patients in different tin canned surroundings had actually done me heaps of good, instead of sitting in a dark corner on Anderson Ward smoking myself silly, filling up with the wrong kind of stimulant and feeling more and more sorry for my pathetic, scabby little self. Shutting out more and more of what I really craved was not a sensible way to move forward. The brain needs exercising and the mind needs stimulating just as any other part of the anatomy does, more so in fact. Feeling suicidal in different stimulating places is far more preferable than being suicidal in one mind numbing place. It sounds like a nutty thing to say but it is so true. It is painfully difficult to make yourself move to new locations and perhaps meet new people, but the harder the effort put in, the better the long-term outcome will be. There is no way that this can be seen or believed when feeling so wretched, but the effort must be made, and that is where tough love comes into its own.

If the depressed person does not at least bother to make even the slightest of efforts, then it is very likely that the caregiver, who has put in an awful lot of hours trying to help raise the spirits, and who could be doing a whole host of far more interesting things, will become increasingly reluctant to continue dishing out their eat as much as you like buffet of encouragement, belief, loyalty and love. It wouldn't be because the care and the concern have suddenly fled overnight, but because we are all human and we all have our own breaking points. How the hell can you expect to help somebody who wont even make a little effort to retrieve the reins of their own life? What I am trying to say is that the severely depressed person has got to get off their bony backside and onto their wobbly legs and try. You will stumble backwards and feel like utter crap, but you have tried. You will often feel a thousand times worse for making the effort, but the rewards will become apparent when they are good and ready. Keep making that effort and the angels in their many manifestations will catch you, or at least soften the blow when you fall, and you will sometimes fall. Within time the landing will become softer due to the layers of confidence that you have earned from realising that the world has not caved in. The layers will keep bouncing you back up onto your feet until you can step forward onto solid ground, into a promising future.

As I mentioned earlier, it took me nearly twelve years before I found the combination of medications that suited me the best. My problem since being diagnosed as having bipolar affective disorder, was that I had a tendency to be overly sensitive to many of their side effects, none of which were particularly serious, but they were long lasting. My depressions since 1990 may have eased considerably by using one or a combination of the vast array of anti-depressants, but there is no escaping the fact that I had to always wait for the devastating storms to blow themselves out. The brain's chemistry can be set right, and then it's left up to you and me to keep occupied both physically and mentally. Trigger avoidance, as I keep saying, is the key. When on the right path, a maintenance dose of antidepressants is usually prescribed to help keep the balance. Make that effort to brush your teeth regularly and take your medications, have some breakfast (another good time to take meds—always read the instructions that come with them), decide what is suitable to wear, attempt a short walk in the fresh air and mingle with another member of the human race other than your caregiver. I recall struggling to make decisions about all sorts of things, especially what to wear outdoors. Going over the simplest of tasks step by step in order to get them right took up lots of my time, leaving me feeling exasperated, but I had no option other than to plod on regardless. Remember, there will always be a creep pointing their critical finger at another person's efforts. Ignore the primitive remarks from ignorant, ill educated, woodenheaded losers and keep on chip-chipping away.

One by one the other patients returned from their Christmas and New Year revelling, some still wearing their presents over their heads, round their necks and on their hands. Two new alcoholics, Jake Millington and Stuart Ridgley, arrived for a three week drying out session. The pair of them had managed to remain on the outside of the hospital for the heaviest drinking session of the year, and now they had three weeks of cleansing followed by regular meetings with Alcoholics Anonymous. If you think that three weeks abstinence is going to make a difference you need to look harder. I knew Jake from childhood as he lived only a few streets away, and he also attended the same class at school as my sister Barbara. In July 2003 Jake—who according to newspaper reports was on at least one large bottle of vodka a day—was imprisoned for life because he slit another man's throat, killing him. Drinking so much of the hard stuff over such a long period of time must have affected his thinking, but that's still no excuse for committing such a heinous crime. Stuart Ridgeley happened to be the son of my former science teacher at the Cavendish School, sharing classes with my eldest Sister Virginia. I know for a fact that both Jake and Stuart flung themselves off the wagon the minute they left the hospital grounds, such a shame, especially in Jake's case as his drinking led to the death of an innocent man.

I continued to stick with my lithium loving water and tea, as I was still a little wary of the plastic jugs dotted all over the ward. There were plenty of times when I would have given anything to have had a heavy session in a pub, a temporary relief as I drowned myself in alcohol. Would the depressant qualities make me feel even worse? Oh yes, eventually. Drinking to try and blot out a depression is a dangerous habit to get caught up in, and I should know because I have done it enough times. Finding out the hard way is not everybody's idea of fun, so why not let people like myself make the mistakes so that you can learn from them? "Fat chance," I hear you cry, but it really is worth thinking seriously about, as it could save an awful lot of unnecessary heartache not only for you but for everybody else. Crying tears into your whisky and then drowning in the mix must be avoided at all costs.

Food, medication and personal hygiene were the only reasons why I ever left the tiny little room, even though I hated it so much. Reluctant distancing ensured minimal human contact. Conversation of more than ten seconds automatically pressed my panic button and sent my nervous system's alarm bells jangling. Believing that I needed a verbal splint, and convinced that my body language was illegible, are most probably the two main reasons why I *did* occasionally stumble and clumsily fumble over nothing at all. It really is inside your head, nestling in an unstable mind. So wrapped up in myself meant that I neglected those to whom I had become close. We trusted and shared, listened and laughed, confided and cried, and now I needed them more than ever before. I was blind to their needs. They may have needed moral support also, so that they could scrub a worry or two off their list. Ian continued to be willingly caught in his own whirlwind imagination, but mine had about as much puff as a fly's fart. Anderson Ward was never a big enough stage for the pair of us to perform simultaneously on full manic throttle.

The caregiver is more susceptible to the jaws of doom than they may think, so they should tread carefully. Being there for an ill person is often all that is needed, leaving the really tough stuff to the professionals. Sometimes all a caregiver can do is be patient and allow the illness to wear itself out before a new life can emerge and develop, fertilised by the recent shitty past. The feel good factor that results in helping others who have been stricken is a priceless one indeed, even when that unwell person has been a total pain in the neck. Helping out in the smallest of ways to inject a ray of sunshine back into the life of another human being, who is at that time less fortunate than you is so richly rewarding. Hard cut up rocks might fulfil the needs of some, but putting the sparkle back into the eyes of somebody who is struggling through their given patch of rough, has on occasions made me and countless others far richer and more fulfilled than our wildest manic dreams would ever allow.

What some people may not realise is that a severely depressed person is capable of stewing so selfishly. They are absorbing so much lumpy doom and gloom that they rarely bubble up to the surface long enough to see and be affected by somebody else's mini or major crises. I would have willingly hacked off my limbs one by one rather than be glued to the bottom of the shaft. I don't mean to offend the amputees and paraplegics for whom that is a fact of life, but this is how I often felt. Come to think of it, how would I be able to climb out of the shaft if all my limbs had been chopped off? Self mutilation is a step up from wanting to end it all, but it is definitely *not* the correct thing to do. These kind of thoughts are *not* uncommon for a depressed person to have, but nobody told me that. I had to figure most of it out as I trotted along. The guilt trips grew longer and began to stick around like fluff on Velcro. You've got to know that a manic-depressive/bipolar affected person is *not* to blame for possessing the genes that cause the chemical imbalances, so there is no need to torture yourself over it. Being a bit different certainly isn't a crime, not in my book.

When I hit the depths of depression nothing much else mattered other than my predicament. Outside influences such as wars and famines may have found a disturbing way into my head, but it is safe to say that nothing else really mattered at that time other than coming up with another way to put a permanent stopper on the agony, or finding a way of squeezing free of an ugly spot in my life. Contemplating what the future would be like if I was trapped in this depression forever took up too much of my time. Picture a bank of twenty television monitors sitting in front of you. We are the editors receiving live pictures and audio from all over the world, images that have been rebounding off satellites. These pictures are edited and then sent back out again in a coherent viewer friendly form. The depressed mind is receiving too many lousy channels, all of them watered down and lacking substance, but they still need to be sifted through and made sense of. It is a tall order that still has to be carried out even when the brain's instinctive processor is on the blink, kaput. An effort of sorts always has to be made. Nothing can be left untouched, even though a bigger tangle may occur as a result. Any sort of willing spirit is better than none, so any failure should *not* be criticised, only applauded. Praise for not trying is *not* being kind. Plenty of successful failures were to come, and yet right now all I really wanted to do was expire as soon as possible, so why the hell should I give a damn about other people's problems, and the monumental cock-ups that self centred mankind has made of almost everything that God has so generously provided? Deep depression is a self absorbent area that encourages you to face and then deal with life's many ingrained truths. It is a very distressing process that has to be dealt with, but the rewards will be worth it. If you can beat a real bummer of a depression, and you will, then you can do anything that you set your magnificent mind to!

The trenches of my mind tried to absorb all that was hurled its way, but the rainy season had set in. My usual arsenal was rendered useless, and the muddied thoughts and ripped threads of reality slid further down into a bath of petrol.

I wanted to create the spark that would light my bath, but I could not even obey that simple little request. More rain diluted all that I had tried so hard to collate, leaving me laying alone in my room, running nowhere and everywhere on empty, full of dried up beans. I was an undiscovered mollusc living miles down in the ruling oceans, misunderstood and under a huge amount of pressure. If I rose too fast I knew that I ran a terminal risk. I was compatible with the beat of today and also with the future pulse, yet unable to merge the two, forgetting the appropriate words, blowing fuses and generally corrupting my mind's entire circuitry. Apart from all of that, everything was just fine.

The big question that I asked myself then was, "Is there a God?" My view on the subject changed like the tides of the sea. Earlier I suggested that we are all part of one spiritual force, a view that still holds strong. How it works exactly is anybody's guess. Why have wars and try to force one persons belief into another person? Being different is healthy, it creates original progress. The prime mover would want us to make the most of our lives and not spend it wondering where we came from and where we are going to. *Now* is what matters. How it all started and where it is all going is a mystery indeed, but I don't think that God would approve of the amount of time spent arguing about something we cannot change. Praise to God is a good thing in every religion, so long as it is conducted in a way that doesn't offend others. Respect for the many different faiths is always in order, because at the end of the day there can only be *one* God. He or "it" has just been divided into different versions, none of which are better or worse. Laying one's religious beliefs upon another person's beliefs sparks the trouble that religion is supposed to be preaching against in the first place! To seize every day and then give something back is all that God wants for his troubles. Why does man complicate matters so much? Evolution or creation? Perhaps God created evolution? Are there living organisms on Mars? Do we share a sixth sense? Are we all capable of telepathy given the right conditions? Where do odd socks vanish to in the wash? How tall is the Empire State building? Why concern ourselves with so much brain cell sapping fascination of the interestingly unsolvable, along with the irrelevancies of our already full to the brim lives? Man's natural curiosity often leaves much to be desired, playing a major role in jamming up many minds, possibly triggering an episode of manic depression or some other mental problem. A little trivia is interesting, but there is no way that I could devote my whole life to something lacking real substance. I am more of a dabbler who finds it hard to see how a person can be so rigid in their ways, without even attempting to see how the grass grows on the other side of the fence. If they do bother to check out the grass they will never find it greener, but they *will* find that it comes in many different shades. It is such a shame that the human race has become so technically brilliant, yet so deaf, dumb and blind to the simple basics than can preserve this planet, and reposition mankind onto a course of peace and harmony.

Any form of expression that acts as a means of steaming open the lid of a burden, letting it out into the open so it will disperse and then disappear forever, is a good thing indeed. Sharing a nagging doubt or a glint of optimism with somebody else worked wonders for me, and it will for you too. There were times when my mind-spring was so tightly wound it took a little longer to uncoil, then allowing the contents a chance to be set free. A mood can be read in many different ways by enlightened caregivers and psychiatric staff alike. My way at this low point was to scribble down a few poems or rhymes, in fact a whole bunch of words in my cut up head that could then be glued together with pure instinct. With the aid of a nervously chewed pencil and a pocket sized notebook, I managed to unload a huge weight. It was nothing fancy, just a collection of thoughts and relevant words in no particular order. I wrote for myself and that was it. Nearly everything made some sense, no matter how I put it down. If the exercise in words gave me a just a brief respite then it was well worth doing. Since 1991 I have invariably found myself reaching for an inexpensive pencil and a pad of paper whenever I felt the need to release some good or bad steam. It works every time for me. The important thing is that it served a purpose just like all of the other therapies on offer. Fortunately, whenever I hold my breath and dive back into my old manic or depressed scribbles, I have been pleasantly surprised at my findings. Possible song lyrics I have in abundance, they are staring me in the face saying, "Use me,"—when I learn to play some guitar chords I will.

All of the social ward activities dried up for me. Tempting succulents that would refresh and stop my whole self from drying out completely were available, but I was too frightened to join in and partake of healthy conversation and laughter as I had readily done before. I had scared myself into believing that if I quenched my thirst for company I may say something wrong, out of line, or worse still I might clam up and retreat further back into my sad little shell. Fear of further knocks held me back from making forward progress. Worries always grew into fear, but as soon I had successfully achieved a task I would wonder why I had worried so much about it. My head never blew up with all of the bedlam taking place inside, though at times it did feel as if my pounding chest was about to.

When it feels as if the world and all that is in it has prematurely shut up shop without prior notice, and that an inbuilt mechanism has predicted a worsening of the situation, no matter how many or what type of precautions are taken, one does tend to overheat and then freeze up. Bipolar affective disorder cannot be learnt entirely from a book. Symptoms and remedies have no other choice than to follow a written pattern I know, but that's about as far as it can go. Hanging on for dear life while riding the storm to its end is the only way out. Apart from millions of other bipolar sufferers, there are only a few people that come close to knowing what it is like to reach the supreme limits of pleasure and pain as I have, so I do *not* take too kindly to know alls who think that they do. When feeling down, there is a small element who feel that they can talk to you like a piece of dirt. They run with those morons who feel that they have the right to regard you as crazy or mad in a very nasty way, so that they can become an even bigger fish in their stagnant pond. Do not do it!

When feeling depressed it is very easy to slump deeper into the trap of taking a negative view of every word that has been spoken to you, and then fearing that the worst will be even *worse* than previously imagined. I have touched upon this already, but I feel it is very important to realise that book after book about depression, references in medical journals and every scrap of writing to be found that relates to how you are feeling, can lead to a further lowering of mood if the magic answer isn't found within. This can instil the false, yet very serious belief that you are an untreatable one off. All you can do is harness inspiration and hope from wherever you can find it, then use it to rise up and out. I'm afraid there aren't any personalised instruction manuals just yet, but you can bet that in the not too distant future every piece of information relating to an individuals condition, their genealogical past and present circumstances, can be fed into a computer programme and a course of treatment will be prescribed, that can include a recommended lifestyle package and a course of the most suitable consumer friendly medication. Perhaps some kind of monitoring computer chip could be inserted into the brain that sends a signal when a chemical imbalance is taking place. Then again, I don't really fancy being connected up to an intrusive bipolar switchboard.

Myself and many other Hillenders continued to lay low with our own custom created version of the "common cold of psychiatry," a phrase coined by the American professionals due to the increasingly abundant number of depression related cases. Depression arrives in so many guises: Post natal depression, the mourning of a dearly departed, the loss of a job, a broken marriage, financial difficulties, drink and drug problems and so on. These varying forms of depression can easily be nurtured into severe clinical cases, or they can be tackled shoulder high and brought to rest. Vincent, the skinny chap who had joined the Anderson crowd as a quivering gibbering bag of knotted nerves, had made a miraculous recovery. He was still in a serious and vulnerable condition, but he had come on in leaps and bounds, not a patch on the pathetic creature that had originally presented itself to the bemused ward. Vincent proved to be genuinely compassionate to the others on the ward, showing off his prized possession of humour that had been stifled throughout his lifelong battle with depression. He remembered that I had offered a few encouraging words, so he attempted to offer me the same in return. If a few words are well chosen it can make the world of difference. Well done Vincent, you didn't forget even when you were down, but *never* out. Sometimes I wonder whether praying for another person can backfire. For that prayer to come true does the prayer giver have to absorb some of the extracted pain?

Unipolar (one-way) *mania* consists of episodic manic attacks that alternate with spells of a more stable mood. Unipolar *depression* is the exact opposite. Bipolar-*one* is an alternation of very high manic periods and severe depressive episodes. Bipolar-*two* is an alternation of mild manic phases (hypomania) and severe depressive episodes. Cyclothymia is cyclical alternation of a high mood along with periods of low mood but without a severe depression. Dysthymia disorder is a neurosis characterised by depression, anxiety, compulsive behaviour and obsession. This last sorry mixture is what Vincent had. It had progressively worsened through his tortuous teenage years into early adulthood. I think the poor fellow was living in dystopia. It is very hard to imagine that Vincent had never had much happiness in his life, unable to raise more than a half-hearted smile on special occasions. Underneath his veneer of deep-rooted sorrow smouldered a wicked sense of humour crying out to be freed. How many of us, myself included, have felt hard done by because life has dealt a few dodgy cards? Compared to Vincent, my existence so far on this planet has been a walk in the Jeckyl and Hyde Park, treading in the odd dog pile of life now and then, but nothing that can't be rinsed off. Vinnie was the kind of human being that rolled over and over in it, but unlike dogs he didn't do it out of choice. This young human must have been Hill End's most successful story during the period of time that I spent there. I bumped into him a couple of years later as he was coming out of Hemel Hempstead's Dacorum College Campus where he was wasting no time in making up for many missed years. I wish him all the very best.

Limited to where and for how long I could roam, I tended to just lay on my institutional little bed and gaze at my same ceiling and walls upon which I used to see living images. I knew that if my depression worsened I would somehow devise a way of being successful in an attempt upon my own life. So much of my mental torture was made up of guilt for having been given a life to live, and now all I wanted to do was throw it all away. How ridiculous it is to be depressed about being depressed. I could *not* lay the misery on any thicker. Do those who are the closest to a suicide victim ever recover? Dying young is tough enough for all concerned, but doing it on purpose adds a whole new dimension that may well prove too hard for the survivors to ever shake off. If I felt brave I would have a day out in the lounge, curling my legs up on a sticky vinyl covered chair from where I would attempt to read somebody's biography. I read the same pages over and over with only depressing thoughts registering. A book enabled me to distance myself from unwanted callers. Any distraction, a smell or a sound, irritated me so much that I never stayed in one place for longer than ten minutes, always giving in to the pull of my little room so that everybody could see the depressed Steadman coming and going. My appearance had become rough, serving as a visual extension of my troubled inner self. The anti-depressant pills that I had been given to help push me into an upright position continued to make me feel ten times worse due to their side effects. They had to be taken though, and patience was required in order for the required effects to kick-in and give the doctors an accurate reading from which to work from.

It was discovered that my lithium level had yet to reach a safe and satisfactory level. I drank gallons of tap water and I ate healthily, even though it wasn't a great amount. Smoking didn't affect the important issue of blood lithium levels, although it did reduce the amount of healthy oxygen mixed up in my bloodstream, not that I cared. I already knew that millions of people had it so much harder than I did, but plenty of well meaning people still made a strong thoughtless point of reminding me. Knowing this only added to my guilt trip. Depressed people have no option other than to survive. It is an instinctive thing. Had I wanted to badly enough I am sure that I would have tried suicide again, but there must have been a part of me that said, "Get up, get up you fool, do *not* lay down and let this thing beat you, get up right now!" Between episodes of mania and depression, the treatment required in order to maintain a healthy balance is a relatively simple procedure. Lithium sometimes combined with a maintenance dosage of an anti-depressant works wonders for me today. There is no need to tell you what my personal medications are. The manic-depressive/ bipolar sufferer on an agreeable package of pills can find that they are still prone to unannounced changes, brought about by stressful situations and/or excessive amounts of pleasurable substances, or by subjecting themselves for too long to the stressful extremities that life presents us with each and every twenty-four indulgent hours of every day, whether it be in the home, in the factory, the office or fields. "You can have too much of a good thing," goes the saying, but for me that simply doesn't ring true, as I force feed myself with life's latest offering until addicted and sick, which I guess *is* too much of a good thing. Too much television news and tabloid sensationalism can tarnish the way we think and behave. A bombardment of advertising, religion, sex and violence etc is also designed to do exactly the same thing, to overload the mind with the same subconscious *and* conscious images that are crying out to be acted upon, so imagine what a bombardment of bad news that is completely out of our hands can do to our minds. It cannot be stressed enough that many sick and violent crimes are triggered by what is seen on television, DVD's and in the warped games that unscrupulous money making executives put out, despite knowing only too well what the end result will be. A cross section of people will believe that normal life means shooting other people's brains out, blowing people up and fornicating on street corners like cats and dogs. Human life is devalued by feeding it with all things evil related.

As far as I was concerned, Hill End Psychiatric Hospitalisation had now ran its course. Twiddled and twirled chunks of my hair were still being yanked out and thrown onto the hard linoleum floor. Prolonged incarceration had long ceased to be of any benefit, if at all. To stay any longer among the lovable mad, happy and sad, tobacco puffing and tea guzzling men and women of Hill End would have been criminally insane. A different lost soul should now benefit from all that was supposed to be good and therapeutic. My turn was over, and I had never felt so bad in my entire life. My continued presence served no beneficial purpose whatsoever. I had been brought back down to an icy earth crater, from where I was reluctant to rise again in case I slipped and fell into an even deeper trough of frozen dreams. My discharge from the hospital was of course going to be another decision that was completely out of my hands. "Don't bother to ask him, he's only the patient," spoke the despicably unfair system. During January 1991 I had put forward the strongest case that I could in my efforts to be released from this hospital hell. The chief consultant psychiatrist Dr. Kananara listened carefully to the expert advice given by the ward staff, all of whom had hardly made an effort to speak to me, let alone make an accurate evaluation of my present condition. A week following my consultation with Dr. Kananara I was free to leave and be miserable somewhere else. A change is always as good as a rest isn't it? Perhaps I am a frustrated rolling stone, stuck in the slushy mud and in dire need of a drier climate to regain my momentum. Where is the cool water going to spring up from when I'm crawling across the base of a salt lake? Where is my happy balance? Gadebridge, Hemel Hempstead, answered my immediate call. The Bahamas would have done nicely, but not even my zany imagination, manic or sad, could stretch that far.

A large quantity of paintings made with manic flare were smashed and ripped to shreds at the crossroads collision between high and low. Some still remained high on the walls of the art therapy room. The overspill art of so many thoughtful minds were kept securely in the art room cupboard. My fellow artists and I never ever saw them again. I hung up my splattered painting apron for the next artist to wear. Another long awaited turn would soon begin for another body of confusion, to unload and lay down the colourful tracks that had lead them there. Danny and myself were to return to the hospital in Springtime as visitors, a move that I could never have envisaged as I prepared for separation. Helen very kindly said that she would be only too glad to come and see me on the outside despite putting her position as a trainee nurse in jeopardy again, but who was going to find out?

With my departure date booked it was now simply a case of waiting out the remaining few days in the best way that I could. All of the tedious arrangements—collecting medications and further prescriptions, booking appointments to see Dr. Hope and also to have my blood extracted and tested for lithium levels—were made without any fuss. I made sure that I packed a large hardback book that documented the history of the movies. This book came to me through Ritchie, but it was of course originally from the generous shelves of the hospital library. When I was manic I could see myself in the photographs, variations of myself, but not in this present life. This book now became just another glossy collection of other peoples fulfilled dreams, yet I still wanted to keep hold of it. That book stayed with me right up until 2000, then I past it on to a movie buff with whom I worked with on night porter duty at St. Albans City Hospital. Just over four months of my life had been spent let loose and holed up inside Hill End Psychiatric Hospital. My admission came at a time when I felt like some kind of immortal Godlike super-being who was ready, with the help of some likeminded recruits, to rescue Planet Earth from some sort of catastrophic disaster. Now I felt crushed to pieces at the bottom of life's bargain basement. This really was the pits. With all of my glorious visions dashed, and with the cold light of day hitting me squarely in the face, it was my turn to take the final walk through the creamy green corridors of no power. The briefest of farewells were made to those who mattered to me the most, along with half-hearted but well intentioned promises of reunions sometime, somewhere. There was to be no looking back. I just needed to get the hell out of there and begin putting in the effort required to rebuild myself, or at least be able to keep my head above water long enough to see dry land. Guts and an unlimited expanse of valuable time were at the top of my shopping list. Time became my empty toolbox. Gathering the kit to fill it would happen sparingly and without any added pressure.

No longer the transformer or the borrower of so many masks and moods, I slid so low on the depression chart that I nearly fell off. This time my journey was to be through the roughest terrain known to mankind in search of the real man, the real me, the true Steadman and not the figment of a previous imagination who hadn't even got the credentials to buy the ticket, let alone fly away to where the sweet Sun burns down on life. Contemplating a transference to a normal and acceptable me (whatever that might be) became a monumental challenge that required an effort like never before. It scared me witless just thinking about what might lay around the next of a thousand corners, waiting to rip any surviving dregs of confidence apart. Taking one small step at a time and not projecting unrealistically into the future was the only option.

Being so depressed means that only the unimportant failings and imagined problematic situations are brought to the forefront, and are given a damaging amount of over exposure. Concentration is a rare commodity among the manic or the depressed. It is so tough to find, and has to be constantly practiced in order to achieve a level of success that can be productively built upon. Persistence and determination are the keys. There is no alternative other than to keep on going and to keep trying and trying, until tiny rays of light start to find their way back into your weakened body and worn out mind.

Dad had parked his car directly behind Anderson Ward. Four or five rubbery faced groups of patients dressed in robes and sporting worn slippers stood and stared goggle eyed at me, as if I had just stepped out of the No.52 spaceship from Planet "Bleep." I recognised the same old faces, but rudely chose to ignore them. All that I wanted was to get inside the family house in Hemel Hempstead as quickly as possible. On the day of my discharge the Sun was shining brightly and the air was clean and fresh, the exact opposite of how I felt. With bones shaking and pulse racing we set off. We drove past the ruins of Keats house, followed by the uneven field in which I performed my fire dancing act, now a dank expanse that still contained the burned patches made by the roaring infernos. Bordering this grassy field was a roughly cut chunk of open space that many years ago served as funny-farmland. A mixed bag of feelings hit me as we rolled up to the exit gate. Keith Alan Steadman had left the old building but my manic fantasies remained forever. I took a part of the old place with me, a very special part indeed that I will never lose nor want to lose. My father did his level best to keep my flagging spirits up and my mind occupied by informing me of all the latest family gossip. He also made a few well intended suggestions regarding activities that we could share in, and places that we could visit together. Every thoughtful offer boarded my battered wreck unenthusiastically, although I did try my best to convey my gratitude. When depressed I often thought that whatever I said was rubbish talk when it really wasn't, so long silences became the nature of my unfunny game. At this stage in the proceedings I simply did not have it in me to even consider having a jolly good time. A pastime is a great idea and should be pursued, even when one's mind is tied up elsewhere with lingering thoughts of death and destruction.

"You can't just sit on your arse all day my old mate," continued Dad. Even when feeling so glum there is still a vacancy for the truth, and not for excessive amounts of soft bullshit that only hardens the effort needed to recover. Later on my father and I did spend some quality time together on the Dorset coastline. Essential trips such as these hurt me like hell. They were agonising affairs that consisted of back to back minutes of solid mental murder. It couldn't have been easy for my father either as he has a slight tendency to lose his patience over petty trivialities, just like myself. Never once did he lose his cool when faced with my negativity. He must have been boiling on the inside though. We did have some special moments, but they were tough to enjoy when my mind was being blitzed by defeatism. It is a selfish world one enters when clinically depressed, yet it pays dividends when the sufferer allows some space around the giver of so much vital loving care. Concerning yourself with another persons well being is a bloody hard thing to do when depressed, and I messed up in that area too many times, so much so that I am extremely fortunate to be surrounded by the same loyal faces today. My team never gave in until the victory was had.

Even if I squared up to a particular demon and kicked the crap out of it, I would still feel just as down, not better. Confidence is very hard to retrieve. It is usually found in stone, densely coated with diamonds and despair. I had to do some serious rock breaking. With no apparent end in sight I kept striding on and on, trying my best not to fold in the uneasy breeze. The realisation that nothing I had attempted to reconstruct had toppled over or blown up in my face did eventually help me to regain self belief and pride, which in turn enabled me to gradually progress to the next stage in the search for the temporarily mislaid me.

As we glided back to my home town, the prospect of a, "Nice bit of steak with mushrooms, spuds and peas—your favourite that Mum is making especially for you," was more than I could stomach. I began to worry myself sick that my nervous belly wouldn't be able to tackle such a feast, and that I would upset my mother's feelings, which wouldn't be a particularly good start. How I dearly wished that those grinding cogs would stop turning even for just a short while, or at least mesh properly and cease grinding my brain into a pulp. I slumped down into my front passenger seat while using my awkward left hand to hide my face from ridiculing street eyes, of which there were none. Paranoia had joined me for the longer haul, although it did have a backhanded way of suggesting that I still demonstrated some self pride. I never stopped caring about the way in which I came across to another human being, maybe if I had stopped caring the pain would not have been nearly as bad as I had encouraged it to be. Everything has to be paid for, but why pay the premium for a package that wasn't even of my choosing? In fear of standing out like a sore thumb, I behaved in such a way that made me stand out like a sore thumb—what a div!

Coupled with the relief of being untied from Hill End Psychiatric Hospital came the soul stabbing fear, the slicing of my pain and the tenderising of my brain. The fear of the outside world became asphyxiating. Tasteless smoke and shivering stress were the two things guaranteed to permeate through my existence from here on in. Only weeks ago I had been the man about town, though limited to the confines of the hospital. Before that I was the man about England, Milan, Europe, the entire planet and beyond, using my lifetime ticket on the Dream Come True Express to its maximum. Such a dramatic transformation so soon must have sent a mild shock wave rumbling up my back tracks and rippling down my system. It was as if I had plunged too far too soon, causing a mental version of the bends to crystallise in a lowly cloud. In my case this took on a life threatening momentum instead of the required lift. Some things just don't happen overnight. My safe mental motel turned me away when I needed it the most. No room for me at the inn, nor at the out. I was glued to the big wheel and welded to the waltzer. What a dark dog, what an absolute bitch, the King and Queen of the rigged pack were back. My grim demons were hungrier now than they had ever been before.

6

Labelled

Returning to my childhood bedroom of dreams and disappointments is always an odd and disconcerting experience. Returning to the home of your youth for prolonged stays is not always the ideal situation, not exactly full of street credibility, but it *is* full of the love and guts needed to get you up and running again. I am dead lucky to be in such a situation. I would enter my old room and ritualistically rifle through the cupboards and drawers to find bits and pieces that had remained in exactly the same place. This usually gave me a feeling of security, safe in the knowledge that some things do not change, no matter where I had been or what I had been doing. My rifling through drawers and cupboards had no effect this time. Everything that I relied on had died or deserted me, except for the human touch, and even that took forever before showing any sign of penetrating my nervous barrier. Returning to the persona of a boy was a move that I had not been looking forward to making one little bit, though it was far better than suffering inside the hospital. I had to convince myself that I was *not* returning to my childhood and that I was an ill adult, an independent man who at this moment in time needed his relations to help steer him through the recovery process. The thought of having to cope with myself terrified me so much that I regularly threw up at the thought of it. Popeye could not have untied my depressed knots. For obvious reasons the professionals strongly advised against attempting a premature return to my own place, advice that I was more than happy to take.

I did my level best to eat as much of the glorious meal my mother had so lovingly prepared, including her deliciously tangy lemon-haze dessert. A huge multivitamin tablet replaced the after dinner mint. When I fancied a smoke I would creep through the side passage door that led into the back garden, praying to God and his assistants to make doubly sure that none of the neighbours could see me. I squashed myself into the bricked corner of our house, and the adjoining house that staggered along a terrace. Below me lay the crazy paving patio that I helped put down when I was a fourteen year old kid. Out of sight and out of sound, I smoked my unevenly rolled cigarette so fast that I barely came up for a breath of crisp fresh air, something that would have done me a far greater service than chugging back whole kegs of cancerous tar filled smoke. It made no difference to me if it was icy cold outside, blowing a gale or pouring down with rain, I still went for my puff. Sometimes I dressed in the most inappropriate clothing such as baggy pyjamas or summer shorts and a singlet. New things to worry over were popping up like weeds in a vandalised flowerbed. For longer than it took me to suck in my golden fumes I would remain stationary and cold, as I fretted over whether or not I had extinguished my cigarette properly. I would crouch down to dribble saliva onto the butt and then search for any burning embers that the wind may have blown away. Then I worried myself sick again that somebody might be watching me. Now I had to tiptoe back into the warm house, making less noise than Marcel Marceau in a monastery so as not to alert the attention of the neighbours, all of whom were busily living their own lives, dealing with their own allocation of problems and enjoying their well deserved personal pleasures. If I was unable to sleep, I would repeat the same diabolical motions in the dark when the neighbours were tucked up in their beds.

You are already more than aware that extreme mania or depression can and often does lead toward a life threatening, confidence shattering climax that will bring tears to more than just one pair of eyes. The knowledge that others are worse off, or were at least on a par with my own depressing heartache made no difference at all. This illness is so disturbing because of its unpredictability. A whole week could pass reasonably well and then things could nosedive without having any idea why. On the other hand, a sudden improvement can be made just as fast. Not knowing how one's mind will work from one day to the next can add to the level of depression. False claims regarding the expiration date of a manic or depressing episode only serves to kick a person harder in the teeth at a time when they least need it. My blotchy head felt as if it was filled with a thousand festering fears, all of them spilling their caramelised puss. My gut was so much on edge that induced vomiting became the only means of escape, briefly freeing me from hell's library, stocked full of the most dreadful horror stories. The slightest relief giving elevation or stomach churning eruption has to be paid for. The only currency that I dealt in was good old fashioned pain. Ten parts pain for one part pleasure is not exactly the kind of balance I would have thought could create a bond strong enough and reliable enough to use in the self building process, but it was a start. Pain and strain for ultimate gain is often the only way. A renegotiation of the present dire situation has to be conducted fairly and squarely in order to achieve a constructive deal, a process that has to be tackled with the greatest of unease. I was the Fort Knox of mental pain, without the key to free my mind of the chaos.

Nothing fits when one is severely depressed. All that remains are ripped up scraps of hope floating around in a dirty puddle of weakened spirit. This is depression. You do *not* want to go there if you can at all help it. Preventative measures can be taken, but who's to know what bad news or self inflicted trigger may be waiting around the corner to gun you down? Helping yourself to slay what will undoubtedly be the most cruel and most soul searching experience of your entire life is the only option available. Harming oneself is definitely *not* an option, but did I take any notice?

The family and friendly support team need reassuring and support themselves. Their most important and hardest work is done in the design offices and on the drawing boards where the early flaws and hitches can be made, then ironed out and strengthened before going ahead with the human building process. Once the caregiver has become committed to the cause it is very hard for them to jump ship, as this can look like desertion or showing a lack of loyalty. If for the sake of their own sanity the carer cannot continue, then they must stop and allow somebody else to take over the leading role. Two ill people in the same frame makes no sense whatsoever. Anybody who is critical of another persons reluctance to continue intense caring in order to self preserve, has absolutely no idea of what is actually involved. We all have our strong points and able areas as much as we do our limitations, and depressed human beings test those fine limits to breaking point. Life does not come to a grinding halt just because one person is temporarily broken in mind or body.

Carefully thought out words were relayed to my bedroom from caring friends and relations. My replies were not exactly personal or detailed in any way. Some were abrupt and slightly abusive. At first I dismissed their supportive visits as prying, that I was some kind of freaky geeky side show to be gossiped about around town. Knowing that I was wrong, and that by shunning them I may have been hurtful toward the makers of so many generous visits, only served to increase the bad feelings that I already harboured inside, and quite rightly so. Nobody was upset at all, instead rising well above and seeing through my shenanigans. How do I know for sure when I am right in the middle of the two extremes? I have been level with my lithium for lengthy periods and still felt rather high or a little low. To see things in a different light can be a rewarding experience or a crushing blow. Returning in person to the actual scene of a high episode can be too much of a let down, as I soon found out now that I had gone full circle and was safely back in Hemel Hempstead, my home town where this whole manic-depressive/

bipolar journey first left the genetic starting blocks—in Gadebridge on September 1st 1964 to be exact. Now I was twenty-six years of age and was relatively new to this level of the human race. I had flown round the bend a few times, and had now been handed the baton that will conduct my progress through the straight and narrow section. It isn't a race, nor is it a game, it is a never ending mystery tour that culminates in many of us tripping over and breaking the tape. Fresh tape stretches ahead of us throughout each and every day, presented differently for each individual. This tape measures us for what we actually are and for how we conduct ourselves before, during and after the mammoth bipolar slog.

The following two months consisted of my unhealthy avoidance of other friendly and well intentioned human beings. If I had an unavoidable appointment looming with my general practitioner or dentist, I would worry for days and days in advance about what might become of me if I failed miserably in putting myself across correctly and thoroughly, giving my general practitioner or dentist the wrong impression that then might lead to the wrong diagnosis, and then to the wrong course of medication. This cauldron of amateur dramatics was not dissimilar to the time when Virginia took me to see the doctor, except this was much worse. Who will I face in the waiting room, or during short walk from the car to the surgery doors? What do I say to somebody that I used to work with? My general practitioner or dentist always alleviated my worries. They were the same old set of reworked hang-ups. It's as if certain underlying fears have an excellent memory, and an ability to resurface like a dormant germ. I often have bad dreams where the repulsive subject matter starts off as a bearable guest but then hangs around, becoming nastier, interrupting my train of thought and poking its nose into affairs that are none of its concern. The following night that very same dream may explode into my sleepy head again, but although the irritating show is the same, I do not always recognise the fact that the bad guy always comes unstuck. To have real progress taking hold, these minor battles have to be fought, won and learnt from. Getting off my backside to beat my simple habits of a lifetime into a semblance of order was tough going to say the very least. Flashbacks of my pre-Milan manic lifestyle came to me thick and fast, welling me up with sadness, embarrassment and worry. I knew that I would eventually have to face up to the second fiddle tunes that I had been banging my drum along to. Right now the instruments that produced my music were still noisily tuning into my brain and practicing their scales in the rumbling pits. An old uninspiring recital of chilling thrills and spills was the last thing that I needed, at least I knew that much.

Now I can look back and see how my life has been all or nothing, never spread evenly like lightly salted butter on a chunk of crusty wholegrain bread. I managed to cram as much as I could into my young life. Musical taste often reflects that life, and it is a pretty accurate measure of present mood. Give a moody person a random selection of music, and the chosen tracks will speak volumes, helping to add to, remove or create a mood. Uplifting lyrics and favourite melodies shed some light on my gloom, by providing reassurances that everything is meant to happen in the way that it is, in order to reach an unknown goal. Is that goal going to be individually modelled, or do we all come together and score with a controversial penalty in extra time?

For about a month following my discharge I could not bear to hear nor see anything remotely associated with Hill End. How can I erase the extraordinary recent past and all of the cock-ups that I had made? Personal regret became anger that pounded on my door before subsiding into sadness. My bleeding past could not be healed nor extinguished by a bucketful of sorry-for-myself tears and a swaddling of prayers, but I tried. I am not ashamed to say that I often cried my eyes out like a hungry baby wearing a crap filled diaper. When those desperate tears dried, I cried inside instead. It took a long time to convince myself that I hadn't done a thing wrong, and that I had a genuine real life illness called manic depression/bipolar affective disorder on which to blame all of my manic and suicidal tendencies. Everybody at Hill End Psychiatric Hospital had their own problems to take care of, so another big headed manic or a bury headed depressive never really made the headline news. The sick antics of a small minority actually helped me to feel slightly better about myself, that I wasn't such a bad bloke after all. As soon as the comparisons with serial killers and wife or child beaters wore off, I slid back into the role of a severely ill, clinically depressed human being.

More than ever before I found that due to lack of physical exercise and a diet of fear riddled depression, my short hairy legs actually shook under my light body weight, especially on those rare occasions when I stepped down the short flight of carpeted stairs to try and eat some food, or to step out for a tasteless sticky throat smoke in the backyard corner. My muscles were wasting away. I was encouraged to at least try and take a short walk when darkness fell around the dimly lit streets of Gadebridge. There was no way whatsoever that anyone could have gotten me out of the house in broad daylight. I always put my hood up and my head down before shuffling off. I preferred it to be raining because fewer people would be out and about, and besides I have always loved to walk in the sweet smelling rain, preferably without an umbrella. The amount of mind mortar that I earned from these excursions accumulated very slowly, but every little scoop on my trowel helped to aid the up and running rebuilding project. My folks always encouraged me but they *never* forced an issue. They were walking along a continuous tightrope, but they kept on persevering despite the perils. Time and again they must have been on the verge of some kind of breakdown, and yet they somehow managed to pull through with unbelievable consideration, composure, control, brute strength and of course generous helpings of unconditional *love*, the ingredient that *should* make the world go round, *not* money.

Hertfordshire contains countless countryside walks. Footpaths that meander through some of the prettiest open spaces are in great abundance, stretching through pockets of scenic wonder such as Boxmoor Common, Gadebridge Park, Ivinghoe Beacon, Dunstable Downs and deer inhabited Ashridge Woods. If water is what you want then go no further than the man made Grand Union Canal, or walk around Tring reservoir. I dragged my bones through and around these beauty spots despite feeling sick inside. Lacking the proud ability to cope with life's routine selection of surprises hurt me to the core. Small body blows often amounted to a knockout, but as time past I began to realise that the distance had been completed and I was still in one piece, a little bruised maybe but still in the upright frame of mind. At first I detested these outings, I couldn't get home quick enough. Unwittingly I was depositing the rewards into my subconscious savings bank, just I had done so before.

On top of everything else I began tormenting myself over how I had been such dull company, and that all I had achieved was to ruin another person's valuable day. Yes, I had been extremely dull, but not to the extent of committing GMH (grievous mental harm) upon my caregivers. Too many worries and problems that really weren't at all, seemed to grow and grow, striking me hard as being so immense and of such high importance that I would collapse under the weight. Personal defence mechanisms were installed in every brave soul who might at some point expect to share the same space as me. It is a wonder that some of them didn't carry an ampoule of cyanide in case things got a bit too much.

One Sunday afternoon Helen Crowhurst telephoned my parent's home to arrange a convenient time to drive over from Harpenden to pay me a visit. Checking my diary wasn't necessary on this delicate occasion. Helen was not supposed to be doing this, but she was a young lady with a strong mind of her own who took the risk of a reprimand fairly nonchalantly. I loved the independent drive that she possessed. Seeing her free spirited entitlement being put into practice in a world of petty rules, refreshed me a great deal. Helen's visits were not about a bit of slap and tickle, my interest in all things sexual had virtually disappeared. Her sweet flying visits were solely to offer some friendly company and a fresh young female face. We would spend the best part of two hours in my sister's old bedroom, rocking together in an upholstered rocking chair. Helen bless her, tried ever so hard to prevent our conversation from slipping down a muddy path. Upbeat light-hearted trivia provided our main course. Following a soft satisfying hug for desert we went for a short walk in broad daylight through Gadebridge Park, an active chapter of my youth, where I once kicked, climbed, fell and threw until my not so innocent young heart was content. Those short walks with Helen were colossal strides for me, because they were the first occasions since returning to Hemel Hempstead that I took a walk in the neighbourhood with somebody other than a family member. Being on show to whoever happened to be sad enough to stop and stare wasn't the disaster that I had imagined. Nobody stopped and stared at me, why should they, did I still believe that my mind could be read? Helen's visits continued for a beneficial month before unsociable working hours and an over protective new boyfriend caused the visits to dry up completely. As is the case with all of my angels, they touch me for as long as God allows and then they flutter off to marry and have Sons and Daughters by a more reliable suitor. Enough of feeling sorry for myself, because my chances have been there and there may be plenty more to come later on—look at Charlie Chaplin!

On the rare good days when I felt bold enough, I would take the four mile drive to Bovingdon with my dad to check my humble little maisonette, and collect the junk mail and free local newspaper. As we inched closer and closer I hid more and more, eliminating unwanted eye contact. Once again, the truth of the matter was that the people I was frightened of seeing were too far into their own lives, and I never even entered their equation, although I definitely felt as if I stood out as the minus symbol. The more I believed that I was behaving abnormally the more I actually would, providing me with a greater imaginary cause for a very real feeling of needless paranoia. I was persecuting myself over absolutely nothing. I sometimes wished that I had no imagination at all, which is of course ridiculous.

The barest minimum of time was spent at my own place before the second leg of this stressful routine went ahead. "Did I shut and lock my front door properly? Were all the windows closed tight?" One nagging thing after another chewed away mercilessly at me in a way that was reminiscent of the previous year, only much worse and showing no signs of improvement. Trips out into the real world could be used as a way of measuring my increase or decrease in mood. My food intake suggested an awful lot as well. You are what you eat, which was very little, bringing me down to around 125 lbs. I was still obese compared to millions of other sick human beings. Mother continued to serve me a regular dinner, sometimes easing back on certain foods. She always made sure that it was waiting there on the table for me. I felt so ungrateful to slouch through the living room into the dining room, before sitting down without uttering hardly a word, take a few mouthfuls, mumble "Thank you Mum," and then trudge back up the stairs for another long haul of being antisocial and incredibly pissed off. Despite desperately wanting things to improve I could not make it happen. It was so hard to build my willpower up to such a level so that it would make a marked difference, allowing everybody the much needed and long awaited lift that they thoroughly deserved. My folks, who were sometimes at there wits end, never ever doubted me. They made sure that the light at my end of my tunnel always shone brightly, and that it was always within a realistic reachable view. There was no stopping them from selflessly helping to prevent any further suffering—now that really is love in action!

When I ponder over the majority of mentally ill or disabled people who have nobody other than themselves, only a compulsory professional and perhaps the occasional personal visitor, I feel deeply ashamed of myself. I will stick to my guns when I say that it is about adapting to one's own personal set of circumstances and that mental pain is pain, exactly the same, no matter whether it is being endured within four small blank walls or in a golden palace. The danger of becoming too distanced from a normal existence is a very real one indeed. For example, in hospital or at home three square meals are prepared as if by magic (if you are lucky), bed linen and sweat encrusted garments are renewed with a crispy soft smell, and in many cases personal finances are taken care of, leaving very little for the patient to control. Knowing when to begin the reintroduction process is a fine line to gauge because the tolerance and attention span needed to carry out even the most straightforward of everyday tasks is so delicate, and the risk of a knock-back is always there. Knock-backs are still an inevitable part of the forward drives. Despite the initial need for no extra worries at the onset of any mentally related problem, the ongoing absence from all of the usual mundane tasks can only make the process of slotting back into the land of the living that little bit tougher. Taking a diversion is always refreshing, whether it be washing the dishes or driving through New England in the rain.

Inadequacy can easily set in when too much is taken away too soon and not replaced soon enough. There was no option other than for my father to take over my monitory reigns at a time when I really didn't know who was doing what, where and when. For a reasonably intelligent human male being in his mid-twenties to be distanced from his routine responsibilities is a huge blow to stomach. Sensing my concern over the added danger of losing touch and then creating more and more hills to crawl up later, my folks made painstakingly sure that even the slightest of transactions—the payment of my electricity bill or household insurance premiums etc—were at my request clearly explained and then dealt with, enabling me to soak up the very important feeling of having an active and purposeful role. The feeling of achievement and self-worth is an imperative factor in the healing process. It also produces a knock-on effect that assists those who are caring for the patient, and are themselves selflessly sharing the agony, just as they will delight in sharing the good times that are always waiting patiently around the corner.

Although severely depressed, I still somehow managed to stumble across the never say die attitude and ability to make the most of the good days. Self imposed imprisonment did *not* help my cause. I needed to be out searching high and low for a timeworn map that would explain the steps needed to negotiate the well trodden road to recovery. If one step forward leads to a situation that sends you two or three steps back, it doesn't matter because you have tried, you have had a go at improving the present predicament. When caregivers can see your effort they will feel encouraged, which can help them to become even more willing to help you out, safe in the knowledge that their patient efforts have not been in vain. Real life is not always a pretty song. In real life ill people do become heavy, especially when they are living under the same roof as the caregivers. How heavy and for how long depends on so many intertwining circumstances. I would probably have sunk to the bottom of the Mariana Trench—the worlds deepest oceanic spot at 10,916 metres (6.78 miles)—in two seconds flat.

Given half a chance, the peaceful white doves soaring above us will try to crap on our unprotected heads. I could not for the life of me see any drops of chocolate covered goodness among the January drizzles. Depression sure takes up a lot of mind-juice, and it is a poor manager of limited energy. That remaining energy is exerted and wasted as the slow healing process tries to configure itself. Positive energy slowly overtakes the negative and is easier to gain as time drifts by, why? because an effort is being made regardless of the outcome, and the realisation is dawning that just maybe the entire world does *not* revolve around one person after all.

The good thing about being a bipolar affected person is that it has strengthened my resolve to make the most out of what I am so fortunate to have been given to work with in the first place, and also to be more tolerant and understanding of others. I can now hold back and think of all the circumstances that contributed so fully to my own emotional climaxes, and actually enjoy watching the process elsewhere, not because I like to see another suffer, but because somewhere in there I can see myself fighting to escape. I know that no matter how horrendous a persons past has been, the rotten devils will eventually be caught and then promptly squashed between Michelangelo's fresco fingers. As is often the case in times of conflict, there may well be some bipolar shrapnel embedded for my remaining days. This is not such a bad thing because it acts as a reminder and also as a warning signal that enables me to continue being the fun loving guy that I am, but without too much of the quick drying complacency and cockiness that to my cost has set me canyons apart in the past. I feel privileged to have already visited a very rough version of my Heaven, even if it was only for a sneak preview. Tiptoeing across the surface of hell *wasn't* the end of the world, in fact it probably did me some good because now I know what's waiting for me if I repeatedly fail to keep my act together. Famine ridden and war stricken zones abound in the real world, and yet myself and millions of others escaped from our comparatively easy extremes, crawling in dust and gratefully yanked out of the debris to resume a normal life, the greatest gift of all. Human on human abuse is still so rife, committed by the so called intelligent race who have too few years to love, give and live. Too many people have set unachievable goals and standards, causing them to stumble under an obstacle too many, or to drown in a rough tough sea of life that they could not quite live up to. Do them and yourself a favour and keep a friendly lookout.

Positioned in the centre of my old bedroom ceiling is a hatch that leads to the attic. Underneath my single bed lived a stubby extendible ladder that would aid my entry into the cobwebbed darkness. After a little fumble and a bumped head I located the light switch, then pulled the ladder up and in to eliminate unwanted visits. This attic used to be the place where I would retreat as a teenager when I felt a bit down in the dumps. I had laid floorboards as well as installing a cold water sink unit and six plug sockets ten years earlier when I was going through my photography phase. I could not help but make the sad comparison between then and the way my life had panned out since. Comparisons and memories are not erasable, they are survival tools as well as working against the grain of life when you need it the least. This cold attic was the last place on Planet Earth that I needed to be as there were memories of happier times scattered all over the place. I sat in silence on an old cushion, with my backbone grazing up against a bare brick wall. With head in hands, helpless in hell, I listened to the sounds of the birds from their gutter perch. Their beautiful songs filled the dingy attic, songs that on a good day I would try to copy, but on this day I wanted to wring their feathered necks because I was envious of their cheeriness. Even natural beauty was taking its toll, now existing only to torment by tactlessly reminding me that it is still all waiting here on a tarnished platter but you cannot eat from it anymore, you swallowed life and all it has to offer much too fast, and so now you must dig in, grit your teeth and suffer in silence. It is true what they say though, that all things pass and that we have a knack of coming out of the other side smelling of roses. The day that happens, and it will, is another matter entirely. Laying flat across the side joists was my old bedroom door, signed by everybody that I invited in from school. I picked Julie's wavy handwriting among many other memory joggers. As far as I could work out, nearly every single one of the scribbled names on that white and blue metallic sprayed door were now married, probably with children in tow and with solid promising careers. Jolly good luck to them all, but why do I do it, why go up into the cold attic and beat myself blue even further with a sentimental trip to a place in history? Why was I having problems accepting that I had hit the canvas, and that right now I had to focus on preparing for a brand new fight using a completely new strategy? Hours upon hours were spent huddled up, only coming down in the evening when I could stand the biting cold no longer. I missed out on too many meals, but water was always plentiful. A dusty downtrodden woollen rug wrapped around my torso kept me reasonably warm, as I sat with my knees pressing firmly into my chest cavity, curled up like a frightened hedgehog who knows that his next journey to the other side could well be his last. I never thought it possible that hell could be as cold as this. Hypothermia became a distinct possibility despite rising heat from the rooms below, warmth that I could quite easily have stepped back down into. It was all very unhealthy, definitely not recommended. This type of behaviour not only reinforced my reluctance to spread my wings in the outside world, but it increased the amount of strain that my illness had already placed upon my folks. How I longed to get up off my bony backside and take a walk in broad daylight with my uncovered head held up high, containing not a single care or worry. Nice in theory, but the green ship I had jumped was now docked for maintenance, leaving me clueless as to the next move, knocking the wind of a lifetime out of my wildly flapping sails. With every new inner rip, I felt more and more powerless. The demons are cowards who thrive on kicking their prey when it is down, but it was going to take something more powerful than that to count me out. I did *not* want to die. At that stage I still yearned for a nice fulfilling life, but when you are at your wits end it is bloody frightening what dark and destructive thoughts come hurtling through your mind. It is the hurting of others that made my attempts half-hearted, because in effect you are taking a part of them with you as well.

Self centred acts such as barricading myself in the freezing attic did little to ease the anguish of my folks, who remained downstairs in the more habitable rooms of the house. My initial belief that the move to the attic would benefit everybody did of course have the complete opposite effect. Now I was at least beginning to display some consistency as far as my judgment was concerned; it always stank to high Heaven. Food shopping day arrived. It was a cold drizzly Saturday afternoon, and this was a particularly bad day for me. Both of my parents decided to take this opportunity to breathe in a lighter atmosphere. At the onset of my depression I tried to tell anyone who would listen how I felt, what it was like for me. This I would repeat in slightly downgraded versions until ears were smoking. Repetition of the same theme from a depressed person is enough to send the recipient into a depression of their own, in fact I have since discovered that my mother had been taking anti-depressants herself all along. Depression drenched, every flat atom that held me together followed their owner's decision to use this opportunity to hang myself with an electric cable. This day was the darkest of them all. I tied the cord around an attic beam. Preparation of the noose took longer. Rather than be calm and collected, the realisation that this was to be the end scared the living daylights out of me. Up onto a kitchen stool I stepped, then with eyes closed I placed the grey extension cable around my skinny neck and pulled the loop tight. Only a three pronged piece of wood stood between my life and my death. Where would I end up? It had been suggested at Hill End Psychiatric Hospital that if there is an afterlife then the act of committing suicide, wiping out the ultimate gift, may make the well hung, poisoned or blown away victim of themselves exempt from any of the benefits.

My not quite dead yet weight pulled tight the noose as I bent my quivering knees. I didn't kick-the-bucket, but I did kick the stool. A fuzzy buzzing sensation came over me and then there was silence, much the same as fainting. Out of this world I briefly went, until I woke up on the bedroom floor having smacked the back of my head again, this time on a dressing table. To my dismay I discovered that the electric cable had snapped. This must have been caused by a lawn mowing or hedge trimming mistake in which a slight cut had been made to the cord. It could be said that I was saved in the "nick" of time. Close shaves with death were beginning to become a regular occurrence. If I had wanted to die badly enough I would have repeated the whole grizzly procedure in a flash, but I'm glad that I didn't feel so inclined. For the next ten minutes, using teeth and some electrical tape, I frantically rejoined the wires in the cable before my folks returned with the weeks haul of shopping. My father had saved my life again because of his love of gardening. I sure was one hell of a lucky cat. This latest display of unintentional escapology simply rammed home the fact that hanging around was not the way to go, not only for me but for anybody else who might be pondering over whether or not they should destroy themselves. *No way is* the right way. A slight cut close to my paving stone scar sprung a minor drop of blood, but it was nothing worth writing home about. Blood smears on my pillow case were the only clue of what had happened, but I was never questioned about it. Later, whenever I saw the cable being used it brought a lump to the same throat that it had once been wrapped around. Not one remark was made in reference to the raised taped section on the cable, probably because there were a couple of other repair jobs on the same reel. To avoid any unwanted accidents the old cable was eventually dumped and replaced. The only foreign object that I place around my neck today is a silver chain that Susan gave me. Exhausting my darkest thoughts one by one and burying my demons with my own pain was quite often the only way forward. Shirking an issue only enlarges it the second time round, so sometimes diving in head first without any headgear, getting stuck into the scrum of depression as soon as possible will result in some sort of a turnaround. Meanwhile, all of you procrastinators out there, expect to suffer like you have never suffered before.

Blotches and rashes kept erupting in the most unlikely of places. It is no use rushing out and slapping on a shelf full of expensive potions and creams without first establishing exactly what's causing your face to resemble a baboon's backside. Many prescription drugs (that often come with a free rash) need a settling in period of anything up to three or four weeks before a credible evaluation of the condition can be made. We are all different, so what may clear up nicely for one person following a brief period of discomfort, may stay put for another. Diet is so important at the best of times, but when your whole system is running low, more attention than usual should be paid to it. Perhaps a vitamin and mineral supplement may be a wise move before leaping straight into the happy slappy land of ointment and cream. There is no substitute for a well balanced diet of vegetables, fruit, dairy, meat and cereals. If you are unsure about the most suitable foodstuffs and supplements to safely take in conjunction with the medications that are fighting their way around your bloodstream, then ask your doctor, consultant psychiatrist or a qualified nutritionist. The natural remedies that can be found on a thousand websites and in hundreds of books work well for me, but try not to get disproportionately disconsolate when remedy after remedy fails to produce immediate results, especially you women who do have the tendency to be a little more sensitive over their hair and skin condition than the average male of the species. Try not to be afraid of showing your true colours. It's a big step toward thinking rationally again. Look around and what do you see? We cannot see what is going on underneath clothing and naked flesh, but everyday we can still observe big bellies and fat wobbling bottoms, no hair, scars, skin grafts, limbs missing, stroke affected people struggling to walk and talk, deaf people, dumb people, even dumber people, blind people, disease ridden people, starving people—all of whom could be severely depressed as well. How rotten must that be? They *will* pull through, we will *all* pull through, even though we sometimes feel so helpless and alone. You have to believe me, you have no choice other than to believe me. What else can you do other than to fight the war and win each battle? You are an extra special person who *will* sail through the rest of your life in relative peace with your emotional side, and madly in love with your present world.

When depressed and stuck in the crap-trap, everything including yourself will look so much worse, the bad points will stand out in 3 D, and the fading eye will eventually become blind to the overwhelming good that there really is in abundance. Good will always prosper, because good easily outnumbers the foul-mouthed bad. We will penetrate the oceans and the highest mountain ranges, and speed around in space before it is time for breakfast. If you search long and hard enough for the bad crap you will eventually convince yourself that you have found it, when all that has really taken place is a poor trick of the distant mind.

Even John Merrick, a.k.a. the Elephant Man, took off his sackcloth head covering. Just imagine what he had to go through during those uneducated bygone days, when brightly labelled products designed to reduce swelling, or lozenges to clear one's nasal and throat passages were not even on the market as they are so readily today. The more a manic-depressive person worships their body (in a healthy way), the better chance they present to themselves of attacking the daily mini and major battles that are waiting like traffic wardens to jump out and assault the mind. It may seem like an eternity to win the war, but every little that is scored strengthens the team, which then instills more and more of one of life's most important qualities—confidence. Get some of that baby inside of you and almost anything becomes possible. Sir Winston Churchill and millions of other great and brave people took over five long years to win the war against evil, so that we could live in the style that we do today. They did it without moaning and groaning too much about minor discomforts, so I think it is safe to say that it's definitely within the realms of possibility that we too are going to be alright and become productive again, without having to put a terrible strain on our loved ones, ourselves or the economy, agreed?

When I was growing up there were plenty of occasions when my confidence slipped drastically, and I would allow it to prevent me from doing what I wanted to do, or going where I longed to go. My clothes, my upper body shape, skinny legs, my hair and the fear of making a fool of myself by saying the wrong thing—

all of these things and other hang-ups and letdowns often dictated the course of my young life. The following week I would be the organiser who dyed his hair bright orange before stepping out and into a roller disco. It always seemed to be the happy medium, the balanced out land of "normal" nutcases that kept on eluding me. But boy, how I tried. Deep down I suppose I have never wanted to be normal, and naturally I am not, but I never wanted to be painfully abnormal either, whether that be too high or too low.

A few extra chopped logs were always placed on my fire when I needed them the most, keeping up the maintenance program until I could do more and more, little by little. Contrary to much of what I have been saying, manic depression is with a few strong exceptions, just one huge collection of activities that rarely have any rhyme nor reason to them, lacking direction and substance, and creating a looseness that is all well and fine but bloody dangerous too, especially when down in the dumps or down in a rush hour subway system. As I touched upon earlier, part of being bipolar means having *too* many contradictory ideas that are simultaneously battling it for supremacy. Exploring anything and everything imaginable when high and having the equivalent amount of excess pressing down on you when low is an explosive situation. Anger and embarrassment usually leads to the avoidance of the paths that were crossed on the way up. Coming to terms—I don't mean wallow in the past manic mayhem—with the upward journey and the old manic thoughts is a vital step, before one can realistically think strong and straight enough to once again head in the right direction. Put on your lucky shoes and take a long hike around the course before attempting to leap over any hurdles.

Getting too carried away with any early progression is understandable but not advised. Each good day, or the better parts of a day should be used as a low springboard to better things, and not as a major leap that cannot always be lived up to. Crashes are inevitable and hold-ups will happen as the rookie or seasoned depressive sets out along a suitable route, to the long lost but never forgotten land of the level-headed. Yes, it can take quite a while to see the results, so long as we sufferers and the caregivers realise and accept that practice does *not* make perfect, but it *does* make pretty good, and that *not* all things, but *most* things become available to those who wait. Get to know your limitations, and don't try to be the big hero or heroine who is always eager to leap over the top. I speak from too many painful and stubborn experiences that were often brought about because of my hatred of being constantly advised and told what to do. I foolishly mistook wise friendly advice as interference from somebody whom I believed was out to steal the credit for my efforts. How childish is that? Sorry, that is a big insult to children as they are *not* as dumb as that. If help and well meant friendly advice is given to you then take it with open arms, use it and learn from it. Do you honestly believe as I did that certain people were using me to earn themselves some extra Brownie points? How selfish and inconsiderate of me to have even entertained that thought when they had far better things to do with their time. Somebody who cares will always say that they regard the time spent in helping you to recover is time well spent, and I would say the same to somebody else, but there is still no denying that we would all rather be doing something different, somewhere else. Treat them with the same consideration as they allow you. Five long months on from that black Christmas of 1990, despite venturing out and about a bit more, and despite having swallowed my regular dosages of happy tablets and lithium carbonate, my spirits remained seized up and sunk.

My late great Nan Duckworth was a very down to earth lady who did not mince her words, a likeable quality. Polite liars serve no purpose at all, but the truth spoken politely is respected whether you like what is said or not. On the inside my nan had a sensitive and warm heart of gold. She had it pretty tough throughout her life, so she had to harden her protective coating in order to survive and raise my three Uncles, Aunt Pauline and of course my dear Mum as best as she possibly could with the little means that she had. Nan had once been Staff Nurse Harris at a general hospital in North London, before she married my granddad Duckworth at 24 years of age. The Second World War did not exactly help their relationship to blossom. Finally they split up, with Granddad moving North to Derbyshire where he married his brother's wife's sister, Anne. Are you still with me? Granddad Duckworth also suffered terribly from bouts of depression, so badly in fact that just before I was born in 1964 he had to be admitted to Derby Royal infirmary for a short period of rest. He was a bit of a worry guts like me, possessing a hot and cold personality that could flare up or coolly ice over at any given moment. I sensed in his last few years that he was happy, but tinged with a little regret over what may have been. It is very likely that the genes I have inherited from him have contributed toward my manic depression/bipolar disorder, but then I can think of so many other distant relations on both sides of my family who have had their fair share of high times and depression, although not recognised back then as being the illness that it is accepted as today.

I spent many happy hours with my nan at her brand new apartment in Elizabeth House, a complex for elderly people that is only a stones throw from Hemel Hempstead's old town. We filled in the football pools coupons, picked out a few horses and tackled the crossword puzzles in the tabloid newspapers. We would discuss every subject under the Sun. When I was a little bit high or low I found that I was able to sit alongside her with total ease. Nan knew a lot more about how I felt than she let on. One evening, only a couple of days before her departure from this life, my uncle Paul came to visit his mum in Hemel Hempstead General Hospital wearing a clothes peg on his nose, because of the smell of urine and faeces that hovered in the sweltering heat of the geriatric ward. Carpeting instead of linoleum had proven to be a smelly administrative mistake. Humour such as this in a place such as that is not to everybody's taste, but it tickled my nan and the nurses right up to the final curtain. Nan and her offspring are made of tough stuff, simply because they had to be resilient for many years before they carved out comfortable lives for themselves. They hurt just as much as the next person, but they have got the ability to rise above and laugh in the face of adversity, which in this case was the impending gallop to rest and peace. I am eternally grateful for her chirpy company and her colourful humour, but most of all for her undying love and for the example she set of always doing her best under the given circumstances without hardly any complaint. Nan could always put things into perspective. She hated moaners, but she applauded those who got on with it and had a go, even if they fell flat on their face trying, sometimes to her amusement. The darkest bruised shades of blue always became determined turquoise oceans of strength following a visit to her humble little home. Spending time with Granddad or Nan when I was either happy, glum or somewhere in the middle was always an enjoyable experience, full of hidden life lessons that I would have been stupid not to have listened and learnt from. The older I get the more I learn from others. I can understand better why they did this, or said that. I guess it's a case of becoming a little more mature and worldly-wise.

Granddad Duckworth liked his couple of pints a day, usually taken in the Bedford Arms pub that was conveniently positioned a narrow roads width away from his tiny terraced house. I often wondered if he chose that particular terraced house in Camden Street, Derby, solely for this beer lit luxury, but I never pried as some things are better left not said, just done. Childish trips to magical Derbyshire were full of happiness and education. We would go to places such as the Blue-John caves where Granddad told me that there were invisible blind fish swimming in the cavern stream. He also told me that he had a pipe installed underneath the road from the pub to his personal beer barrel located in his kitchen pantry. Both yarns I gullibly swallowed. The Derbyshire Dale's and Matlock, along with Sherwood Forest in neighbouring Nottingham were just a few of the fun days out that we all enjoyed together, and like most things that we did as children they were extensively recorded by my father on cine film and also on 35 mm film. The trip to Derby in 1991 lacked the old magic. My 6 year old Niece Emily, and my 4 year old Nephew Joel came along on that visit, a visit that we all hoped would produce a magical cure in fond surroundings. Like hell it did, although it was much healthier mentally and physically than venturing nowhere except into the dreary attic. Excursions such as these were painful affairs. I felt as if I was mourning all of the memories that I so badly wanted to resurrect and relive. Granddad hurt along with me. I think he may have felt partly to blame for supplying me with depressing genes; a nonsensical way to think, because as I have already mentioned I am made up of so many people who were all happy and sad a long long time before me. *Nobody* is to blame, why blame anything or anyone for my present plight? It sure isn't going to change anything. Poor old Granddad, he wanted to provide his eldest Grandson out of four with a guiding remedy. He would have willingly swapped places with me to quell the pain that gnawed away. Since 1991 I have spent a lot of quality time in Derby, sometimes to redecorate a room while he and Anne were Olde English sheepdog sitting at my second cousin Desmond's home. The last quality time that we shared was not long after his frail wife Anne's passing in late 1993. As is often the case, my dear old Granddad deteriorated rapidly afterwards, spending his last days clutching on to every struggling breath, and also on to his trusty little Adidas sports bag full of personals. He was a deep thinking man, and I bet he was wondering what might or might not be awaiting him once he had taken his final gasp of oxygen. Derby City Hospital took great care of the old soldier, a man small in stature but great in every other sense. He survived the D-Day battles in which he and many other men—to whom I am eternally grateful— gave all of themselves. Two months before his final breath, Mother had the idea of having him move in with her. She had built a downstairs bathroom complete with an enclosed shower, toilet and sink so that he could enjoy a convenient stair free life. For medical reasons the arrangement never materialised, but the gesture had been made and appreciated which is what mattered more than anything. That downstairs bathroom is now affectionately known as the "Albert Room." How delightful it must be to have such a room named after you when everybody else gets a music hall, a statue or even a park bench. I bet he is smiling about it now, wherever he may be.

In 1991 following the Derbyshire trip, I came down too hard on myself for failing to make a miraculous over night recovery. Had I of done so, the medical books would have needed to be painstakingly rewritten. There was definitely some improvement. My temper erupted with a healthier regularity, verbally flowing over the obscuring rocks and drowning out the occasional negative thought. Over and over again I would tell myself to stop wasting so much valuable time worrying about what other people think of me, and give up worrying about the future until it arrives, or better still stop bloody well worrying, period! Live my life for *now, not* for yesterday or tomorrow or for somebody else who couldn't give a shit about me. There were many times when I went flying over the top, telling the world and its peculiar contents to, "Get lost, go take a running jump and leave me well alone." This was an unreasonable and fruitless way to carry on, especially when my own unsettled chemistry was to blame. Compressed steam escaped with more and more purpose, slowly generating my creaking mental motor as it pursued the precision that was to recondition and run my forward looking life. Going overboard with anger and frustration is fine and dandy so long as nobody gets hurt in the works. I told myself that if anybody dares to get in the way of my life or causes me grief from now on in, then they were going to suffer. Of course it was all tough talk without the plaid trousers to match.

It was time to rinse out the rubbish that my mind had attracted, rinse it out real good so that I would feel lighter, brighter and alive. These occasional bursts of fury had me roaring like a lion and revved up sufficiently, before putting myself out of the house to take more and more walks, even in broad daylight and in full view of whoever cared to look. "Wow, big deal," some of you might be sarcastically thinking, I understand. To a severely depressed person, overcoming or at least attempting to eliminate what may appear to the layman as being a thing of trivia is an enormous deal, something to be encouraged and praised. To ridicule and to mock a fellow human being who is struggling to perform in the manner that today's selfish and critical society accepts can be devastating, a killer blow even, delivered with no real purpose other than to make the deliverer feel as if they have gained something that is seriously lacking from their own smeared make-up. The tongue is probably one of the most evil components in a person's armoury, and it should be used very carefully at all times, especially when you are perfectly aware that sensitive and temporarily unbalanced people are in the vicinity. You may well become one of them one day, although I sincerely hope that it doesn't take such an extreme measure for us all to think twice before shutting our big well oiled mouths. My two beautiful Sisters know only too well just how vicious a loose tongue can be because I used to mouth off at them, spewing out torrents of undeserved abuse. Mind you, they are more than capable at volleying abuse back into my court. It is never too late to change one's ways, but never lose sight of the old remarkable you! Males especially tend to psyche themselves up before embarking upon the latest sporting bout or work related problem by using aggression, huffing and puffing like the wolf so that they can knock the other man down and provide for their family—a condition probably best described as a natural instinct in what is now an unnatural environment. In the dog-eat-dog world, every man, woman and child has to find and develop their own unique pumping up technique, that will lubricate the survival strategies and self defence mechanisms that are often needed just to keep afloat.

Pumping myself full of aggression is not the only method that I employed in order to help further my onward and upward roll. Relaxation, the complete opposite to mouth frothing aggression has to be the most beneficial addition to the depressives arsenal. Sporting activity combines the two, especially swimming. Indoor games can be the start of what can then lead to outdoor activities, enabling the mind to accept encouragement and to be reminded how to focus on the task in hand, not allowing it to wander into an imaginative tomorrow and then dragged through a worrisome past. We all have to find our own techniques and then practice them with a regularity that will eventually make a dent of difference. Making that initial effort to help myself has got to be one of the toughest jobs that I have ever had to do. Thankfully it has come on in leaps and bounds, but back then I gave in far too easily if I didn't achieve an immediate result. Time is a healer and a teacher if you will allow it to be. Time spent in a depression taught me the true value and importance of patience, and that an excessively gung-ho approach just creates an inevitable and disappointing mental mirage of a craving that is not yet ready to make an appearance.

Real friends do not deserve to be neglected if they make the effort to call up. Real friends care, real friends remain quiet when something deeply personal and private is confided in them, real friends never lose sight of the human being who is having a temporary rough time of it, real friends have often been there themselves and understand what their unwell friend is going through. They feel bad because they know that there is no magical cure to offer. Friends offer their loyalty and time, although they need to protect themselves from an excessive amount of depressive exposure that radiates from off the sufferer. There is no use in having two fighters shot down in flames, when a little extra time spent planning the forthcoming raids on the depressed areas could protect both souls.

Spring made a most welcome appearance, bringing with it the perfect warmth and soft light that gently encourages every living thing to wake up and display their full glory. Extended daylight hours created a whole new atmosphere. The worst of my 1991 depressive episode had blown itself out, although I was still feeling way below par. Despite the crappiness, I could still feel the irresistible pulling power of natures annual rebirth. My spirits rose with a greater frequency, inviting me to join in with the human race again, to walk through Gadebridge park and smell the first cuttings of the lush damp grass, a therapeutic aroma that

I wanted to bottle so that I could smell its scent all year round. How I yearned to be free in my mind so that I could run out into the park that I have always regarded as my back garden. I drooled at the prospect of whistling along with the wildlife that sat high up among the branches, in the very same trees that were there long before I entered the worldly scene, and will still be around long after my present body of sixty percent water finally dries out. I wanted to be able to enjoy the seasonal lift to its fullest by inviting it to peacefully infiltrate every part of me, kicking out the miserable lodgers of my busy mind in the process, but I still found it an extremely difficult step to take. Sure, I would take the two minute walk to the park without too much mental discomfort, but when I was there I simply couldn't relax. I felt as tense as the swinging ropes and as rigid as the silver steel slide in the children's playing area. A baby bird might feel similar when it is about to leave its nest for the very first time, leaping out into the big wide world without a parachute, not knowing for certain if its unused wings are going to get into a flap or if they will freeze, letting you down and down. It's a bloody long way to drop when being watched by the local cats, ready to pounce on every mistake. I was always teetering on the edge of my branch, terrified that an awkward situation may arise out of the breeze, a chance meeting perhaps that could knock out cold what little confidence I had accumulated, putting the little yet solid forward progress that I had made way back somewhere behind the starting line, complete with its winding roads and blocks of glue.

Peace of mind and good physical health are requests that I used to think only those over the age of fifty made, but I quickly changed my tune when bipolar affective disorder came thudding at my door. Freedom, love and understanding will creak open Heaven's ancient gate that little bit more. Could it be that the odd drop of oil, crude or refined, will be our saviour or our downfall? Perhaps we will have to wait for a heated conversation in 2012—only five years from today's rising emotional waves—for the far strung web to sort things out, to catch the impostor, or for our arachnid friends to become tangled up in their own doing.

Due to being wrapped up in myself for so long, I had neglected to reply to the many letters that Sue had sent me from Long Island, New York. Those cards and letters meant so much to me, lifting my sagging spirits when I needed them hoisting the most. Amazingly she was already able to comfortably tap into my innermost thoughts and feelings. The occasional telephone call always came when it was needed the most, *always*. Sue listened to my depressed droning with the patience of a Saint before conveying her own personal experiences, hitting the relevant spots in such a clear, precise and uplifting way. Having been through episodes of manic depression herself, Sue knew only too well that there is no miracle quick fix. My waiting miracle was definitely going to happen someday, but first there was going to be one heck of a long hard slog. Susan's reassuring words, coupled with a genuine concern and overwhelming generosity, were major contributory factors in assisting me all of the way through, and then out of my bipolar struggles. Sue remains a calming influence whether I'm up or if I am down, or living my life somewhere in the socially acceptable no mans land. Everybody who has ever had the privilege of knowing Susan would have experienced inspiring examples of her generous and caring nature. A regular churchgoer and soprano in the St. Patrick's Church choir, Smithtown, New York, and now at St. Isidores in Riverhead, Sue is a devout Catholic who refreshingly practices what she hears, reads and decides for herself, by getting off her backside and doing something practical such as volunteering at Riverhead's modern Peconic Bay Medical Centre. Susan and I have marinated together through thick and thin for all of these years, and there will be many more because she is my best friend and loyal partner. Innumerable transatlantic journeys have been made in order for us to be together as often as possible, and attempts to make it a permanent situation have fallen through on many occasions due to unforeseen personal circumstances and huge reels of red tape. This unlikely pairing has produced a strong operational team, who have fought the battle together, emerging far happier and a whole lot wiser for their combined efforts. The battle has become more of a scrap these days, just enough to keep us on our toes. Today we are a couple of seasoned campaigners who keep a welcome and watchful eye on each other's well-being, and at this present moment in time our beings are very well indeed thank you!

Low moods were definitely rising. My identity waited, clearly in view now, primed and ready to be retrieved and renewed. What still ate away at me was my temporary inability and lack of drive to rise up and make my own stand, to follow my own convictions, to carve out my own route and simply be a D.I.M. (Do it myself) kind of guy. My long term failure in satisfying my mind—to fully express my collection of thoughts and opinions through a suitable job or art form, or by being in the wrong place with the wrong people for far too long—may have contributed towards my 1990 diagnosis. The frustration of being unable to express my thoughts in the same way that they were playing in my head could have boosted my growing fondness of alcohol. Manic depression had of course been bubbling away in the background ever since my conception in December 1963, so if I had grown up to become an average teetotaller, the final explosive manic/depressive outcome would not have changed, instead materialising in some other way. Booze and other drugs, financial difficulties, relationship problems, current affairs—they can all trigger an episode, but only if the manic-depressive seeds have been planted at the onset and the mind's handbrake is released, causing random thoughts to run wildly away with themselves. Thoughts, theories, half-baked conclusions and solutions such as these kept rerunning through my downtrodden head with hardly any let up. Even so, things were noticeably improving. Thousands of questions and very few tattooed answers. Why did I torture myself so? It must be the nature of the beast. Lack of stimulation through conversation and healthy activity left more room in my hard driven brain for stale mixtures of negativity, an urgent situation that had to change fast.

Assisting with the household chores was at first a colossal effort, but as my confidence and concentration grew I even attempted a small amount of basic interior decorating, painting mostly. Setting my mind to anything was bloody tough at first. Over and over again I repeated the instructions in my mind of how to do a job that I could once do blindfolded. The level of concentration required for an ill person to claw their way out of depression, by whatever means, is so high that it is exhausting for a caregiver to even watch. An understanding of what is not visible to the naked eye makes all the difference when it comes to those who are trying to help the sufferer. A greater understanding of any mental problem makes life much easier and more tolerable, thus enabling a caregiver to box blind and still be capable of smacking the illness into submission. It did not matter one single little bit if it took all day long to peel one King Edward potato or to dust my bedroom. The boost that each little successful activity provided may seem small from the outside looking in, but as I mentioned earlier, every achievement is a priceless contribution in the delicate process of rebuilding some semblance of sanity, and also to the ongoing maintenance of what once felt like an irretrievably decimated life. Small acorns baby.

Fear of failure has always been my Achilles heel. This irrational fear held me back from what should really have pushed me toward bigger and better things. In 1991 as I stumbled and fell back onto the track, this fear stood out the most. Failure is a condition produced by a mind filled with nothing but negative thoughts. The measure of success is set by you and judged by you. Failure is to *not* even make an attempt. Success is to *make* an attempt and cocking it right up. If you succeed in attempting a task without too many cock-ups then the sky's your limit! When I was severely or mildly depressed, every effort that I made, no matter what the outcome, offered me no medals or cream cakes, but those efforts *did* provide me with plenty of sizeable personal success stories that I took from my many mini achievements. These stories and achievements are kept in an open safe, always available for those gloomy days, void of sunlight and flying sparks.

Inactivity is to be avoided at all costs. If the brain cells and body do not receive adequate stimulation and exercise, they will slow down and prove to be much harder to get moving again as precious time marches on, just like a garaged car that hasn't been taken for a decent drive in ages. Overcoming my mind's love affair with all things detrimental to my pursuit of a full recovery was tough. It didn't happen overnight, instead slowly and surely over a period of many difficult and trying months, full of false summits and tempting titbits of true elation. The ever perceptive Doctor Hope was able to accurately gauge any changes in my mood within a fifteen minute appointment. The three to four week gap between visits enabled my doctor to see and hear a considerable shift in both my physical and mental condition. Having been scared witless for days leading up to my appointments, I would now come away from the surgery with my head held a little higher. This rejuvenation process would last for a few days and then the same old nonsense would come knocking again, asking me to play black-ball just as we had in the bad old days—a flogged to death request that I was ignoring more and more. My visitor from the bad old days knocked less frequently as time passed, but there was still a lot of hard work to be done. Pieces of the key to my life were not being forced as much by conflicting opinions, and instead were slowly slotting back into place.

My mind's sickly eye continued to project macabre Technicolor displays onto surfaces such as walls, floors, buildings and so on. These imaginary images hindered many tasks because they took my concentration away, causing me to drift from the main event. The task would have to be repeated as if it was an obsessive compulsion, which usually causes some irritation which leads to frustration and anger, that most probably will be taken out on an undeserving human being who hasn't got a clue what the commotion is all about. It was not until I had eliminated the highly defiant intruders from my equation that I was able to resume doing whatever it was I had originally intended to do, if I could still remember. The brain is capable of producing so many wondrous delights and despairing doubts. It will never cease to bemuse and bedazzle. The brain is home to approximately one hundred billion neurons, the body impulse conducting cells that are transmitted by chemicals which can become unbalanced. It is fascinating that the human brain is the least explored, or extensively researched organ out of all the organs contained within the human body. Maybe we are one entity already, or are we all part of the entity known as God and possibly the devil too? Are we battling among ourselves, super-braining in a draining orgy of chemically enriched water and pulsing spiritual electricity, throbbing pure and innocent, violently dirty and used, incestuously sick and insane? Shocking isn't it, but it never fails to get me thinking.

Pain remains no matter where one goes, but there was a marked improvement when my father and I spent a week together in Dorset. Spurts of happiness sprayed lightly over me, only to be blown away briskly by the fresh sea breeze. My heals always dragged as I prepared for another long day ahead. Dad was always immaculately groomed and smartly attired long before I had brushed my teeth or decided what clothes would be suitable to wear that bright or dismal day. I tackled one basic task at a time, sometimes feeling as if it was my very first experience. Focusing solely on one thing at a time was an imperative key issue that needed to be returned to my bunch as soon as possible, as this base key would affect practically everything else that I attempted to do. Mornings are so awful when feeling down, so it took sheer guts and willpower to plough my way through. I needed a Shire workhorse to pull me as I pushed. My old man became my hard but fair task master, giving me just the right balance of tough instruction and encouragement. This was exactly what the good Dorset doctor ordered!

The Golden Cap is the highest cliff peak along the entire Dorset Jurassic coastline. I knew it well from previous trips, but on this occasion I could not stop dwelling upon the availability of an instant drop, my smashed body left to leak its bloody ending over the rocks, to be scrubbed out courtesy of the abrasive English Channel. All that I could realistically aim for would be to just keep on going, allowing no room nor time for caving in. Striving forward in the hope that I would wear my way out of the heaviness was my only real option. An everyday trek it may well be for the locals who were walking their dogs, but for me it was a huge undertaking. It was obvious that my helpless father was having to display a brave face, masking his own agony with every step and with each long silence.

Exercise is such a good spirit lifter, even if it seems like a killer to begin with. My physical strength gradually began to build, making me feel as if I had a little more control over my life. The temptation to over do it when I was on an uplifting roll was hard to ignore, resulting in a few minor setbacks that are all part and parcel of the depressed persons comeback tour. If the healing process is pushed too soon and too far, the hard work could be knocked all the way back to the beginning. It was so tempting to milk to death any good moment that came my way, and why not? Instead, tempted though I was, I had to teach myself some self discipline and take only a tiny swig for starters, then slowly increase the dose.

The big problem with me is that I hate to hold back and be told what to do. A stubborn awkward blighter, that's me down to the ground.

Two miles West is the larger coastal town of Lyme-Regis. It was here in Lyme that I could practice mingling with the human race again. All of them were distracted by their melting ice creams, or were simply keeping an eye on the kids as they played on the sandy beach. This was an agreeable situation to integrate myself back into. For the first time in ages I felt released from my imaginary fear of being spotted by someone that I knew, somebody who might go and tell everybody back home that I was acting like a complete jerk. Of course nobody would bother talking about me even if I was spotted in the crowd, or if I was as pathetically odd as I had wrongly convinced myself that I was. It takes a while to realise that despite feeling sick, gawky and awkward inside, the outside appears much the same to another human being. There really is *nothing* out there to be afraid of.

I had reached the stage where I clearly knew the difference between an irrational and a rational thought, but I still had a great deal of trouble shaking off the former. Now my optimistic forecast blew crispy hot and then bitterly cold, lifting me up and up before dropping me like a rotten habit. Rapid mood swings are part of the recovery process, and now I was regularly sensing golden opportunities to climb out and back up onto my thick skinned feet. Cascades of workable and unworkable thoughts still tumbled loosely in my mind, all of them blowing hot and cold and ready to pounce.

One day as we were about to climb the Golden Cap, my old man commented on the abundance of seagulls flying around the car park, and how they had splattered every car windscreen in sight. "They had better not dump one on me," remarked my fate-tempting Father. Soon enough the squawking birds decided to dive-bomb my father who took a direct splash of white and grey seagull slop all over his short sleeved shoulder. I hadn't laughed so much since my manic days on Anderson Ward. A jolly good laugh always provides a lift, so perhaps a visit to a comedy show or watching a funny DVD would be an excellent choice of alternative medicine (many elderly people put their longevity down to having a good sense of humour, and not taking everything that life throws your way too seriously.) This time the climb to the Golden Cap wasn't nearly as traumatic, instead it was more achievable and fun—always best to use the positive description rather than the traumatic negative. It occurred to me later that our merriment had succeeded there and then in turning my attention away from the cliff edge, dissuading me from making any future plans to soar off it if my depression took another downward spiral. From that day on the Golden Cap became known as the Golden Crap.

With only my father and myself together for the week it meant that equal weight would be required to make as light work as possible of the cooking and cleaning. It's not a great deal to do I know, but apart from washing up and laying the dining room tables on Anderson Ward I had done hardly anything to contribute, instead it had all been done for me. An element of lethargy that can lead toward laziness does set in when feeling low, but with a little effort it isn't very hard to break free from that idle habit. Little by little I regained the incentive and confidence to take full care of my surroundings and of myself, without being put under any sort pressure. All of the domestic skills come flooding back when the operator's out of order sign has been removed, dismantled and placed out of sight. My irrational nagging fear of losing personal belongings, especially keys, waited patiently in the wings to give a dominating performance. Heckling from all sides of the imaginary fence was not unheard of. Every minor accomplishment, painful though it may have been, kept adding that extra spark toward the recharging of Steadman's lithium powered battery. Dad was never unnecessarily critical. He remained constructively critical when it was due and beneficial, a vital role that isn't at all easy, yet somebody has to play it. Praise and encouragement came when it was due, without going artificially over the top. A temporary pleasant gloss smeared on to a flaky surface is not the way to go, ask any painter. Depression takes its own time to run out of gas, so please don't force it. The support and love that my father has unselfishly given to every member of his family is truly phenomenal, and sometimes he doesn't get the credit that he so richly deserves.

As the final few days in Dorset approached, I found that I was actually looking forward to returning to the caravan in the evenings to tuck into some fresh fish and chips, play some music, read a little, watch some television or chat lightly about anything that took our exerted minds off the heavy stuff. At around 10 p.m. without fail Dad would take a couple of well deserved shots of his favourite Scotch whisky. The aroma of his tipple gave me tempting ideas that I knew should never be fooled around with. I was beginning to feel so much better, and although I had been existing in the land of the living, I now felt as if I was starting to actually *live* and belong in it again. My stretched mind, still tired from recording the bygone day in its entirety, was able to ease up and relax at my command more so than before, but it was still on involuntary over time, staging unscheduled rehearsals for what might lay ahead. My unhealthy obsession of pointlessly dissecting and scrutinising everything and everyone, trying against my better judgment to find a hidden or obvious flaw, had finally run its course and faded. Now I was carrying a much lighter load with which to build my solid wall of strength, using the fragments of my daily recovery as a preliminary foundation. Those remaining three days in sunny Dorset were anything but. Now I wanted nothing better than to rush out and enjoy the elements that I had been sheltering from. Walking in the pouring rain is something that I have always loved doing. The heavier it's tipping down the better. Five years earlier I had sat alone on Folkestone's beach, Kent, feeling down in the dumps because I had just lost my third seaside job and a beautiful girlfriend, both on the same miserable day. Now I can laugh at how I thought the end was nigh and that my circumstances couldn't possibly become worse. Sitting on that beach helped me put that little crisis into some sort of perspective. Men are the soppiest species on the quiet, especially when they lose their woman. A trip to the beach will lift even the most depressed of the depressed, even if it is only for two seconds. Two seconds and a little effort are better than none at all. Solo sessions are by far the best, but if a person is suicidal then it is strongly advised that they have some alert company standing close by; we don't want anybody jumping to their depressing conclusions now do we.

We spent hours watching nature do its natural best, giving us a variety performance, a never ending spectacle complete with a continuous array of changing scenery and mood evoking light displays. The greatest show on this planet is free, but it does demand great respect and constant maintenance. We sat back from the beach and gazed in awe at the matinee performance, always live and very well presented in Lyme Bay. The realisation dawned on me that we were only two small fry in a great big pond, two grains of sharp sand in a pinprick of time. One day I wouldn't mind meeting the orchestral brain behind it all, but there certainly isn't any hurry. Maybe we are all assistant managers? One thing that *is* for sure is that every single one of us has the responsibility of caretakers.

The caravan and camping park has an excellent heated indoor swimming pool, that if I felt daring enough I would use. I made sure by peering through the windows that hardly any other campers were using the facility before I dared myself to enter the building. The obligatory lifeguard was often the only other person in sight, but when another swimmer showed up my pulse increased. You see, I have always been very self-conscious of my inverted chest and also of the white patches of vitiligo that are splashed across my body like a Jackson Pollock painting. Before ending my swimming session I made certain that the pink chlorine eyes still bobbing about were diverted, so that I could scurry up the pool steps and quickly grab my jumbo sized towel. I always positioned it close to the waters edge so that I could limit the amount of seconds that my naked flesh would be on display to what felt like the entire prying world, as if they hadn't anything better to do. You may well laugh in disbelief, but many of us have similar hang-ups and phobias that we keep hidden for years and years, secretly suffering every time an unavoidable occasion arises.

When I began to feel my mood rising, an urgency to bite off more than I could chew set in. I needed to tackle and finish off the previous years projects that had been brushed aside by depression and mania. Long before my admittance to Hill End Psychiatric Hospital my sister Barbara had requested my capable, if not super quick, decorating services. I had already tackled most of the other rooms in her house with reasonable results, and so I agreed to take on this job. When the heavy swing of depression hit home, my unfulfilled promise played on my conscience. Barbara wasn't bothered in the slightest, but the depression blew my fears way out of proportion. I even began to think that she was angry with me, which was of course utter nonsense. Barbara and her then partner Roberta were only concerned that I made a full recovery, so they told me to, "Forget about the decorating, that stuff isn't important and can wait until later." I also recalled having an upbeat conversation on Anderson Ward with a softly spoken Berkhamsted publican called George Lambert, whose Grand Union Canal-side pub was in dire need of a gardener. After discussing all of the other odd gardening jobs that I had undertaken, he offered me the part time pint and a pie, cash in hand position at his pub, The Rising Sun. Running before I can barely crawl is a pursuit that I have been fortunate enough to get away with in the past, but now I was wary of the possible consequences. Instead of dismissing the opportunity altogether I decided to place the offer in trust, then sit back for a while and see what might or might not become of it. These and many other positive thoughts were now entering my recovering head, but I still needed more time to piece myself together so that I could work out a sensible forward strategy.

My father and I drove back across the beautiful Salisbury Plain to Hemel Hempstead in an elevated moodmobile. I had a long way to go mentally, but the signs were good and all things were at last looking brighter. Awaiting us was my mother and a full Sunday roast dinner, the best meal that I had attempted to devour for quite some time. My appetite was now clawing its way back into the limelight, so every meal from then on consisted of a healthy mixture of all the foods that I love the most. It was as if my taste buds had died and had now been resurrected. Those sweet and sour buds were born again. The very same thing gradually happened to each of my other senses, all of which had been on a life support system since my fall from manic grace. Now that I was able to see and feel the world famous light at the end of the tunnel looming nearer and nearer, I began to over eagerly and somewhat prematurely question my folks about when it might be a good time to resume driving my ladder laden Volkswagen, and even reuniting myself with my luxury maisonette in Bovingdon. All of this would allow myself to be reacquainted with independence, a man's best friend along with his hound. Sprinting before I could stride is one thing, but biting off more of life's spice than I was able to chew and then swallowing it whole, might just make me plain sick again. Up until now the only ghastly light that I could make out in the tunnel were the headlights belonging to a speeding intercity express train. This speeding sick bucket had rattled the tracks at me once too often, while clutching in its fist of steel my sixth class ticket to hell—a rotten service that I'll always pray will never arrive at my station again.

A couple of days after we returned from Dorset, Dad and I decided to give my car a run to my maisonette to pick up the mail and check that all was shipshape. I felt so much better about visiting my own home now than I did a couple of weeks earlier. It is odd to see everything the same, but in yet another different light. You could say that my dimmer switch was carefully increasing the brightness. One turn of the Yale lock and I was back in touch with my castle. Greeting me was the usual pile of advertising junk and a giant redwood's worth of free newspapers, none of which had my name sprawled across the front page. Laying underneath this extensive and expensive pile of nonsensical waste was a beautifully hand written envelope from Susan, 3600 miles away. I placed it carefully in my inside jacket pocket to read later. I swear to God that I could feel the warmth of her letter permeating through my bomber jacket and resting deep inside my heart.

At long last a once lost but never forgotten friend came back into my life. He had been knocking impatiently, yet he was too timid to shout. His knocks became harder, and his bloody red knuckles sorer. In his madness he had forgotten that the easy key was either under the mat or safe with the trustworthy neighbours. That friend was me, and he decided there and then that he wanted to remain where he was, on solid level ground.

My mind bank surrounds me, and it is open 24 hours for whenever I need some advice, or a boost of confidence. Teachers are found everywhere, although they sometimes might not even be aware of their own influential powers. All of us are teachers and caretakers. By doing wrong you can bring home to others what is right, so can you lose? yes, if you do not at least make a reasonable effort to reform. There is also the risky possibility of a naive younger or older somebody picking up new and attractive bad habits that often become very sticky, similar to having gum stuck in your hair. Learning from an experienced professional or an old campaigner can make that wrong a sensible right, which is just as much fun and a whole lot safer. When we all get our acts together, everything else will fall into place, choreographed nicely to keep life interesting and fresh. Controlled extreme behaviour will still remain available but *without* the dire consequences, at least that's my dream and I'm sticking to it. We will realise that everything goes full circle and that recycling does not just apply to old newspapers, clothing and liquor bottles. I hereby rest my case, and shall now step down from my soapbox before I slide off and bang my head again.

Returning to my life was like coming out of a terrible trance. Perseverance was the keyword if I were survive and thrive on my own two feet again. I also needed to be a little selfish. The buck had to stop here. Apart from having no option, I had never before been so determined to pull my finger out and do something positive for myself. Having the conviction was one thing, possessing the power and current ability to follow it through was something else altogether. When the bitter end of hell came into view and the taste of life returned, it was so sweet that I wanted to devour it all at once. One careful step at a time in order to avoid tripping over and having to restart, was the only way to catch up and maintain a steady pace. There were to be the down days full of disappointing results and overwhelming despair at the enormity of the job in hand. There were to be the up days full of excellent results and delicious sensations of achievement and hope. The two extremes had to wear down a little and then merge somewhere in-between. It is in my nature to step up to the plate and throw caution to the wind by swinging at every pitch in search of the home run, but now I had to display a touch of conservatism while remaining firmly focused on my prioritised short term goals. The knots and gum wedged in my hair would eventually pull through or grow out, and the importance of issues would at long last be drastically filed down into an acceptable and manageable pile. My mental batteries trickle charged thanks to a trip to the local shops or a brisk daylight stroll in the park or woods. I could roughly gauge by the amount of pages I had read of a book without losing concentration how I was coming along. It didn't always improve. Sometimes my walks were shorter than the previous day but so what, it was better than nothing at all. So long as I had a therapeutic aim, something that would play its part in the overall healing/confidence building process, I would get there. Becoming fully charged seems to take forever, but the best sides of beef are always cooked nice and slow, then checked on a regular basis until the clear juices are running just dandy.

Driving a car was a skill that I was particularly wary of, not because of my ability to drive but of finding myself stranded somewhere out in the sticks, or being involved in an accident and unable to handle the situation properly. Up until then I had never experienced even a minor crunch, or even a major scratch. Considering that in 1986 I spent a year selling Ford automobiles in Harrow Weald, North London, that's not a bad achievement.

I gradually managed to grind my motoring skills back into gear, far sooner than we had anticipated. Short runs to and from my maisonette in Bovingdon sufficed at first, followed by gentle drives around the local countryside lanes. Since 1992 I have on two occasions had my driving license revoked because I was having a bipolar episode, so why didn't I have it taken from me in 1991 when I was at my lowest ebb? This is yet another barmy example of bureaucracy and officialdom gone mad. When they revoke your license it is a bitch to get it back again. It didn't necessarily mean that I was unable to drive throughout the ridiculously long processing period, but it did involve stinking heaps of forms to be filled in, as well as medical reports galore that were apparently supposed to be private, and *not* passed round the DVLA offices by a bunch of pimply teenage pen pushers who couldn't tell their arses from their elbows. Same old stuff, same old bullshit, but I guess it's a small price to pay in the scheme of things. Having to visit my general practitioner, consultant psychiatrist, pathology laboratory and pharmacy, as well as dealing with the skin problems and weight gain that my medication can cause, are all lifetime requirements that I am more than happy to tolerate, but everything else is *poppycock*. I am so hugely grateful to have such fine team of highly professional and dedicated human beings around, including the doctors, consultants, financial advisors, scientists, support workers, pharmacists and haematology technicians to help me take control of my own life and maintain its balanced course.

According to the results of my many blood tests and by the positive indications that I had shown, it appeared at long last that my lithium medication had been at the correct and safe level for quite a while now. At the same time, the natural effects of this manic-depressive/bipolar episode lost their grip on the old rope, falling away in big burnt out lumps, leaving only a few scorch marks seared on my brain. My lifeboat still floated in the corrosive Dead Sea, firming my faith as I placed my own stake in our future. I felt my freedom return, then I realised that it had never even left, it had just been temporarily mislaid, overshadowed by an illness, that's all. Anyone who has experienced the sheer relief of having any kind of load lifted knows exactly what it feels like to be freed, to be removed from deaths door and given a renewed lease of life. It can be so tempting to jump back into the old fire pit of excessiveness when you think that the situation is licked. Making up for lost time is the attraction awaiting a recovering bipolar person, but the ideal way to go is to take whatever presents itself in your stride.

It is easy for me to say today, but abiding to the basic rules of recovery, some of which will be hard to stomach, and by showing plenty of maturity and self discipline you should land yourself on a level winning streak.

Appreciation for what has been done to aid recovery cannot be better displayed than by showing some responsibility and self restraint, which in my case meant abstaining from large quantities of alcohol, or better still none at all. One of the many pieces of valuable advice that the hospital staff relay to a patient when they (unlike me) make a healthy discharge from a psychiatric unit is, "We hope we never ever see you again," because if they do then that means a breakdown of self discipline has taken place, a needless case that could easily have been prevented. Unavoidable returns are inevitable, but if you have the tools to prevent a disturbance of the mind, get them out and put them to work, don't be lazy! Somebody else who is ill for the very first time may not receive as much attention as they deserve, all because of the self centred undisciplined sloppiness of a returnee patient. I was one of the worst offenders.

Coming through a manic or a depressive episode despite the heavy cost of ammunition, often gives an onlooker a valuable insight that may one day come in handy. Every manic-depressive or bipolar affected human being has in effect been given a gift to be used wisely. They can see through a wider scope, make sense of the ins and the outs of the unbelievable ups and the depressing downs, and generally have a deeper clearer insight and a better informed understanding of life itself, possibly even death. Travelling through the university of life is a never ending adventure full of lessons to learn, mistakes to make and final scores to boot into practice at the appropriate time. I for one do not intend to sit back and moan, "Why me, it's not fair, I'm so hard done by, dear oh dear, woe is me," and all of that gutter drivel. Immediate commitments and relationships were best avoided, or so I thought at the time. Settling into a job of work and becoming involved with an American lady 25 years older than myself nearly had me fleeing in a cloud of dust, but I was constantly reminded that there was *no* pressure or any time limits to make decisions such as these, not until I had really got my scabby head screwed on right and tight.

Naturally I had the occasional flat mental tyre. Over revving in certain situations is so tempting, when all of the time I should have been running myself back in gently, so that everything would slot into place without any damage. Because this was the first time that I had experienced episodes of fully blown manic depression, there were going to be plenty of typical reactions that I would have to adjust and acquaint myself with if I were to enjoy a low key journey back to some semblance of normality. This preferable arrangement didn't want to play ball with me, probably because I never accepted a particularly "normal" life even when I was supposedly normal. If somebody said one thing I would have to be stubborn and say or do the complete opposite. I used to prefer being on the side of the rebellious underdog, the people who have got guts enough to stand up and say and do what the flock of critical sheep dare not. These days I am a little wiser, now possessing sufficient commonsense to know that by having and putting to use that attitude I will get nowhere pretty damn fast. A caregiver might take it upon themselves to read about what they might expect to encounter during certain stages of recovery. They may wish to discuss the subject with trained medical staff, or with members of organisations such as the Manic Depression Fellowship or Mind. There is always bound to be a level headed seasonal manic-depressive at these places and usually family members and friends of existing active cases. These people can give the best advice of all, and I am sure that they would be more than happy to help out with your current plight in any way that they possibly can. All the talking in the world will not fully prepare those close to the recovering depressive for the irritability and antics that the mini mood swings within the pendulum upswing will bring. Because a mood is on the up and up, and the relief that it brings is already lapping at the heels, extra tolerance is dredged up by those who have had a stake in the proceedings. The resulting smiles will further strengthen the current takeover bid, and then pay out dividends to the deserving.

It took six to eight weeks following the Dorset break before it was in every-body's best interests to hand me back my car and dreaded keys. Driving myself to my own home after such an eventful and lengthy lay off was an emotional step, a colossal moment. The last time that I had driven my car without a passenger by my side was on the way to Heathrow Airport, from where I soared to one of the fashion capitals of the world. This homecoming was a move that could and should have waited, but I could only do what felt right at the time, and anyway despite having manic genes and a small drop of Gypsy blood swishing around inside, my short-term predictive powers were inoperative.

I went straight out and drank the little money that I had in the local pubs. On my return I would purchase the cheapest and most cheerful bottles of cider and beer to continue my gut rotting sessions into the early hours of the morning. Acid reflux didn't deter me one little bit. A welcome home blast is to be expected I suppose, but it is also supposed to stop so that life can continue in moderation. I should never have drunk again, let alone embark on a bender. My medication could have done without the abuse as could my soaked liver, but I carried on from where I left off, using my recovery as an excuse. When that excuse ran its course, I rallied round and came up with another equally feeble guilt free reason why I should be allowed to behave indoors like an alcoholic lout. Alcohol could very well trigger me off again, especially at such a delicate time, and here was I firing my lubricated machine gun, trying my hardest to annihilate the recent past. When I drank I very rarely took my medication = trouble waiting to happen.

I attempted to acquire a few odd gardening and decorating jobs to help out with my modest household and car expenses. Food became the last entry on my list of priorities, while making doubly sure that each day I had enough money to score a satisfactory level of drunkenness. This was such a stupid and irresponsible way to be conducting myself, throwing caution and three sheets out into the wind. This unreliable pattern of odd jobs and heavy drinking went on in much the same way from 1991 right into the new millennium. Booze was a big player as far as trigger pulling is concerned, but it is not always the main culprit. If I am heading up or down without taking my medication I will still go up or down, booze or no booze. It is the neglectful and addictive aspect that ruins everything for everybody. If I decided against taking my lithium carbonate and anti-depressants, as well as failing to inform my general practitioner of any sudden mood changes, I would be in *big* trouble. In the back of my mind, as any manic-depressive will tell you, I knew that my doctor would try his level best, and quite rightly so, to put the kibosh on my antics and sever the supply to my roaring senses. I was feeling too good too soon, but I thought I would keep it under my cap and have a bit of fun for a change. My bipolar inexperience made me turn a foolish blind eye to the dangers of sudden highs from the recovering lows, and sudden lows following a high. Most of this I had a vague commonsense idea about, but I didn't think it would apply to me—a fatal mistake!

The higher I felt, with the aid of drink, the less medication I took. Whenever I became a little low I drank too much to combat the bad feeling, which meant that even if I did take my medication it wouldn't have a hope in hell of doing my system any good. There were many long periods of time when I did everything right, and then I would go and blow all of the good work in one fell swoop. Trying to emulate the feeling of a manic high with dangerous quantities of booze has been the downfall of many respected manic-depressives/bipolar affective sufferers before me, so like an idiot I flung myself fully into the same two faced claptrap. Feeling fantastic did not mean that I should neglect my medicine, the very same medicine that had successfully helped to pull me out of the sticky fix that I had been in. A common belief among manic-depressives is that by omitting the prescribed lithium and other necessary medicines there is a strong possibility of becoming high again. We are always being reminded to, "Keep taking your medicine, don't forget to take it when you go away somewhere," which does keep us on our toes. The temptation still remains, *always*. There is no sure way of knowing which direction such a risky business will send you, but if Russian roulette of the mind is your sort of thing then who am I to stop you. A depression will always be waiting for you whether you get high or not, so what's the point of becoming high when it is such a long way to come crashing down? Either way you could overstep the mark and end up in the fridge with a tagged toe.

Friends and relations must have been pulling their hair out knowing that I was indeed heading for another rough ride, a journey of self destruction that could explode at any given moment. At that tentative time it took a brave and extraordinarily caring human being to exercise their rights and confront me on the subject of medication and alcohol. A Jeckyl and Hyde attitude toward this subject left those in my company completely baffled and slightly on edge. My temper became unthinkably nasty with the minimum of effort, in a very short space of time, in much the same way as I could suddenly turn and become an amicable fellow. The trick was to catch me somewhere in the middle. When I was nice I was very nice, and when I was bad I blew people to shreds with the sheer velocity of my inconsiderate and over enthusiastic speech. I could easily win them over with a smile, and then make their day with a cocky grin. It was my poor mum who received the brunt of my ear-bashing (Mothers always do), and it was she God bless her who gave back as good as she got. Sometimes she hurled the nearest coffee mug or ornament across the small room with an impressive accuracy. My big fat mouth avoided any direct hits, but the message hit home hard. As I became higher and higher my verbal diarrhoea flowed with an effortless coarseness. I thought that my whole tirade and Mother's accurate pitching was one huge joke, and that we were both acting out a part. It certainly wasn't a comedy or a West End play for her. When I smiled and smirked she occasionally lost touch with the end of her tether, leaving her teetering precariously on the edge of her own sanity, an edge that I honed too finely and too often in the past for everybody's peace of mind. When things settled down I could lay on the charm of a prince. In my mind, high blood pressurising incidents such as this were often wrapped in joy, happiness and lashings of what can only be described as tough and hard to swallow, yet tender, warm and baked to perfection, homemade sweet Mother love. Well that's how I felt, she probably wished I was wrapped up in brown paper and shipped off to Australia's outback.

Doing whatever pleased me in Bovingdon felt wonderful, but I was still a big risk to myself, a problem waiting to happen. The tugboats can only go so far before having to return to their safe harbour, allowing me to breeze single handed through the turbulence that my life never fails to throw up. Unlike Titanic, the only ice that I came into serious contact with was at the bottom of a whisky tumbler. Gossip has a habit of spreading like wildfire in tightly knit villages around England. Simple basic truths often become distorted, but nobody is to blame. Establishing the true facts before dragging a defenceless name through the dirt is imperative, otherwise shut up! Information regarding my Bovingdon comeback was relayed mostly by rumour and hunch. A few ridiculous rumours were squashed, such as whether or not I had died or been sent down for a stretch, perhaps even holed up like Howard Hughes. Nobody really knew, and I don't suppose that many really cared apart from a handful of well intentioned souls. Whatever I did, I did it with the aid of alcohol. The noise coming from my mai-sonette rated way up alongside the party I once threw at my parent's house when I had just turned 17 years old. I consumed the cheapest version of every liver rotting alcoholic beverage available, giving them all a thoroughly good seeing to in the moronic search for something resembling my darling high. It feels as if nothing much gets in your way when you are on a bender, and if it does you don't care. It's a large case of steamrolling through a party-pooping bunch of boring killjoys, then watching all of the hard work put in fall apart brick by selfish brick. Learning all over again—not that I was particularly good at it to begin with—that there is a time and a place for everything, was not going to be at all easy. I figured that the time was whenever I said it was time, and that the place would be wherever I wanted. This was such an inconsiderate, people repelling attitude, but *I* was the one who had been through something that most people couldn't possibly even begin to imagine, let alone experience fully and then come out the other side. So I became a, "Get off my case and leave me to my own devices, if you know what's good for you," kind of guy. Lacking charm and manners made me utterly repulsive, but I couldn't care less because I felt that I had put in so much effort, this world at least owed me my little pleasures as scant reward for what I had believed wholeheartedly in.

What exactly would the benefits be of working within a shared spirit on an I'll scratch your back if you'll scratch mine basis, minding out and drawing in from one another? The answer is a greater understanding, realisation and usage of what is good—love and peace. By putting together a big positive project for me, such as this little book for you, I might be able to help other likeminded people in a small way. It will hopefully encourage and make more people aware of the fact that manic depression/bipolar affective disorder, or *any* mental difference, lethal beliefs, true colours and foreign cultures, no matter how distant and irrelevant they may seem, are large pieces of the puzzling hop, skip, and a jump toward a beautiful future. Let's pray that the world doesn't explode like a head brimming with mania before things can be put right again, but if that's how it will be it will be. 2012 is around the next few blockheads of power. A bigger and better way of life has always been right here, staring us in the face. We are the childish knock-knock jokes that we thought we knew all the answers to, but we were never really at home that often, completely missing the basic messages. Believe me when I say that as soon as you have woken up and have experienced first hand your version of the whole spiritual enlightenment extravaganza, you can *never* forget it, and nor will you have any desire to, but you *will* want to share it out, because the more people that are turned on naturally and in their own good time, the better the purity of our existence will be.

The world is to share and protect as equals with unique personalities and strengths. One huge garden and each of us a gardener that cultivates, harvests and shares. If each and every one of us stops being so greedy and power mad, and open our honest eyes and then offer out our heart simultaneously we be in Heavens high, no question about it. You cannot buy true happiness and spiritual contentment, you are the creator of it yourself. We have been given the correct tools and unlimited opportunities, so rather than talking into thin air why don't we patch up the planet and stop the leaks before we drown in guilt and saltwater. God's marriage to Mother nature has sometimes been an explosive affair, but that was many moons ago, so why don't we use their forgiving example to put things right. Take a good look at how everything keeps on returning and giving, passed on by Mother nature to grow again. See how forests burnt to ashes still return. Death's release will always act as the ultimate example of a valuable spiritual lesson, and only God knows how long this has been going on for. It doesn't need over explaining, or excessive knowledge of the exact dates of when this and that began, it is right *now* that counts, because right now you can reach out and touch it, smell it, taste it, hear it, and then see it all miraculously return to an updated form. This present existence has twisted, turned and gone full circle from the day that God woke up with a sparkle in his eye and a grand plan in his hand.

7

Loose Screws, Tight Nuts and Lightening Bolts

"Nervous-breakdown" is a widely used term that despite being a polite way of describing somebody who is a complete fruitcake, or whose turn it is to wage war with the demons, is not one of my favourites because it can mean absolutely anything at all. Mismatched terminology can open the back door for a thousand different tongues to wag off a thousand different poorly informed case histories, tongues that would not have a clue or a notion about one single lotion, potion, pill or painkiller, but they suddenly become experts in the world of psychiatry. They may mean well but boy can they make it harder for the sufferer if they get it wrong, and they do. Jumping to conclusions is done only on dangerous ground, jump too hard and it will swallow you up.

The party of one could only last for so long. I knew that I would have to get out more often other than to just stock up on booze from the local off-license. The man who lived at the top of Box Lane was not a fool, but he often felt like one. He felt trapped, unable to pierce through with his real point of view about life and where it is going, always running into barriers that have held back the creative expression that bubbled away inside. Instead of taking a few plunges in the real world, he did it instead by drinking his way through a bottle, travelling to places in his mind that he longed to be. Wherever I roamed in my mind or with my feet, I still couldn't find someone who felt comfortable about pulling a cracker with me, and I can't say that I blame them. Re-establishing myself was not going to be a bed of roses, a vineyard perhaps but definitely no blooms. One warm summer evening my doorbell rang. I was in a good mood so I opened the door. A bad habit of mine for many years was to simply ignore the doorbell and pull the telephone cable from out of its socket, so that I could do my own thing without ant interference. Hiding away from friends and from life is not my true style, so I was more than happy to welcome with open arms the three people on the healthy side of my front door, John Carter, Glen Robinson and cuddly Christine who sadly past away in 2002. "Do you fancy coming down to the Bull with us, there's a karaoke on tonight if you're up for it?" It took two milliseconds for me to cave in and join them for the short walk down Vicarage Lane, through St. Lawrence's sweetly scented Churchyard, past the cottage on the left with the crooked chimney and in the beery rear entrance of the fully charged up Bull. The experience was nowhere near as painful as I had anticipated. When the correctly chosen time came to explain my absence from the local social scene, the news was greeted with interest and understanding. When Hill End Psychiatric Hospital was mentioned I was pleasantly relieved by their reactions. They weren't stupid. They had sensed what was going on because of my increasing manic behaviour leading up to my jaunt to Milan. "Ah yes, old Sam went there didn't he when he was very down after losing his wife, and my aunt Flo who had a drinking problem went there too, and what about that chap you were playing pool with the last time we saw you Keith, he turned out to be schizophrenic, though you would never have thought so would you," and so it went on. A selection of friends put across in a kind, well timed way that they regarded mental health as just another form of illness, and that it was in fact far more common than I had originally thought. There was no shame whatsoever in having to go over to St. Albans for a "rest," in fact it wasn't that different than spending time in a regular hospital. In this day and age with so much advancement and pressure, it is increasingly likely that more and more people will be shot in the head with some sort of mental problem. More and more advances are being made regarding the existing treatment of mental illness, which is a good thing because more and more people are cracking up, flipping their lids, or breaking down in helpless despair within an increasingly materialistic and violent society. Considerate reactions from John, Glen, and Christine helped me enormously to quite rightly hold my head up high in public again, without displaying any shame or spirit crushing embarrassment. They also helped me to dispel the stigma that I had needlessly attached to myself. Instead of being my own worst enemy, I had to learn how to become my own best friend, a transformation that doesn't happen overnight.

Good luck to the fortunate few who can travel through this life with a content mind that behaves itself and remains safely docked, but there is no escaping the fact that in an awful lot of cases it is those who have lived a little, been around the block a few more times than most, that are the most susceptible to a twinge or tweak of mental irritation. Too much baggage collected along the way needs to be lightened at some point, otherwise the handle will break and may never be retrieved. I did it on the steps of the *Stazione Centrale* in Milan, giving away my belongings and surrendering my soul for something that I knew I desperately needed, though not sure exactly what. Some of us have to blow ourselves apart in order to find out what we are made of and what we are capable of achieving, so it is very important to be surrounded by loyal human glue, that for some will create a reliable lifetime bond.

Somebody threw a long list of karaoke songs onto our beer slopped table, along with a white slip of paper. After a bit of cajoling I settled on *Hey Jude* by the Beatles. What a difference a pub full of jovial people and a belly full of beer makes. Over the coming years there were to be many late night after pub musical nights back at my maisonette. These homely musical moments were to come later, but tonight, just a few months on from my second depressing half hearted suicide effort, I would attempt for three whole minutes to be a small part of the evenings entertainment. It made a comfortable change to have a microphone attached to the end of a cable instead of my neck. Everything that I did could only be a plus from then on. I knew that there was no way in which I was going to die in front of everybody, so when my name was called out I flew up onto the tiny stage. I suddenly realised that I didn't like it one little bit, but I carried on. Sensing my discomfort half way through, the entire pub joined in with the "Na-Na-Na—Na-na-na-na, Na-na-na-na, Heyeh Jude" sections until the music faded. The pub goers carried on enjoying themselves, enjoying and applauding every effort made by everyone. God bless the lot of them. True to old form, I staggered home alone back through St. Lawrence's Churchyard and up Vicarage lane, where I grabbed a bottle of something strong and stayed up until three or four in the morning playing records. More than ever before I didn't want the party to stop, especially after what I had been through.

I didn't relish the thought of enduring another dull minute even though dull times are part of a human beings life. Squeezing out every last drop of pleasure was all that mattered. It was pointless trying to knock any sense into my thick skull at that time because I felt strongly and completely wrongly that I was now owed for all of the mental exertion and suffering that I had put in. It was a bit like demanding an unconditional payout from my bipolar insurance company. I thought that I had the right to play doubly hard, but wanting it all too soon is a recipe for disaster.

I needed a purpose to get my arse out of bed. It had to be something that was not going to be too taxing on the brain, so I took up the previous offer made on Anderson Ward from the depressed Berkhamsted publican George Lambert. George had lost his wife a few years earlier and had been taking it very hard, especially around the time of her birthday and their wedding anniversary. A couple of small decorating jobs came my way too, thanks to my association with the pub regulars. The problem with working cash in hand was that most of it was drunk in George's pub. My time there was spent replanting new beds in the adjacent walled garden, creating traditional hanging basket displays of cascading blooms, grass cutting, yacht varnishing the wooden benches and tables, and I even degreased and repainted the kitchen to satisfy the health inspectors that had been getting on George's back. George suggested that I might represent the Rising Sun pub in a sponsored mini marathon. The run was on behalf of the Marie Curie Cancer Relief Charity, an organisation that meant a lot to George because it was cancer that took his beloved wife. George supplied my baggy running shorts with the long slit up the sides, and a vest with *The Rising Sun* emblazoned across it. Although I had been exercising by walking from Bovingdon to Berkhamsted and back (an 11 mile round trip), I really wasn't conditioned to take on, yet alone complete the ten mile run. Had I been high I could probably have completed it in record time, backwards! This was to be a perfect example of running before I could jump, but I couldn't stop myself. The will was there to move my upper body forward, but my lower half struggled to keep up. The run was never meant to be taken seriously, but try telling that to the other participants. I began the run well but after a mile or so the other athletes flew past me, until I was left at the bottom of the pack. A cooling rain fell at Camelot R.U.F.C (the halfway mark), but I still wasn't happy. Nothing on this planet was going to prevent me from completing the course, even it did mean coming in last out of about 300 participants. Sure enough, I came in last with my dripping head held high with pride. We were all winners because we all did our little bit for the cancer charity. My folks cheered me on, knowing how much it would boost my confidence and self pride if I finished. As I crossed the finishing line I punched the wet sky and shouted, "*Yes!*" I felt proud of myself for gritting my teeth and attempting to do something so positive following such a traumatic period in my life. My joy and delight at being able to stick my middle finger defiantly up at depression was shared by my folks. Making them happy makes me happy, just as causing them unhappiness eats away at me like an incurable disease. Not a single one of the regulars from the Rising Sun pub bothered to cheer me on, not even George or one of his three sons. That hurt a little, but I wasn't about to sit back and let a bunch of snotty nosed old farts ruin my priceless moment. When I had changed into dry clothes we decided to pay the pub a visit. I wasted no time in approaching them one by one to collect my sponsorship money in full, and even then there were a pathetic few who were reluctant to honour their pledge. Too many people sit back and criticise those who do remarkable things for others, but I bet they won't find fault when they are dying of cancer, and are resigned to live out their final days in a hospice that is kept running with the help of monies raised by the rained on fun running human beings of Hertfordshire, Bedfordshire and Buckinghamshire.

Sometimes it has to take a serious problem or illness in order to discover who your true friends are. A few I lost and a few were gained, but that's life. In years gone by, mental illness has often been a taboo subject, despite some of the world's greatest minds proving themselves to be frustrated geniuses who were wrestling with a way to expel their important message. It wasn't all that long ago when we hid away our mentally ill in dark asylums. The aristocracy went to great lengths to cover up any madness that might be rearing its alternative head among their ranks. Very often the misused word *mental* conjures up the false image of somebody who is stupid, thick, backward, slow, a dunce or a moronic oaf. If you believe any of these descriptions then they are describing you. Childhood has to assimilate all of these descriptions and hopefully come up with a well reasoned impression, but cheap thoughtless use of such words brands the wrong impression on the uneducated brain, something that has got to be changed at home, at the workplace, and at especially at school. Better education at an early age about things such as mental health is extremely vital. Knowing for certain instead of always wondering as a child why a person is behaving in an offbeat way, will pave the way toward a better understanding and a greater tolerance within future generations. Harmless awareness can only contribute to the production of future harmony, productivity and trust. The word *mental* describes anything pertaining to the mind, pertaining to the intellect, so for starters it is true to say that we are all mental. It is essential that we choose the words that follow *mental* very carefully. Mental deficiency is a condition characterised by subnormal intelligence. A mental age is the degree of mental development or intelligence of an individual in comparison with the average intelligence of normal children at different ages. Mental healing is the healing of any ailment or disorder by mental concentration and suggestion; a complex task performed by a skilled hypnotist or psychotherapist. I have never come across anybody referring to mental arithmetic as being loony, crazy, mad or backward mathematics, have you? Or when asked to create a mental picture, you either describe your state of mind verbally or extend it through an art form. I defy anybody to describe the great British heavyweight boxer Mr. Frank Bruno, who knocked out 38 of his 45 opponents, as being a stupid mental case. This brave and exceptionally kind and generous man also suffers from bouts of manic depression. If you ever feel worried or uncomfortable about spending time, or being associated in one way or another with a fellow human being who has a form of mental illness, then there is no need to be, in fact why don't you try talking to them, and I am positive that you will come away feeling pleasantly surprised with what they had to say. You may also become a better rounded, more illuminated person for the painless experience. Try not to worry yourself over something that is never going to happen, instead just remember that quite often it is in fact all in *your* mind and *not* in theirs.

Danny has remained a good friend, and I still see him from time to time. Not long before it was demolished we used to enjoy driving over to Hill End Psychiatric Hospital to have a good look around the old place. Many of the same rubbery-faced patients wearing the same clothing and scrounging cigarettes were still to be found wandering over the leafy grounds or through the creamy green corridors that echoed memories happy and sad. Returning to the hospital was a safe and comforting experience for me, and I think also for the others. The good memories struck me more than the recent bad. The human mechanism has an ability to eliminate certain bad memories, to edit them out of one's mind, or at least throw a bucket of cold water over them fast to save oneself from repeating the performance too soon; similar to the initial disinterest after orgasm, although you know that later on you will be back for another helping. Even though my final days in the old building were terribly distressing, the better ones shone through, causing me to make many more trips to the far side of the old Roman City. We spent most of our time back on Anderson Ward conversing with some of the regulars whose whole life consisted of spells on the outside, followed by a routine readmission to the place where they were quite happy to be waited on hand and foot, and would proudly call their home. If I didn't have the support team or a place to go then who knows, I might have become one of them, but I doubt it very much because my pride would not have allowed the situation to stretch that far. I found that I was able to see for the first time the hospital and its occupants without being in a manic or a depressed state. Control over my own true emotions had come to settle. Self control throughout my entire life had always been a rare luxury. Mr. Sensible I was not, but I am working on it without wishing to put my true personality in jeopardy. The duty staff didn't seem to appreciate our visits, preferring instead that we try and put the more recent chapters of all our lives well and truly behind us, which is understandable. We chose to do it this way in order to make the separation less severe. We had friends that were still on the wards of Hill End Psychiatric Hospital, friends and acquaintances that none of us will ever forget. Ritchie Smith remained, still carrying a heavy weight from the second he woke to when he fell back into another disturbing sleep. I attempted to speak to him, but anxiety would descend out of nowhere like a mental meteorite.

Lisa, who still lived nearby, very kindly paid a visit to Ritchie nearly every day. On a personal level I felt that I owed him a favour for being so kind and generous, taking me under his wing so soon after my return from Milan, but nothing could be said or done to shift the weight that bore down on this undeserving hairy little man.

Taste the highs and nothing else ever compares. From then on life becomes a case of being grateful and thankful for what one has been given the second time round. The "real" world is wonderful in so many ways, but it is also despicable and mindless in others. A high, if it could be tamed and controlled to be productive, is a trillion times more attractive. Fear of the unknown always puts the mockers on things. It is no wonder that history always throws up human examples of what the naive and narrow minded look upon as approaching mad. Many of these earlier misunderstood examples were mentally unwell human souls who had the living daylights banged out of their busting heads when their hearts were still pounding a thousand drums. They are heard so much clearer now that the beating has stopped, and the sweet echoing of their combined minds reverberates up the dead ends of every ignoramus's finger pointing alley.

Lisa was offered a modern apartment of her own in Hemel Hempstead, so I helped her move a few sticks of furniture in and put up a couple of curtain rails. One day when I visited Lisa there was no answer at the door. A pungency filled the corridor air. By peering through her letterbox I could see a limp body sprawled over the couch. She had set fire to various pieces of furniture and then taken a prescribed pill too many. I smashed my way through the door and put the smouldering articles out. Plastic stinks something rotten when it is burning. The fire brigade were summoned by an elderly high-rise neighbour, but they were too late to witness the latest instalment from one of the all time attention seeking greats. Lisa later married a man with plenty of money after a whirlwind affair, how convenient and so romantic. She could be a Mother by now and living in a huge mansion, and good luck to her if she is. One thing is for sure, she will still be wearing black ski pants with a gaping hole in the crotch—way to go Lisa!

Manic Ian and his beloved mountain bike had also secured a lovely little brand new flat, built upon the site of Hemel Hempstead's old St. Paul's Hospital. None of us saw a great deal of Ian outside of Hill End. He valued his privacy and made no secret of the fact that he desperately needed to disassociate himself with all things relating to Hill End Psychiatric Hospital and of all the baggage, tags and labels that travel with it. He struggled to come to terms with the bipolar facts of his life, but time would eventually help him to find an inner peace. One must fully respect another person's personal wishes at times such as this, and try to understand the adjustments that they are working very hard to make. All of us need a select collection of cogs and a drop or two of high grade oil to help us get through this life as efficiently as possible, reducing the chances of a major mental failure. Ian, more than anybody I knew was determined not to lose his old face and his old standing in society, so he went about it in a way that may seem aggressive and ruthless, but it was the natural way for him to survive at that time. He would soon come to realise that he had nothing to be ashamed of, and nothing to hide, but for some people these things take time to figure out, and they have to be figured out by the person themselves. Young Jenny moved back to her mother and taxi driving stepfather's home in Hemel Hempstead for a short while, before moving into a small flat of her own. We all lived within a couple of miles of each other, forming a mini network in which to share good times and bad. I was delighted to learn in 2004 through her website that she has two little boys, a loving husband and a wonderful life—no thanks to that filthy scumbag of an old man, the sickening specimen of a parent that she had to endure, the monster whose creepy image appeared on my art therapy paper. Jenny's father may have been biological, but he was dirty as hell!

George Lambert's pub cleaner, Fat Pat The Chat (a rather rotund lady who would not stop talking), asked me if I would paint the exterior masonry and woodwork of her Berkhamsted house in lime green and white. It stood out like a gangrenous thumb, but that's what she wanted so that's what she got. The job went very well, adding confidence. This was followed by some unfinished decorating business at my sister's house. Barbara wanted me to ply my trade in her small entrance hallway and stairwell. The trouble was that instead of taking the occasional tea break, I took an alcohol break. I would steal a teeny drop from this bottle and a tiny slug out of that bottle, not bargaining for my sister's beady eye and healthy sense of smell. Slowly decreasing levels of a widespread assortment of beverages did not go unnoticed, but she resisted any sort of confrontation, allowing me the opportunity to come to my senses. I should not have been so selfish and put her in such an awkward position. I didn't actually intend to take advantage of Barbara and Roberta by using my recent problems as an excuse to get away with such behaviour, but I suppose that is exactly what I did end up doing. Using any kind of medical condition to prod a generous loved one into a no win corner is inexcusably nasty and unfair. Fortunately I saw the errors of my ways before Barbara, who is no pushover, lost her cool and severely reprimanded me. A problem drinker will think up and try every trick in their thick destructive book in order to steal and sneak a drink, or use manipulative measures so that they can be in an alcohol flowing environment as often as possible. You can never pull the wool over the eyes of those who know you the best, you will just be making an even bigger fool of yourself than you already are. It takes years of drunken practice to convince yourself that you have perfected the art of what is a self destructive deception, to believe that you have refined the lies that will eventually turn around and hit you in the face with the inevitable alcohol induced depression. Liquid despair always catches up and makes the consumer pay dearly for all of those well thought out excuses, laced with quadruple measures of deceit and liver rotting denial.

I have always been more than capable of handling my own personal and financial affairs without a hitch, but at that yo-yoing time in my life I did have a little difficulty. Fortunately there were enough people rallying around me to ensure that my life could move along as freely as possible. Never for one second did they let me sit back and lose my grip on realities spanner, an adjustable screw type that kept life's nuts and bolts nice and tight. Caring people are more willing to assist if the person requiring assistance helps themselves until they are up and running again. Certain sluggish people that I had the misfortune of meeting in Hill End Psychiatric Hospital exist solely on getting as much out of others while doing as little for themselves as they can get away with. I have had my belly full of cockroaches like that. They insult you behind your back when they don't get what they want. Only so much tolerance and benefit of the doubt is available, though I very much doubt that they care. For me, enough is enough. I have to preserve and nurture my existing sanity so that I can contribute something, give some hope back from deep within my heart. It would be nice if I could do my bit to help create a greater awareness and understanding of the world in which a bipolar affected human being, and all of those who have ever been touched or are yet to be touched by any strain of mental illness, inhabits. The effort that one puts in is usually rewarded somewhere down the wavy lifeline. I get so annoyed with the never-have-a-go slugs of this world who live unnecessarily in squalor, despite having a ton of money coming in, most of which is spent on take away junk food, tobacco and luxury cruises. There are still an unhygienic few who either miss life's plot without genuinely realising, or they simply couldn't give two hoots about anything, and in doing so they become a greater burden on so many other decent hard working people.

Immediate family cannot help from being over fussy and protective toward a loved one who may be going through a testing mental trial, despite having committed no serious crime. Although being subjected to constant scrutiny and assessment can be rather aggravating—always having my side of a conversation put under a highly powered microscope, leaving my straightforward and level headed words unrecognised—I had to come to terms with the situation, and keep reminding myself that it is a very small price to pay for everybody's peace of mind. It was up to me to try to understand what it must be like on their side of the fence, knowing that I could erupt at any God given moment, putting everybody in a real fix.

The autumn of 1991 was drawing to a close and my progress was very good. Booze still played a major part in my life. It was to blame for the ruination of a couple of days out at Lord's cricket ground, London, with my friend Harry, Aunt Pauline's partner. Actually I was the one to blame, not the booze, because I was the one who didn't behave responsibly and maturely. Alcohol is not the culprit, it is the addictive mentality of the consumer.

A trained eye could see that my brakes were once again failing to slow my speeding mind, a mind that had begun to stock up with illogical racing thoughts. Mania would be far too strong a word to describe how I felt at that time, but hyperactive bordering on hypomania would be a fair description. My reflexes, coordination and memory all worked super well, although they did occasionally race away, briefly leaving me in an anxious mental limbo that I somehow always managed to claw my way out of. No matter how often I lost and then retrieved my manic powers I always panicked slightly, wondering if I was stuck in that anxiety zone forever. It was very easy to forget the past times when the mania switch had been flicked off and then flicked straight back on again, always with a slightly higher wattage bulb burning brightly for all to see, and for some to beware.

Halfway up the ladder to psychiatric Heaven is an agreeable position to be in, which is exactly where I found myself stuck for a few weeks. I felt a definite affinity with the Grand Old Duke Of York and his 10,000 men. The Duke had an army, but I had only myself to rely upon on the way up. I did have an army to put the pieces back together again if I fell off my previously built wall, but that would be a completely unfair and totally selfish burden to bestow on another human being. Perhaps egghead Humpty and the Duke were manic-depressives, or at least their creators were, who knows? Half way up and relatively stable meant that I could lap up the cream until my heart was content, but it never was content, always greedily searching for the next exhilarating mind episode. Adaptation and adjustment was required in order to fool all of those around me into believing that I was actually being myself. Exactly what *myself* is supposed to be

I am not quite sure, but that's cool. It is so true, the world *is* a stage and we *are* all actors at some point in our lives, some of us are playing the leading roles and some of us as understudies, with an audience of billions. None of us arrived on this planet with a book of behavioural instructions carved in stone, did we? Perhaps the Bible fits that bill, but there are still numerous versions and meanings of the same scriptures. The ten commandments make perfect sense, but someone always invents a loophole so they can be conveniently broken for their own gain. Acceptable social behaviour varies so much from culture to culture, so who is right and who is wrong? Just so long as an individual doesn't hurt members of their own race as they pursue their fulfilling and productive existence on this planet, then I cannot see any problem in freeing oneself from the claws of acceptability and boldly conducting one's own tune in whatever key feels honest, right and proper. A colossal ingredient in being myself involves plenty of pretending to be someone other than myself, if that makes any sense. Adaptation is probably a better way of putting it, something we all have to do in order to deal with whatever life slings at us. I reckon that I must have become Oscar material as the years progressed. The world is not only a stage, it is also one huge circus in which bipolar affected people work the tightrope and trapeze, sometimes with a network of support in case of a slip up, and at other times without a soul to catch them as they come crashing down to earth.

Autumn through winter 1991 were very agreeable days for me indeed. My disguised inner manic buzz appeared to stay loyal, assisting me through every flawless day as I flashed around Hemel Hempstead in my Volkswagen. Lack of sleep, little food, too much booze and playing my vinyl LP's at full volume were the first tell tale signs that a long overdue sting was imminent, and that I was back on the rocky road, rapidly heading toward more irresponsible and unnecessary manic mayhem. I had grand plans dashing in and out of my mind. No sooner had I begun planning and playing in my head a wild idea, when another twist or turn took over. Everything looked bright and alive again. Auditory hallucinations persistently played the same melodies over and over in my head. *Amazing Grace* drove me up the wall and almost back into the attic. Of course I committed the cardinal sin of omitting my lithium carbonate from my daily schedule, instead flushing them down the toilet. I had also been taking anti-depressants up until then, but although I was on a low dosage they may still have contributed their little bit toward my manic cause. Even during a routine appointment with Dr. Hope I was somehow able to suppress my buoyancy as I surfed the electric waves. This I can assure you is no mean feat, as not much escaped Dr. Hope's finely meshed medical net. Out came the prescription pad. Next stop was the small pharmacy in Warner's End shopping centre, just around the corner from the surgery and a stones throw from the Top Of The World pub. When my prescription had been made up I made a beeline for the pub where I drank and smoked, doing all of the things that deep down I knew I shouldn't really be indulging in, not to that extent at least, and then like a complete imbecile I recklessly drove my car back to Bovingdon, where I am ashamed to say that I flushed all of the pills and all of the hard work put in by Dr. Hope, the pharmacist, and by myself straight down the toilet. How could I be so blinkered when it came to the serious issues of my health, and the responsibilities that go arm in arm with it? It just goes to show that I can be one hell of a stupid prick; an observation that I was reluctant to make when flying into orbit on the wings of a wild white horse. My stars kept shining brighter and brighter with every passing second, as I allowed myself to be marinated in mania. The manic addiction is like gravity, you can't pull away from it, and yet you are soaring further and further out of your mind, rocketing and rolling somewhere in Bonkersville. When high, or even half way high, everything can be twisted and moulded like Plasticine until it fits perfectly. If you are blessed with a vivid imagination to begin with you can quickly see through the haziness and generate a clearer image of what you believe to be really important. Have yourself a manic inspired laugh at everybody running around like worker ants, tooting their own horns, bossing each other about, worrying themselves over nothing, and tripping over the simple and uncomplicated basic clues and rules. Reality really is for people who lack a vivid imagination.

On numerous occasions a pretty female B.B.C newscaster took the full brunt of my lusty busty imagination. I had convinced myself again that I was actually transmitting live on air, causing her succulent buds to become erect, and for her to squirm with the throbbing and tingling between her firm thighs as she swivelled deep into her black clammy leather chair. She always had her mind blowing orgasms when footage of a journalists report from a far distant country came onto the screen. Primetime with a dangerously sexy slice of decent under the desk exposure, great! My TV license fee was suddenly worth every single penny. Was it the pulling power of Heaven's ninety-nine percent proof of perfection, or fear of hell's well oiled gates? Who cared. I kept knocking back the hard stuff even though I was rising faster than Jesus Christ tripping out on sildenafil citrate.

Early one morning I decided to switch on my television set. Channel 4 ran a live show called The Big-breakfast, and I decided to take part and hopefully win a popular daily competition called "More Tea Vicar?" The idea was to guess how many cups of tea there are in a picture, and whoever gets it spot on after being prompted up and down, wins. I succeeded in getting on the show, but was told to wait by my telephone in front of the television set until the competition began. I hadn't slept a wink all night, instead staying up listening to one track from a vinyl L.P, discarding it, then another and another, so that I ended up with even more black discs than before strewn across my living room carpet. Another favourite manic repetition of mine, which must have driven my poor neighbours completely crackers, was to play over and over again a video tape of the legendary rock group Queen performing live at Wembley Stadium, North London in 1986. This show was extra special because I sat in the special enclosure along with a dusting of stars: Mick Jagger, Twiggy, Errol Brown to name-drop a few. Now I was as high as a shimmering star, and out of my brains. I sat naked in my cold living room waiting for my turn. The reason I was naked was because I had taken to nude dancing; freedom of expression and movement, and all of that hippie type stuff with a kinky naturistic edge to it. The entire nation would soon hear my voice as I thought they should, and already could. Before the game got underway I regretfully announced to everybody listening that I was sitting in the nude; an announcement that is enough to put anybody off their sausage and egg and reach for the muesli instead. The host of the show announced to the United Kingdom that, "Perhaps you need specialist help my friend," followed up by the compulsory bellow of laughter from everyone inside the studio, including the crew. Suffice to say I was beaten by a young Irish lady who knew exactly how many cups of tea there were. When I was off air I asked the person from channel 4 television—whose job it was to be nice to sad fools like myself—if she could ask the winner if I could possibly share her fly drive trip for two to Boston, New England? "No," came the quick reply. The Irish were lucky again. Now, if I had been a wiser type of fool I would have drunk a few mugs of that tea instead of the stronger sauce, then I might have found myself on the way to a manic tea party in Boston. On second thoughts, the outcome of the TV game probably spared myself and the Bostonians quite a headache if the Milan experience was anything to go by. I didn't need to convince myself that it was a blessing in disguise, the sort of blessing that has somehow kept coming my way ever since that sunny September 1st afternoon in 1964 when I popped out for some independent air.

Many of us are often attacked by the fear of the unknown. Cloning is a scientific breakthrough that scares and disgusts me, as it is venturing *too* far into a dangerous and unnatural territory. One thing they will never be able to duplicate is the mentality of a person, or will they? I used to be frightened and unsure for many years of so many things, blaming myself for so much, taking on more weight than my shoulders could bear, until I finally crumbled and stumbled into a bar or hid away inside my maisonette. I have lost count of the times I have wandered around central London by myself, either in a great mood or in a low mood, sometimes in-between. Over the years I have met hundreds of new faces, but I could relax in the knowledge that I would probably never see them again, so I could say whatever I needed to say at the time without any comebacks. Oddly enough I often gravitated toward somebody, male or female, young and old, who had a similar psychiatric background, or somebody would gravitate toward me. Beautifully written transatlantic letters from Susan kept falling with a welcome regularity onto my doormat. I replied without fail. The volume of heartfelt concern and spot-on support that Susan offered me from across the pond left me overwhelmed. Our transatlantic closeness became closer with every cherished word and with every softly spoken breath. An awful lot of those early communications were regretfully repaid by telling white lies regarding my present mental state, and the administering of my level-headed medication, lithium. My ridiculous alcohol intake was another one of the lies. I learnt very quickly how, when and in what quantities to dish out the misleading devil within me, in order to placate those who were only showing a deep concern for my welfare. The generous people offering me this exceptionally high quality of kindness need not have bothered. If they knew exactly what I knew they probably wouldn't have done, except for my close family and a certain special lady from New York called Susan Steck Corradi. My little white lies slowly developed into huge black deceitful lies. Being slightly dishonest at first about my medication and alcohol intake was grossly unfair and terribly feeble, especially when she was always open and honest with me regarding every aspect of her own turbulent life. As our verbal and written relationship progressed, old wounds were sealed for good. Our enriched souls inspired a new love that developed more and more with each new day. We were like two ends of a fractured bone that kept growing new bone until they would meet in the middle, creating an even stronger bond than before, a bond that would be capable of absolutely anything. The trouble was that my mind was still plastered. Love was not the only thing to build up, as my telephone bills paid testament to. I have always been a hopeless liar, not such a bad thing as it prevents me from getting away with too much that would ultimately end in tears. Pangs of guilt shot through me every time I didn't tell Sue the truth, the whole truth and nothing but the truth. That Beauty from Bayside had a sharp conscience pricking intuition and a warm perception, not to mention all of those other womanly senses that men struggle to fathom out. The 25 year advantage over me very rarely let her down. Sue could read me like a pop-up picture book, even from the very early telephonic stages. She was the one that I needed, but being typical me, I had to do things in an unorthodox way. We have always wanted to live in the same country and be of a similar age, but we never dwell too much on a situation that for the time being is beyond our control. The age half of our relationship definitely can't be altered unless the human anti ageing gene is mastered by the genealogists. The other half remains a strong possibility.

Susan subtly chose her moments in a letter or during a transatlantic telephone chat to let the stories of her own experiences with manic depression flow. She described in detail the effect that her illness had upon the disintegration of her 25 year marriage to Henry. I would be all ears, paying a respectful attention to the personal sequence of events that she had endured, and was now sharing with little unknown me, showing faith and trust as she unloaded little by little the heaviness that she had been carrying alone for far too long inside her delicate head. As successful couples delight in doing, Sue and myself have since erased and eased each other's burdens, worries and doubts, about the past, present and future. We have been fortunate enough to have shared so many pleasurable experiences that this gift of life has to offer. It certainly does take two to tango. Sue and I still rock slightly on life's ocean but who doesn't? Ever since we lifted ourselves and came together we have been on a roll, sharing realistic goals of being happy, healthy, productive and content with what we have, giving what and when we can so long as it is not detrimental to our personal well-being. Susan will feature more prominently a little later on, providing us with a slightly different slant and a delicate feminine curve on the intricate world of bipolar affected disorder.

If it was not for Terrence Dawson—the manager of the Ember-Echoes youth soccer team, the man who through personal grief and adversity had the goodness and determination in him to take a team of 15 and 16 year old kids to New York in the Summer of 1981 for the Smithtown Kickers tournament—I would never have stayed as a guest with the then 40 year old Susan and her welcoming family. Terry became involved with the Echoes soon after he had lost his daughter outside The Cavendish School, Hemel Hempstead. She was hit by a speeding car when crossing the busy road.

Jack, Susan's only son, played a key role for the host team. Jack Corradi Ph.D. later chose to enter the field of scientific research, studying genealogy and extensively researching the possible causes, prevention and ground breaking treatments of a wide range of mental illnesses, especially mother inspired bipolar affective disorder. I wouldn't attempt to explain in detail the scientific stuff that takes place behind the scenes, so let the expertise of Jack and his colleagues write that book, and put together the medications for which we should all be eternally grateful. Today Jack is involved with bioinformatics (information science) for a large pharmaceutical company based in New England U.S.A. He is now happily married to the attractive, fun loving Angela. The pair of them are proud and protective parents to a pretty little chatterbox called Nicole, and also to independent Amy, for whom the entire family flew to China to adopt when she was just one priceless year old. Susan also has two adopted daughters. Dawn the eldest married the artistic Luciano, and her younger Sister Leigh married Lenny. Tragically, Dawn passed away at the beginning of 2005.

Most of our telephone conversations focused on a possible reunion either in England or in the United States of America. I played around for a few weeks with my distorted manic vision, trying to picture what it would be like if we actually did go ahead and meet. I was a little wary in case the image in my head—I don't mean looks—was dashed if we actually met. There was a comfortable feeling of having the safety of the slightly unknown, similar to developing a warmth toward a radio disc-jockey, but without the commitment that a proper friendship entails. We all know what often happens to many couples after they get married, they tend to lose some of the old magic. At least most married couples who have lost their wand had at least met each other in the flesh from the very beginning. Was this to be just another first that flutters away never to be seen again, or was this to be the beginning of something extra special that might continue to this day, so long as some slightly unconventional ingredients are stirred in with the conventional? Having had so much pain in the recent past, I didn't want anything to go wrong with a rushed meeting. This attitude was not something I wished to get into the habit of, otherwise I would end up as peculiar recluse. I had to do what my head and my heart insisted upon. This was all part of the rebuilding process, I knew that, but was Sue, who was snarled up in a divorce settlement, and myself attempting to climb a skyscraper before taking a preliminary walk through Central Park? In much the same way as selling a house or a car, we had to believe in ourselves and aim realistically high. In this way, a drop in expectations would pan out into a valuable and more than satisfactory start. Susan had the unenviable task of distinguishing between the many moods of me. Comparing moods in order to get a ballpark assessment takes time for the caring party, and it is a task made none the simpler when I was struggling to come to terms with my own true personality. Susan assured me that she had been levelled successfully by lithium carbonate and a few other mood stabilisers for well over a decade, and that any drop in mood that I may detect through her voice, or in her award winning high school handwriting, was only because of the stress thrown up by the ongoing divorce procedure. I was to take any of her abnormally sounding upbeat moments as natural elation at yet another legal step forward. The difference between being high and simply having a great day, along with getting out of the bed the wrong way and sliding into depression, will always continue to be a tough call for those close to the manic-depressive to make. It is tough enough for the B.P.A.D person themselves to register a genuine bipolar slip or lift, so how others can pick up on the signs so quickly is a truly amazing feat, requiring a strong familiarity and plenty of attentiveness. If in doubt then the manic-depressive must be allowed a free rein.

Too many delightful ups and desperate downs took place up until the summer of 1993. Sleepless lonely nights with my bottle and Bowie music became second unnatural nature to me. I had my telephone line to anyone in the world, but I still felt cut off and distanced. Susan remained on the scene, but neither of us had made the decisive move to see one another. A strong friendship was developing, but I didn't at that stage feel the need, nor did I particularly want to show much loyalty when it came to members of the opposite sex. My priority was to be sent back up into orbit just enough, so that I could be with friends with whom I could communicate on a similar level with. Self importance also needed to find it's big-headed way back into my life. I needed a higher level where the wavelength is the same for everyone, but only the few manic-depressives who have paid an exorbitant price to get there can tune in. I wanted it all without earning it in the regular way. Technological and scientific breakthroughs will bring the high cost paid by the likes of Susan and myself rapidly down, so that just like everything else happening the highs will be legally achievable and embraced by the golden old nonbelievers. Returning to an old favourite haunt is not always as sweet a trip as it was originally cracked up to be, we all know that. My effort to recapture the essence of 1990 was no exception.

In 1993 I could *not* be told a thing, and if I were I would probably go and do the opposite. Being too big for one's own boots only creates splits in a person's personality. It is the things that I did in order to get where I didn't really want or need to go that turned me into many different un-tethered characters, some of which I still secretly enjoy playing and some, usually the nasty one's, caused untold grief to the recipient. The Hemel Hempstead constabulary received a disturbing phone call in the early hours of one 1993 morning. My cousin Leona had introduced me to her friend Heather when I had visited Leona's daughter in Hemel Hospital following a meningitis scare. She was, unbeknown to me, dating various members of the local police force. Still a little high and still in constant communication with Susan, I arranged to spend an evening with Heather at her Hemel apartment. So off I went to her place with a large bottle of cheap white wine and a protective pack of three—how charming of me. We had a nice little half an hour chat before we got down to doing what we both knew I had been invited round to do. She came to my place a few days later and a repeat performance took place. The next time that I went to her apartment, this time uninvited, I noticed a police car parked outside. I saw right through her behind-closed-door excuses as I yelled through the letterbox, knowing full well that she was giving Policeman Plod some enjoyable leg-overtime. We had no agreement or loyalty to speak of, I just wish that she could have been honest with me. Honesty would have won the day. I left the scene and returned home from where I telephoned her. She admitted everything, which was fine because she hadn't done anything seriously wrong except tell a small lie. After her apology she snidely had to slip in the fact that her policeman friend just so happened to be in some sort of special police unit, and that he drove an extra fast car and carried a handgun under plain clothes. Paranoia immediately set in. I felt as if all the people I had wronged or upset were coming to get me, starting with a gun toting cop. My front door was soon barricaded, although that would never have stopped somebody who was armed and meant serious business. All lights were switched off. There I was, a little high and all alone, crouching below window height when moving about, or laying down in the darkness. I had done a good job of convincing myself that I was about to be shot in the head, weighted down with Hertfordshire pudding stone, and then thrown into the Grand Union Canal. Because my execution was carried out by a policeman, the sordid details would be covered up. What a ridiculous state to get in, but it felt so real. The condition of my mind had become so distorted that I was becoming my own prisoner, a free man barricaded in his own castle. Tangling myself up in knots is rather an odd behaviour for somebody who is repulsed at the thought of being shackled, yet there was I in my mind-stitched straightjacket waiting to be annihilated by an uninterested off duty policeman, who only cared about his next conquest and certainly not about a little pissed shit living in La-La land who goes by the name of Keith Alan Steadman. I telephoned Glen at his mothers house at 2 a.m. Despite the fact that he was probably cursing under his own beery breath, he calmly persuaded me to collect my paranoid packet of thoughts together and sling them into the rubbish bin where they belonged. I remained awake in my pitch black front room, tightly clutching my wooden Louisville-Slugger baseball bat that I had brought back from New York in 1981. More phone calls were made to Heather, and also to the police station, creating a big fuss over absolutely nothing at all. Never mind "burning my boats," as far as getting back with Heather was concerned I had well and truly burnt the whole damn armada.

A Universal menu waited patiently to be used and then recycled. Manipulating manic thoughts into an answer faster than an Internet search engine, and then squeezing the resulting gem into an attractive space between my ears, was a manic skill that returned with ease. There would be polished moments of shining inspiration, and new awakenings that would further excite and delight.

Remaining open minded to change, and having the guts to admit that you may have been wrong is healthy and refreshing. It is so stubborn and unattractive not to budge from one's views even if a watertight argument is presented by another party. Open mindedness in a person may be a contributory factor toward the regulation of a persons capability and potency within a manic or depressive episode. It makes perfect sense to me that if a mind is wide open then more information, good and bad, can fall into place or just as easily fall out. Play your cards right and you will find your key to a free spirited paradise on Planet Earth. You will then have to display a huge amount of dedication in order to make it fit the lock, that when opened will direct you and me into the next chapter of our heightened level of existence. One day there will be *no* keys and locks to access the magnificent mind. We will be free minded souls with a roaming spirit. Every nation will be welcoming without a passport, in fact there will not be separate nations, instead just one Planet Earth containing one race of human beings. This is my dream that I know will one day become reality. It *will* happen if you can believe that it will.

8

Gentle Touchdown

When a bipolar affected person is manic, it is often very tempting to use what you believe to be special powers in a crafty, manipulative way. More often than not I did exactly that, irrespective of the feelings of those around me. There were so many occasions when I achieved my own way without really knowing how I did it. I tested to breaking point the already exhausted patience and restraint exercised by my loyal, though emotionally battered corner. An inbuilt mechanism usually alerted me when my demanding and trying alter-ego was pushing those the closest to their finest limits of tolerance, when all it would have taken is an out of turn moment too many to make them crack, snap and even breakdown completely.

An awful lot of blind selfishness takes place when one is manic, despite believing that every oddball thing you do is for the benefit of mankind. All along you have had your head stuck halfway up your backside, and are totally incapable of finishing to any satisfactory degree every prophetic piece of philosophical claptrap that has been thought up and uttered to the imagined masses. There is an element of reality within that mind mayhem, something beyond genes and chemicals, but try telling that to the poor people who have had to contend with myself and similar minded manic-depressives who sing their "make them up as you come and go" tunes, and run around town trying to figure out how to get the most out of the little money that has been sensibly allocated by a sane member of the species. Try telling those caring folk who can still hear the haunting sound of our combined voices echoing through the creamy green corridors of Hill End, an indelible memory. Maybe a safe manic reality is a just a pipedream after all, but I cannot, and do *not* want to admit to it, such is its alluring pull.

This episode was of course part of the biggest manic test that I had ever had to contend with. This was being screened and seen, scene by scene behind my back by an immaculate network of future thoughts and historical shock waves, choreographed and hysterically staged by my outgoing mania. You were all in on this serious joke, but you had to remain incognito.

Picking germ ridden cigarette butts off the floor, then smoking them in full view of busy shoppers was perfectly alright. I believed without a shadow of doubt that they were all on my side, willing me to past the latest test. I cannot express how amazed and grateful I am for being tolerated so much during those pleasurably tough sessions when I would run from pillar to post like a lost lunatic who had just been sniffing crazy glue. The truth was that the majority of shoppers were probably looking at me in utter disgust, but I was seeing and interpreting everything to suit my latest manic requirements.

A good understanding of the beholder of any kind of affliction, mental or otherwise, helps the caring individual or group to address, cope and expel their own personal stresses instead of fighting the unknown battle, which could ultimately drag the caregiver under so much that they run the risk of drowning in the residue of the ill persons mental stew. God only knows what a nightmare of hellish proportions it must be for a depressed person who, through no fault of their own lifestyle or personality, have not got a single person apart from a qualified medical professional with whom they can pour out and share their most intimate feelings and temporarily dashed hopes and dreams with. I had helping hands placed in turn underneath my quivering chin, propping up my lowly spirit, keeping my ravaged head above boiling water when I felt desperately sunk, submerged in life's increasing pressure cooker. I was exceedingly fortunate.

The isolation of severe clinical depression, any depression in fact, has on too many occasions been the anchor tied so tightly around the defenceless wreck of a human neck with barbed wire, a chain of thorns or even a length of electrical cable, daring you to move in any direction in case even more unbearable damage is inflicted. Sadly there is an abundance of unheard screams and sodium tears that fade into nothingness, away to a place conveniently forgotten, a place where happiness never seems to notice the empty space where a priceless body of potential once stood with a squeaky clean vision, leaking energy that only needed a little direction and a friendly patch in the past to grow into the future, to be a part of what is now a world of technical revelations, that in some cases have been made null and void by man's inhumanity to others. Being polite and courteous to those we meet on the way up—we all have our own versions of life's up and downs, your up might be my down and vice versa—or in whatever direction life's journey maps out, is the true direction to head toward, not just because it is the done thing and makes the moment harmonious, but because one can never know for sure who you may be appreciative of on the way down.

Initially I had been prescribed 1200 mg of lithium carbonate salts, but that was reduced to 800mg because my routine blood test had showed that my level had been slightly too high. So I had gone from being too little lithium to too much and then back down a smidgen until I was on the level. I still felt high, not mouth foamingly so, but still a bit too buzzed up for my or for anybody else's own good. About one week before my blood tests, when feeling high, I would diligently down the prescribed amount of lithium in the hope that this would position me on the lithium equator.

I busied myself throughout most of the winter by taking on a variety of odd jobs, but nothing that was too far out of my depth, except for a slightly manic attempt at boarding out the attic for friends of my parents. This resulted in blowing the electrical wiring system to pieces, a hiccup remedied by an available neighbour who just so happened to be a retired electrician. I brought him out of retirement before realising my lonesome limitations, packing up my tools and leaving the scene. The job was left half finished. I had tackled loft tongue and groove boarding perfectly well before, but that incident had dented my confidence. These projects should really involve two people and a liability insurance policy, so in a way it taught me a valuable lesson.

All that I had to get around town with was my old drop handlebar pushbike, an infrequent public transport system better known as the No.52 bus, and not forgetting my experienced legs. Very kindly my dad added my name to his car insurance policy, which enabled me to share his car despite having the small inconvenience of occasionally having to drive him to and from his place of work. Dad worked as a quality control chief supervisor at Lucas Aerospace Ltd, now demolished. The Lucas site was very close to the Buncefield fuel depot that blew up toward the end of 2005, making the news headlines throughout the world. This was the very same area that I had walked back to from Hill End in 1990, not only once but twice. Car sharing worked extremely well for the pair of us, so long as I made doubly sure that I collected him on time and put some petrol in, otherwise that little luxury would have gone up in smoke just like the fuel depot. The generous nature of my family as a whole was rarely taken for granted. When a favour is done it is supposed to be done out of the goodness of one's heart and not with any ulterior motive. This golden rule applied among the people who were the closest to me, but no matter whether I was up, down or somewhere in the middle, I would always try my best to make a mental note of repayments in kind, or where appropriate in pounds sterling. I cannot stress enough just how important it is to keep one's sense of pride intact, and *not* to become too reliant on others. As soon as you begin taking advantage of another human being's generous nature, in whatever shape or form that may manifest itself, you will very quickly discover just how lonely this world of billions can become. Independence is the aim. Making any contribution, big or small, is one major part of the healing process, because standing on your own two feet will be so much easier with the least amount of independence taken away, and with the most amount added—simple maths once again!

Drinking was becoming more and more of a sneaky problem. I hated to be sneaky about it, but when addled with drink I invented a self satisfying reason for every ounce of deceit used. Being at a certain high level was often unsatisfactory, and so I craved an even higher existence. Too many times I abused the hard work of my loved ones and the friendly but serious advice given by my wonderful general practitioner Dr. Hope. I could sometimes last a week or two without drinking vast quantities of alcohol in one sitting. The condition of my skin and hair improved considerably when I abstained. Bowel movements were firmer. A healthier appetite returned. More money for better things remained in my pocket for longer. Staying clean of stimulants for a short burst of time proved that I could and should knuckle down and do more of the same. Unfortunately, short bursts were about as far as it ever went. It was as if I was kidding myself into an early grave. Everybody around me saw more than I thought, they sensed what was going on, but they needed to catch me in arm bending action. They certainly knew their onions, but I didn't wish to face the tissue issues of my liver. The fact that I was pretty much always penniless through binge drinking—rendering me useless when it came to being productive and earning some decent money—forced the stopper on what I am sure would have been a lethal cocktail had I been better off financially. More often than not these dry periods were half hearted affairs, strategically staged to show just what a clean living kind of guy I really was (not.) I knew in the back of my mind that it would be just a matter of time before I stepped back into my old methods of mass destruction. The only way an addictive person can beat their particular demon is if they truly want to, otherwise all the treatment and advice is completely wasted. Being manic in the early nineties, and having so many narrow escapes in my life up until that point made me believe, as I have already mentioned, that I was totally invincible. I believed that I could not and would not ever die, and on top of that the conviction resurfaced that some of us were the special chosen few in a higher position, and that the rest were running around playing catch-up. Holy smoke, things were cranking up again!

Mankind has always worked hard, and has always fought with contradiction over the meaning and direction of life. Using the stimulating by-products of an abnormal brain chemistry set to their full potential is possibly the only way in which to step through that big door, to where the answers to our universal existence and future lay. The bipolar expeditionist then takes a good look around before returning to base control, so that the reports for the medical profession can be prepared. A natural fully blown manic high under controlled conditions is the best form of transport to get to where the answers are, *not* through a truckload of whisky and cocaine. There are answers out there to questions we have yet to think of, and when those questions are answered our present limited understanding will seem insignificant, and our brains will suddenly become fully operational, making anything possible, instilling the realisation in everyone that evil will never work. What we need is a character such as Captain Crackpot, a super zero-hero who can save the world from self destruction. I am willing to take on the mission whenever a reliable grounded control is in position and ready to launch. It's a dirty job, but somebody out there has to go and do it.

Whenever I resumed boozing I always threw myself overboard in order to make up for lost time. I was the person who had to get in a pint and two double shots when the last order bell rang, forcing it down within the allocated drink up time. At the end of a pubby evening I was always standing. I could become rather mouthy after a few too many, but nothing that the other regulars couldn't handle. Hundreds of times have I gone the distance in a pub and then dashed back to my place for another bout with the heavyweights: Captain's Jack and Morgan, Vladivar, Beam, Walker, Napoleon and all of their mates. I took them all on and downed the lot in one fell slurp. Quite often I mixed it real bad, felling two or three in the same tumbler. Once I used a cranberry glass vase so that I didn't have to keep refilling my glass. The high maintenance that a habit of alcohol required was killing me in the pocket as well as mentally. I hardly ate, perhaps a slither of apple or a slice of dry toast to last me all day long, if that. Food became my last priority so that I could have a little more cash to blow away on the demon drink. Drinking in moderation and having the occasional blow-out on special occasions is not such a bad thing if it is done socially and responsibly. Good luck to all of those who do not need to sink a few in order to feel more at ease in social situations. Two or three squirts of alcoholic mouth oil (A.M.O) can help a normally placid person to open up and make a pretty accurate evaluation of a given situation, enabling them to latch onto and learn far more in one session about another person than they had ever done before. More often than not a slightly exaggerated version of their true character emerges, and those shy nagging points and opinions finally find the Dutch courage to be released into an unsuspecting world.

Lots of work was needed to self improve, but instead I kept finding any excuse to indulge in solo parties. If Sue called from the States I would celebrate, if the clock struck nine I would celebrate—hopeless! Being a relatively new manic-depressive meant that boozing was the last thing I should be partaking in, but I wouldn't have any of it and instead increased my intake instead of reducing it. Because of all the depressing days, weeks and months that I had spent curled up praying that I could die—when everybody else around held down decent jobs, bought fancy homes, got married, had kids and smiled a lot when I was going backwards—I figured that I had not so much of an excuse, but a valid reason to get hammered whenever and wherever I felt like it. Self pity is *not* a healthy nor attractive route to pursue, although I must admit that I had plenty of it in reserve to get whatever I needed. Sometimes I just felt like shouting out to the world, "Go screw yourself," but I can't go to those extremes because if I did, the men and women in white coats would be summoned. I did not look forward to this sort of future one little bit, a future where even if I farted in the wrong place and in front of the wrong people, the world around me would point their ill qualified fingers and announce that I am high, followed by a harsh section order issued by an authority who strips away human rights with the same blasé attitude as they dish out drugs. My philosophies, prophesies and theories remained sketchy and erasable depending on my manic level. Brainwaves were tidal. They came crashing down on top of me. When there was a ripple of calm I drunk and sunk until fully recharged with artificial happiness. Real happiness means that harmful stimulants are not required in order to have a nice day. This strongly suggests that despite my mania, I was not a happy camper.

So much for equal opportunities and discrimination within the workplace. Many employers stick by their word but in 1990 the Royal Mail certainly did not. My mood had begun to level out somewhat, despite still treating my medication with disdain. Even a sloshed high can become tiring after a while. It actually felt good to be back on a level pegging with everybody else, although I don't think that any of us are truly ever on the exact same wavelength, otherwise we would be nothing more than a bunch of boring robotic sheep. I sat through an extensive interview and aptitude test, that in my humble opinion went very well indeed, and I should know because I have successfully sat through many interviews and tests in my time that were a whole lot tougher. I knew right away that I had made the fateful faux-pas of being upfront and honest in my efforts to become a postman. Failing to omit from the medical questionnaire the truth about my recent dalliance with bipolar affective disorder certainly tipped the scales, but not in my favour. It didn't make an ounce of difference if five years ago I had won the postman World Championships. To them I was a taboo subject, painted from head to toe in a stinking stigma that stole from me a fair chance of rejoining and progressing productively within society. This was the very first time that I had come face to face with cold, hard hitting discrimination. I learned there and then what an unjust body blow really feels like. They were frightened of the unknown, preferring to employ the softer options and give me, the mental case, a harsh warning of what to expect in the wonderful future. Fortunately I was able to secure various other positions, in fact since my Cavendish Schooldays I have had more positions than the Karma Sutra, always starting at the bottom and working my way up until I succeed in blowing the situation again. I decided that for most of my future interviews I would stick to being honest and up front, although this brave approach usually warranted an extra grilling from the bosses. In early 2000, when I applied for and secured a position at Hemel Hempstead's General Hospital as a porter, I still had to experience the indignity of being evaluated by a psychiatrist before commencement. My male evaluator looked madder than most of the lovable nutty patients with whom I had been associated with in Hill End. Anybody out there who is thinking about, or has already applied for a fresh start in a new job, do *not* be palmed off by unsubstantial reasoning. You are not second class, you are a *first* class citizen in possession of a unique mind that deserves priority treatment. Prospective employers will eventually latch on to your unique qualities. If you know a trade then why not try to redevelop your skills and work for yourself? Apart from keeping the books there is no form filling in or prying interviews, and you will keep the profit instead of having a boss making a fortune from off your breaking back.

Courses on many subjects are now available to enrol in over the internet, or you could sign up for an interesting course at your local college, without any obligation to rush out on completion to put your newly discovered knowledge to work. To keep your hand in and your mind ticking over, why not consider doing some voluntary work that could also lead to future employment, because even if you did not decide to follow through with the type of voluntary work you chose, it shows a prospective employer that you haven't been sitting around on your fat arse all day long eating Mars bars and Indian takeaways.

Mentally ill or ex-mentally ill people have never had it as good as they do today. Awareness and acceptance of such needlessly difficult and occasionally challenging mental issues is improving right across the board. There is still a long way to go as far as social education is concerned, especially among the younger community. Ignorance of mental illness has got to stop right *now*, which is why further education is essential. Everybody would benefit if only fifteen minutes a week was subtly included within the school curriculum. If you went up to someone and asked them if they, or anybody they knew had been touched in some way by a mental problem and they replied, "No," I would call them a bloody liar. How many people have seen movies that were based upon manic depression or any other form of mental illness, and were not touched by the moving story? Is the word *mental* too set in one's mind as being crazy, thick and stupid? Therefore, should we have a few alternatives such as: Genetic-headache, thought-overloaded, chilled-out-mind, on-a-psychological-journey or unsteady-head?

Being told to look at the other person who is far worse off does not always make the intended difference. Should I be rejoicing because in the explosion I lost one arm but the person next to me lost two? The person dishing out this advice is usually always the person who was nowhere near the explosion in the first place, and has two upper limbs still firmly attached to a torso. I have often found that being made aware of someone who is far worse off than myself has prevented me from wallowing too deep in pointless self pity. Not only the inhabitants of your local leprosarium, but anything or anyone that is capable of removing a manic drunk or a depressed person's mind away from itself has to be sought. If that other wretched soul needs help then what better way of distancing yourself from your own imagined, magnified woes? When the pros and cons are weighed up I would have to say that I am a much richer, wiser and a more understanding pupil of life's innumerable lessons, it is just that because I am human I sometimes forget them when they are needed the most.

Occasionally I attended a weekly gathering of ex-Hillenders at St. Johns village hall in Boxmoor. Slouched and stiff on moth eaten armchairs were a raggedy collection of people who represented the broad spectrum of mental torment. The gathering only seemed to attract the fed up, and it didn't take long too discover why. All ages did their best to ensure that the miserable participants to begin with left feeling even worse, and that the rest of the funny-farmers were driven further insane. Most people with a mental disorder would be hard to detect in the street, as they have made an effort to conduct their lives in a perfectly normal fashion, but these, often through no fault of their own, were the sorry exceptions. Off-loading a bag full of mentally affected tales is fine in moderation, but after a while it made me feel so glum to be subjected to so much negativity and pessimism. Some of the more optimistic, less troubled of the huddle, brought with them an empty plastic carrier bag into which they tried to place the tiny snippets of a hopeful guiding map, along with a reluctant compass and a few titbits of diluted encouragement. Camaraderie and a positive support structure are vital factors for anyone, but they are even more crucial to those who are finding that the old familiar hills have turned into distant mountains, too steep to climb, let alone get a decent foothold on. Those old faithful boots had traipsed through the valleys of life so many times, they had lost their permanent grip on reality. A renewed soul was in order.

Even though I smoked, I found it such a relief to get back outside, away from the dense room. These weekly gatherings became terribly nauseating and depressing, so I decided to drastically cut the frequency of my visits to a big fat zero. Perhaps if more of an effort had been made by everybody else to make these cancer contracting sessions a little more upbeat, and with some kind of project to look forward to or places to visit, then it might have been different story. Nobody was prepared to take the initiative and do something to help themselves. I suggested a few things but all that I got back were a few grunts and moans. Planting a positive seed and then tending to it so that it grows into something sustainable, is imperative to the rehabilitation process. Life, to a depressed human being, then becomes worth getting out of the sack for in the mornings. Appreciation returns when the pleasurable gifts in life—gifts that have always been purposely placed in our path from day one—are reopened and acknowledged for the beauty and perfection that they possess. The many doorways to a Heavenly existence have to be opened by you and me in order for us to have the most appreciation, and to feel the greatest sense of independence and freedom of mind, body, spirit and soul.

I worked with two severe groups of irreparable mentally disabled cases in 1992, but that position of support worker did not last for as long as I would have liked, in fact the initial rewarding experience had an adverse affect toward my own mental state. The rejuvenation of my drinking to excess, brought on partly by the stresses of being in such company, didn't do me any immediate or long term favours. The irony is that so many people in the medical profession are driven to drink and tobacco, maybe even recreational drugs, in order to dampen the unnatural volume of personal stress that their profession inevitably brings. Whenever I see a nurse or doctor smoking I feel a little put out and shocked, but at the end of a long gruelling day they are human beings just like the rest of us, except that they deal with matters of life and death and get paid too little for their expertise. Knowing only too well how appalling any form of depression is, I would go out of my way to offer any kind of support and encouragement that I possibly could. Most probably you or someone you know who has suffered from depression feels exactly the same way. If I was put in a small imposing room with a dozen people, all of whom were moaning and whining though thoroughly capable of helping themselves but adamantly will not, I would go bananas and start screaming at them. A severely unwell person can be guided through the maze, but it is up to them to at least do the walking instead of being carried too far. Regaining self-esteem only happens under one's own steam.

My self-preservation was and still is a must, otherwise coming from so far back into a recognisable picture would have been in vain. I have come this far with the help of so many, but mostly through my own efforts. I am going to be wary from now on of the poisoned arrows that are flying around my mind like an eager beaver sperm waiting for the right opportunity to get inside the delicate egg, impatient to breed unplanned irrationality instead of a reasonably pure and innocent life. It is my responsibility to take my pills and thoroughly protect my position at all sensible and realistic costs, so as not to be an unfair burden on others who have their own priceless life to live.

As winter bit in hard, my handy little gardening number at the Rising Sun pub ended. In order to be prepared and alert for whatever was lurking for me around the next twist and turn I had to be mentally stable. There is nothing complicated or more obvious about that observation on paper, but at that particular time of thinking I was probably up to fifty percent manic and enjoying the best of both worlds. Any remaining fireworks had to be kept dry and preferably not removed from their box. A single triggered spark could erupt all of the good work, leaving an untold amount of damage in its wake. Foolishly, I figured that one blast at a time would do, but I did not account for the residual effect that this would have. Had I followed the official book of bipolar rules and held my cards closer to my chest, I would have been far better equipped to put on a more controlled display, but it is me that we are dealing with here remember. Theory is one thing, and putting a plan into action is quite another. I seemed to be attracting so many jolting sparks that I ran the serious risk of being electrocuted or internally combusting, or was it me alone who was creating so much friction that my modest fifty percent would flare up Milan style? There was always that one spark too many that could not be drowned, even when propped up against the bar or when bottling it down home alone. I felt like an underwater welding torch. Bars, jars, illegal cars—they were all filling the tank with disasters waiting to happen.

Alright, so a manic person does tend to go way over the top with their vivid imagination, but they have tasted what everybody else within all religions and society preaches about, and they are only trying to take it a step further. The problem with mania is the lack of tools to make these fantasies come true, leaving the manic person to play pretend games, to imagine a world of unbridled joy and peace. It is the basics that will send us to the place we all strive to be. If we mercurial, temperamental explorers have to be idiots in the eyes of some in order to play a tiny role in pushing us there, then so be it. I will stare the devil and his moronic followers in the face and never back down, because I know that even if they kill me I will still be alright. It hurt like hell to realise that valuable and comforting fact. I can put the pieces together now and see with greater clarity that a large part of my mania involved having to push myself to the utmost limits. I had to die alive and high in order to confirm my lifelong hunch.

Why do some of us put ourselves through so much self-destruction? Is it a subconscious penance for all of the things we did that were bad before we were born into this present life, for the crimes that occasionally flash back into our brain for no apparent reason? Dreams are funny things that say much more than we know. We conveniently forget most of what was so surreal in our sleep, otherwise we would blow our minds and freak out. Salvador Dali succeeded in capturing the most spectacular dreamy visions. I was fortunate enough to attend an exhibition of his on London's South bank, and I remember thinking to myself what it would be like if all of us were constantly manic and just as uniquely talented. There is more to everything than meets our blind eyes and limited brains, and that *more* really isn't all that complicated. Look too hard, too far and you will miss what's staring and laughing in your face. Why do some of us treat our body not as a temple but as a bus-stop to nowhere, not knowing when to hop on or off, preferring instead to spend a life watching the No.64 go by in a flash?

That entire winter was spent balancing my personality like a cirque du soleil high wire walker. When I was locked in the solitude of my Bovingdon abode I could really let my hair down, living out my extreme emotions and far out/in fantasies. There were many times when I painted my face with coloured pastels, and fiddled and farted around with my hair to achieve so many ludicrous styles, all of which had an added significance, a time and a place, ultimately bringing me a step closer to a person or emotion that was figuring strongly in my manic thought of the minute. Just as they had before my musty clothes suddenly became desirable and trendy, fitting my slender carcass so well, as if tailor made by a Jewish illusionist. My old television set remained on most of the time. I only had the four main channels: BBC.1, BBC.2, ITV.1 and Channel 4. God only knows what I would have made of cable television had it been available to me then. Controlling the set with my manic mind was great fun at the time, but it is really a sad indication of my deteriorating mental state. I still remain firm that manic depression/bipolar affective disorder is the sort of illness (or condition) that messes up, due to the unbalanced chemistry of the brain, the forced reality that the sufferer has grown accustomed to throughout their previous block of life, but at the same time introduces the sufferer to a fresh new world that they were already sensing and sniffing out since the day that they were born. We all sense and sniff similarly; it is our psychogenesis that reveals vital clues and secrets that can explain why and how our paths and ways are so different. In my case, awaiting me were a muddled huddle of spiritually uplifting adventures, whereas the next person is just as ecstatically happy, but doesn't scream off into orbit in quite the same way. Each individual has there own party piece, a manic speciality that sets them apart, the big mouth with a plan to save the universe just like Superman or Flash Gordon, the prolific deep thinking artist who has difficulty converting ideas into music or pictures fast enough, or the self proclaimed sex God with delinquent delusions of swollen rampant grandeur. The depression side wipes out the entire spiritual side of a manic episode, but it does serve to display by the severity and depth, just how high the manic human being had clambered in the first place. A *manic* depression often hits home first, followed by euphoria in similar proportion to the depression. In my particular case the melancholia—an Ancient Greek word meaning "black"(*melas*), and "bile"(*chole*)—always came on as a late act to support the manic highs. The highs and the lows can just as easily *not* be in proportion to each other, nor in proportion to any given trigger that might have set the bipolar ball rolling out of control in the first place.

My music spoke to me more than ever before, or did I play the songs purposely so that they would deliver the desired effect? Every single word sung was intended for me and about me, offering and occasionally insisting that I take the advice on how to conduct myself in accordance to my privileged manic status. Often, I just sat quietly with my drink of the day and a cigarette by my side, contemplating the whole manic situation. Who was I? Where was I really born? Who really are X, Y and Z? Did I have a previous life? At one point, as I touched upon earlier, I even thought that I was the only person on Planet Earth with a personality split of billions! That particular manic belief stuck with nearly every manic episode that I have had up until the present day. I often thought that my brown eyes provided the only canvas that viewers could see through their television sets. The viewers became me, creating a feedback effect like an electric guitar and amplifier, but when I turned to see myself the vision had been cut. Strategically placed mirrors didn't help much either. Talk about being wrapped up in oneself. Being manic is being larger than life, it is fancying yourself far too much for the comfort of everyone concerned, it is exploring the unexplored recesses of one's mind, and it is finding the part of that mind that sees and suggests fresh appeal in rotten fruit, picking out the old pips among the maggots, replanting new seeds of thought and then selling the fresh produce to a waiting world.

My two budgerigars, Boycie (blue) and Marlene (yellow), were my feathered angels. They became flying steadicams when I had been high, and flying crap bombers when I was low. The poor things spent many an evening locked out of their prison cell, wishing that they could get back in because I delighted in pinging elastic bands at them. I missed most of the time, so there is no need to call the Royal Society For The Protection Of Animals. One day Boycie flew out of my living room window never to be seen again, except for his photograph in the local newspaper. His young captor kept him, and I gave Marlene and the cage to an elderly neighbour. I can't blame him for escaping from me and my multitude of moods.

Hundreds of letters were written to Smithtown Susie. Photographs were exchanged as well, not only of ourselves throughout various stages of our lives but also of our respective families, friends and contrasting surroundings. More than a decade had passed since Susan's last manic-depressive episode. Her husband Henry had struggled to deal with her condition, but through no fault of his own he found it very difficult to come to terms with. Each of us have our strengths and weaknesses, but living with someone who is prone to mood swings can occasionally tip the scales, such is life. Around this time, Susan was trying desperately to keep her emotional head above water. To counteract the upset of divorce proceedings she threw herself headfirst into a new venture. She decided that she would set up from scratch and then run a children's apparel store in Saint James, Long Island, NY. Sue had always worked hard for others in and around New York City, as well as bringing up her three children. Now, instead of working for the rich men and women, she decided to embark upon a project that would instil in her a feeling of self worth that had been sadly absent in recent years. The shop was to be called "Kids Wear It's At." Susan did almost everything except lay the child friendly carpets and install the jazzy lighting. She made many trips into Midwest Manhattan to the Javitt's Convention Centre where she would have a ball purchasing stock for the new shop. A catchy advertising jingle was expensively produced that enjoyed plenty of primetime on Long Island's Magic FM radio. Mrs. Corradi even went to the trouble of sending me a tape cassette of the jingle, along with a snazzy black sweatshirt with the Magic FM logo emblazoned across the front. Kids Wear It's At came to life in the summer of 1993, and it was a much needed breath of fresh air for the little lady. Before the grand opening it had been arranged that Susan would visit England for a two week vacation. The plans for this trip were made rather too hurriedly, and also at the same time as my manic enthusiasm began facing up to a slow painful puncture. The show had to go on. A whole picnic of places to go and people to see had been laid out on the two week timetable, but already I was dreading that May day when I had to attend that multilingual hive of activity, otherwise known as London's Heathrow

Airport. Terminal 4 is where I would meet her for the first time since the scorching New York summer of 1981. Sharp sounding, fun filled days were now becoming blurred, and my crystal sharp thinking lost its edge again, becoming dull and uncertain. My mood sunk and then sunk some more. As if I needed to offer any more proof of how idiotic I could be in a downward crisis, I turned even more heavily to drink. I was living in the blind hope that alcohol and roll-ups would blot out all of my misplaced fears. The booze just multiplied and magnified my overblown fears of life and its entire contents. The tortuous claws of depression mercilessly clamped themselves around my entire being. Slowly the inevitable paralysis of my mind set in hard like mental rigor-mortis, causing everything that I treasured to lose its sweet taste and soft comforting texture. "I know," I thought, "wouldn't it be a jolly good idea if I start taking my lithium again, only this time on a regular basis." Now I knew just how foolish I had been when I was becoming manic to have given up on the medication, that had up until then been successfully balancing out my life. Why I dismounted my winning horse—let us call the filly "Madame Lithium"—I will never know. Stability had been presented to me, but I just hated to remain within the confines of that sane stable when my mania riddled friend kept calling me out to play in the green meadow. Mister head-case Steadman was far from ready.

In 1949 John Cade, an Australian scientist discovered that lithium carbonate could be used as a successful treatment of manic depressive psychosis. It took a while to get going due to the fear that table salt substitutes might lead to toxicity or even death. Later in the 1950's U.S hospitals began experimenting with lithium carbonate on their patients. Reports started to appear in the mid 60's regarding the effectiveness of lithium, but it wasn't until 1970 that the U.S. Food And Drug Administration approved its use. *Never* stop taking lithium just because you feel good, for it is this light alkali metal that stabilises and maintains a natural level of well being by enhancing the uptake of norepinephrine and serotonin into the synaptosomes. Ever since my time in Hill End Psychiatric Hospital I have taken 1200, 1000, and now 800mg of sustained release tablets. Fortunately for me I have had no toxic side effects from lithium, but there are 10,000 reported cases of it per year in the United States alone. The CNS (central nervous system) is affected the most. The common signs of toxicity to watch out for are: Nausea and vomiting, diarrhoea, weakness and fatigue, lethargy and confusion, tremor, seizure, vertigo and tinnitus. Sodium polystyrene sulphate, sodium bicarbonate and a polyethylene glycol bowel preparation, are all used to enhance the lithium binding and renal elimination process, necessary to prevent serious illness and even fatality due to lithium toxicity—if this doesn't explain why regular blood level tests are so important then nothing will.

We must all do exactly what the good doctor says in order to prevent ourselves from falling flat on our faces into every nightmare we ever had. At the first sign of a manic-depressive episode whether it be up or down, the person concerned should make an appointment with their doctor, or if stubbornness sets in as it had done with me, especially on the way up, then the nearest person should, if they truly care, be bold enough to make the first medical move for the affected person, even if that person spews out a torrent of verbal obscenities at the loving suggestion, and believe me, more often than not they will. It is when the pointed sticks and sharp stones start flying that a seriously professional force full of medical expertise needs to be urgently deployed.

It is during those early days of departure into a depression that you would imagine help of any kind would be embraced with open arms. Curiously, I did my uneven best to hide away from what felt to me like a backstabbing, double-crossing world. My telephone remained unanswered, unless it rang at a prearranged time when I knew for certain that it would be Susan on the other end. I kept the front door closed, ignoring bell ringers and knockers, and I gave up frequenting the local public houses of Bovingdon Village. I still wanted at that stage to do so much out in the open, in public, but I was too scared of doing it in case I made mistakes and was criticised. I suppose I had a fear of something happening that would make me even more frightened. When feeling down it was so hard to believe that the opposite might happen and that something might take place that will help alleviate my imaginary fears. Distancing myself from family and friends was not the brightest thing to do, because it just made me feel lousier and lousier until I was a mush of words and a splintered wreck of nerves, a distant faded shadow of my former happy go lucky self. My conspicuous absenteeism from every previous scene did not go unnoticed. My folks and friends are *not* fools, soon sensing that something bad was up, or should I say they sensed that somebody very close to their hearts was down, though *never* out!

Susan being typically Susan, and pretty typical of most females, soon picked up the tone of my hard to disguise voice and tried to fill the silences with soothing words, softly spoken in a Queens County, NY accent. It didn't take long before she was on my battered case, vowing that together we could and would close it. All of this giving, despite having so much already to contend with at her end is typical of Susan, and I believe that there are too many people out there who take her goodness for granted without ever giving anything back, apart from more of their self inflicted grief. Even though she didn't know them, I still pleaded with Susan not to tell my folks about this latest deflation. She reluctantly agreed, but only under a few concerned conditions; "Make sure you go and see your doctor and get some anti-depressants or something before you sink too far, and don't forget to tell him the truth, tell him everything you told me, write it down so you don't forget."

Like a complete idiot I had once again flushed my prescribed anti-depressants down the toilet. Regrets jumped out of every situation. There wasn't any time to dwell upon what I should or should not have done, it was now that mattered. Nervously, I promptly made my promised appointment with my General Practitioner, Dr. Hope. Before the surgery hours had expired I was squeezed in as a VIP (very ill person) who was more than capable of being a threat to himself. Anti-depressants were prescribed by Dr. Hope, along with firm instructions to get back in touch with him whenever I felt the need. Panic took a deeper root as the little daggers prodded away, reminding me with each piercing push of gut churning anxiety of the putrid sewer into which I had been sucked before. I had never allowed my mental mortar to dry out fully, and now the brewing storm had hit home hard, but alas, this one had ignored the teacup. Playing host to a forthcoming depression—having already had one rotten enough to convince me that suicide was the only pleasurable release on offer—is something to dread with an added passion. My main concern, apart from a possible reunion with the polar devil, was the looming visit of my newfound angel, Susan. Of all the times there are to visit and we chose the time when I would be boringly downbeat and depressed. Would this get together become a blessing in disguise? "Why did she have to go and pick a time like this to clip on her long haul wings?," I thought so self absorbingly. It would turn out to be perfect timing.

Why had I foolishly neglected myself when things seemed to be getting so good again? "The whole trip has got to be a no-go," I thought with a renewed negativity. I never considered at this stage in the proceedings that although the ingredients of my present life were being mixed up and blended to a pulp, I would one day be feasting on angel cake—now that's a thought to sink your teeth into! In 1993 I was not aware of that special lady's dogged determination and sheer gritty spirit when it comes to getting done what needs doing, even if that objective is pleasant or sad, good or bad. This time we were in the sad category. Taking into account her own vulnerabilities and present circumstances, Susan's love driven flight took on an extra special significance.

I pleaded to Sue to change her plans as far as accommodation was concerned, as I couldn't bear the pressure of having her staying at my private little hellhole in Bovingdon, knowing that I would then be on depressing display 24/7. Sue was due to touchdown on an early May day at London's Heathrow Airport to commence in the flesh what would become a beautiful long lasting relationship.

I admit, it may not be your average run of the mill situation because of the age difference and so much salty water in-between, but we are more than happy and contented, and as far as we are concerned that's all that counts. On a good day, playing the host with the most and giving my all to Susan would be such a joy, a privilege, an experience to be cherished. On a good day, I would proudly show her around the London sights, and also introduce her to my family and a small circle of friends. This daunting feeling could not be helped, so I began to wish that something harmless would occur that might prevent her from making the transatlantic trip, letting me off the hook. I did not have the heart to tell her the truth. I worried that if she knew what I honestly felt about the trip, she would be extremely upset and hurt, thus creating a guilty party that I knew I could not bear to be the host of. How could I disappoint her? She already had an unfair amount of her own problems to put right in America, plus she needed a break from the divorce chaos in order to protect her own sanity. Would two negatives together produce a positive? Sue soon figured out my doubts and concerns, as she had of course been there before. She put herself in my shoes and flew across the Atlantic Ocean to show and share with me her deep faith, understanding and unconditional love. Sue never once felt the need to press me into revealing any nitty-gritty details, nor did she judge me because the underlying yucky feeling of depression is universally felt, and Susan the empathic Queen from Queens had tuned in and could feel my pain. The fear of the pain awaiting around every greased corner pushed me to fight my way forward. Disturbing flashbacks of agonising pasts spurred us on and geed us both up. Nothing, and I mean nothing was going to deter this wondrous woman from her mission, thank God!

Gaining a happy balance is something that I have struggled with throughout my entire life. It is understandable that so many acquaintances simply cannot and do not deserve to take my nonsensical behaviour for too long, so either I leave or I am nudged unapologetically to one side. When I was an eleven to sixteen year old pupil attending the Cavendish Secondary School, there were an awful lot of hot and cold moments. Now I can clearly pick out blocks of time, an entire term or a single afternoon, into which I submerged myself because of insecure think-ing, when really I had nothing to worry about at all. I worried that I wouldn't be popular enough to be included in boyish group pranks or athletic enough to be a member of the sports teams, not to mention my academic performances. The class clown usually acts as such in the hope that their performance will win over their fellow pupils. Schoolwork suffers as a consequence and most of the other pupils, who may well have laughed the loudest and egged the clown on, secretly think that you are a complete dickhead. A form of jealousy even surfaced when I was at my worst. If a good friend decided to sit with somebody else in class for a change I would feel a little jealous, as well as imagining a completely false situation in which nobody cared to include me in anything anymore. Now I am aware that it was only a form of insecurity and a lack of confidence that made me feel that way. My schoolwork suffered considerably during these blips, but when I pulled myself together I managed to excel in all subjects, making up for the lost schooldays that were duly attended, but without any attention. Worrying about something that may not even happen is a crippling condition, culminating in a phobic fear of not wanting to touch or attempt to do anything in case it breaks or fails. When these fears are stirred into such a frenzy, nervous mistakes are more likely to happen, causing the whole experience to appear ten times worse than it really is. All of my worst fears *never* came true because although we had our usual fallouts, my school friends were too closely knit and far too loyal too ignore a fellow pupil. My companions from Cavendish stuck up for each other, and in doing so they created a trustworthy class of camaraderie and companionship—I love them all!

Enemy No.1 was me, unpredictable and mildly dangerous, existing in an imaginary fish bowl of unfounded fear. The amount of precious childhood time that I had wasted by secretly fretting over nothing must account for at least a quarter of my entire schooling from the tender age of five. When I felt up and alive again I sometimes managed to be one of the leaders, an instigator, attempting to organise activities such as an evenings ice skating at Richmond's rink in London. I would have to say that on those better days I was rather outgoing and inventive. Popular? I think so, though not an out and out attention seeker, just a turned on kid who was simply trying to recapture and make up for his turned off days. Today, I wage a more subdued war with my mood swings, not so much with fully blown mania and depression, but with the light hearted sensations of being bubbly, the life and soul of the party, followed a week later by feeling a little withdrawn, still an attendee at the party but pooping all night long. We have all been there, but not all of you have experienced the rapidity and severity of change that some of us have to put up with. My minor mood swings are not particularly rapid, nor are they a great deal different from the average person's mood, but they are still simmering with no sign in sight of evaporation. Not only that, these unannounced changes strike at the most inappropriate of places and at the most inopportune of times, meaning that on Friday a party invite is received and agreed, but when Saturday evening comes I might have to scrape the barrel again for another lame excuse so that I can sit at home alone with a bottle and compact disc, getting rat-arsed to rock—*not* recommended. It is far better to be miserable in the company of a familiar face, because they may become the crow bar that prizes open your mind's safe, releasing true happiness and dispersing the depression—*highly* recommended!

Two weeks remained until Susan touched down on English soil. Bottle after bottle, can after can of cheap but definitely not cheerful alcohol found its way into my foodless stomach and around my senseless brain. Hardly a potato peel or a slick of baked beans were to be found in my plastic dustbin, instead it was filling up with the empty sounds of glass and tin. My diet had become so poor, lacking the essential vitamins and minerals. My facial skin became blotchy, my entire body ached and my weight had dipped, although not as much as when I was running wild through the sleek streets of Milan. One evening when I was drunk, I dared myself to face the world again so that I could stock up on even more booze. This time I decided to cycle along Vicarage Lane in the dark, turning right at St. Lawrence Church until I came to the general store in the High Street. There were no lights on my old boneshaker but I wasn't deterred. The lane was so dark it was almost impossible to see where I was going. So far so good, but the return leg was not quite as straightforward. With a heavy backpack loaded with strong fluid, I slowly wobbled my way back along the same route. I had nearly made it home when I miscalculated the no-mans land that separated the hard lane from a small soft ditch. Arse over tit I flew, scratching myself to ribbons in the overgrown bushes. My immediate concern was not about any possible broken bones or nasty cuts, but whether or not my liquor supply had survived the tumble. Fortunately, depending on how one looks at it, neither the booze nor myself came to any serious harm. I knew that by pickling myself now, I stood a bloody good chance of later creating a downer of greater intensity than the initial pleasure rush, soon to be supplied to my hideaway head. When 10 p.m. arrived, a feeling of extra safety and distance from undesirable human contact settled in. The daunting visit of Susan ate away chunks of my time, not spent in planning interesting fun things for us to do, but in worrying myself sick. Could I live up to the tall order of providing adequate hospitality?

Putting a stopper on the bottle and not on the proceedings would have made a sensible start, but my commonsense had vanished down the toilet. Somehow I forced myself to charge up in readiness to play host to Susan. I did try. I tried until I cried, leaving me feeling a little better for putting in the effort. Despite many a lengthy transatlantic conversation, you have to remember that this was to be our first coming together since the soccer scorcher of July/August 1981. Susan must have also been feeling the nerves as she made her determined solo journey from Smithtown, Long Island, New York, to John F. Kennedy International Airport, and then on to London's Heathrow Airport. This extraordinary lady had more bottle and spirit than I had ever downed and discarded in my entire alcoholic binging career. This special woman sure had an abundance of all things beautiful and bright!

Dressed from head to toe in black and reeking of beer and tobacco due to staying up most of the night fretting, I patiently waited alongside my father in the Terminal 4 arrivals hall for Sue to emerge. This was my first time back at the world's greatest airport since my manic trip to Milan when I was in search of Julie, little Tommy and a brand new world. Now somebody was flying to me, this time somebody real with a true purpose. She had taken a British Airways night flight, 5 hours into the future. When she came into the arrivals hall it was tricky to get a full view of her, because the mountain of flowery luggage that she was carting hid her petite 5ft 3" frame. She carried a big golden grin from ear to ear that gently caressed our butterfly collection. Dressed in a yellow polka dot dress and propped up on snow white heels, Sue looked the epitome of femininity, much younger than her sprightly 53 years might suggest. She had arrived.

The usual "How was the flight and the food?" questions were asked as the three of us made our way back to the multi-storey car park. I sat in the back of the car next to Sue as we made our way clockwise around the M.25 motorway toward Hemel Hempstead. Susan had pre-booked a room at the Black Lion Inn, in St. Albans, but first we headed for Gadebridge to pick up Mother. The usual cup of tea and a biscuit session took place before we all piled into the car and headed for St. Albans. Drinks were had at the Inn, and arrangements made for the following morning. The offer for Sue to stay at my folks house was understandably declined, besides at the Inn she would be able to indulge in her favourite vodka tonic tipple whenever she felt the inclination. I would often inconsiderately leave Susan at the Black Lion early in the evening to fend for herself, so that I could return to Bovingdon for an early night and a lonely drink. Sue looked after herself despite some obvious attention from curious pub regulars. The fourteen days were a struggle, but Sue understood my unsocial ways and allowed for it without forcing home any issues. Every tense evening I returned home and drank myself into a daze, unready to fight another day of sightseeing and conversation. More and more guilt set in because I wasn't being as accommodating as I would have liked. The hospitality shown by the Corradi crew back in 1981 was phenomenal, but all it did for me in 1993 was to drag me further into the shameful dirt.

Lacking wheels of my own, apart from my beaten up old bike, I had to catch the early No.52 bus into Hemel Hempstead town centre. From the town centre bus station I hopped aboard another bus, filled to bursting with rowdy school-boys who blew gum bubbles, farted smelly farts, and burped ever so loudly in the hope that they may impress the schoolgirls of a similar age, most of whom were dressed and made-up like miniature tarts, yet under the illusion that they looked so adorable and mature. Normally I enjoy being among a rabble of lively children, but on that first full day with Sue it was all becoming a bit of an unneeded nightmare. My drop zone was only a short walk from the Black Lion Inn. I seriously considered staying onboard the bus so that I could make a cowardly return journey. On arrival I was full of trepidation, but a powerful determination and an inbuilt fighting spirit helped to carry me off that noisy bus and onto the sunny street. With weak legs trembling and heart double pumping, I slowly began to walk toward the Black Lion Inn. My stomach rumbled nervously for the much needed food that I could not face. A beaming Susan stood in the car park. She wore blue jeans and a turquoise short sleeved blouse. Light and tight summery numbers and a countless supply of beautiful warm smiles appeared to be Susan's trademark.

Expectant sunshine greeted us on that first morning, producing a lively light that forced positive energy out of me for a change, energy that I reasoned would make her believe I was enthusiastic about the whole fortnight affair. Susan is no mug though. "Have you eaten?," Sue asked, "Oh Yes," I lied hopelessly. "Guinness is food surely?," I thought with an alcoholic brain, but it was still only 9 a.m., not that the time of day would have made any difference to me had I been left to my own devices. Being the soft touch that I am, Susan prized the truth out of me in record time. In a way I was rather pleased that she did suss me out, although I was rather annoyed at my feeble attempt at a lie that I knew would only make me feel guilty later. "Come inside and help me finish off my breakfast, they have given me *so* much," insisted Sue, who knew only too well from her own valuable experiences that food and sleep are the vital factors of any natural body and mind repair process. We had touched upon a variety of topics over the telephone, some were light and others heavy, but when we were face to face a whole new dimension emerged. Our conversation over the breakfast table was earthy and open, covering her past and present relationships, health problems, fun times with friends and family, travel, her new children's apparel retail venture and so on. She took me briefly away from my misery, but when my mind flashed back to the same old nagging demons it hurt even more than before. Sue listened intently to my tongue-tied stories, trying to make me feel relaxed even though it felt as if I was addressing millions. Her energetic never lay down and die attitude shone through stunningly, accurately shooting me in the heart and soul with trigger happy sunrays, moonbeams and golden hope. This special woman was good news indeed, because it was she who managed to put me at more ease over that pub breakfast table than I had been throughout the past month, except for when I was totally drunk, and even then the anxiety vultures would swoop down and rip out that short lived spell of topped up of relief.

Sue wasted no time in extinguishing my flaming concern that I was nothing but a burden, a wart on the obese backside of society. For a few fleeting moments she had been victorious in the alleviation of some of my lingering anxieties, but then I would attack myself again. Sue had a huge scrapbook of her own problems to be concerned about, and so far it had all been about me. On the other hand she did want to get away from all of her own problems, and she did know what to expect with me. Focusing on another can remove yourself from your own woes for a while, which is exactly what Sue was doing. Sitting opposite Susan, with the morning Sun streaming through the small paned windows, I knew something was so right. Beautiful gut feelings hopped out of my stomach and skipped around a timeless room. Right there and then I sensed that Susan Carol Rose Steck Corradi—a true Catholic Church going, choir singing, living breathing angel in ankle breaking Fifth Avenue heels—was not only going to be a very good friend to me, but perhaps become my saviour as well. This was rather a large conclusion to have arrived at after such a short period of time, but when the letters and phone-calls are also taken into account, it really wasn't such an unusual or amazing thought to have after all. An angel in my eyes she may be, but we still required four wheels to get around with, so we hired a small Vauxhall Corsa hatchback from a nearby hire company. Driving the car scared me to death at first, but Susan reassured me that I would be just fine. After a few silent prayers we were back on track, both desperately seeking a nice day. Getting my coordination and vital reactions together took some doing. At times I felt so disorientated that I had to pull over to recompose myself before having another try. On that particular day there was no way that I should have been behind that wheel, but what the hell. Lack of energy and interest made those first few weeks together since 1981 extremely hard work, but I was determined to keep on going. Constant company of a preoccupied downer on human legs must have been both physically draining and mentally taxing on Susan, but to her credit she never let on, instead remaining typically cheerful. Adjusting accordingly in order to deal with somebody who is mentally despairing is an art form in itself, and Susan certainly mastered it. She took on the role of stimulator and motivator. She took my noisy mind off the dull grinding repetitiveness, and then pointed out where it needed to belong. I tried to give back what I could spare so that she too could be as far removed from her own predicaments as possible. I found it to be hard graft, but excellent therapy. This unforced arrangement came together so naturally, and it especially helped me to retrieve the key essences of life. Believing that my world was *not* about to cave in all around me if I messed something up big time, served as the base from which to improve. More and more activity became the order of every day. Sometimes I felt very wary of stopping in case the persistent madness and badness from the past caught up with me, which of course it sometimes did, and when it did it hurt like mad.

One clement day we decided to catch the train into nearby London to check out all of the usual tourist places: The Houses of Parliament, Downing Street, Trafalgar Square, Green and Hyde Parks, Buckingham Palace, Royal Mews, National Gallery, Covent Garden, St. Paul's Cathedral, Soho, Leicester Square, Piccadilly Circus, Wardour Street, Gerrard Street (Chinatown) Regent Street, Heddon Street, Oxford Street, Shaftesbury Avenue and so much more, all on foot! We could have used London's excellent bus and tube system, but there was always something else to see just around the corner, so we didn't bother. Little wonder our feet bled and blistered. Poor Susan's size threes and little legs put in twice as much effort as I did. Cobwebs were well and truly blown away during that busy day. Just being surrounded by hoards of similar minded human beings served as a blockage release and as another solid brick on my home base. For the remainder of Susan's stay we had to hobble about in a happier agony. Sue's historical knowledge of all things British put me to shame, especially in history steeped London and Oxford. St. Albans didn't escape her knowledgeable scrutiny either, and I must admit that I found all of it a very interesting and enlightening experience that helped me to divert my wandering attentions back to a subject that was real and present. When we returned to the familiarity of the Black Lion Inn I would stay for only 15 to 20 minutes, before dashing back to Bovingdon where I could sink more than a few strong beverages without any criticism.

As I have already touched upon, it is easy for me to see today that a huge portion of my life since my mid-teens had been masked by alcohol. Learning to act the part to fit the role became a stressful and unhealthy drag as the years passed by. Eventually my facade became transparent and disintegrated, leaving me feeling awkward and a shade distant, not quite as confident in social situations as I would like to be. Today there is plenty of room for self improvement, and I know that my social skills and confidence will improve naturally as time marches on. I must either be myself and believe in myself one-hundred percent, or risk becoming just another stiff statistic. I intend to be around for a lot longer!

Stamina and Susan go hand in hand, and so naturally she wanted me to go here, there and everywhere in the evenings, but one drink in the bar was plenty, before making my way back to Bovingdon where I would wash my medication down with something stronger than willpower. Of course I felt rotten about leaving the little lady alone in St. Albans, in an unfamiliar country surrounded by unfamiliar locals. A tough cookie with a soft centre is our Susan. Sure she enjoyed some conversational attention, but only on her terms. Despite Sue suggesting a few times that I show her my maisonette, she never did see it until a few years later. I did not want the image of my untidy, boozy home life to interfere with the amount of good that we had already built up in such a short period of time. Material surroundings would not have mattered in the slightest to somebody who sees the person for what they are, irrespective of what has accumulated around them during a low period in their life. Critical eyes and awkward questions jabbing away at me when my guard was down, were just what I endeavoured to veer away from if I could at all help it. No awkwardness would have displayed itself, but it was still early days and I for one was definitely *not* about to take that chance to blow the goodness to smithereens. Yes I worried myself silly that I had hurt her feelings, and yes she understood fully and was not fazed in the slightest. Flying all that way to be with a person whom she knew in advance was well below par, speaks volumes about just how extra special she really is. How refreshing it can be to witness a human being actually putting into practice exactly what they preach, instead of self indulgently talking about it in the false belief that a few hymn songs and a token prayer alone will secure them a first class ticket to the next stage of existence.

When the day arrived for Susan to pin on her wings and fly back across the deep blue pond to New York, I have to admit that although I knew for certain that I would miss her company enormously, I felt a sense of relief. Before long I began to miss Susie like crazy. When my depressing mood lifted all that I wanted was to be with her again, a union that we have been fortunate to join and renew on many occasions since 1993. A strong bond had formed from out of the most unlikely of circumstances. As we parted at Heathrow Airport with a cheeky kiss, and as I watched the little lady disappear into the departure lounge, I knew for sure, right there and then, that I had at last found my soul mate. As far as I was concerned she wasn't leaving me at all, she had only just arrived, right on time. From that day on, no matter how many miles apart we may be, no matter what goodies or adversities either of us may be experiencing, Sue and I would always be together. Both of us will be taking our bipolar medications morning and night for the rest of our lives, which is no big deal when one considers the quality of life that such a tiny painless chore can bring. In my book *love* is the sweetest drug, and I am proud to announce that Susie is still, and always will be, my lovable little dealer. Hallelujah!

Take care.
Keith